no new. ed. 11/2016

BestCredit
HOW TO WIN THE CREDIT GAME

Amazon
7109
$30

BestCredit

HOW TO WIN THE CREDIT GAME

DANA A. NEAL

Paladin Press · Boulder, Colorado

"Credit Repair: Self-Help May Be Best."
—Federal Trade Commission

BestCredit:
How to Win the Credit Game, Second Edition
by Dana A. Neal

Copyright © 2006 by Dana A. Neal

ISBN 10: 1-58160-501-3
ISBN 13: 978-1-58160-501-3
Printed in the United States of America

Published by Paladin Press, a division of
Paladin Enterprises, Inc.
Gunbarrel Tech Center
7077 Winchester Circle
Boulder, Colorado 80301 USA
+1.303.443.7250

Direct inquiries and/or orders to the above address.

PALADIN, PALADIN PRESS, and the "horse head" design
are trademarks belonging to Paladin Enterprises and
registered in United States Patent and Trademark Office.

Visit our Web site at: www.paladin-press.com

CONTENTS

Small-Claims Court
Service of Process
Prepare to Win

DISCLAIMER

This book provides information on techniques the reader can use to improve credit and/or reduce debt. Those actions are the full and total responsibility of the individual, and no guarantees or warrantees are provided. It is the responsibility of the reader to evaluate the accuracy, completeness, or usefulness of any information, opinion, or other content available in this book; check with an attorney; and review applicable local, state, federal, and any other laws. The author and publisher are not engaged in rendering any legal advice or accounting service. The services of a professional attorney are recommended if legal or financial advice or assistance is needed. The author and publisher disclaim any responsibility for personal loss or liabilities caused by the direct or indirect use or misuse of any information presented herein.

FOREWORD

Most consumers don't even realize the impact their everyday behavior has on their credit standing and thus their everyday lives. As a loan officer at a mortgage brokerage firm, I see people every day who are affected in various ways by their credit rating. There are those who are in excellent standing and have the best rates, programs, and services available to them, and then there are those who pay a premium for their loans—or don't qualify at all—based on their credit report.

Many of you already know that when you want to do anything in life, the people who are in a position to help you will likely use a critical eye and look at three things: credit, character, and collateral. Otherwise known as the Three Cs, they're all connected, but the first two are deeply connected, since prevailing perceptions are that you can't have one without the other. That's why *BestCredit* is so important, because fixing your credit will prop up the perception of character, and then, over time, the collateral will follow.

The reality is that a good credit score is achievable for everyone! As you'll soon discover, *BestCredit* takes the guesswork out of the credit scoring process and provides a clear, methodical plan for making your credit the best it can be. It's the most comprehensive program that I've seen for reestablishing credit or improving your score.

The opportunity to work with the author on my own credit improvement plan and preview *BestCredit* has been a tremendous asset to me, not only personally but professionally as well. The ability to effectively advise my clients on how they can improve their scores is no small thing, and it's rewarding to see them empowered—obtaining the financing they need to accomplish their life goals.

Dana Neal's frankness and clarity are not only refreshing, but they make the information in *BestCredit* easy to understand, digest, and implement. His use of specific, real-life examples lets you know that this former bill collector really knows what he's talking about. Furthermore, he brings a certain class to a genre that's filled with unsavory characters and dubious advice.

If you are the type that cuts corners or skims paragraphs, don't do it. There's much to know and many nuances, but the breadth and depth of information are a positive testament to the thoroughness of this book.

Once you've applied the tools the author provides, apologies or excuses for your credit will never again be necessary.

— T.J. Mehan, Loan Officer
Consumer Financial

PREFACE

Why a second edition? There are many reasons, including the December 2003 passage of the Fair and Accurate Credit Transactions Act (FACTA), which amends the Fair Credit Reporting Act (FCRA). In addition, identity theft continues to rise, and there are some new strategies for dealing with it; the Bankruptcy Abuse Prevention and Consumer Protection Act (commonly referred to as the Bankruptcy Reform Bill of 2005) was passed into law on April 14, 2005 (taking effect on October 17, 2005), making bankruptcy far less appealing; and my knowledge of credit restoration tactics and strategies has grown significantly in the two years since the first edition of *BestCredit* was published.

All these things are good for the consumer and collectively improve the chances for do-it-yourself credit restoration. And yet one of the most dramatic changes has to do with a decision by Fair Isaac and Company (FICO) to release detailed information about its credit scoring model. This is no small thing, since 75 percent of mortgage lenders use the FICO credit score to assess risk, more than 90 percent of credit card issuers use it in their lending decisions, and 70 percent of all lenders use it for all lending decisions.[1]

In this edition, I've also included new information that was requested by readers of the first book. This includes a greater explanation of legal remedies, what to do when swimming in debt, what really happens when a credit bureau receives a dispute letter, and how to go about removing public records. I have also broken down things in a way that's more easily understood, and I've developed what I call situational and collective assessments. These are really nothing more than a series of relevant questions, ones that will take the important issues and connect them with real-world circumstances, enabling you to grasp your own situation and more readily create an individualized road map to clean credit.

Taking steps to improve your credit rating and reduce debt is truly commendable. It isn't easy, and your initiative and commitment to improving your credit situation will ultimately enhance not only your credit but your life. It's this commitment, mixed with perseverance and the tools I'll provide, that is key to attaining your goals.

And yet it's easy to feel bad when your credit is poor; guilt, shame, and even depression often accompany a bad report. Furthermore, every time you get denied, it's a sobering reminder of an old mistake—a festering wound. But don't be disheartened, because you'll begin to feel better just as soon as you act to do something about it. Believe me, empowerment is very therapeutic.

Doing something begins with learning and having an open mind. Many people are misinformed about their rights concerning debt collections, credit reporting, and debt reduction. As a former bill collector, I learned firsthand the cold, hard facts about debtors and creditors. Having been on both ends of the spectrum, I have gained a keen understanding of the many facets of credit reporting and the powerful tools that are available to get you out of trouble. My goal is to arm you with this knowledge in order to turn things around and get you going

---

1. Brian Deagon, "Fair Isaac's New Scoring Service Attracts Banks," *Investor's Business Daily*, July 25, 2001; Betty-Lin Fisher (quoting Fair Isaac spokesperson), "It Pays to Know the Score: Credit Bureaus Reveal Where You Rank," *Detroit Free Press*, April 22, 2002.

on the right track. Each method I present is tried and true; there isn't anything here that I haven't tried personally.

So why do I do it? It's my belief that credit reporting is inherently flawed. Why? Because there are extenuating, life-altering circumstances that often lead to financial changes and thus financial risk. These occurrences are often outside the control of individuals. Yes, the credit reporting system is there for lending institutions to assess risk in determining whether to extend credit, but the risk assessment and the credit extended are based on a set of circumstances that can ultimately change. Yes, an individual's "creditworthiness" may have changed, but only as a function of how much credit to extend, not whether or not he or she is actually a good credit risk.

A rational financial-risk-assessment process is not linear, as life-altering events can change the equation. A loan officer looking at an individual's creditworthiness after he or she has suffered a financial disaster, in effect, does not see the same person that another creditor saw when extending credit to that individual prior to the disaster. Creditors should take past credit history into account when assessing current and future risk, but they don't; they only see the current credit report. This seems patently unfair and unrealistic. The current system of credit reporting only concerns itself with whether or not a debt was paid and when. The underlying assumption is that people either pay or don't pay based on their character—and all that this entails. A debt collector (and the system as a whole) does not distinguish between a crack user and a victim of a terrible accident. With brutal efficiency, the credit score and report will treat each case the same, with equal doses of callousness; the cause of lateness or default is of no consequence.

This measure of creditworthiness is far too simplistic, which is one of the reasons I wrote *BestCredit*. It is intended to serve as the great equalizer, since it provides the tools necessary to balance out the inherent inequities of the credit reporting system.

It's disturbing just how debilitating negative credit can be—it can leave you paralyzed! Even a small amount of negative credit can hamstring you, affecting the interest rate on your car or home loan, your approval for a home lease, a cell phone application, whether you land a job, and even your auto insurance rates. Many people are denied a checking account due to bad credit, which makes it extremely difficult to get back into the credit system. That's why it's more important than ever to make sure your credit is perfect, or at least the best it can be.

From every possible angle, this book provides the remedy to lackluster credit.

BestCredit is about covering all of the bases—reestablishing and repairing credit simultaneously, reducing debt, and using your rights to your advantage in order to take your credit rating to a higher level very quickly. All you need to do is follow the guidelines that I lay out for you, and your credit will soon be the best it can be—and more than likely flawless.

As you will soon discover, debt-consolidation and debt-settlement companies will likely cause harm, as many place their greed above the needs of their customers, and few truly understand credit restoration, or even care to understand. Credit repair agencies are also notoriously unreliable, by charging exorbitant fees and making dubious claims, claims that cannot be lived up to. Self-help insulates you from disreputable companies—pseudo nonprofits that seek only to make money from the misfortune of others. *BestCredit* teaches solid debt-reduction methods that you can employ on your own terms, based on your unique situation.

Both debt reduction and credit restoration can and should be performed simultaneously and without the illusory help of anyone. The two ideas aren't mutually exclusive; they work in harmony, one to complement the other. The application of credit restoration tactics that cover every possible angle is a powerful approach when woven together with a tailored debt-reduction strategy, enabling the best possible outcome. This fusing of credit restoration and debt reduction is what I call Debt Fusion™.

Debt Fusion™ isn't complicated. By learning all there is to know about the credit reporting system, overlaying your individual circumstances, and then devising the best possible outcome, you can achieve incredible results. The following statement is posted on the Federal Trade Commission (FTC) Web site: "Credit Repair: Self-Help May Be Best." I'm here to tell you that self-help *is* the best, since few people will ever know as much as you will after reading this book, and even fewer will understand your personal situation as well as you do. Certainly nobody will take the care and put forth the effort that you will on your own behalf.

The material in this book is very comprehensive, and it's important that you read each section carefully so that you can apply the various techniques in the most effective manner. Since each individual's situation is unique, the best way to benefit from this information is to apply it to particular situations. While this book offers many strategies and examples, the ideal student of credit improvement will take from it a great deal more than just an ability to apply a solution to any particular type of credit problem. He or she will be able to devise techniques independently. Although this book provides many answers, there is no substitute for improvising, being creative, and using a new spin on an old wheel. This "alchemy" will allow you to formulate the most potent mixture for addressing your individual credit concerns.

Again, the information I provide herein is based on my own experience, both as a collector and a debtor. Keep in mind that my mission is not to make judgments about decisions regarding your credit—right or wrong. I'm simply the purveyor of knowledge that is intended to illuminate and educate, enabling you to make powerful decisions about your credit and your future. Every situation has a specific set of circumstances to consider, and you must decide for yourself whom to pay, how much, and under what terms.

There are various other books available on the subject of credit repair, many of which offer flow charts or tables that illustrate your prospective chances at negative credit removal based on such factors as patterns of lateness, type of debt, and so on. This may all look interesting, but the bottom line is this: every item that is derogatory has a high probability for removal. The major factors that will affect your success rate are how well you learn the lessons contained in this book and how hard you're willing to work at solving your credit problems.

As I've already mentioned, some readers of the first edition requested more information on legal remedies, and I have responded to that request in this edition. But please don't be intimidated by my numerous citations of legal manuals and the law. Though the vast majority of readers can successfully restore their credit without the use of the courts, I address the subject in detail for those who need it. I'm fully aware that the credit repair genre is filled with a lot of useless pap and false information, and the references exist in order to show that what you're reading is, in fact, the truth. And while few people will ever want or need to perform legal action of any kind, being prepared is far better than the alternative. It's always helpful to know where to begin to look in any event.

It's important to me that readers not only have success in their quest for perfect credit and debt reduction, but that they also feel that *BestCredit* really helped them improve their lives. If you have any ideas on how to improve on the information provided, feel free to log on to www.bestcredit.com and send an e-mail via the contact page. Of course, I get many e-mails and cannot respond to every one, but I do read all of them. And from time to time my Web site offers new products and services, so be sure and check those out as well.

Some will call me a renegade and others a humanitarian. That's up to every individual to decide. But if I can make a difference in some small way, to champion the cause of the little guy, then I'll have accomplished my goal. It's my sincere hope that all readers will become a force to be reckoned with, empowered to lift themselves up from whatever position they find themselves in.

CHAPTER 1

CREDIT REPORTING—
THE SYSTEM AND
THE PLAYERS

The credit reporting system has many parts. Primary among them are credit reporting agencies (aka credit bureaus); furnishers (those that feed account and public record information to the bureaus), including collection agencies, creditors, and service bureaus; and users of reports.

This chapter will focus on the major players of the credit reporting system and provide an overview of how they operate together to affect your credit. When you consider the complexity of these bureaucracies along with the myriad personalities found in each, it's easy to see how overwhelming and frustrating bad credit can be. Yet knowing how the system really works and separating fact from fiction will enable you to navigate what often appears to be a hopelessly complex maze. In fact, the credit reporting system is a shrewd game of strategy, and understanding the playing field is your first, critical step to positioning yourself to play along, even the score, and ultimately come out a winner.

CREDIT REPORTING AGENCIES

The Fair Credit Reporting Act is the federal law that governs credit reporting. It defines a credit reporting agency[1] as "any person which, for monetary fees, dues, or on a cooperative nonprofit basis, regularly engages in whole or in part in the practice of assembling or evaluating consumer credit information or other information on consumers for the purpose of furnishing consumer reports to third parties, and which uses any means or facility of interstate commerce for the purpose of preparing or furnishing consumer reports."

The primary agencies that collect public record and credit account information and furnish consumer credit reports on a nationwide basis are known as the Big Three: Equifax, Experian, and Trans Union. According to the strict FCRA definition, a nationwide credit reporting agency is one that not only regularly compiles and maintains consumer information and makes it available to third parties but also collects both public record information *and* credit account information on consumers nationwide. So while the Act's definition technically includes other agencies besides the Big Three, the term "nationwide" is intended to apply to them and no others.[2]

There are also hundreds of regional agencies, which likewise compile consumer information on a regional basis. Such agencies may compile the same type of information found in the national bureaus, yet may also be more specialized in the data they compile. For example, some provide specialized consumer reports, including business/ commercial reports, employment, check approval, and tenant screening.

Medical information can also be compiled by national bureaus as well as specialty agencies, though the release of such information is prohibited when a report is used for employment, and if the report is for a credit, an insurance, or a direct marketing transaction, then medical information cannot be disclosed unless the consumer

---

1. The FCRA uses the term "consumer reporting agency."
2. See 140 Cong. Rec. 25,871 (1994) (remarks of Rep. Joseph Kennedy); Brinckerhoff, FTC Informal Staff Opinion Letter, June 29, 1999.

consents.[3] The Fair and Accurate Credit Transactions Act was passed into law in December 2003. (FACTA simply amends the FCRA.) It removed the FCRA requirement that medical information be *obtained* only with the consent of the consumer, yet FACTA strengthened disclosure rules without the consumer's consent.[4]

One such medical specialty agency is the Medical Information Bureau (MIB). Many medical insurers are members and will use adverse medical information when underwriting for life or health insurance, or disability policies. Even activities that are considered hazardous may be compiled, such as hang gliding or piloting airplanes.[5] There are also resellers and affiliates of each national bureau, and those will be explained in more detail in Chapter 5.

For the purposes of this book, we will focus on the national credit reporting agencies, as well as the major players in the check reporting arena. Virtually every major bank and collection agency reports to one or more of the Big Three, and most of the smaller reporting agencies get their information straight from one or more of them. The Big Three also compile public record information. As such, consumers who wish to improve their credit rating will have to focus on Equifax, Experian, and Trans Union independently. Yet keep in mind that any credit reporting agency as defined by the FCRA will have to abide by the rules of that Act as well as any state FCRA rules. The information provided herein is universal in that regard.

Credit reporting agencies store information regarding your credit and public records in a data warehouse (or "repository"). This data is

---

3. 15 U.S.C. § 1681b(g), as amended by Pub. L. No. 104-208 § 2408, 110 Stat. 3009 (Sept. 30, 1996). States have enacted their own laws concerning the disclosure of medical information on consumer reports, such as California, which prohibits the inclusion of medical information for employment, insurance, or credit purposes without consumer consent. Cal. Civ. Code § 1785.13(f). Check your state laws.
4. 15 U.S.C. § 1681a(i), as amended by Pub. L. No. 108-159 § 411(c)(2003).
5. National Consumer Law Center (NCLC) *Fair Credit Reporting* § 4.5.5 (5th ed. 2002 and 2005 Supp.). Under FACTA, the MIB is now considered a nationwide bureau, and the FTC has yet to determine the timetable for when the MIB will be required to make a free report available to consumers once per annum. But in the meantime, if you're interested in what's in your MIB file, contact MIB at 160 University Avenue, Westwood, MA 02090-2307, 617-426-3660.

provided by *furnishers*, including current and former creditors and service bureaus (agencies that scan public record information). Creditors feed the credit reporting agencies with account information and such personal history as date of birth, employment data, and address information. Service bureaus scan public record documents (found at courthouses and county offices) that contain such information as judgments (court documents declaring that one party owes another money), bankruptcies, liens, and criminal records. The service bureaus furnish this public record information to credit reporting agencies, which house it in their databases.

When a credit bureau compiles a consumer's record from its database, this is often referred to as a credit report or credit file. The credit report contains personal information, such as age, date of birth, and past and present addresses; trade information, such as credit accounts and their payment history and status; public record information, including liens, bankruptcies, foreclosures, arrests, convictions, and judgments; collection information for delinquent accounts; and a list of inquiries (requests for a credit file.)

Upon request, the credit bureaus supply consumer credit reports to *users*. These users may or may not be actual subscribers (those who have open accounts with the credit bureaus and thus have the ability to furnish information as well as request it). Users then apply the information in determining creditworthiness or in consideration of employment and certain types of insurance.[6]

The Data Bucket

In reality, at any given moment there isn't any such thing as a "credit report." The credit bureau's vast database is like a data warehouse that contains information about you and millions of other consumers in the same general pile, and what comes out in a consumer's credit report often depends on who happens to be doing the scooping. When viewed in this way, a credit report is really just a query of the bits and bytes of information in the bureau's database.

---

6. Under the FCRA, life insurance underwriting policies can consider credit history, while medical insurance cannot.

When a consumer requests a credit report directly from a credit bureau, he or she must provide very specific identifying information. Known as "match data," this unique identifying information, which includes name, date of birth, exact address, current and former employers, and Social Security number (SSN), ensures a reliable query when the credit bureau matches the data against its repository of consumer financial history.

However, to make the system work as expeditiously as possible for themselves and users, credit bureaus place far looser match data requirements on subscribers, their biggest customers, than on nonsubscribers, you and me. In fact, the bureaus only require a subscriber's query to match seven of the nine digits of a consumer's SSN. Further, if a subscriber provides the consumer's full SSN, then the bureau uses a modified query that permits significant discrepancies in last name, street address, city, and state.[7] A wider net is therefore cast, increasing the odds of picking up erroneous data, usually in the form of accounts that belong to people with closely matching names or SSNs.

Furthermore, when creditors supply consumer account information to a bureau, the consumer's SSN may not even be included. Thus, when the bureau runs a query, the resulting report may attribute information to you that is not necessarily yours. For example, a collection agency may furnish information to a bureau about a collection account for someone with a name and street address that match yours, and the modified query, with its relaxed standards for accuracy, will pick this account up when a subscriber requests a report. This merging of your financial data with someone else's is known as a "file merger" mistake, and it's estimated that such errors occur in 10 percent of all credit reports.[8]

Plenty of case law exists on this subject, since many people who have been wrongly denied credit as a result of the bureaus' carelessness have sued to recoup losses. As Evan Hendricks points out in *Credit Scores & Credit Reports*, in 2002 a federal jury awarded Judy Thomas $5 million in punitive damages and $350,000 in compen-

---

7. Evan Hendricks, *Credit Scores & Credit Reports*, Privacy Times, Inc., 2004, 125.
8. Consumer Federation of America, 2002.

satory damages for negligence on the part of the bureaus. Although the judge reduced the punitive damage award to $1 million, the original award illustrates the way in which juries are viewing the big, bad bureaus.

Cloaking and Reinsertion of Data

When an item is considered "obsolete," it is deleted from a consumer's credit file. The obsolescence period varies based on such factors as the reporting statute of limitations (explained in Chapter 6), which varies by type of entry; e.g., late payments are seven years from the date of delinquency, while judgments vary by state. An item may also be obsolete simply because it's inaccurate. But when an item is deleted, most often it is not actually purged (the procedure known as a "hard delete"). Instead, it's stored in the system in an effort to provide the information to users that meet the data-retention exception, a provision within the FCRA that enables credit bureaus to retain information for a longer period than normal. The exception to the standard seven-year data-retention period applies when certain types of inquiries are conducted, as when a consumer is applying for a loan exceeding $150,000. There are other exemptions as well, and this is fully explained in Chapter 6 under "Credit Reporting Statute of Limitations." This storing of otherwise obsolete information that is made available to creditors under certain circumstances is known as a "soft delete" and is often referred to as "cloaking" or "suppression."

Although it would seem logical that any obsolete information that's supposed to be deleted in accordance with the FCRA ought to be purged, bureaus are permitted to store such information at their discretion. (Hendricks claims that they often keep the information on file in an effort to suppress incoming duplicates—entries that the bureau previously soft-deleted that are once again provided by a furnisher. He believes that bureaus use the retained information as a makeshift flag that serves to filter out unwanted incoming data. I'm not sure I buy this explanation, since there are many database management methods available that can be used to filter out incoming furnisher data without retaining information in the primary database.) It's not clear why, but sometimes bureaus set soft deletes to expire after a certain period. Set on a timer, these items will reappear in the database upon expiration.[9]

Unfortunately for consumers, the cloaking system often fails. Since agencies routinely receive uncorrected information from furnishers, reinsertion occurs. Part of the problem is that a furnisher may report information that a bureau has previously cloaked using a different subscriber or account number. Creditors often sell debts to third parties, and they each have different subscriber numbers assigned by the credit bureau, thus defeating the cloaking system if the credit reporting agency hasn't put in place adequate filters to catch any refurnishing. Also, buyers of debt will often intentionally furnish under different account numbers than those of the original creditors in order to undermine the credit bureaus' filters. By ensuring that a debt shows up on a report, this puts pressure on debtors to pay on a debt, whether they actually owe it or not. This is just one of the many reasons it's so important to check your credit report at least once every six months—and at least once a quarter if you've been having problems with inaccurate information being reported.

By law, the bureaus are required to adopt procedures to prevent the reappearance of obsolete material, except as specifically allowed by the FCRA (more on this in Chapter 6 under "Credit Reporting Statute of Limitations").[10] In cases where a consumer disputes an item and the credit bureau is unable to verify its accuracy within the allotted time as prescribed by law (usually 30 to 45 days; see "Bureau Reinvestigation Procedures" in Chapter 4), the bureau must delete it.[11] And a soft delete may not comply with the terms of the FCRA, which require the agency to *delete* the information. In at least one lawsuit, a court found Trans Union's cloaking procedures to be unreason-

---

9. NCLC *Fair Credit Reporting* § 7.5 (5th ed. 2002 and 2005 Supp.). My attempts to discover an answer for the use of a timer have failed, and I can only surmise that it may have something to do with items under dispute or review.
10. 15 U.S.C. § 1681i(a)(5)(C).
11. 15 U.S.C. § 1681i(a)(5)(A)(i).

able under the FCRA.[12] Among items that agencies are required to delete are fraud-related activities and reinvestigations.[13]

Identity Theft Enablers

When the credit reporting agency receives a dispute (a formal complaint disputing the validity of information contained in one's credit file), it must conduct a "reinvestigation." To do this, the bureau communicates the dispute to the furnisher of the information in question through the use of a consumer dispute verification form (CDV) or "611 notice." There's also an automated (electronic) version of the form, known as an ACDV.

The ACDV system was developed by the Big Three, collaborating through the Consumer Data Industry Association (CDIA)[14] to create E-OSCAR (Online Solution for Complete and Accurate Reporting). This computer system takes the place of manual reinvestigation, and consumer disputes are translated into computer codes. This is all done in the name of accuracy, yet, as you will see, the use of this system results in verification, not reinvestigation.

Both CDVS and ACDVs rely on dispute codes to communicate a dispute to a furnisher. When a bureau receives a consumer dispute, someone who would otherwise be flipping hamburgers is tasked with entering it into E-OSCAR. These bureaucrats have quotas that require them to process a certain number of disputes per hour. A former employee of Trans Union testified in a civil trial that she was required to process a dispute every four minutes, or 15 per hour.[15] Since the average consumer dispute involves an average of three items,[16] the

12. *Cousin v. Trans Union Corp.*, 246 F.3d 359 (5th Cir. 2001); NCLC *Fair Credit Reporting* § 7.4.2 (5th ed. 2002 and 2005 Supp.).

13. *Andrews v. Trans Union Corp.*, 7 F. Supp. 2d 1056, 1075 (C.D. Cal. 1998) (presence of inquiry, resulting from identity theft, that suggested that the plaintiff had applied for credit raised issue of material fact as to whether listing of inquiry was misleading), *aff'd in part, rev'd in part on other grounds sub nom. Andrews v. TRW*, Inc., 225 F.3d 1063 (9th Cir. 2000), *cert. granted*, 121 S. Ct. 1223 (2001).

14. CDIA, www.cdiaonline.com.

15. Deposition of Regina Sorenson, *Fleischer v. Trans Union*, Civ. Action No. 02-71301 (E.D. Mich. Jan 9, 2002).

16. Evan Hendricks, *Credit Scores & Credit Reports*, Privacy Times, Inc., 2004, 141.

actual number that must be entered is 45 per hour. (Hendricks claims the number is 30 to 36 per hour. Whatever the number, it's a lot.)

The dispute is converted to a code using the CDV/ACDV, but the nature of the dispute almost never is, and meanwhile, the actual letter from the consumer often ends up lost in space.[17] (Note that Equifax doesn't even hire employees in the United States to perform this work. It outsources it, using offices in Jamaica. Trans Union and Experian are also looking to move this area of operations to either the Philippines or India.)[18]

Most often, the bureaucrat codes the CDV/ACDV using a two-digit identifier, which simply indicates that the consumer disputes the validity of the entry, which may be account information (a tradeline, as it is known in the industry) or public record information. And while there are several different two-digit codes, one could mean "not mine," while another could mean, "wrong balance," for example. When the furnisher receives the CDV/ACDV from the bureau, someone—with similar skills to those of the bureau letter handler, and who would likewise have quotas to meet—is tasked with one single thing: confirming whether the last information they provided to the credit bureau matches the information the furnisher currently has in its computer database. If so, then the disputed entry is affirmed as correct. If not, then the data is resubmitted to the credit bureau as reflected in the furnisher's database. The bureau will always defer to the furnisher, reporting whatever the furnisher instructs. (This illustrates the importance of getting a creditor on board to report desirably, even when an account is seriously delinquent, detailed in Chapter 9.)

Now I ask you, just where in this dispute scenario might someone who has fraudulently obtained new credit using someone else's identity be discovered? And more importantly, where in this scenario does a victim of identity theft have any adequate recourse? The answer is nowhere. If the identity thief is granted new credit by using the victim's SSN (the consumer's identity, for all practical purposes), then

---

17. CDVs and ACDVs are often communicated without the documentation provided by the consumer. NCLC *Fair Credit Reporting* § 3.10 (5th ed. 2002 and 2005 Supp.).
18. Evan Hendricks, *Privacy Times* 23, no. 17 (Sept. 12, 2003).

this new credit is reported to the credit bureaus—eventually as a delinquent account when the thief fails to pay the duped creditor. When the victim attempts to dispute the information with a credit reporting agency, the bureau will contact the furnisher and request verification. The dispute handler at the furnisher will then verify the debt as valid and owed by the victim. And therein lies the key to why identity theft is such a growing and attractive crime: the credit bureaus perpetuate it, since there is no mechanism within the furnisher-bureau interface to deal with it.

Trans Union reports that 52 percent of its data furnishers participate in the ACDV system.[19] This does not bode well for consumers, but on the on the upside, FACTA has provisions to assist consumers with combating identity theft, summarized in the next chapter.[20]

The Snapshot/Frozen Scan

Information in a bureau's repository is always changing. This is due to the internal factors inherent in the database itself, such as items automatically dropping off after the data-retention period expires or closed accounts dropping after 10 years. (Credit bureaus are not required to keep positive information any longer than they do adverse, yet their common policy is to retain nonadverse closed accounts for 10 years.) Database information can also change due to external factors, including the direct modification of the data by virtue of deleting or changing existing entries or adding new ones.

Since a credit report is a living record that is constantly in flux, bureaus need a way to go back and view the report *the way it was* at a specific point in time. Using this archival system of data retrieval, often referred to as a snapshot or "frozen scan," assists them in discovering the source of errors and other problems and is particularly useful for rooting out identity theft or file merger mistakes. There are at least two types of snapshots.

---

19. Statement of Harry Gambill, chief executive officer, Trans Union, LLC, before the Subcommittee on Financial Institutions and Consumer Credit, June 4, 2003. *Fair Credit Reporting*, 5th ed. and supp. (Boston: National Consumer Law Center, 2002), § 3.10.
20. Chapter 11 details practical steps for identity theft prevention and recovery.

The *monthly* snapshot is created every 30 days automatically. This data has actually proven extremely valuable in lawsuits against the bureaus, where it has served to demonstrate systematically how bureau mistakes and shoddy database management have negatively affected large groups of people. What I refer to as a *general* snapshot is generated any time an inquiry is made on your credit report—including one you make when you run a credit report on yourself, either directly from a bureau or through a third-party credit report provider. Should discrepancies arise, this enables the bureaus to go back in time and look at the exact report that existed at the time of the inquiry if necessary, in order to deal with any problems. However, when you pull a report for yourself through a third-party credit report provider, such as FICO, a snapshot is not taken. (A Trans Union manager made this claim, though I question its accuracy.)

This is a shame, since it's the FICO score that matters most because it's the one most lenders use. FICO is closely associated with the Big Three, providing the national bureaus' reports directly to consumers and tying in its software scoring model to those reports in order to generate a FICO credit score. (Chapter 3 explains FICO scoring in detail, while Chapter 5 provides detailed information on obtaining personal credit reports.) You also want a snapshot in the bureau's database because it can be very useful when attempting to have changes made to your report. It will also prove helpful in any legal action that you may embark on later. For this and other reasons that will be explained later, always get your Big Three reports directly from FICO, but also obtain the individual reports directly from each of the Big Three at the same time. It may seem redundant, but the creation of a snapshot in the bureau's database is important in light of common bureau errors and identity theft.

Prone to Errors

As you can see, it's important that you take steps to protect yourself because the credit bureaus' basic modus operandi is inherently flawed. It is designed to serve their ends, with no concern for accuracy or integrity. As a result, consumer credit reports are fraught with error. In 2002, the Consumer Federation of America (CFA) and the National Credit Reporting Association (NCRA) conducted a study of 502,623 consumer credit reports, doing an extensive review of 1,700 of them. In examining 3-in-1 reports (merged reports containing data from each of the Big Three), researchers found that on 29 percent of them, the FICO scores for each individual bureau report ranged by at least 50 points, and on 4 percent the scores ranged by at least 100 points. The average range of the three scores was 41 points, and the median range was 35 points.

Upon conducting a more detailed examination of 51 files, researchers uncovered various reasons for the differences in scores: "Common errors of omission were the failure to report a negative event—for example, a delinquency or charge-off—or a positive event—for example, payments on an account. Seventy-eight percent of files were missing a revolving [credit card] account in good standing, while one-third (33 percent) of files were missing a mortgage account that had never been late." The report further found that "more serious errors of commission appeared in a significant portion of files. In 43 percent of the files, reports on the same accounts conflicted in regard to how often consumers had been late by 30 days. In 29 percent of the files, there was conflicting information about how many times the consumer had been 60 days late. And in 24 percent of the files, conflicts existed about 90-day delinquencies. Reported delinquencies have a large effect on credit scores."

Since FICO credit scores are the primary determining factor lenders use to assess your creditworthiness, the flawed credit reporting system at the root of such discrepancies may well result in your paying a higher interest rate or receiving a flat-out denial.

Credit Bureaus Are the Enemy

Credit bureaus don't care about you. They are in business to make money, period. They make the bulk of their money by providing services to subscribers, which pay them both to report and to pull credit reports. They also make a great deal of money by selling information (names and addresses used for marketing) to prospective lenders and others. They lose money every time they deal with you, the consumer. Never forget it. Legal action is usually the last thing they want, and they have no interest in tangling with you over something they are really indifferent about.

And yet letters from lawyers on behalf of clients in disagreement over reported information are becoming less and less effective. Perhaps bureaus figure that most people don't have the *cojones* to follow through and sue them when they screw up. I'm hoping you do; if enough people stand up to them, then and only then will things change. In 2000, the FTC fined the Big Three $2.5 million for preventing millions of consumers from discussing the contents of their credit reports by placing hurdles that made it difficult to contact them.

Be forewarned that credit reporting agencies have been known to shut down a consumer's credit file in response to a lawsuit. When this occurs, any inquiry from a potential creditor will yield "file under review."[21] This retaliatory action is intended to intimidate and frustrate, and yet there are remedies for any breach of the FCRA, as you will soon learn.

Now that you have received an introduction to how the credit bureaus operate, which is really only the tip of the iceberg, you might appreciate the following statement the chief executive officer of Equifax made to the Commonwealth Club of California on June 27, 2005, expressing his chagrin with FACTA's requirement that the bureaus provide consumers with one free credit report per year in an effort to curb identity theft:

> Our company felt, and still does . . . that it's unconstitutional to cause a public company who has a fiduciary responsibility to return profit to shareholders to give away the product . . . Most of my shareholder group did not think that giving away our product was the American way . . . That's like turning on the smoke alarm once a year.

In fact, the so-called product he's referring to costs the credit bureaus next to nothing to make and deliver. It's the subsequent consumer disputes, filed in an effort to correct *inaccurate information,* that

---

21. *Thomas v. Trans Union, LLC,* 2002 U.S. Dist. LEXIS 7451 (D. Or. Mar. 21, 2002); *Thompson v. Equifax,* 2001 U.S. Dist. LEXIS 22640 (M.D. Ala. Dec. 14, 2001).

cost the bureaus money. God forbid their product should be made accurate—that would cut into shareholder profits and executive bonuses!

In my opinion, the credit reporting agencies are *the number-one cause* of identity theft. It is their failure to adequately investigate consumer disputes, which is a product of *their greed*, that enables identity theft to work. It simply would not work otherwise.

The credit bureaus don't want consumers to know about their rights, and there's plenty of evidence to support that claim. Just go to their Web sites and search their so-called education sections. They don't even list the word "reinvestigation" in their glossaries. You won't find the word "validation" or "verification" anywhere either. Nor will you find detailed information on the statutes of limitations on credit reporting. And you certainly won't find detailed information on how to improve a FICO score or one of the Big Three's proprietary scores. (Reporting agencies have their own scoring models, detailed in Chapter 3.)

Furthermore, here's what Experian's Web site says about credit repair clinics:

> Some consumers pay so-called credit clinics hundreds and even thousands of dollars to fix their credit report, but only time can heal bad credit. Experian credit reports contain easy-to-follow instructions for disputing information at no charge. Information proven to be inaccurate will be changed or deleted. Federal and state laws mandate the amount of time that various credit information remains on a credit report. If you need help repaying creditors, managing debt or setting up a personal budget, consider contacting a nonprofit credit counseling organization that offers budgeting and credit management training.

Only time can heal bad credit? That's simply not true. And notice Experian's careful choice of wording with regard to what federal law mandates with regard to "the amount of time that various credit information remains," subtly implying that not *all* information can be changed or deleted. As for the helpful suggestion about the so-called nonprofit credit counseling agencies, you might as well forget that; they're as crooked as anyone, as you will soon learn.

Let's face it: the biggest threat credit reporting agencies face is an educated consumer, because each and every one cuts into their bottom line. Such a person, especially one who has read this book, is the last thing the bureaus want to deal with.

FURNISHERS OF INFORMATION

How does account information end up on your credit report? The answer to this can get complicated and depends on many factors, including what type of account it is, who the creditor is, whether the creditor is a subscriber to a bureau, whether the creditor is affiliated with an association that is a subscriber, what service bureaus feed to which credit reporting agencies, and whether the account has been turned over to a collection agency. Members of credit reporting agencies can pull reports, while subscribers can report as well as run credit checks.

Large to midsize creditors have subscriber accounts with the bureaus; they pay fees for the right to report consumer account information and separate fees for running inquiries on consumers. Although it's unclear what large to midsize creditors pay, smaller creditors can often open up accounts with the bureaus, paying a setup fee of around $300 and a monthly fee of $50, which enables them to report at will.[22]

Equifax and Experian do not deal directly with landlords, so landlords must set up accounts with an organization the bureaus already do business with. In the case of Equifax, this is the National Association of Independent Landlords (NAIL), a third-party landlord reporting organization, which charges its clients $60 per month. In turn, NAIL will furnish the information to the credit reporting agencies. This enables landlords to report at will. Experian likewise does business with a couple of third-party companies—Landlord Protection Services and Allied Residence.

---

22. Equifax's business office claimed that it doesn't release exact guidelines for opening a business account and approves or denies applicants at its discretion. Although Equifax is a private company, its deep integration into the credit and banking system could make it susceptible to all sorts of federal consumer protection laws. A case for legal challenge? It should at least be required to post guidelines.

As an interesting aside, when NAIL reports an item as delinquent and then a landlord later requests that the item be removed, NAIL will not remove it. NAIL claims it will only report such an account as a zero balance but not instruct Equifax to remove it. There's no justification for this position; it's another case of the bully syndrome. NAIL is simply a purveyor of information from the original creditor (the landlord) to Equifax. If NAIL does this in practice, such meddling is in direct violation of the FCRA and probably also violates state Unfair and Deceptive Acts and Practices (UDAP) statutes. If you run into this problem with NAIL or any credit reporting agency, be sure to notify the FTC and the attorney general (in your state and Texas, the state in which NAIL operates) immediately, and consider a legal remedy where appropriate. (Credit reporting agencies have no problem with a furnisher's instructing them to change information—whether from negative to positive or visa versa—or delete it entirely.)

Those who are not landlords can set up a subscriber account with Experian, but the account holder must report 500 individuals per month regardless of company size. Experian also has a member program that enables companies to pull credit reports, charging a $165 one-time setup fee and a $500 security deposit, and requiring a $50 monthly minimum. After one full year of membership (pulling credit reports), this can be converted to a subscriber account with no reporting minimums. Yet the company must be in the business of extending credit to clients.

Trans Union will permit companies (and landlords) that report at least 100 accounts per month to open a member account. It charges its subscribers a $305 setup fee and a $95 annual renewal fee. It also does business with third-party vendors, since many companies simply can't meet the minimum reporting volume requirement. The middlemen will roll up several smaller company accounts and report to the Big Three for them. InterCept and The Service Bureau are two such vendors, both of which report to Trans Union. (Both InterCept and The Service Bureau are credit reporting agencies as defined by the FCRA.)

Some credit bureaus are also unwilling to set up accounts with companies that are in certain lines of business. These include credit repair and debt consolidation firms, bail bond companies, and even lawyers who aren't in the sole business of collections.

As I've shown, since individuals and small businesses usually can't report delinquent accounts or run inquiries without being a subscriber of a bureau or a member of some sort of association that reports for the bureaus, they'll often turn to collection agencies and third parties—which have subscriber accounts with bureaus and report diligently.

In addition to third parties reporting account information to the reporting agencies on behalf of clients, other companies known as service bureaus scan public records and contract with the credit bureaus to provide this information on a regular basis. (Some reporting agencies own service bureaus.) This means that when you are being sued, have a judgment against you, have a lien against your property, get arrested or convicted, or file for bankruptcy, it's likely to appear on your credit report. The problem is these service bureaus are careless and prone to mistakes such as transcribing names, addresses, and SSNs incorrectly.

Data Transfer

Some furnishers report their customers' account data to credit reporting agencies via magnetic tape, delivered by courier, but most transmit the data electronically. Since 1997 the industry standard has been Metro 2. Metro 2 is simply a format created by software called Credit Manager, which is produced by The Service Bureau. It uses more identifiers (match data) than the older version, Metro 1, and while Metro 1 was transmitted solely by courier, Metro 2 permits the transfer of data to the bureaus over the Internet. As with all things, the industry treats this information as a state secret, though some of it has come out in lawsuits through the process of discovery. Although not all furnishers use Metro 2 to transfer their data electronically, the credit reporting agencies report that up to 80 percent of their subscribers or furnishers have converted to Metro 2.[23]

One problem with tapes is that they can be lost or stolen, whereas data transmitted over the Internet is encrypted with very high security

---

23. *Fair Credit Reporting,* § 3.3.1. The NCLC manual (5th ed. 2002 and 2005 Supp.) provides detailed information about the use of fields and segments in Metro 2. It's the sloppiness of collectors with regard to data entry that often causes errors, particularly as debts are bought and sold.

UNIVERSAL DATA FORM

General Help (F1)
This form has been approved for reporting or updating account information.

☐ New   ☐ Change   If Change makes trade current, is previous delinquent history to be deleted? ☐ Yes ☐ No

☒ Delete (By checking Delete, tradeline will be removed)

(Do not include security passwords with codes below.)

Subscriber Name: **Bank One, Delaware, N.A.**	EXPERIAN Subscriber Code: XXXXXX
Subscriber Address: **201 North Walnut Street, DE1-1024**	EQUIFAX Subscriber Code: XXXXXXX
Wilmington, DE 19801	TRANS UNION Subscriber Code XXXXXXX

CONSUMER INFORMATION

Surname	First	Middle Name	Suffix	SSN:			DOB
NEAL	DANA						

Current Address		City			State	Zip Code	
■■■■■■		■■■■■■			■	■■	

Previous Address	City	State	Zip Code

Current Employer Name	Occupation	City	State

Co-Applicant Information

Surname	First	Middle Name	Suffix	SSN:		DOB

Address (if different)	City	State	Zip Code

Employer Name	Occupation	City	State

CURRENT HISTORICAL ACCOUNT INFORMATION

Account Number	Present Status				24-Month Payment History	Type Acct/ MOP
	Date Open	Date	Balance	Past Due	☐ MOP History	
■■■■■	/ /	/ /				

Metro Status Code	Orig. or Credit Limit Amt.	Terms/ Amount	Date Last Pay	Maximum Delinquency			Status Closed Date	CCC	CII	SCC	ECOA
				Date	Amt.*	MOP					
		/	/ /	/ /			/ /				

Type of Loan	High Credit	First Delinquency			Historical Status						
		Date	P & L Amount	MOP	No. Mos.	30	60	90	120	150	180
		/ /									

*Must be present when reporting a charge off or repossession.   ☐ Automated   ☐ Manual

When you sign this form, you certify that your computer and/or manual records have been adjusted to reflect any changes made.

Reason for deletion or status change from adverse to favorable:

DELETE TRADELINE - CORRECT RECORDS   3RD REQUEST - PLEASE RUSH AND CONFIRM

Authorized Signature: _____	Date: ■■■■■
Please Print Name: ■■■■■	Telephone: ■■■■■

Figure 1.

and is not likely to be compromised. In 2005, Bank of America lost computer tapes containing the financial and personal data of 1.2 million government employees, including U.S. senators. Those tapes contained all sorts of information that identity thieves would love, including SSNs and account information. And in June 2005, Citigroup claimed that UPS lost its computer tapes, which housed account information and SSNs on 3.9 million customers.

When a furnisher/subscriber contacts a bureau requesting a specific adjustment to account information, usually a correction, that request can be performed manually instead of waiting for the Metro 2. That is, furnishers can contact the bureaus at any time, using a standard form known as a Universal Data Form (UDF). There are different variations, but essentially this form is designed to streamline the communication process between the bureau and the subscriber. The UDF consists of standardized information that enables the bureaus to quickly cut to the chase and perform whatever action the furnisher chooses.

The use of the UDF is important to consumers, because they often need information corrected in a hurry. Metro 2 "dumps" are only performed one a month, whereas the UDF makes it possible to have information updated or corrected in less than three days. There's a paper and an automated version (electronic) of the UDF form. I always require a paper copy be provided to me as a condition in all my written settlement agreements (see Chapter 13). You should do likewise.

USERS OF REPORTS

Users are individuals, businesses, agencies, or institutions that request consumer credit files from credit reporting agencies to determine creditworthiness, among other things. Under the FCRA, they can utilize credit report information to determine creditworthiness or in consideration of employment and certain types of insurance. (Life insurance underwriting policies can consider credit history, whereas medical insurance may not.) Of course, sometimes furnishers are users of reports, and vice versa. Existing creditors will often use reports to extend additional credit, to assist in their collection efforts, or to engage in risk-based pricing (i.e., set interest rates based on credit history). Credit reports may be used as follows:[24]

1. to determine eligibility for credit or insurance that will be used primarily for personal, family, or household purposes
2. for employment purposes
3. for other permissible purposes, which are specified as follows:

    *   to review or collect current accounts
    *   to establish eligibility for government licenses or other benefits
    *   to evaluate credit and repayment risks of existing credit obligations
    *   to respond to a legitimate business need for the information in connection with a transaction initiated by a consumer. (Those with whom you are doing business have the right to pull your credit file, period. Providing them with your SSN equals your implicit approval of the inquiry. It's just that simple. In all cases, they can pull one or more bureau files to assess your creditworthiness.)
    *   to set or modify government-mandated child support payment levels
    *   in response to a court order[25]
    *   on written instruction from the consumer

Users have a duty to safeguard credit report information, and failure to do so constitutes a breach of the FCRA. Users may provide a copy of the report to the consumer, though this isn't required.[26]

---

24. NCLC *Fair Credit Reporting* § 2.3.6.1 (5th ed. 2002 and 2005 Supp.). The manual indicates there are a lot of gray areas with no satisfactory answers.
25. Courts have held that judgment holders can also obtain a report on a consumer, and the FTC commentary concurs. Employment purposes are acceptable, as are considerations for promotion, reassignment, or termination. There are others. *Fair Credit Reporting,* § 5.2.4.1 - 5.3.7. (5th ed. 2002 and 2005 Supp.).
26. The big, bad bureaus used to force users into contracts that forbade such disclosure, but this was outlawed with the 1996 amendments to the Act.

Civil penalties exist under the FCRA for impermissible purposes (anything that falls outside of the permissible purposes listed above), up to $1,000 per occurrence for knowing noncompliance. Some states have additional laws, such as the California statute that provides damages up to $2,500 for pulling a report for an impermissible purpose.[27] Criminal penalties also exist for knowingly and willfully obtaining a report under false pretenses.[28]

ABUSIVE PRACTICES IN AN UNFAIR SYSTEM

Not only is the credit reporting system flawed, but it is also inherently unfair, fraught with abusive practices that enable the players to prey on consumers. Among them are risk-based pricing and predatory lending.

Risk-Based Pricing

Often people tell me that creditors are putting the squeeze on them for no reason. They claim that while they've always paid their bills on time, a particular creditor will sometimes double or even triple its interest rate out of the blue. This is a product of risk-based pricing, which is what lenders use to justify raising interest rates and late fee terms in midstream. When lenders perform inquiries, which they can at any time, they can raise consumers' interest rates based on their track record with other lenders. This is known as "universal default." Credit card companies can also raise their interest rates simply because consumers have high balances with other lenders, as reflected on their credit reports.

Just so you're clear on this, let's break it down to its lowest common denominator. A consumer may be struggling with a particular creditor, either due to a large balance or late payment. When a second creditor performs an inquiry on this consumer, whose account has always been in good standing, the large balance or late payment that

---

27. Calif. Civil Code, § 1785.19.
28. 15 U.S.C., § 1681q.

shows up on the report creates the perception that the consumer is a higher risk overall. This causes the creditor to raise the consumer's interest rate—making it even harder for him or her to pay bills and thereby raising the odds of default.

Brilliant.

And just how much interest can the banks charge? In 1979, South Dakota banks were having a hard time coping with double-digit inflation and a recession, as they were borrowing money at 20 percent while the interest rate cap on consumer credit cards was 12 percent. Money was very tight, and banks were not extending many home mortgage or loans of any kind. South Dakota repealed the cap, known as a usury law, permitting banks to charge consumers unlimited interest rates. And since a 1978 U.S. Supreme Court decision known as Marquette[29] permitted banks to apply interest rates to consumers based on where the credit decision is made—or in the state in which the bank resides—banks in South Dakota could now charge unlimited interest to all of their customers. Former South Dakota governor Bill Jenklow claims that within a few months of the repeal of the interest rate cap, he was meeting with the CEOs of Bank of America, First Chicago, Chemical Bank, Chase Manhattan, Citibank, Manufacturer's Hanover, Bank of New York, and others. Shortly thereafter, Delaware also lifted its interest rate cap, and banks, such as MBNA, began moving there.

In 2004, banks in the United States made $30 billion in profits from the credit card business—a record (and this while interest rates were at a 30-year low).[30]

Predatory Lending

Not even members of Congress know quite how to define predatory lending, but it generally refers to consumer loans with high rates of interest and/or high fees, and/or the use of underwriting policies that enable consumers to obtain loans they have little likelihood of being able to repay.

---

29. *Marquette Nat. Bank v. First Omaha Corp.*, 439 U.S. 299 (1978).
30. CardWeb, www.cardweb.com.

The Mortgage Bankers Association identifies the following practices as predatory: "(1) steering borrowers to high-rate loans; (2) intentionally structuring high-cost loans with payments that the borrower cannot afford; (3) falsifying loan documents; (4) making loans to mentally incapacitated homeowners; (5) forging signatures on loan documents; (6) changing the loan terms at closing; (7) requiring credit insurance; (8) falsely identifying loans as lines of credit or open-end loans; (9) increasing interest rates when payments are late; (10) charging excessive prepayment penalties; (11) failing to report good payment histories to credit bureaus; and (12) failing to provide accurate loan balance and payoff amounts."[31]

These practices are widespread among some of the biggest players in the banking arena, particularly credit card issuers. For example, the FTC went after Citigroup (parent of Citibank) for deceptive lending practices, and Citigroup agreed to pay a $215 million settlement in September 2002.[32]

Jodie Bernstein, director of FTC's Bureau of Consumer Protection, said, "They hid essential information from consumers, misrepresented loan terms, flipped loans, and packed in optional fees to raise the costs of the loans."

One area where predatory lending is rampant is in preapproved college student credit offers. Creditors extend lines of credit to students without requiring any type of income or credit track record, knowing full well that the students probably can't repay, yet hoping that parents will step in and pay the balance—along with exorbitant late fees and interest.

More examples of predatory lending can be found in the fine print of cardmember agreements issued by creditors such as Discover Card. Discover has an arbitration clause in its terms of service credit card contract that bars consumers from taking part in class action lawsuits. In my opinion this is a predatory practice, and the California Supreme Court agrees: it has ruled such clauses unenforceable and

---

31. Andrea Lee Negroni and Nick Koufos, *Predatory Lending Laws Trickle Down from Congress to City Hall,* Goodwin Proctor LLP; "AMBA Unveils Mortgage Reform Plan," *Real Estate Finance Today,* June 19, 2000.
32. The FTC action was against one of Citigroup's companies, First Capital.

unconscionable.[33] However, other courts have found the practice acceptable, as in the case of *Jenkins v. First American Cash Advance of Georgia, LLC* (No. 03-16329, 11th Cir. 2005), which upheld the class action waiver.

Discover imposed the class action waiver on those who had existing accounts, sending out notices to cardholders concerning the change in their rights and giving them the option to close their accounts if they didn't like it. That's hardly an option at all. The class action waiver says, "Arbitration: The Cardmember Agreement provides that we may choose to resolve a claim relating to your Account by binding arbitration, in which case, you will not have the right to have that claim resolved by a judge or jury." In my opinion, Congress should ban the use of such language outright. Note that Discover doesn't even provide the Cardmember Agreement on its Web site, which simply states, "You agree to be bound by the terms of the Cardmember Agreement, which will be sent with the Card. You also agree that the Cardmember Agreement and the Account are governed by Delaware and federal law. The Cardmember Agreement, which includes the rates and fees, is subject to change." In other words, "You agree to our terms—and then we'll tell you what the terms are. And by the way, the terms can change—unfavorably—but you'll have the option to close your account if you don't like it." When I contacted Discover's new accounts department and requested the terms, they claimed they would mail them to me. As expected, I never received them; it's safe to say that they were never sent.

The FTC should intervene and at least require that the entire agreement be readily disclosed to those applying online.

Given Discover's practices and subsequent mixed rulings by the courts, I recommend that consumers avoid the Discover Card.

---

33. 105 Cal. App. 4th 326 (Cal. Ct. App., 2d Dist., Jan. 14, 2003); the California Supreme Court determined that California law does prohibit class action waivers and can be enforced; therefore, class action lawsuits are not preempted by the Federal Arbitration Act. However, the court ruled that the choice of law, California or Delaware, had not been determined by the lower court, so the decision was remanded. The appellate court then ruled that choice of law was governed by contract (in this case, Delaware law); Discover won its petition, and the class action was not permitted.

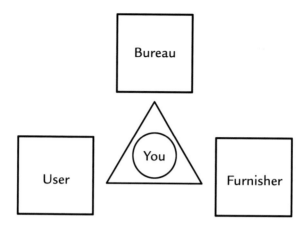

Figure 2.

THE TERRIBLE TRIANGLE

FCRA attorney Leonard Bennett testified before Congress in 2003 as a champion of consumer rights and in advance of FACTA,[34] which was due to go before Congress in December of that year.[35] In that testimony, he referred to the game creditors and reporting agencies play as a "shell game." I couldn't have come up with a better way to describe it. Plenty of case law exists to back his statement up, and if those aren't enough, his full testimony before Congress should remove any doubt.

Have you ever contacted a credit bureau about something erroneous on your report, only to be told, "Contact the creditor," and then contacted the creditor only to be told, "Dispute it with the bureaus"? Meanwhile, your potential lender is saying, "We can't approve you until this matter is resolved." Back and forth it goes, round and round,

---

34. Fair and Accurate Credit Transaction Act, Dec. 2003; amends the Fair Credit Reporting Act.
35. Leonard A. Bennett is a FCRA attorney who often represents consumers in their suits against credit reporting agencies. See Leonard Bennett's full testimony, Appendix B.

until temporary insanity begins to creep in. You are caught up in what I call the Terrible Triangle.

The Terrible Triangle comprises the reporting agency, the furnisher, and the user (potential lender), all manipulating the system to serve their ends, with you caught in the middle. But the shell game they are playing only works because consumers are uninformed. A 2003 study conducted by the Consumer Federation of America found that only 3 percent of Americans could name the three national credit bureaus.

Only the educated consumer is immune to the shenanigans of the Terrible Triangle, and you can soon count yourself among the inoculated. Even those who don't believe they are playing are indeed playing, most of them poorly. Play well, and you will surely win.

CHAPTER 2

YOU—THE PLAYER

I'm a player. Are you?

I became a player out of necessity. When I was medically retired from the military, the Veterans Administration (VA) took a very long time to 'fess up. Meanwhile, finances began to deteriorate substantially, and by the time my ship came in, it was too late for my credit report.

As I explained in the Preface, it seems patently unfair to place the creditworthiness of someone with an illness or injury on par with that of a deadbeat crackhead. If a tragedy befalls someone, then there should be provisions in the FCRA that make reasonable allowances for that.

For example, if it can be shown that someone has an illness or injury, either through a doctor's certification or similar document, it seems only fair that he or she be permitted have any adverse history expunged once any debts are paid back in full. As it stands, any temporary illness or injury will haunt the person for many years.

I speak from experience. I was a good citizen and soldier, and yet the way I was treated by collectors and bureaus alike goes beyond the pale. But instead of moping, I reached down, grabbed myself by my bootstraps, and pulled myself up.

Was it work? You bet it was. But the injustice only angered me, motivating me to fight back and turn the malevolent system on itself.

Tenacity. Relentlessness. These are things that can come from an angry person with pride and purpose. And in the end, I won the credit game—not only for me but also for others who have taken *BestCredit* and made it work for them.

And yet some will claim that what I teach isn't fair, and that it undermines the integrity of the credit reporting system; "it's accuracy that's important," they'll say.

That's laughable. As I have shown, the very people who make such claims—those deeply entrenched in the reporting system who are reliant on making money—have no interest in accuracy whatsoever. Don't listen to what they *say*; look at what they *do*. Since when has any credit bureau ever been interested in accuracy, or fairness for that matter? Is risk-based pricing fair? Is credit scoring fair? Is predatory lending fair? Banks charge exorbitant fees for returned checks; is that fair? And what about their absurd ATM charges? Is it fair that credit reports, with all their inaccuracies, are used to qualify people for employment? Is it fair that consumers got screwed with the passage of the Bankruptcy Reform Bill of 2005 as a result of trillion-dollar-industry lobbyists twisting the arms of self-centered politicians? Is it fair that members of the Terrible Triangle play a shell game and lawmakers won't put an end to it?

Fairness is not an issue, and neither is accuracy. What's at issue is the almighty dollar. Don't ever forget it.

So be it. Knowledge is power, and each and every person who learns what I know will in turn become a force if they share my audacity.

Credit restoration is not a team sport. It's an individual game that you can win or lose all by yourself. It's lonely. It's frustrating. But, as with any game, there are rules and regulations that govern the way it's played. And though I've shown that reporting agencies and creditors don't follow the rules, this very fact only serves to strengthen your chances at winning.

Ever see the comedy *DodgeBall*? There were basically two teams, one with the good guys and another with the bad guys. At the end of the film, it appeared that the good guys had lost in a forfeit because a player failed to show up. Yet one of the good guys always had his head buried in the rule book, learning every little nuance. Everyone thought he was just a pencil-neck, but in the end, it was he who pulled out the rule book and quoted a little-known rule that enabled the good guys to get back into the game and ultimately win.

The same holds true with credit restoration. There are things so seemingly inconsequential and obscure that matter. And I'm the pencil-neck who's drilled down into every aspect, every possibility. All you have to do is be a good student, while playing by the rules and forcing the malevolent players of the Terrible Triangle to do likewise.

REGULATORY AGENCIES AND FAIR CREDIT RIGHTS

The FTC is the regulatory body that oversees and, to some extent, enforces laws concerning credit reporting. The Federal Reserve Board and other federal agencies also play a role in regulating the system, though that involvement is centered on banking oversight. To some extent, attorney generals of all 50 states also play a role in the enforcement of consumer credit laws, but this is geared mostly toward insuring compliance with the laws of the individual states they serve. Whenever you experience any violation of consumer protection statutes, particularly if it's credit related, you should file a complaint with both the FTC and your state attorney general.

Your Rights under the Fair Credit Reporting Act

It's important that you know your rights under the FCRA. The FCRA is designed to help ensure that credit reporting agencies furnish correct and complete information to businesses to use in evaluating your credit or loan application. The following is a summary of the Act:[1]

* You must be told if information in your file has been used against you. Anyone who uses a credit report or another type of consumer report to deny your application for credit, insurance, or employment—or to take another adverse action against you—must tell you, and must give you the name, address, and phone number of the agency that provided the information.

---

1. FTC, www.ftc.gov, or write to: Consumer Response Center, Room 130-A, Federal Trade Commission, 600 Pennsylvania Ave. NW, Washington, D.C. 20580.

- You have the right to know what is in your file. You may request and obtain all the information about you in the files of a consumer reporting agency (your right to "file disclosure"). You will be required to provide proper identification, which may include your SSN. In many cases, the disclosure will be free. You are entitled to a free file disclosure if

  - a person has taken adverse action against you because of information in your credit report;
  - you are the victim of identify theft and place a fraud alert in your file;
  - your file contains inaccurate information as a result of fraud;
  - you are on public assistance;
  - you are unemployed but expect to apply for employment within 60 days;
  - you are entitled to one free disclosure every 12 months upon request from each nationwide credit bureau and from nationwide specialty consumer reporting agencies.

- You have the right to ask for a credit score. Credit scores are numerical summaries of your creditworthiness based on information from credit bureaus. You may request a credit score from consumer reporting agencies that create scores or distribute scores used in residential real property loans, but you will have to pay for it. In some mortgage transactions, you will receive credit score information for free from the mortgage lender.

- You have the right to dispute incomplete or inaccurate information. If you identify information in your file that is incomplete or inaccurate and report it to the consumer reporting agency, the agency must investigate unless your dispute is frivolous. (See www.ftc.gov/credit for an explanation of dispute procedures.)

- Consumer reporting agencies must correct or delete inaccurate, incomplete, or unverifiable information. Inaccurate, incomplete, or unverifiable information must be removed or corrected, usually within 30 days. However, a consumer reporting agency may continue to report information it has verified as accurate.

- Consumer reporting agencies may not report outdated negative information. In most cases, a consumer reporting agency may not report negative information that is more than seven years old or bankruptcies that are more than 10 years old.
- Access to your file is limited. A consumer reporting agency may provide information about you only to people with a valid need—usually to consider an application with a creditor, insurer, employer, landlord, or other business. The FCRA specifies those with a valid need for access.
- You must give your consent for reports to be provided to employers. A consumer reporting agency may not give out information about you to your employer, or a potential employer, without your written consent given to the employer. The trucking industry is generally an exception, however. (For more information, go to www.ftc.gov/credit.)
- You may limit "prescreened" offers of credit and insurance you get based on information in your credit report. Unsolicited prescreened offers for credit and insurance must include a toll-free phone number you can call if you choose to remove your name and address from the lists these offers are based on. You may opt out of receiving these offers with the nationwide credit bureaus at 1-888-5-OPTOUT (1-888-567-8688).
- You may seek damages from violators. If a consumer reporting agency or, in some cases, a user of consumer reports or a furnisher of information to a consumer reporting agency violates the FCRA, you may be able to sue in state or federal court.
- Identity theft victims and active duty military personnel have additional rights.

States may enforce the FCRA, and many states have their own consumer reporting laws. In some cases, you may have more rights under state law. For more information, contact your state or local consumer protection agency or your state attorney general. Table 1 lists the federal regulatory agencies for various types of business.

If any problem exists regarding violations of the FCRA, a complaint should be filed with the appropriate government enforcer from the table provided and the attorneys general of both your state and the

FEDERAL ENFORCERS

TYPE OF BUSINESS:	CONTACT:
Consumer reporting agencies, creditors, collection agencies, and others not listed below	Federal Trade Commission: Consumer Response Center—FCRA Washington, D.C. 20580 www.ftc.gov; 877-382-4357
National banks, federal branches/ agencies of foreign banks (word "national" or initials "N.A." appear in or after bank's name)	Office of the Comptroller of the Currency Compliance Management, Mail Stop 6-6 Washington, D.C. 20219 www.occ.treas.gov; 800-613-6743
Federal Reserve System member banks (except national banks, and federal branches/agencies of foreign banks)	Federal Reserve Board Division of Consumer & Community Affairs Washington, D.C. 20551 www.federalreserve.gov; 202-452-3693
Savings associations and federally chartered savings banks (word "Federal" or initials "F.S.B." appear in federal institution's name)	Office of Thrift Supervision Consumer Complaints Washington, D.C. 20552 www.ots.treas.gov; 800-842-6929
Federal credit unions (words "federal credit union" appear in institution's name)	National Credit Union Administration 1775 Duke Street Alexandria, VA 22314 www.ncua.gov; 703-519-4600
State-chartered banks that are not members of the Federal Reserve System	Federal Deposit Insurance Corporation Consumer Response Center 2345 Grand Avenue, Suite 100 Kansas City, MO 64108-2638 www.fdic.gov; 877-275-3342
Air, surface, or rail common carriers regulated by former Civil Aeronautics Board or Interstate Commerce Commission	Department of Transportation Office of Financial Management Washington, D.C. 20590 www.dot.gov; 202-366-1306
Activities subject to the Packers and Stockyards Act, 1921	Department of Agriculture Office of Deputy Administrator—GIPSA Washington, D.C. 20250 www.usda.gov; 202-720-7051

Table 1.

state in which the violator does business. Violations of the Fair Debt Collection Practices Act (FDCPA)—dealing with debt collectors—will be addressed in a later chapter.

Recent Amendments to the FCRA

As explained, FACTA was adopted in December 2003 as an amendment to the FCRA. Though it was touted as consumer friendly, and not entirely without good effects, it was really nothing more than a feel-good bill that left the industry holding all the cards.

The FCRA was about to lapse. Consumer groups wanted a complete overhaul and, in particular, sought to get rid of a provision in which federal law preempted state action. This is significant, since under the pre-FACTA FCRA, federal law prohibited most types of class action lawsuits against the bureaus; certain federal rules of civil procedure made it impossible, since each party to a class action has to have incurred damage that is "measurable." (How do you measure damages for credit reporting errors, especially considering FICO and others won't release their complete scoring algorithms, i.e., step-by-step problem-solving procedures that use established and recurring computations?) Many states sought to remedy this by creating their own rules concerning class actions, but the preemption provision was kept intact with the passage of FACTA, and consumers lost big time.

Imagine if class actions were permitted on such a scale. *Consumer Reports* magazine estimates that 48 percent of all credit reports have errors, and I suspect that number would shrink to less than 1 percent after a class action or three.

On the upside, FACTA did include some new provisions that are useful:

- *Right to dispute credit report information directly with furnishers.* Consumers can file formal disputes directly with furnishers of information.
- *Opt-out notification requirement.* Affiliates (i.e., business partners) of the bureaus are now required to provide clear and conspicuous notices to consumers of their intention to share

marketing information and to provide consumers with an opportunity to opt out.

- *Risk-based pricing notification requirement.* Creditors that engage in risk-based pricing must now provide notice to customers when they create new terms that are "materially less favorable than the most favorable terms available to a substantial proportion" of their new customers. The FTC has yet to define "materially less favorable."

- *New accuracy standards for furnishers.* Furnishers must now establish reasonable policies and procedures to ensure the accuracy and integrity of the information provided to credit reporting agencies. They are prohibited from providing information that they know or have "reasonable cause to believe" is inaccurate.

- *New requirements for users of consumer reports.* When a consumer credit report uses a substantially different address from that in the consumer's file, the bureaus are required to notify users of the reports. When notified, users are required to have in place reasonable procedures to confirm a consumer's identity. In addition, users are required to dispose of consumer report information in such a way as to preserve its security and confidentiality. The FTC has yet to define this.

- *Rules prohibiting the use of medical information in underwriting decisions.* Creditors cannot use or obtain medical information unless the information is obtained and used pursuant to a specific federal banking agency, FTC, or state insurance agency regulation permitting such use.

- *Bureau and furnisher interface requirements.* Bureaus are required to notify furnishers when they receive a report of identity theft, and furnishers are required to modify or delete information resulting from identify theft. Furnishers are also required to provide notice to consumers that they intend to report negative information.

- *Provision for fraud alerts.* It used to be that this was only available to California residents, but now all consumers may place a fraud alert on their credit files. A fraud alert notifies users of a credit report that the consumer may be a victim of identity theft and requires such users to take specific steps to obtain authorization from the consumer before establishing new credit or raising a credit limit on behalf of that consumer. (More information on fraud and active duty alerts is available in Chapter 11 in the sections on identity theft prevention and recovery.)

- *Provision for active duty alerts.* Military personnel can request that the bureaus place an active duty alert on their credit files. This notifies users of a report that the consumer is an active-duty member of the military and requires such users to take specific steps to obtain authorization from the consumer before establishing new credit or increasing a credit limit on behalf of that consumer.

- *New receipt handling rules for merchants.* Businesses that accept payment by credit (or debit) cards are prohibited from printing more than the last five digits of the account number and the expiry date. This provision is effective December 2006 for cash registers in use before January 1, 2005, and for newer machines it was effective January 1, 2005. If you ever get a receipt with the full account number, inform the merchant of the new law and cross out the last four digits using a pen. If the merchant is intransigent, you can always notify the FTC and state attorney general if you're so inclined.

- *ID theft remedies.* Businesses that have extended credit to someone who used a fake identity to obtain such credit must provide the ID theft victim with copies of the thief's application and any related business records.

Now that you understand some of the basic rules of the FCRA and how to go about enforcing them, it should be clear that there are many laws to protect you and a great deal of recourse available to you. As such, you don't need to recruit others to help you; you just need to have the intestinal fortitude to force the reluctant compliance of others.

Although collection agencies (those that are in the sole business of collecting debt) are not covered here, they will be addressed at length in Chapter 7.

CREDIT COUNSELING, DEBT CONSOLIDATION, AND CREDIT REPAIR

The term "credit counseling" used to mean debt management help. These days, however, the term more likely refers to companies that are in the business of debt consolidation or debt settlement. I've yet to hear from someone who has benefited from such "services," and often I hear from those who have been hurt.

I received the following e-mail just as I began writing this chapter:

From: blank@noneya.com
To: support@bestcredit.com
Subject: HELP!
Date: 06/18/05

My husband and I agreed to "hire" Trinity Debt Management to help us consolidate our debt. We paid them $679/month for two years.

When I had to stop working (I was diagnosed with chronic fatigue syndrome) in February of this year, I had some time to research what was happening. I found that there was a $7,000.00 difference in what Trinity took out of our checking account and what our creditors show was paid.

My husband wants to hire an attorney to go after them since they can't give us a detailed answer to our questions.

Since I am not working, we are struggling BIG TIME. We don't want to file for Bankruptcy, but are desperate for help (we have hired "Credit Attorneys" to clean our credit up, but we still need to know how we can get a consolidation loan with payments that won't kill us. We currently own our home, but only have ~8K in equity built up. My husband is an ordained music/worship pastor and started selling health, life and p & c insurance when I started to have health problems. We have five children, but only one 20 year-old still at home.

Can you direct us? I want to buy your book, but we just don't have the money right now. Any advice you could give us would be GREATLY appreciated.

Thank you!
Regards,

[Name Withheld]

And my reply:

From: support@bestcredit.com
To: blank@noneya.com
Subject: RE: HELP!
Date: 06/19/05

Hi [Name Withheld],

Your problem is not uncommon. First, file a complaint with the FTC
and your state attorney general. The FTC's Web site is here:

http://www.ftc.gov/ftc/consumer.htm

You can also contact the attorneys general in the state which
Trinity does business. Make sure all of your complaints are in writing
(use their Web form if available).

And finally, you'll need to hire an attorney. Your best bet is to
search for one on the National Association of Consumer Advocates
Web site: http://www.naca.net.

Wish I could do more, but once someone takes on a debt settlement company, there isn't much I can do for them. Particularly
when the whole situation is made worse by misdealings. Filing suit
will likely be your only recourse, but it's important that you file the
complaints, as the FTC and attorney general can ultimately shut
Trinity down if they get enough of them.

Good luck,
Dana Neal

Once someone gets into such a situation, he or she truly is beyond
my help. It happens all too often. Hundreds companies are out there
making a great deal of money on the hardship of others. The FTC is
shutting down many of these organizations, even nonprofit companies.
The FTC raided the National Consumer Counsel and closed its doors
in May 2004, and AmeriDebt is currently under investigation for
defrauding consumers. AmeriDebt's Web site is offline, and it looks as
if the company is all but finished. Shady operations like these abound,
and they cause legitimate companies to struggle with draconian laws
meant to shut the bad ones down.

The "nonprofits" are the ones the FTC is currently targeting, since they obtained that status to avoid being bound by the Credit Repair Organizations Act. Such immunity precludes them from having to comply with certain disclosure and other consumer protection requirements. Not only is the FTC going after many nonprofits, but the IRS is also unlikely to grant 501(c)(3) (nonprofit) status to credit repair companies. In fact, it hasn't granted the status to any credit repair organization since April 2003 and has actually revoked the status of four of them, with more being targeted for revocation. Debra J. Kawecki, an IRS attorney, told the Association of Independent Consumer Credit Counseling Agencies in July 2005 that the nonprofits are being shut down for deceptive and fraudulent practices, including high fees, high-pressure tactics, and inadequate educational services.[2] Unfortunately, this hurts legitimate companies as well as consumers.

I've tested some of the nonprofits to see for myself what they're hawking. On June 3, 2004, I contacted 1800creditcarddebt.com (aka 800creditcarddebt.com) as directed by a link on the AmeriDebt Web site, which says: "Unfortunately, AmeriDebt is no longer accepting new clients. However, if you are looking to get help with your debt, you may want to consider 800CreditCardDebt.com."

The customer service rep I spoke with informed me that the company had two programs to choose from—debt consolidation and debt settlement. He explained that debt consolidation would roll all my debts into one and reduce my interest rate, not to exceed 9 percent, while debt settlement would permit the company to negotiate with creditors on my behalf, and I would end up paying 75 cents on the dollar. He said that the company would pay creditors whatever it could negotiate and then keep the rest of the money. (In other words, if the company negotiates 65 cents on the dollar, it keeps the 10 cents.) He said, "The debt settlement will hurt your credit, but don't worry, because we're going to set you up with a credit repair program afterward, and they'll get all of that removed." When I asked more about the credit repair program and how much it costs, he told me it's out-

---

2. Caroline E. Mayer, "IRS Revokes Tax-Exempt Status of 4 Credit-Counseling Agencies," *Washington Post*, July 17, 2005, A10.

sourced to a law firm. When I asked which law firm, he refused to answer and then was evasive, giving me a bunch of double talk.

But there was a lot of bunk in the whole conversation, especially when I asked him to provide a copy of the contract and he refused, saying that I had to fill out several forms and agree to go into the program before a contract would be provided. Then he actually claimed he didn't have a copy of the contract! After a great deal of smooth talking, he realized that I wouldn't join without seeing the contract, so he relented. The contract indicated the company's true name: Debt Set, Inc. I get e-mails all the time from people who claim they've been hurt by this company.

As I've said, the "nonprofits" are often the worst—contrary to what some may tell you. But I've yet to discover one debt consolidation/credit counseling organization that's on the level, nonprofit or otherwise. I can't recommend them for any reason. Creditors often have their own credit counseling and debt-repayment plans. Accounts are often reported to the bureaus as such and will likely cause you to be denied.

Recently a young lady who was attending a local college told me that her finance teacher was advising students who were in financial trouble to seek out nonprofit debt consolidation organizations. Unfortunately, this teacher is seriously misinformed, and it's a shame that impressionable minds will soak up such dubious advice.

Debt Consolidation: A Tactic You Can Use

Just because most debt consolidation companies are crooked doesn't mean that you can't or shouldn't consolidate your debt. Many people take out second mortgages or home equity loans as a way to consolidate their debt. Should you consider this route? Perhaps; it can be helpful in many respects, but it's a tool like any other—one that can be advantageous or detrimental, depending on your situation. Certainly the interest rate will likely be lower than what you're paying on your existing debt, and the interest is tax-deductible. In this respect, debt consolidation can be beneficial. But you must look at other things, such as closing costs and other fees.

If you can get such a loan without paying off existing creditors, then you can hold the money in your bank account and then use it as leverage to get the derogatory credit history removed from the accounts you plan to consolidate. This is described in more detail in Chapter 8.

Later, I'll show you how to negotiate the best terms for each individual account, by getting your debt reduced *and* getting the bad credit removed—what I refer to as Debt Fusion™. Once this is accomplished, that's the time to consolidate the remaining debt if you think it will benefit you. The main attraction at that point will be for a better interest rate, but bear in mind if you close the accounts that you consolidate, it could lower your FICO score. This will depend on the overall distribution of your score and how much a benefit will offset a negative. Reducing the balances on revolving accounts can be very positive, especially if the accounts are kept open, while the negative effect of new credit on a score will diminish quickly over time.

But don't race out and get a home equity (or other any other) loan until after you've read this entire book and you've found a way to maximize its benefits within your credit restoration/debt reduction framework. Then do the math and determine your best course. Always remember, the credit game is a puzzle, and you, with your cunning, have to piece together your future credit report and build the masterpiece you envision. Once you've performed both situational and collective assessments, as described in Chapter 8, things will look much clearer.

If you opt for debt consolidation, always use a reputable lender, i.e., a bank or credit union. (Contact me at www.bestcredit.com/debtconsolidation/ for assistance with self debt consolidation.) Never use alternative sources unless all other avenues have failed and you have no other choice. Most of the reasons were mentioned previously, but I'll add another: bad financial decisions look bad to reputable lenders, making them question your judgment. And as explained in the next chapter, a subpar lender will lower your FICO score.

Credit Repair Organizations and Credit Consulting

Credit repair organizations perform the credit repair themselves (if you're lucky) and will most often charge you a monthly fee for this service. Credit consultants, on the other hand, will perform an analysis of your situation, make recommendations on ways you can fix it yourself, and often walk you through a workable debt consolidation scenario.

With consultants, you get to see firsthand how much work is being performed on your behalf, and you get personalized attention. But with credit repair organizations, there's no way to know exactly what efforts are being made, if any. And although some may guarantee results, the fine print can be very complicated. For example, some will say they'll return fees paid after a year of service, by multiplying the number of deletions by a figure of $50 each, for example, and then returning the difference between that number and the total amount paid. But the problem with this is that there are often many items that can be deleted when someone gets into this situation, since many tradelines contain numerous fields, such as date opened, status, late payment, and so on (explained later). Further, what if they fail to deliver? The contracts are often have very restrictive damage remedies, and the venue will likely be in another state. Who wants to get a lawyer in another state? Surely none will take such a small case, one that will likely be limited to actual damages, without a retainer of thousands of dollars.

Soon I may offer a credit coaching service that won't charge clients recurring monthly fees or rely on someone else to perform the work. I'll simply analyze each individual situation and provide recommendations. If you're interested in such a service, feel free to contact me at www.bestcredit.com/creditconsulting/.

If you do elect to hire a third party to handle your credit matters, the Credit Repair Organizations Act is there to protect you from crooked operators. In summary, the law dictates the following:

- Written contracts are required, with full details of services to be performed and estimates.
- Under federal law, consumers may cancel within three days of signing an agreement. (Some state laws permit cancellation during the contact period at any time.)
- A disclosure spelling out the basic terms of the Credit Repair Organizations Act is required.

There are exemptions to this Act, such as for nonprofit organizations. Again, in recent years the IRS has changed its policy regarding the issuance of such exemptions for credit repair agencies in light of all the fraud. And many states have additional regulations concerning credit repair organizations that greatly restrict their operation. Many states also permit exemptions for attorneys and mortgage brokers. And some allow companies that perform credit repair as a secondary and connected service exemptions. Still others have bonding requirements (required to post money with the state as insurance against loss). Check your state laws.

STAY ON POINT

It's easy to become angry about the system, and many people become frustrated.

But have you ever played poker? If you have, you'll often see players making remarks grumbling about the weak play of others. It's kind of silly if you think about it. After all, it's the poor play of others that puts money in their pockets.

The credit reporting agencies can be viewed in much the same way. While people will gnash their teeth, cursing the unfairness of the system, they forget that this same flawed system is the gift horse of someone attempting to remove accurate derogatory data from his or her credit report. As you'll discover, if it weren't for the screwed-up system of data storage and retrieval, the twisted queries and filters, and the impossible workload of those in the system, many attempts at credit restoration would simply fail. If you play your cards right, you can take the same flawed system that has worked against you and make it work for you.

So don't get hung up on what's wrong with the system. Focus your energies on what really matters: the deletion of any bad credit. *Play the game.*

One way to get a leg up on the game is through credit scoring. By understanding its many subtleties, you can even the score long before the real game of credit restoration even begins.

CREDIT SCORING
AND LOAN APPROVAL

FICO's decision to release detailed information about its credit scoring model in 2002 came as a result of intense pressure from Congress and consumer advocacy groups. It has given consumers a significant leg up. Now we don't have to make as many guesses about how to improve our credit score. For example, in the past it was assumed that a person's age played a role in scoring. This was a reasonable conclusion, since older people had better scores overall. But in reality, it's the age of the credit report that matters—an important difference. New knowledge such as this can prove very powerful in devising individualized tactics and strategies for improving credit scores.

Credit scores are derived using software that analyzes the data contained in a report. This software uses algorithms to come up with a solution for analyzing a finite number of variables. One big advantage to this is that everyone is treated equally by the software, as the software does not discriminate as people sometimes do; it is indifferent to someone's religion or hairstyle, for example.

Don't be alarmed when you order your credit reports and find that your credit scores from each of the Big Three bureaus are different. The discrepancies can be attributed in part to the fact that certain accounts either don't show up on each report or are reported differently. It's also because the bureaus use different scoring models. Equifax uses the FICO score, while Experian and Trans Union use their proprietary models. Yet you can obtain a FICO score for each of the individual Big Three reports directly through the consumer arm of FICO, myFICO (www.myfico.com) or one of its affiliates. There are many FICO affiliates, though by purchasing from All3Reports (www.all3reports.com), you're supporting a BestCredit partner.

In addition to the FICO score, which Equifax markets under the name Score Power, the other two credit scoring models used by lenders are Trans Union's TrueCredit and Experian's Plus Score. To illustrate how confusing this can get, compare the following scores, all calculated for the same individual in the same hour (and note how each compares to the FICO score calculated for the same set of data):

Experian/Plus Score (Range: 330–830)
Plus Score: 702
(FICO Score: 711)

Equifax/Score Power (Range: 300–850)
Score Power: 687
(FICO Score: 687)

Trans Union/TrueCredit (Range: 400–925)
TrueCredit: 644
(FICO Score: 688)

At first glance, the different scoring ranges might appear to be an issue, but upon further examination, Experian's scoring range is 500 points (330–830), versus 550 for Equifax/FICO (300–850) and 525 (400–925) for Trans Union. Experian's Plus Score has nearly the same range as the FICO, so it's basically a wash, and Equifax uses FICO, so range is not an issue there. The big discrepancies and problems arise with Trans Union's proprietary score. If the scoring algorithms are indeed similar, then the TrueCredit score should be around 770, not 644. The range of the TrueCredit score is 525 points, while the range of the FICO score is 550 points. Though I'm no mathematician, I simply took the 688 Trans Union FICO score and converted it to 388/550, which is 70.54 percent of the range. Using the TrueCredit range of 525, I then took the 70.54 percent of the 525 range, ending up with 370, and added it to the 400 TrueCredit floor for 770. (Although this doesn't take into consideration that the starting point is 400 for TrueCredit versus 300 for FICO, it's close enough for government work. It serves to illustrate the main point, which is that TrueCredit's score doesn't jive with FICO's at all, falling within what TrueCredit considers to be a poor range, while the FICO score for that same report falls within what FICO considers a good range.) From what I've seen based on my own observations and anecdotal evidence, it appears that TrueCredit assigns derogatory history more weight than FICO does overall, since FICO is more forgiving over time, placing more weight on *recency of lateness.*

Of course, this is just one set of scores, so my research method doesn't exactly qualify as scientific. On the other hand, this example is useful for demonstrating that differences can exist. Fortunately, few lenders use Trans Union's TrueCredit score. As such, don't get hung up on it. It's the FICO score that consumers should be most concerned about, since it's the one the majority of lenders look at in determining creditworthiness. Besides, if you can get your FICO score to within acceptable levels, then the other scores will likely follow suit. Gear your efforts toward FICO, and you'll come out ahead in the long run.

As an aside, the bureaus also each have a proprietary FICO score. Equifax is known as Beacon, Trans Union is known as Empirica, and Experian is known as Experian/FICO Risk Model. Of course, Equifax's Score Power is basically the same thing as a Beacon; the others are not made available to consumers, though lenders may obtain Trans Union's Empirica and the Experian/FICO Risk Model scores when they pull consolidated reports.

Lenders use the FICO score primarily as a tool for early detection of potential credit problems. By analyzing past data, they believe they can predict future results.

This has some merit, but as with all computer algorithms, the FICO score isn't without flaws. Unfortunately, that's outside your control. For now, all you can do is play along. The name of the game is improving your score.

National Distribution of FICO Scores

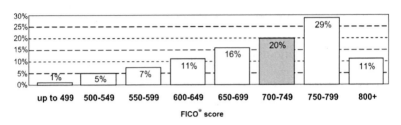

Figure 3.

Delinquency Rates by FICO Score

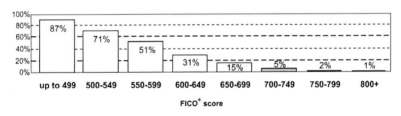

Figure 4.

FICO'S METHODOLOGY

By looking at previous credit report data and default rates based on that data, FICO believes that by matching an individual's credit report to those of other consumers with similar entries, it can more accurately predict default rates. They match people in this way and then assign them to categories. Based on the category in which the consumer is placed, he or she is then given a scorecard. Each consumer's credit history is initially assigned one of ten scorecards based on his or her worst credit entry and is sequentially passed through multiple scorecards. People who have filed for bankruptcy in the last year, for example, are assigned the worst initial scorecard, as are those with recent late payments.

This is why it's not necessarily beneficial to have all adverse entries drop off your report. Because of the way scorecards work, you may have worked your way up to the highest level within a given scorecard, and when entire tradelines fall off (due to the statute of limitations for adverse reporting, for example) you end up in a different, "better" initial scorecard, which can actually lower your score overall. That is, the lesser initial scorecard has a ceiling that goes higher than the floor of the next highest scorecard. People with a sparse credit history in particular are more susceptible to this anomaly, since the weight of a longer credit history counteracts the dropping off of an old account— one that is holding up a score because of its age. Yes, length of credit history counts substantially, which is explained shortly.[1]

FICO scores range from 300 to 850, and, assuming that your total debt-to-income ratio falls within the acceptable limits (i.e., your total monthly debt, including the new loan, doesn't exceed 45 percent of your gross income), a score of 620+ will get you approved with a mainstream mortgage lender. To get the best interest rates, however, you will need a score of 720+. If your score is 780+, mort-

---

1. FICO claims, "Bad credit hurts you more than age helps you." My experience does not bear this out. FICO's Nexgen model is supposed to eliminate this problem. And yet, if FICO claims that it's not a problem with the classic FICO scoring model, why does it then claim that Nexgen fixes the problem?

gage lenders will fight over your business, perhaps offering even better terms, such as reduced points (each point is equal to 1 percent of the total loan) or closing costs. A score of 500–619 will get you a B or C loan (alternative loan, often referred to as "subprime") with inflated interest rates and other undesirable terms, such as higher closing costs. Even if your score falls within their acceptable range, subprime mortgage lenders will usually decline you for 12 months following a bankruptcy. Add another year if you've had a foreclosure. By comparison, it takes two years to get loan approval from mainstream lenders following a bankruptcy and three years following a foreclosure.

Tip: Most mortgage lenders will pull all three credit reports and scores and then use the middle score. Some will even take the average of the top two scores and throw out the worst. Reputable auto lenders will most often take the highest FICO score, though some banks and credit unions will only pull the reports from bureaus to which they subscribe. Find out in advance of any auto loan application by checking with the dealer's finance department (or the bank or credit union if you're obtaining the loan directly).

Why Care? Higher Scores Can Save You Money

The importance of improving your FICO score cannot be overstated, and the biggest jumps in savings occur in the 620–700 range for mainstream mortgage and auto loans.

Using FICO's Loan Savings Calculator (www.myfico.com), it's easy to see what kind of savings someone seeking a $200,000 mortgage can expect from a small change in his or her credit score. Figure 5 shows an example from June 6, 2005.

Someone with a score of 674 versus 700 can expect to pay $222 more per month ($1,378–$1,156), $2,664 more per year ($222 x 12 months), or $79,914 more over the life of the loan ($296,207–$216,293). But 26 FICO points doesn't really tell the story. Note that

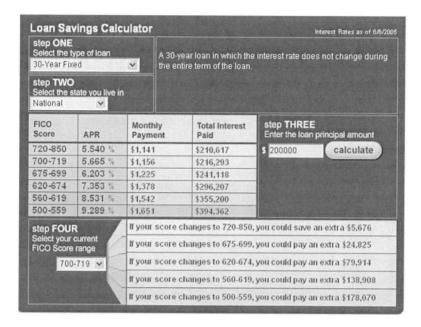

Figure 5.

Copyright © 2005 Fair Isaac Corporation. Fair Isaac, the Fair Isaac logo, and the Fair Isaac product and service names are trademarks or registered trademarks of Fair Isaac Corporation.

all you need if you have a score of 674 is one point higher in order to go to the next tier, the 675–699 tier, which represents a savings of $153 per month ($1,378–$1,225).

FACTORS THAT AFFECT YOUR FICO SCORE

FICO's scoring summary (www.myfico.com) lists five categories that affect a score: payment history, amounts owed, length of credit history, types of credit used, and new credit. Each category is further broken down into subfactors, for a combined total of 22 factors. The process of generating is a score is what FICO refers to as a "multi-variant analysis." I guess this is just a fancy way of saying that multiple variables are analyzed. Here is the exact language from FICO's Web site showing how each factor is weighted:

Payment History – [35%]

- Account payment information on specific types of accounts (credit cards, retail accounts, installment loans, finance company accounts, mortgage, etc.)
- Presence of adverse public records (bankruptcy, judgments, suits, liens, wage attachments, etc.), collection items, and/or delinquency (past-due items)
- Severity of delinquency (how long past due)
- Amount past due on delinquent accounts or collection items
- Time since (recency of) past-due items (delinquency), adverse public records (if any), or collection items (if any)
- Number of past-due items on file
- Number of accounts paid as agreed

Amounts Owed – [30%]

- Amount owing on accounts
- Amount owing on specific types of accounts
- Lack of a specific type of balance, in some cases
- Number of accounts with balances
- Proportion of credit lines used (proportion of balances to total credit limits on certain types of revolving accounts)
- Proportion of installment loan amounts still owing (proportion of balance to original loan amount on certain types of installment loans)

Length of Credit History – [15%]

- Time since accounts opened
- Time since accounts opened, by specific type of account
- Time since account activity

New Credit – [10%]

- Number of recently opened accounts, and proportion of accounts that are recently opened, by type of account

- Number of recent credit inquiries
- Time since recent account opening(s), by type of account
- Time since credit inquiry(s)
- Reestablishment of positive credit history following past payment problems

Types of Credit Used – [10%]

- Number of (presence, prevalence, and recent information on) various types of accounts (credit cards, retail accounts, installment loans, mortgage, consumer finance accounts, etc.)

Please note that:

- *A score takes into consideration all these categories of information, not just one or two.* No one piece of information or factor alone will determine your score.
- *The importance of any factor depends on the overall information in your credit report.* For some people, a given factor may be more important than for someone else with a different credit history. In addition, as the information in your credit report changes, so does the importance of any factor in determining your score. Thus, it's impossible to say exactly how important any single factor is in determining your score—even the levels of importance shown here are for the general population and will be different for different credit profiles. What's important is the mix of information, which varies from person to person and for any one person over time.
- *Your FICO score only looks at information in your credit report.* However, lenders look at many things when making a credit decision including your income, how long you have worked at your present job and the kind of credit you are requesting.
- *Your score considers both positive and negative information in your credit report.* Late payments will lower your score, but establishing or reestablishing a good track record of making payments on time will raise your score.

Payment history accounts for 35 percent of the total score, meaning it's essential that you pay your bills on time and remove the worst of bad credit from your credit report. But the remaining 65 percent of the pie comprises amounts owed (30 percent), length of credit history (15 percent), types of credit used (10 percent), and new credit (10 percent). That means you can have a perfect payment history, and two-thirds of your credit score is still blowing in the wind! It's also important to note that since FICO bases its scoring summary on the *average person*, the weight given to certain factors can shift depending on the individual. For example, payment history might account for 70 percent of a total score if other aspects of the credit report warrant it—such as an abundance of new and subpar accounts or short age of the credit history (explained shortly).

Let's dissect each of the five scoring elements and consider them in terms of their relative connection to practical, real-world actions you can take to improve your score.

Payment History

As explained, payment history is the most heavily weighted factor, comprising 35 percent of the total credit score for the average person.

1. The last 12 months of payment history carries the most significant weight, so recent late payments are the worst. One recent late payment on a single account can lower a score by 15 to 40 points, and missing one payment cycle for all accounts in the same month can cause a score to tank by 150 points or more! This puts a score well below loan-eligibility range overnight. Those 150 points won't come back overnight, though, I assure you. Bills must be paid on time.

2. It's estimated that each judgment and collection account entry can reduce a FICO score from 15 to 40 points. The severest detrimental effects come from entries that involve public records, such as judgments, and information from an original creditor, such as tradeline information. That is, an entry such as collection account (an account past due 90 days or more) from an original creditor (the issuing bank of a credit card, for example) will carry more weight than a collection account

from a third-party debt collector that is collecting on behalf of an original creditor. Collection accounts and judgments—even paid judgments—are worse than a bankruptcy that's two years old (assuming a good track record since the bankruptcy), so it's important to avoid or remove judgments and collection accounts at all costs. You can still get approved for a home mortgage at the very best rates within two years after bankruptcy. The road to a good credit score is very similar after bankruptcy but a bit trickier. This is explained in far greater detail in Chapter 12.

3. The number of tradelines that are "paid as agreed" will raise a credit score, though not by very much (unless they're adding to an average of the total credit history, explained shortly). It's important to make sure at least three accounts in good standing appear on your credit report, since the more accounts in good standing, especially open, the better.

4. Public records are factored into the FICO payment history category, including such things as judgments and liens. As such, all adverse public record information must be removed from your credit report.

5. Consecutive late payments hurt your score exponentially. In other words, the first late payment isn't weighted as heavily as the second, the second as heavily as the third, and so on. This is particularly true for lateness occurring in the 12 months prior to scoring. Keep this in mind when prioritizing the removal of adverse information, as you may want to first remove items of recent and multiple lateness (especially from the same furnisher), which may yield the greatest benefit in the shortest amount of time.

6. Lofty scores are more volatile and will be impacted more by recent lateness. For example, for someone with a score over 800, one 30-days-late entry can reduce it by 100 points, whereas someone with a score of 650 may see a change of only 25 points for the same entry. This is another reason to place recent lateness at the head of the pack when prioritizing bad credit removal.

7. FICO does not include adverse payment history when an account is shown as in dispute by a consumer. For information

on how to have credit bureaus show an account as in dispute, see "Four Times When Furnishing Is Limited" in Chapter 4.

8. Although participating in a credit counseling or debt repayment plan with a creditor can get you denied by most lenders, it is neutral to a FICO score.

Again, the 35 percent weight that the FICO scoring model gives to payment history is for a typical person. This weight can rise substantially if the credit report contains recent delinquent tradelines, collection accounts, or public record entries. For example, with the other factors (amounts owed, length of credit history, types of credit used, and new credit) in a very good state where FICO is concerned, I've seen recent delinquent accounts with a recent bankruptcy take a score down to 450 in weeks! This would put the weight of payment history at more like 70 percent; such a score is only 30 percent of the range theoretical maximum of 850 (150 points of the 550 range, 300–850, is 27.27 percent, leaving roughly 70 percent affected by the payment history).

This knowledge is helpful in understanding how recent lateness can be a huge detriment, and certainly should be prioritized accordingly when removing bad credit.

Amounts Owed

Few people understand the enormous impact their balances can have on their FICO scores. Yet this is the second most weighted factor in the credit score, at 30 percent.

1. The more owed relative to the credit card limit (cap), the lower a FICO score. And there are cutoffs or segments, meaning that within certain ranges of a balance percentage there's no effect, and then a change when a balance hits a cutoff. The cutoffs are as follows: 0–19 percent, 20–39 percent, 40–59 percent, 60–79 percent, 80–99 percent, 100+ percent. Each increasing cutoff harms a score the same amount as the previous (e.g., if a balance goes from 39–40 percent, it will harm a score at the same rate as its going from 79–80 percent would). (Many "experts" claim 50 percent of the credit limit is a magic number. But as you can see, this is wrong.) Keep all balances

on your revolving (credit card) accounts below 40 percent of the credit limit, and never exceed that amount. If possible, never exceed 19 percent.

2. The "amounts owed" factor not only takes into consideration all accounts, but each individual account as well. The FICO model will first look at the revolving account with the highest balance relative to the limit and weight this heavily. It will then look at all the accounts (including installment loans, which are fixed payments, such as on an auto) relative to the cumulative limits. If you carry a balance, try to keep it to only one account if it can be below 20 percent. Otherwise, spread the debt around to all the accounts, keeping each one below 40 percent. And if you know when your creditor is reporting, time your payments accordingly; the balance will be lower during the reporting period. Unfortunately, the bureaus only report the date and month, not the day on which an account is reported. But if you are serious about finding out when a creditor reports to the bureaus, you can subscribe to a credit monitoring service (see Chapter 11), which permits unlimited new credit report access over a period of time. You may check this daily to discover when creditors report to any of the Big Three (though a separate subscription for each individual bureau is required for unlimited access to each of their reports).

3. As a top negative factor, FICO will often report, "You have no recent revolving balance information being reported." In general, moderate and responsible use of revolving credit accounts will boost the score slightly. Research shows that consumers with very moderate usage of revolving credit accounts (charging low balances and repaying them on time) have slightly better repayment risk than those who do not use revolving credit at all. Responsible, frequent use of credit increases a score, so use your credit cards regularly (as long as you keep the balances below 20 percent of the credit limit), since not using them will hurt a score.

4. Mortgages and other installment loans (e.g., auto loans) are also considered in terms of "gap" (that is, balance relative to amount originally borrowed), though not to the same degree as revolving debt. However, Fair Isaac will not say how much

of a role this plays. Paying down installment loans below 40 percent will help.

5. Those holding second mortgages may technically have a "line of credit." It has been generally assumed that such accounts are treated as revolving accounts and can decimate a score if the balances are high. However, Craig Watts of Fair Isaac explained that the FICO model accommodates this by assuming those with very high home equity lines of credit (HELOCs) are using them as second mortgages. He says that someone with a $10,000 HELOC will have it treated as revolving debt, while someone with a $100,000 HELOC will have it treated as installment. He wouldn't say what the cutoff is, even going so far as to say it would change if the secret ever got out. (Many would simply go after a HELOC right below the cutoff, which he claims would be manipulating the system.) My wild, safe guess is that the cutoff falls between $30,000 and $60,000. The best bet is to dump the HELOC if there's a large balance relative to the limit and get a second mortgage if practicable. (Of course, someone who is serious about scoring could check his or her score, close the HELOC, make sure it's reported closed with the credit bureaus, and then check the score again. HELOCs can usually be reopened within a couple of months of closing. Ask your lender.)

6. Mortgages and other installment loans (e.g., auto loans) are also considered in terms of "gap" (that is, balance relative to amount originally borrowed), though not to the same degree as revolving debt. However, Fair Isaac will not say how much of a role this plays. Paying down installment loans below 40 percent will help.

Credit History

Weighted at 15 percent, credit history is no small thing. For a FICO score to be calculated, your credit report must contain at least one account that has been open for six months or more and at least one account that has been updated in the past six months. The older your credit accounts, the better your score.

1. FICO scoring takes into account both the oldest credit account and the average age of all open accounts, so it makes sense to keep accounts that are in good standing open (unless they are of the subpar variety; see "Types of Credit" below). Closing accounts not only lowers your score by reducing open account history, but it may also affect the "amounts owed" portion of the pie by lowering the total credit available so that remaining balances weigh more in terms of a percentage of the total available credit. If you've already closed some very old accounts, some creditors will permit you to open them back up (under the same account number). Reopening an account that's far older than anything currently open or reopening a couple of old accounts may be worth a try if doing so will increase the average age of all open accounts. Just bear in mind that before reopening your accounts creditors will perform an inquiry, which will put a small downward pressure on your FICO score. Yet the benefit of adding an aged account should override this, especially for those with a sparse or short credit history.

2. Recent activity helps your score, so use your accounts. If you have several revolving accounts, rotate using them every couple of months or so while keeping the balances below 40 percent of the cap or paying them off in full every month.

Are you beginning to see how one of the five scoring elements can affect one or more of the other four?

Types of Credit

The types of credit and creditors account for 10 percent of your credit score. The best scenario is to have a mix of secured and unsecured credit and installment and revolving accounts. Secured credit is simply when collateral is used, such as a house or car, while unsecured credit is when no collateral is used, and the credit extended is guaranteed with a simple signature or promise. The ideal mix appears to be a couple of credit cards and a mortgage or an installment loan on a car.

The quality of the lender also matters. There are captive and general lenders. Auto manufacturers are captive lenders—they loan money on their product only; the FICO scoring model treats them the same as a bank, which is good. Credit from auto manufacturing companies such as Toyota Motor Credit and General Motors is fine. But be wary of outside dealer financing; it's often from a finance company. Finance companies, unlike banks, are general lenders; they loan money on anything and are to be avoided because they will hurt your FICO score.

FICO's scoring algorithm attempts to detect if a consumer is making poor credit decisions—that is, getting poor credit terms such as paying a higher interest rate. It's assumed, with some merit, that consumers who use general lenders are making bad credit decisions, and thus any lender that has "Banc" or "Finance" in its name will lower your credit score.

Appliance and electronics stores are always offering "90 days same as cash," or "no payments for two years." That type of credit is almost always provided by outside finance companies and is harmful to a FICO score. The exceptions are department stores such as Sears and Macy's, which provide branded credit cards using Citibank and Chase Manhattan, respectively.

New Credit

Though it's weighted at only 10 percent, obtaining new credit impacts a score far more than most people realize.

1. Anytime you apply for credit of any kind, the potential lender performs an inquiry. These compound, with each successive one taking more points off your score. Inquiries have a greater impact on those with a shorter credit history and/or fewer accounts because FICO assumes that the newer you are to credit, the more likely you are to overindulge. FICO also claims that those with six or more inquiries in a two-year span are eight times more likely to declare bankruptcy than those with no inquiries (this claim was made prior to the Bankruptcy Reform Bill of 2005 taking effect). Many department stores try to lure you into applying for a credit card in exchange for 10 percent or more off your purchase. Don't do it! Don't apply for any credit unless you absolutely need it!

(Exceptions would be the rebuilding of credit, explained later, and those needing to establish credit for the first time.)

2. Some inquiries don't count against your FICO score, including those you perform yourself and those coded PRM (permissible purpose), which include preapproved credit offers, those considered to be "routine account reviews" by existing creditors, and employment-related inquiries. Further, "rate shopping" (going to multiple lenders in search of the best rate on a car or home loan) will only count as a single inquiry if the multiple inquiries were made in the same 14-day period (though each inquiry will still show up on the report). In addition, the FICO score will ignore all inquiries made in the 30 days prior to scoring, so it will be completely unaffected by rate shopping.

3. In 2001, FICO developed a new scoring model called Nexgen. It is supposed to be a more accurate predictor of consumer behavior, but few lenders have adopted it because of the cost involved in fielding the new software. Moreover, lenders are reluctant to adopt something that Fannie Mae and Freddie Mac (explained later in this chapter) have yet to endorse; it took them six years to endorse FICO's original scoring model. Nexgen does a few things better, like permitting 45-day rate shopping verses 14. This is excellent, as it allows those in search of a home or auto to take up to six weeks as opposed to two when deciding on what lender to do business with and not be penalized for multiple inquiries during that period.

4. Each time you actually obtain new credit, it will affect your FICO score, most likely in a negative way. The more new accounts you have relative to the total number of accounts reported, the worse the effect on your score. New credit will be most detrimental to someone with a shorter credit history. If you've had past credit problems, getting new credit will harm your score in the short term, but it will help you in the long run if you get the right type of credit and pay on time. In the best-case scenario, someone who has a stellar record and hasn't applied for new credit in many years

(say 10 or 15) can actually boost his or her score by opening up a new account.

5. Unsecured new credit will do more harm than secured new cred-
    it. Be cognizant of this, and obtain unsecured credit judiciously.

6. FICO scores both secured and unsecured cards the same way.

Caution: When you receive credit card offers, bear in mind
that only "preapproved" is preapproved. "Preselected," "pre-
qualified," or similar terms do not mean approved. Even
some preapproved offers have additional conditions; read
the fine print. Applying for these cards will generate an
inquiry that counts against your credit score. Further, auto
dealers are notorious for performing inquiries without
approval. Don't give them your SSN unless you fully intend
to buy a car and are certain to get approval. (You can be certain when you have good credit and your debt-to-income
ratio is within their acceptable range.)

People often ask if auto insurers may perform an inquiry on a credit report. They may, unless state law specifically precludes it.[2] Inquiries
will be covered in detail in Chapter 10.

IMPACT OF ADVERSE ENTRIES

In FICO's summary, notice the fine print: "The importance of any
factor depends on the overall information in your credit report."

There's no perfect way to predict what variable will change the
weight given to any of the five scoring elements, which is why FICO's
algorithm is often referred to as the "black box." However, certain gen-
eralizations can be drawn, and, with respectable accuracy, a range of

---

2. Many states have adopted laws that regulate the practice, such as the score not
    being the sole determinant, as well as disclosure rules. See the National
    Association of Mutual Insurance Commissioners Web site (www.namic.org) for
    more information.

point change can be roughly predicted for many of the possibilities, particularly those involving payment history. After all, it's this category that can move a score very quickly—and in ways that aren't subtle.

FICO states that "the importance of any factor depends on the overall information in your credit report." As I've shown, FICO uses stair-stepping scorecards, which are assigned to people based on many factors and which can change with a slight modification of credit report data. Any extreme entry (a recent bankruptcy, for example) can skew a person's score by placing him or her into a different, undesirable initial scorecard. And since the importance of any one factor in determining your score changes as the information in your credit report changes, it's impossible to say exactly how important any single factor is in determining your score. What's important is the mix of information, which varies from person to person and for any one person over time.

This makes perfect sense. Someone with very few accounts, for example, may be more negatively impacted by a late payment than someone with many accounts. Likewise, someone with new credit may be more negatively impacted by lateness than someone with no new credit. Keep this in mind when trying to raise your credit score. Of course, removing anything *recently* negative will always help some and will often help a great deal. I've seen one *BestCredit* student with a 12-year credit history remove one 30-day late installment payment that was 18 months old—her only adverse entry—raising her FICO credit score 40 points, from 638 to 778! Now that's money.

When disputing negative entries on your credit report in an effort to have them removed, you will have to exert a certain amount of time and effort for each item, and the priority you give to each entry will vary according to your situation. Some entries may be more severe than others on their face; for instance, a paid judgment that's three years old may look more adverse that a late payment within the last 60 days. Yet the latter will impact a score far more. *If you want to obtain a loan in the near term*, you might consider targeting entries that affect your score the most. However, this may not always be possible, since different factors may play into the probability for removal, such as whether money is owed or not. Again, this will become clearer later, especially when you perform collective and situational assessments, as outlined in Chapter 8. But in the mean-

GENERAL EFFECT ON FICO® SCORE BY **SEVERITY OF PUBLIC RECORD OR TRADELINE**		
LOW	**MEDIUM**	**HIGH**
• Bankruptcy 3+ years	• Bankruptcy 2- years	• Bankruptcy 1- year
• Paid lien 3+ years	• Paid lien 2- years	• Unpaid lien
• Paid judgment 3+ years	• Paid judgment 2- years	• Unpaid judgment
• Paid collection account 3+ years	• Paid collection account 2- years	• Collection account
• Paid charge-off 3+ years	• Paid charge-off 2- years	• Current late
• 30+ late 2+ years	• 30+ late < 180 days	• Charge-off
• 60+ late 2+ years	• 60+ late < 180 days	• 30+ late < 60 days
• 90+ late 2+ years	• 90+ late < 180 days	• 60+ late < 60 days
• 120+ late 2+ years	• 120+ late < 180 days	• 90+ late < 60 days
• 3+ inquiries < 1 year	• 4+ inquiries < 1 year	• 120+ late < 60 days
• 4+ inquiries < 2 years	• 6+ inquiries < 2 years	• Multiple late 1- year
• Multiple late 3+ years	• Multiple late 1–2 years	

Table 2.

time, Table 2 shows how various negative items rank in terms of their general impact on a credit score.

Keep in mind that I don't know for sure what entry is worse than another on a FICO score; this is just my opinion based on anecdotal evidence. Again, since the severity of a mark is dependent on score-cards and algorithms, each item's impact can shift up or down, depending on other factors that have nothing to do with payment history.

Credit Score Estimator

The FICO Score Estimator, available on the Bankrate Web site (http://origin.bankrate.com/brm/fico/calc.asp) is a useful tool in my opinion. Although it gives only ranges, it coincides with the real world in my experience; real-world scores seem to consistently fall near the middle of the FICO Estimator ranges. And while it doesn't interface directly with your individual credit report, it is useful for running hypothetical scenarios. Give the Estimator a try, changing a single variable and running multiple scenarios, to get an idea of what you can accomplish by modifying or deleting certain hypothetical entries and paying bills on time (over time).

Credit Score Simulator

In addition to the Estimator, FICO has also provided a tool called the Simulator (www.myfico.com). It goes beyond the hypothetical, serving as a personalized simulator that interfaces directly with your report, and you can peer into your future report by changing some variables. Although it doesn't give you the ability to simulate the deletion or alteration of tradelines and public records, using it in conjunction with the Estimator may give you some idea about where you can take your score and how fast, perhaps assisting you in the prioritization process.

Here are some generalities I've noticed with regard to FICO scores and reports that I've studied over time, viewing various credit reports and simultaneously toying with the FICO Score Estimator and Simulator:

- A current or recent late payment will affect a score a great deal more than a bankruptcy that's been discharged for three years or more.
- Creditors who've had their accounts included in bankruptcy by a debtor will tag such accounts on a credit report as "included in bankruptcy." Removal of these accounts from a credit report has some affect on a score, around 10 points on average for each when a score is within the 600–730 range.
- For credit reports with a very bad entry, like bankruptcy (more than three years old), yet no other bad marks, there's a FICO score ceiling (maximum) that falls around 730. This is true for someone with an average-length credit history (15 years), and the score doesn't improve much once three years have elapsed post-discharge. (Yes, it's possible for someone to have a bankruptcy and no other adverse entries, since those with a bankruptcy who are in the middle of credit restoration will remove

the other bad marks first if they've read my book, and then remove the bankruptcy in accordance with Chapter 10.) I ran the FICO Score Estimator to test this and noticed the bankruptcy variable was set to a max of three-plus years, which supports my theory. The Estimator listed the maximum under this scenario at 760, but I've yet to see a maximum of a range ever attained.

- Using the scenario above, I simply removed the bankruptcy from the Estimator, and the FICO score maximum was then 790, only 30 points higher than the FICO cap where a bankruptcy was three years old.

- Continuing with the same scenario, I changed another variable and added a single recent collection account to the 3-year-old bankruptcy. I listed it as a $250–$499 debt, plus indicated that it was currently late, and the score went to a range of 595–645, dropping the maximum by 115 points and the minimum by 105.

- Although the Estimator doesn't ask about credit limits, it does ask for total nonmortgage debt and then asks about balances as a percentage of that debt. This seems odd. If the Estimator is to be taken at face value, then there's something it is using regarding total nonmortgage debt that should be discovered. Taking a closer look, I ran it using the max range of $20,000+ for the nonmortgage debt and then ran it again using $0. The score range was actually the same, 730–780. Suspecting that the debt would have an impact if there was recent lateness, I ran the Simulator again, simply changing a variable to include one recent late payment, and the ranges were still the same. And yet again, the same for high balances. I kept trying to get the simulated increase in debt to move the range but couldn't. This is consistent with my own experience: it doesn't appear that having a lot of nonmortgage debt and lots of accounts is a big issue; at issue are the balances relative to the limits, which are even more weighty if there's derogatory history in the mix. (Though a lender can deny for having too many open accounts.)

- The biggest downward moves come with recent late payments

or collection accounts, recent bankruptcy, and high balances relative to limits.

- Multiple late payments will make payment history worse on a magnified scale, particularly if they're more recent. Within the last 90 days is the worst but will gradually carry less weight as time passes, especially up to three years.

THINGS YOU CAN DO RIGHT NOW
TO IMPROVE YOUR SCORE

There are some easy things you can do immediately to improve your score, not least of which is to *begin to pay your bills on time, now and forevermore*. You'd be surprised how rapidly things improve once you do this one thing.

Moreover, there are five additional steps you can take: (1) make sure positive information gets reported, (2) reestablish years of good credit where none existed before, (3) remove adverse information that you know to be false, (4) have credit limits raised, and (5) remove inaccurate adverse information.

Make Sure Positive Information Gets Reported

Got a college loan with a perfect payment history that isn't on one of the bureau reports? Perhaps you have an old credit card or installment loan that didn't make it on the reports. Items that are in good standing often go unreported, and it's up to you to make sure they get on your report. Since many lenders use credit scoring, the good stuff can boost your score, and you should make every effort to ensure that it is factored in.

If you have evidence of such accounts, contact the bureaus by mail and request that they add this information to your report. If you don't have evidence, simply contact the creditors, and they'll usually be more than happy to provide you with a letter (get a copy for yourself and have them send a copy directly to the bureaus). To be certain that the positive account gets reported, you should send a copy of the creditor's letter to each of the bureaus along with your letter. In addition, ask the creditor to begin reporting the account to the bureaus.

Bureaus aren't required by the FCRA to add positive information, but they usually will. Although there's no civil remedy under the FCRA if the bureau fails to do so, there may be a remedy using state UDAPs. Credit reporting agencies may also charge a fee to add positive information at the request of a consumer.[3]

Obtain Credit from Those Who Report

Did you know that many creditors don't report your accounts to the credit bureaus? In fact, credit unions are notorious for this. Few report to all bureaus, and most only report to one. If you're looking to obtain new credit, ask the lender which bureaus they report to before you apply and only apply to those that report to all three. This is especially important if you have filed bankruptcy and are attempting to build new credit or are new to the credit reporting system and need more positive entries.

Target Scoring Anomalies

Certain banks (e.g., Capital One) are notorious for failing to provide a credit limit when they furnish account information to the bureaus. This failure can potentially hurt a score, according to Watts:

> All three credit bureaus organize consumer data differently, so there is no one-size-fits-all solution for FICO scores to the relatively minor problem of a tradeline missing a credit limit. Generally speaking when this situation comes up, the FICO score algorithm looks first to see if the credit report does list the high balance for that tradeline. When high balance is present, the algorithm substitutes it for the missing credit limit when calculating the tradeline's credit utilization rate. It's not a perfect solution, but we've found that it results in a more predictive score than simply ignoring the tradeline altogether. If the tradeline has neither credit limit nor high balance, then our algorithm will ignore the tradeline for certain calculations used in producing the FICO score.

---

3.   FTC Official Staff Commentary § 611 item 3.

There are many problems with FICO's approach. First, if someone hasn't reached his or her credit limit (or it hasn't been reported as such because the balance was paid off before the information was furnished to the bureaus), then the calculation is erroneous. Second, notice the last sentence: "If the tradeline has neither credit limit nor high balance, then our algorithm will ignore the tradeline for certain calculations." For certain calculations? That means that although FICO attempts to make adjustments for no high balance or credit limit present, it puts downward pressure on a score *to some extent* regardless. As such, any creditor who fails to report a true credit limit is causing a reduction in the customer's FICO score.

One way to counter this is to notify the bureaus as to what the limit is and have it added to the tradeline by simply requesting it in writing in accordance with Chapter 10.

Figure 6 shows where Capital One didn't report the limit to Equifax. When I contacted Capital One and asked it to report the limits, it refused. I asked for that refusal in writing, and Capital One provided it (Figure 7).

Although you can ask the bureaus to add the limit, they may not elect to do so. Of course any request should be accompanied by the bankcard statement that shows the credit limit. Any dispute should be crafted to include the statement "Do not delete the tradeline," since bureaus will often nuke the whole thing if they choose—which can hurt a score. If they do delete the tradeline, there may be a legal claim against them for doing so, since anything they remove at their discretion that's positive must balanced by negative removals.[4]

Watts claimed that the lack of a credit limit hurts a score very little. He said the scoring model will look to see if there's a credit limit, and, if not, then it will take the highest balance reported and use that as the cap. This can be very bad for someone with accounts that haven't come anywhere near the credit limit. Watts also says that if there's no reported high balance and no credit limit, the account is ignored for

---

4. Anything that would skew a consumer's file negatively may be considered a violation of Unfair and Deceptive Acts and Practices (UDAP). There may also be FCRA breaches, depending on the situation surrounding the removal.

Open Accounts

Account Name	Account Number	Date Opened	Balance	Date Reported	Past Due	Account Status	Credit Limit
CAPITAL ONE	486236249417XXXX	11/2004	$0	05/2005	$0	PAYS AS AGREED	$0
CAPITAL ONE	517805234706XXXX	08/2003	$99	05/2005	$0	PAYS AS AGREED	$0

Figure 6.

Capital

Capital One Services, Inc.
P.O. Box 85015
Richmond, VA 23285-5018

July 14, 2005

Dana A. Neal
PO Box 8094
Bend, OR 97708-8094

Re: 48623624941
Creditor: Capital One Bank

Dear Dana A. Neal:

Thank you for contacting us on July 13, 2005, concerning your Capital One* account. I am glad to fulfill your request for credit information.

We provide the following account information to the credit bureaus:

Date account was opened:	November 3, 2004
High credit (highest account balance):	$4,665.79
Present balance:	zero
Date last paid:	July 12, 2005
Minimum payment due/terms:	3.00% or $15.00

This is to confirm that as of July 14, 2005, your current credit limit is $5,000.00. Of the total credit limit, $1,000.00 may be used for cash advances. It is Capital One policy not to report credit limits to the credit bureaus. I hope the information provided meets your needs.

If you have any questions, please do not hesitate to call our Customer Relations Department toll free at 1-800-955-7070.

We value you as our cardholder and look forward to our continued financial relationship. Thank you for choosing Capital One.

Sincerely,

Rhonda Copeland
Customer Relations Account Manager
Capital One Services, Inc.

Figure 7.

the "amounts owed" factor. Rather than trust the scoring model, have the credit limits added using credit bureau disputes.

The Capital One accounts shown here are my own. I disputed the credit limit entries with the Big Three, with poor results. Experian responded to the disputed accounts as "updated" yet didn't change a thing. Trans Union responded with "new information below," a term it uses for updated/changed, yet also failed to list the limits. Equifax responded with, "The creditor has verified that the high credit/limit is being reported correctly."

Back when I was a young lieutenant in the army, an old commander used to have a saying when someone failed to do his job: "If you're not part of the solution, then you must be something else." The only reason Capital One could possibly have for reporting accounts in this way is self-serving and callous: intentionally hurting the FICO scores of its paying customers. Yet when I contacted a local FCRA attorney about the problem, he claimed that it's so minor an infraction that it's not worth pursuing. Although he may be correct, such a case would be a nice add-on when pursuing a credit reporting agency for other breaches. Furthermore, a good attorney with knowledge of scoring should be able to get a federal judge to order Capital One to stop this practice. There's not much money in this Samaritan type of work, however.

If you find yourself in this situation, do as I have done and dispute the item with the credit reporting agencies. If that doesn't work, then contact your congressman, the FTC, and the state attorney general in your state and in Virginia (the state in which Capital One does business).

It can be assumed that American Express and Discover cards without a limit (some of their cards have limits while others do not) are also bad for a credit report, as they don't report credit limits either.

I suggest you check your reports carefully to ensure that credit limits (and any original loan amounts from installment loans) are reported. Again, it's all the seemingly little things that add up!

Reestablish Credit

You can start down your road to recovery right away by placing as much distance as possible between you and your bad credit. The specific actions you can take toward this end are as follows:

- Always pay your bills on time, without exception.
- Open two (but no more) unsecured credit card accounts. If you can't get unsecured cards, then seek the help of a cosigner. (Unsecured and secured credit cards are viewed the same by FICO, but unsecured cards often have their limits raised automatically, which is good for FICO scoring.)
- Convert secured credit cards to unsecured ones when possible. This usually becomes an option only six months after opening the account, provided there haven't been any late payments.
- For those with poor credit who are unable to obtain unsecured cards, open secured cards, which require a cash deposit. With secured cards, your credit limit is often the amount on deposit but can be less or more. Piggyback secured cards, if need be, by taking out a cash advance on the first credit card you open and then depositing that money in another bank in order to get approval for another secured card. Just be sure to obtain the secured cards from creditors who report to all the bureaus and ones that also report their secured accounts as unsecured to the credit bureaus. (See "Getting Approved under Adverse Conditions" below for more information on banks that do this.)
- You can also get a debit card (also known as a check card), which basically takes any purchase right out of your checking account, making the balance in the account your limit. Although debit cards aren't reported to the bureaus, they can make it easier to function by providing a way to conveniently pay for things, such as online purchases, for example. Further, when attempting to reestablish yourself, it helps to have a checking account to pay bills in a cost-effective fashion. Studies have shown that those who've opted out of the banking system entirely due to bad credit end up paying a lot more in transaction fees (e.g., the added cost of money orders, payday lenders, check cashing stores, etc.) than those that remain in the banking system. If banks will not permit you to open an account because you have a bad history with ChexSystems (a checking account credit reporting agency), get back into the

banking system as soon as possible using the techniques spelled out in Chapter 10.

- Make sure that you have both a savings and checking account, and use the checking account to pay your bills. Never, ever write a bad check. Get online bill-pay, as this will assist you in making payments on time. Online bill-pay enables users to automate recurring payments and set up e-mail reminders, among other features.

- Get overdraft protection if possible. You can either use a credit card with that bank, or many banks now permit anyone with a debit card to overdraft-draw from a credit card issued from any bank. Overdraft protection is useful for many reasons. Those you write checks to won't ever receive a bad check, and you can avoid ever having to pay insufficient funds fees to both your bank and the receiving party. Further, banks that provide overdraft protection to their issued cards will often report them as a line of credit, which is another tradeline entry generated on your credit reports. And finally, those who have insufficient funds are often reported to ChexSystems, and this can be avoided when overdraft protection is in place. Just be advised that any request for overdraft protection directly from the bank is a request for a line of credit and will generate a credit inquiry. (Of course, if the bank permits the use of an existing credit card for overdraft protection, then no inquiry is generated.)

- Open a certificate of deposit (CD), which is a good way to establish good relations with a bank. The minimum CD is usually $1,000 with a six-month term, which means that you can't take the money out before the term is up or you'll pay a penalty. Immediately or within a short period after opening a CD, you can borrow against it through the bank you opened it with; that is, obtain an installment loan using the CD as security. The bank will report this to the bureaus as a secured installment loan. Make the payments on time without fail.

- Stay put! If you can avoid it, don't change jobs. This affects your ability to get credit, particularly if you have bad credit already.

> **Tip:** For many different reasons, those with a checkered credit past—even those with a lot of money—often drop out of the credit reporting system altogether, opting instead to use cash to pay for everything. Even if you have a bad credit history, this is the last thing you want to do; it just makes things worse. It's something people inevitably regret, since credit approval involves not only good credit but also recent credit. Keep two or three accounts open and in good standing, preferably a mix of revolving and installment accounts (e.g., one or two credit cards and one auto loan).

Establish Years of Good Credit Where None Existed Before

This little-known secret absolutely takes the cake. It's so simple and powerful, yet hardly anyone knows about it! Simply follow these steps:

1. Locate a friend or family member with a Visa or MasterCard that is in perfect standing.
2. Convince him or her to assign you as a secondary cardholder. (You might do so by agreeing to turn over the card once it comes in the mail so you will never use it. Or use whatever means of negotiating a deal that you think will be most effective.) This is referred to as a "user account." Be advised—the one responsible for any charges is the account holder, not the added user.
3. Once you've sealed the deal, get a copy of the person's credit report and make sure the account is in good standing. This may seem presumptuous, but (a) if he or she is willing to do such a thing then you're already darn familiar anyway, and (b) you can't risk adding negative credit to your own.
4. Once you're satisfied that the account is in good standing, have the person send a letter to the card issuer requesting that you be added to the account as a secondary cardholder and stating in writing that he or she will take responsibility for paying the balance.

5. The new card should arrive within a few weeks, or you may just receive an application or request for additional information. Either way, it is usually sent to the primary cardholder. If an application is required, you will fill out the coapplicant part. The card should arrive soon!

6. Wait 90 days and then order a copy of your report. It should show the credit card in good standing, open for as long as the original primary cardholder had it. Nuts!

Caution: Keep in mind also that if the primary cardholder becomes delinquent, the negative history shows up on your report! Moreover, balances can negatively affect your score; if the primary cardholder carries large balances, this can be harmful to your credit score. And while any new credit can harm a score initially, it would appear that this doesn't show up as new credit, since the opened date will be that of the original cardholder's account. Be aware that an inquiry will likely be performed on your credit report, though the benefits for someone needing to generate a longer good credit history will far outweigh any downside.

FICO scores user accounts, and since they add points for length of credit history, length of open credit history, and good payment history, it makes this technique all the more powerful.

User accounts can be deleted from a person's credit file at any time, because bureaus aren't required to report individuals who aren't contractually liable for a debt. In this way, the "user" of a user account gets to have his cake and eat it too, as he can have it reported when in good standing and deleted if things go south.

Have Credit Limits Raised

Contact your creditors and ask them to raise the limits on your accounts as much as possible. Although they'll perform a credit check, such inquiries don't affect a credit score. Account limits can usually be raised every six months, up to a cap determined by the issuing bank.

Most standard cards have a cap of $5,000, while platinum cards are often capped at $25,000. Banks are more likely to raise credit limits for those with good credit, of course, and for those who report an increase in income. Incidentally, they don't verify increases in income for existing customers.

Remove Inaccurate Adverse Information

One of the fastest ways to improve a score is to remove any inaccurate adverse information, including late payments and public records. There are many ways in which inaccurate data can end up on your report, including a mistake by a furnisher or a credit bureau database glitch. Identity theft may even be the culprit if someone has stolen your SSN and obtained new credit in your name. Erroneous information can come in many forms, such as duplicate accounts, the reporting of obsolete information, and entries that are simply not yours. Detailed information on how to remove inaccurate adverse information is covered in Chapter 11.

Request Rapid Rescoring

In the event that you discover something on a report is erroneous when you're in the process of seeking loan approval, there's a quick remedy, provided you can prove the information is invalid.

To have rapid rescoring performed,

1. you have to be a prospective customer of a lender or mortgage broker,
2. the lender must be a customer of a reseller (one who partners with a credit reporting agency to provide credit reports), and
3. the lender must request the reseller's help on your behalf.

Since very few lenders use resellers, this is difficult. Further, a conflict of interest exists, since the lender actually makes more money if the interest rate is higher due to a client's lower score. If approval will occur in spite of the negative entry, then there's little impetus for the lender to request a rescore. Reputable lenders will always get the best deal for their clients, of course.

Resellers are also often versed on scoring and may be able to come up with a game plan for raising your score. However, the main requirement for rapid rescoring is that the consumer must provide proof (e.g., court documents, payment receipts, or letters from creditors) to the lender that accounts are reported inaccurately. The lender will then forward the documentation to the reseller, which will then make changes directly to the individual's bureau files within a three-day period.

Each change will often run from $25 to $100, for an average of $200 to $300 total per client, and the bureaus have rules that prohibit these fees from being passed on to the borrower. As such, the lender must absorb the cost. Though there's no way for the bureaus to know if their rules are being followed, discovery of any breach can always occur as the result of a consumer's interfacing with a bureau on the issue, and bureaus can either warn any offender or simply close the reseller account at their discretion.

BEYOND THE CREDIT SCORE: LOAN APPROVAL

When it comes to loan approval, lenders will use different criteria for different situations. Unsecured debt is riskier than secured debt in general since there's no collateral involved in unsecured debt. You see, it's all about "what happens if you default?" A house or auto is collateral, and if you default, the lender can always come and take that collateral to mitigate its loss. If you're getting a good deal on a car and putting money down, you have a better chance of getting approved than if you're paying above book value and putting no money down. Once again, if the lender repossesses the car due to nonpayment, then it can mitigate its loss if there's equity in the car. Likewise, if you already own property and have equity, then you are a better credit risk than if you don't.

If you have an established relationship with the lender (i.e., it has extended credit to you previously, or you have a checking/savings account with it), it helps. It also helps if you deal face-to-face with a loan officer at your bank, because you become more than just a name. Some banks can still approve loans at branch level, so ask the branch manager about this before you fill out an application. However, most underwriting is no longer preformed by a branch, but at a corporate office—where you're just another name on a piece of paper. In such cases your credit score and your debt-to-income ratio will determine your creditworthiness, period. This is not necessarily a bad thing. Such an approach helps to ensure that people are treated equally, as do restrictions imposed by the federal government, which provide a minimum standard for loan underwriting. This not only helps to keep a certain level of fairness in play but also provides a way to keep overzealous loan officers from making bad decisions, i.e., loaning to people who are high risk. This keeps the entire financial and banking system strong and also ensures that the secondary markets are not faced with a financial crisis due to an increase in loans that go unpaid by homebuyers.

The secondary market is in place to ensure that there's plenty of money available for banks to make home loans. Let's say the consumer mortgage division of a bank has $100 million to loan. If they loan it all out, how can they continue to make loans? This is where the secondary market comes in. Once a bank loans you money, it will likely want to sell that note to the "secondary market," so that it can get additional capital to loan again. The largest secondary market purchasers of these mortgage loans are the Federal Home Loan Mortgage Corporation ("Freddie Mac") and the Federal National Mortgage Association ("Fannie Mae"), which are publicly traded private companies, congressionally chartered entities that are known as "government-sponsored" enterprises. They buy home loans from banks and other lenders and then wrap them into mortgage-backed, publicly traded securities (stocks), which are sold to investors. The federal government has guidelines about what loans can qualify to be sold on the secondary market, such as the 45 percent debt-to-income ratio, which is why banks' hands are often tied when it comes to loan approval.

Freddie Mac and Fannie Mae are the only secondary market enterprises, since they're the only ones Congress chartered to serve the secondary market, keeping money available for banks to make home loans. It's a circle, put in place so that the lending system continues to work.

Some banks offer another type of mortgage, the portfolio loan. If you have bad credit but have 20 to 25 percent to put down, you can buy property under this method, providing you place the property into a separate business entity, such as a corporation or limited liability company (LLC). This option won't hurt your credit score as a subprime loan will, and such a loan will be reported on a business credit report, not your personal credit report (unless the loan becomes delinquent, in which case it may be reported on the personal report of anyone who is a guarantor of the note).

Also be aware that those who get their middle score to 700-plus can often use "stated income" to get the mortgage they desire. Such an approach is attractive, since the use of stated income permits the borrower to forgo revealing previous tax returns.

Of course, alternative sources of home mortgage loans are available to those with poor credit, but the interest rates are often several points higher and the terms undesirable. As explained, having these subprime lenders on your credit report will hurt your score as well, since FICO classifies them as undesirable. I don't recommend these types of loans, especially considering that if you wait and repair your credit, you can obtain conventional funding anyway. One exception would be a subprime loan used as leverage in any Debt Fusion™ plan (see Chapter 8).

Getting Approved under Adverse Conditions

Of course, the best thing you can do for a score is to take the time to remove the bad credit and pay your bills on time. But if you can't wait for that or you lack sufficient credit history, you still may be able to obtain an auto loan or credit card using quality lenders.

I used to recommend Ford Motor Credit for auto loans, but it has since toughened up its policies. I also used to recommend Capital One secured credit cards, but since it doesn't report high limits and is screwing 48 million customers, I cannot in good conscience recommend the firm. I used to recommend American Pacific Bank's secured credit cards, but it has since been bought out by Riverside Bank and no longer offers that card.

Since things change so rapidly, I think it's best to just send you to my Web site, www.bestcredit.com/badcreditlenders/. There you will find the best bad credit offers available. And, of course, if you have any knowledge of such lenders, let me know and I'll post it.

In closing, by understanding the various components of FICO scoring and lender criteria for loan approval, you can begin formulating a coherent strategy for raising your score. Of course, this doesn't begin to address the removal of bad credit. Far more complex, credit restoration requires a great deal more knowledge, the foundation of which is an understanding of some fundamental ground rules.

GROUND RULES FOR BUREAUS AND FURNISHERS

Credit reporting agencies and furnishers alike have to play by certain rules put in place by Congress, and when you know the rules, you can use them to your advantage. Some of the most important regulations revolve around the handling of consumer disputes and the reporting of certain types of information as decreed by the FCRA and the Fair Credit Billing Act (FCBA), while the FDCPA and the Real Estate Settlement Procedures Act (RESPA) restrict certain reporting as well.

BUREAU REINVESTIGATION PROCEDURES

Any item on a credit report can be disputed, and FCRA regulations require the bureaus to handle all cases of disputed accuracy in a certain way. Foremost among them is the requirement that the bureaus perform a reinvestigation and either verify the accuracy of the entry or delete it, generally within 30 days of receiving a consumer dispute.

Because it can be very difficult to verify data within this time frame, it can really pay to challenge any derogatory data that appears on your report. This is particularly true when the disputed item involves public records. Service bureaus are the primary furnishers of this type of information, and they have no vested interest in the way in which something is reported. After all, adverse reporting is designed to force payment to the creditor; what's in it for the service bureau? And if the service bureaus must verify something with the courts, the courts are very slow to respond. With some county records it's nearly impossible to verify the accuracy of the reported data within the 30-day reinvestigation period.[1] (The procedure for disputing public records is covered in Chapter 10.)

Since there may be variations, not only in *how* the Big Three report individual tradeline and public record entries but also in *which* items they report, you must challenge entries on your credit report with each bureau separately. This process is known as *verification*.

> **Note:** The term "reinvestigation" is a misnomer; it's the same as an investigation. But since credit reporting agencies consider any compiling of a report to be an investigation, they therefore refer to the process of verifying that data as a reinvestigation.

The FCRA provides for a maximum 15-day extension of the reinvestigation period if the disputer contacts the bureau with new information during the dispute period.[2] Many people feel compelled to call the bureaus and discuss the issues, add an issue, or whatever. They also sometimes believe that sending new information that they forgot to attach will be useful. The bureaus have interpreted this to mean that all the items listed in the same dispute are

---

1. 15 U.S.C. § 1681i(a)(1)(A). FCRA limits reinvestigations to 30 days.
2. 15 U.S.C. § 1681i(a)(1)(B).

now extended by 15 days, so don't contact them again until the 30-day period has elapsed.[3]

Can every bureau and/or furnisher meet this 30-day deadline? Clearly the answer is no, since they're required to contact the furnisher in accordance with the FCRA whenever a dispute is received, and many furnishers are simply far too busy to respond to every single dispute. When a bureau can't verify an entry as accurate, the law requires that the information be deleted from the report. Furthermore, if the furnisher provides incomplete information or simply fails to respond to the bureau's request for verification, the item must be deleted.[4]

Unless a 15-day extension is allowed (due to a consumer's supplying more information during the 30-day window),[5] a furnisher will normally have 15 to 23 days to respond to the notice of the dispute.[6] Further, state law may set a maximum number of days that the credit reporting agency has to contact the furnisher, and the more restrictive statutes will apply. This can be useful for residents of Nevada, Vermont, and Washington, where the maximum is five days.[7] States can also set a maximum number of days for a reinvestigation; howev-

---

3. The following states prohibit a 15-day extension to perform reinvestigations: Arizona, Maryland, Massachusetts, Nevada, New Hampshire, Rhode Island, Vermont, and Washington. Maine has a 21-day cap to perform reinvestigations and immediate notification that a dispute is deemed frivolous. Maryland requires notification within seven days if information is considered accurate or inaccurate and seven days if determined to be frivolous. Texas requires items disputed found inaccurate or incomplete investigations to be corrected within five business days; Texas also requires that consumers receive notice if there is insufficient time to conduct a reinvestigation within 30 days. Washington and California permit reinvestigations to be completed within 30 business days.

4. 15 U.S.C. § 1681i(a)(5)(A)(i). ". . . any information disputed by a consumer, an item of the information is found to be inaccurate or incomplete or cannot be verified . . ." This is extremely useful and often causes accurate adverse data to be deleted. Notice that there's a requirement to notify the furnisher if any data is modified or deleted as a result of a consumer dispute.

5. This assumes the reports were purchased, since the law extends the reinvestigation period to 45 days for reports that the bureaus provide free of charge.

6. NCLC *Fair Credit Reporting* § 3.12.1 (5th ed. 2002 and 2005 Supp.).

7. Nev. Rev. Stat. § 598C.160 (five days); Vt. Stat. Ann. Tit. 9, § 2480d (five days); Wash. Rev. Code. § 19.182.090 (five days).

er, at the time of this writing there is only one state that has a more restrictive time requirement: Maine allows only 21 days![8] New Hampshire also requires bureaus to notify consumers of results within 10 days following the 30-day reinvestigation period.[9]

And FACTA requires that bureaus notify consumers who dispute information of their right to request a description of procedures used to reinvestigate, including the name, address, and telephone number of any person contacted within 15 days of receipt of the request.[10] This is extremely useful for those disputing information, whether accurate or not. The fact that disputers can always go back and demand this information from a reporting agency following a reinvestigation that has an unfavorable outcome (i.e., one that verifies adverse data so that it remains on the credit report) places a labor burden on the bureaus, which may cause them to delete the information.

Note: Contrary to popular myth, disputed credit bureau entries aren't temporarily deleted during the reinvestigation period, but they can be shown to be in dispute. Bureaus don't show a consumer's version of events, though there isn't anything in the law that prevents them from acknowledging a consumer's version of the dispute.[11]

Any foot-dragging on the part of the bureaus should call you to action. They generally have 30 days from the date they receive the dispute to complete their investigation. (This is why your dispute letters, like *all* correspondence with the bureaus, must be sent via certified mail with a request for a return receipt; the return receipts will provide proof of the date the bureaus received the dispute.) If you don't receive a response from any bureau within the allotted time, send a follow-up

---

8. Me. Rev. Stat. Ann. tit. 10, § 1317(2) (West).
9. N.H. Rev. Stat. §§ 598C.010 to 598C.200.
10. 15 U.S.C. § 1681i(a)(7).
11. NCLC *Fair Credit Reporting* § 7.3.6 (5th ed. 2002 and 2005 Supp.).

letter demanding that it remove the item(s) or you'll lodge a complaint with the FTC and state attorney general.[12]

Reinsertion of Verified Data

When a bureau can't verify data within the time required by law and deletes it, the information will stay off your credit report until the furnisher can verify its accuracy. But the rules for reinsertion are a little stiffer than those for a furnisher verifying information during a reinvestigation. (This reinsertion isn't to be confused with the cloaking/suppression system working improperly; that is, when a credit reporting agency inadvertently reinserts information that it had intended to filter out.)

The relevant part of the Act reads, "The information may not be reinserted in the file by the consumer reporting agency unless the person who furnishes the information certifies that the information is complete and accurate."[13] Certifying that data is accurate is a tricky business for furnishers. If any *i* is not dotted or any *t* not crossed, they could be opening themselves up to a FCRA lawsuit, maybe even with punitive money damages attached. This puts a lot of pressure on them. Since certification has legal liability associated with it, some furnishers will forgo it, particularly with smaller debts and those that are beyond the statute of limitations for collection (explained in Chapter 6).

Frivolous Disputes

There's a provision in the FCRA that permits bureaus to claim a disputed item is frivolous, and under such circumstances they don't have to perform a reinvestigation.[14] It's simply a way for the bureaus to deal with letters that read something like, "I hereby dispute every negative thing on my credit report. If you don't remove it, I'll sue your

---

12. In addition to attorney's fees, the agency is subject to actual damages in the event of negligence, as well as punitive damages for willful noncompliance. 15 U.S.C. §§ 1681n, o.
13. 15 U.S.C. § 1681i(a)(5)(B)(i).
14. 15 U.S.C. § 1681i(a)(3).

pants off!" This is nothing to be concerned about, since reporting agencies must assume that a consumer's dispute is bona fide unless there is evidence to the contrary.[15]

However, "a consumer's lack of precision as to the item being disputed is probably not a sufficient reason not to reinvestigate.[16] But if the consumer does not provide a bureau with a clear statement that the accuracy or completeness of specific information is 'disputed' or 'challenged,' the consumer's statement may not be construed as an exercise of rights under the Act."[17] In other words, you must make sure that your dispute letter is coherent and specific as to the item in question and why you are disputing its accuracy. Anything specific will be treated as both sufficient and relevant, as long as it's credible on its face.

It should also come from you directly. Many people like to have their attorneys write letters to the bureaus, reasoning that such correspondence will carry more weight. In fact, the opposite is true. Technically, the FCRA maintains that credit reporting agencies don't have to accept any letter from a third party. The inclusion of this requirement was an effort by credit bureaus to detect or curb the use of credit repair agencies, which are a thorn in their side. If an attorney writes and signs a dispute, then it should also be signed by the consumer.[18]

A formal consumer dispute must also go directly to the credit bureau and not to a third party, such as a furnisher.

Expedited Dispute Resolution

Believe it or not, when a bureau receives a dispute, it doesn't even have to perform an investigation. That's right. The bureau can delete the information altogether at its discretion, foregoing any attempt to verify its accuracy. This is known as an expedited dispute resolution; the bureau has three business days from receipt of the

---

15. FTC Official Staff Commentary § 611.
16. Equifax, Inc., 96 FTC 1045 (1980), rev'd in part on other grounds, 678 F.2d 1047 (11th Cir. 1982).
17. NCLC *Fair Credit Reporting* § 7.3.2.2 (5th ed. 2002 and 2005 Supp.).
18. NCLC *Fair Credit Reporting* § 7.3.2.2 (5th ed. 2002 and 2005 Supp.).

dispute to perform the deletion if it exercises this option.[19] Agencies will often do this when documentation that supports a consumer's claim accompanies the dispute, provided the documents are considered authentic. However, they can also forgo an investigation and delete the information in question without such evidentiary support *at their discretion.*

Notification to Parties

When a consumer initiates a reinvestigation, the bureau must notify the furnisher of the disputed information within five business days.[20] When a bureau completes a reinvestigation, it must notify the consumer of the results within five business days.[21] If a bureau determines that a claim is frivolous, it must notify the consumer within five business days of such a determination, though it is not required to notify the furnisher.[22] With expedited disputes, the bureaus must notify consumers within five business days of completion of such a determination, though, here again, they are not required to notify the furnishers.[23] When reinserting previously deleted material, the bureau must notify the consumer within five business days of reinsertion.[24]

Any users that received previous information from a report that was subsequently corrected due to reinvestigation will receive a copy of the corrected version *at the consumer's request.*[25] This is *not* automatic. Such notice will indicate what items were deleted. The notice request from the consumer must specify the recipients (the users that previously received a credit report containing erroneous information), and they must have received the report within the previous six months (or two years if the report was used for employment purposes).[26] Any consumer whose file is corrected as a result of an investigation will receive

---

19. 15 U.S.C. § 1681i(a).
20. 15 U.S.C. § 1681i(a)(2)(A).
21. 15 U.S.C. § 1681i(a)(6)(A).
22. 15 U.S.C. § 1681i(a)(3)(A).
23. 15 U.S.C. § 1681i(a)(8)(C).
24. 15 U.S.C. § 1681i(a)(5)(B)(ii).
25. 15 U.S.C. § 1681i(d).
26. 15 U.S.C. § 1681i(a)(8)(C).

a corrected copy at no charge.[27] Bureaus are also required to provide a full, corrected copy of a credit report to the consumer upon the conclusion of any reinvestigation.[28]

Creditor-furnishers are also required to notify consumers when reporting adverse information. "If any financial institution that extends credit and regularly and in the ordinary course of business furnishes information to a consumer reporting agency described in section 603(p) furnishes negative information to such an agency regarding credit extended to a customer, the financial institution shall provide a notice of such furnishing of negative information, in writing, to the customer."[29]

Many types of notification requirements can be changed by governing statute, with the exception of those that are preempted by federal law, as explained in Chapter 6.

FURNISHER REQUIREMENTS FOR DISPUTED INFORMATION

In the event of a consumer dispute, the FCRA requires the furnisher to participate in the reinvestigation process, except for claims that a bureau has determined to be frivolous and expedited dispute resolution claims.[30] Upon receiving a notice of dispute from the bureaus, furnishers may not instruct the bureaus to simply delete the information instead of performing an investigation.[31] This is a good thing, because there are many legitimate disputes where consumers are requesting a status change (e.g., Paid, Never Late) but wish to have an account remain for scoring purposes.

The FCRA requires all furnishers, including debt collectors, to note (somewhere within their entry/tradeline) when information they report

---

27. 15 U.S.C. § 1681i(j).
28. 15 U.S.C. § 1681i(a)(6)(B)(ii).
29. 15 U.S.C. § 1681s-2(a)(7)(A)(i); "The notice required under subparagraph (A) shall be provided to the customer prior to, or no later than 30 days after, furnishing the negative information to a consumer reporting agency described in section 603(p)," 15 U.S.C. § 1681s-2(a)(7)(B)(i).
30. 15 U.S.C. § 1681i(a)(2), § 1681s-2.
31. *McKeown v. Sears Roebuck & Co.*, 335 F. Supp. 2d 917 (D. Pa. 2004).

to a credit reporting agency is disputed by the customer.[32] However, any failure to do so carries little consequence for the furnisher, since no private FCRA civil remedies are available for noncompliance.[33] However, a debt collector (third party collecting on behalf of another) falls under different rules altogether, in addition to those imposed by the FCRA. Debt collectors who fail to note that an entry is disputed by a consumer are subject to suit for damages and other relief under the FDCPA.[34]

When a furnisher performs an investigation as a result of a consumer's dispute with a bureau and finds errors, it must disseminate any such information to all the bureaus within the same time frame within which it is required to notify the bureau that initiated the reinvestigation. Noncompliance with this requirement is a violation and may subject furnishers to civil liability.[35]

Furnishers must block information when it is unverifiable so as to prevent its reappearance on a consumer's credit report. That is, when a consumer files a formal dispute with the bureaus and the furnisher cannot verify the accuracy, future reporting on the part of the furnisher is prohibited, and reasonable steps must be taken to modify, delete, or block that information to preclude reappearance.[36] "Nothing in FACTA appears to prevent consumers from enforcing this provision."[37]

As an aside, note that as of December 1, 2004, FACTA requires that financial institutions notify a customer when they're furnishing negative information about a consumer,[38] and they must do so within 30 days of providing it to a credit reporting agency.[39]

---

32. 15 U.S.C. § 1681s-2(a)(3).
33. 15 U.S.C. § 1692(e)(8); NCLC *Fair Credit Reporting* § 3.3.4.2 (5th ed. 2002 and 2005 Supp.).
34. *Brady v. Credit Recovery Co.*, 160 F.3d 64 (1st Cir. 1998); NCLC *Fair Debt Collection* Chapter 6 (5th ed. 2004 and 2005 Supp.).
35. 15 U.S.C. § 1671s-2(b).
36. 15 U.S.C. § 1681s-2(b), as amended by Pub. L. No. 108-159, § 314 (2003).
37. NCLC *Fair Credit Reporting* § 3.11.3 (5th ed. 2002 and 2005 Supp.).
38. 15 U.S.C. § 1681s-2(a)(7), added by Pub. L. No. 108-159, § 217 (2003); 16 C.F.R. § 602.1(c)(3)(xii), added by 69 Fed. Reg. 6526-31 (Feb. 5, 2004).
39. 15 U.S.C. § 1681s-2(a)(7)(B)(i).

RESELLER REQUIREMENTS FOR
DISPUTED INFORMATION

Resellers (financial institutions that extend credit and furnish financial information to the Big Three; more on this in Chapter 5) are basically exempt from reinvestigation requirements.[40] However, since December 1, 2004, they do have to follow certain rules regarding consumer disputes. In particular, within five days of receiving a dispute, a reseller must determine whether the item is inaccurate as a result of an act or omission on its part. If so, it has to either correct or delete the item within 20 days of receipt of the consumer notice. If the reseller determines that no act or omission on its part has resulted in inaccurate reporting, it is only required to notify the consumer reporting agency of the consumer's dispute.

Although there doesn't appear to be any legal recourse for consumers when resellers fail to adhere to this law,[41] any such failure on the part of the furnisher should be reported to the appropriate enforcement agency (as listed in Chapter 2), as well as the state attorney general.

FOUR SITUATIONS WHEN FURNISHING IS LIMITED

Under certain circumstances, furnishers may not report delinquent accounts even if the information is accurate, and in such cases consumers can sometimes use the law to their advantage in an effort to prevent adverse entries. In addition, furnishers must indicate when an entry is in dispute under certain circumstances, which, as I've shown, can be a positive thing since FICO doesn't include disputed entries.

Credit Card and Open-End Accounts

By using the FCBA, a consumer may be able to have an account placed in dispute for an indefinite period. This applies to open-end accounts, such as credit cards and lines of credit.

---

40. 15 U.S.C. § 1681i(f)(1), added by Pub. L. No. 108-159, § 316(b); 16 C.F.R. § 602.1(c)(3)(xviii), added by 69 Fed. Reg. 6526-31 (Feb. 5, 2004); paraphrased from NCLC *Fair Credit Reporting* § 3.15 (5th ed. 2002 and 2005 Supp.).
41. 15 U.S.C. § 1681s-2(c)(1), as amended by Pub. L. No. 108-159, § 312 (2003).

When a consumer complains to a creditor about a billing error, such as the way in which interest is calculated, the creditor is only permitted to report that the account is in dispute and may not report any delinquent information unless and until the consumer fails to pay the bill after the creditor has complied with all the requirements of the FCBA (namely, investigating the dispute, sending written notice to the consumer of the determination, and then allowing the consumer 10 days to pay whatever is owed). After receiving a billing error dispute from a consumer, the creditor may not threaten—directly or indirectly—to report the account as past due to any person or credit reporting agency.[42] (Though the billing dispute is not required to be in writing, it's what I recommend in all things.)

During this 10-day period, the consumer has the right to contact the creditor again and state that he or she still disputes the bill. In this case, the FCBA forbids the creditor from reporting the account as delinquent unless it (1) also notes the account as in dispute when it subsequently furnishes information to the credit bureaus and (2) notifies the consumer in writing of the names and addresses of everyone to whom it is reporting information about the disputed amount. Furthermore, once the creditor has reported the delinquent account, it must also provide notification of any subsequent resolution of the dispute.

This labor-intensive requirement is one that creditors find tedious, and they often don't report such accounts as delinquent, but instead report them as in dispute even after completing their investigation.[43] The furnisher isn't required to notify the bureau of the ultimate resolution of the dispute unless it had previously informed the agency that the account was delinquent, so if the account was only reported as in dispute in the first place, then the bureau (and any users) may never be informed that the consumer was correct and the amount was never owed.[44] Although the furnisher is obligated to correct and update any information to a credit reporting agency, its liability is restricted in this case.

---

42. NCLC *Fair Credit Reporting* § 3.3.4.3 (5th ed. 2002 and 2005 Supp.).
43. Geltzer, *Current Practice Under the Fair Credit Reporting Act*, Quarterly Report, Conf. on Personal Fin. Law 94, 98 (Fall 1976); NCLC *Fair Credit Reporting* § 3.3.4.2 (5th ed. 2002 and 2005 Supp.).
44. 15 U.S.C. § 1666.

There are many ways for a cardholder to dispute a bill. Among the best is to contest the way the creditor calculated interest after raising the interest rate. Often credit card issuers will not respond to a billing error dispute properly, and such failure could potentially open up an FCBA claim. And if after filing such a dispute, a consumer learns that the creditor hasn't complied with the FCBA reporting requirements, he or she may then file a formal reinvestigation with the credit reporting agencies disputing the information furnished by a creditor. In response to this, a creditor may affirm the reporting as accurate, which is a violation of the FCRA and opens up liability. Any failure on the creditor's part to report accurately can also be used as leverage in negotiating.[45] (Although it may seem as if disputing directly with the bureaus in the first place would be the best recourse, by disputing with the creditors in this manner, a consumer can head off adverse reporting before it ever begins, while possibly setting up a scenario where the creditor-furnisher has broken the law. They usually do.)

Charge-Backs

Under the FCBA, when a consumer contacts his or her credit card issuer to dispute the amount a merchant has charged, the cardholder may withhold payment of the amount in question until the issue is resolved. However, for this to be allowed, the cardholder must have attempted to resolve the dispute with the merchant directly. Also, the amount must exceed $50, and the purchase must have been made within the consumer's state or 100 miles from his or her residence.[46] If the cardholder pays the amount in dispute, then the right to dispute is lost. While a charge is in dispute, interest cannot accrue on the disputed amount.

Once the consumer notifies the credit card issuer of the disputed charge, the creditor may not report the disputed amount as delinquent until the dispute is settled or a judgment is rendered, though it may

---

45. The NCLC reports that the FCBA may apply to closed-end loans, 15 U.S.C. § 1666 does not explicitly limit its scope to open-end credit. But see NCLC *Truth in Lending* § 5.8 (5th ed. 2003 and Supp.).

46. The last two requirements are waived if the merchant and card issuer are closely connected. See regulation Z, 12 C.F.R. § 226 note 26; NCLC *Fair Credit Reporting* § 3.3.4.3 (5th ed. 2002 and 2005 Supp.).

report the amount as in dispute.[47] The creditor can continue to collect on the disputed amount, including pursuing legal remedies, but the consumer can raise misconduct on the part of the merchant as a defense.[48] This dispute process is often known as a charge-back, and the card issuer will often side with the consumer and simply hold the merchant accountable for all or part of the amount in dispute.

Tip: Consumers are not responsible for any unauthorized or fraudulent charges to their credit cards for any amount exceeding $50.[49]

Disputed Mortgage and Home Equity Loans

Under RESPA, the consumer is granted additional rights that preclude credit reporting during a 60-day dispute period. This covers virtually all loans secured by a first or junior lien on residential real property.[50]

The borrower must send a qualified written request, which is a letter (not permitted to be written on a payment coupon or other payment medium provided by the servicer) identifying his or her name

---

47. Federal Reserve Board (FRB) official staff commentary regarding Regulation Z, § 226.12(c)(2)-1; NCLC *Fair Credit Reporting* § 3.3.4.3 (5th ed. 2002 and 2005 Supp.).
48. NCLC *Fair Credit Reporting* § 3.3.4.3 (5th ed. 2002 and 2005 Supp.).
49. Fair Credit Billing Act § 161. Any dispute of charges must be made within 60 days after the bill containing the charge is mailed by the creditor. The creditor must respond within 30 days and resolve the dispute within 90 days.
50. Family dwellings of one to four units, 12 U.S.C. § 2602(1)(A). "The loan must involve a federally insured lender; must be guaranteed by FHA, FmHA, VA, or other federal agency; must be intended to be sold to FNMA, Freddie Mac, or GNMA; or the creditor must have more than $1 million a year in residential real estate loans. 12 U.S.C. § 2602(1)(B). The major area where RESPA may not apply involves a private individual who makes a small number of mortgage loans, even though a major institution acts as a broker for that and numerous other individuals who are acting as lenders." NCLC *Fair Credit Reporting* § 3.3.4.4 (5th ed. 2002 and 2005 Supp.).

and account and either (a) explaining why he or she believes the amount owed is in error, or (b) requesting in sufficient detail (specific to the request) other information (such as how interest or late fees were calculated, or proof that the loan was purchased).[51] Within 60 days, the servicer must make any necessary corrections to the account or provide the consumer with a statement as to why it believes the account is correct. If the consumer merely sought information, the servicer must provide such information or explain why it's unavailable.[52]

During the 60-day period, the servicer may not report any derogatory information regarding overdue payments that relate to the qualified written request, and even if the servicer responds before the 60 days have elapsed, such reporting is prohibited.[53]

The same protection is afforded a consumer when the debt is transferred from one servicer to another. The homeowner may send payment to the old servicer, but as long as the old servicer receives the payment by the due date, the new servicer may not impose a late fee or report the payment as late.[54]

RESPA has its own rules concerning noncompliance, including the recovery of attorney's fees, actual damages, and up to $1,000 in statutory damages.[55]

Debts under Validation

When a debt collector initiates collection action, he or she does so by sending out a validation notice to the debtor. This begins a 30-day validation period, and if during that period the debtor sends a written notice that disputes the debt as owed, all collection efforts must cease

---

51. 12 U.S.C. § 2605(e)(1); NCLC *Fair Credit Reporting* § 3.3.4.4 (5th ed. 2002 and 2005 Supp.).
52. NCLC *Fair Credit Reporting* § 3.3.4.4 (5th ed. 2002 and 2005 Supp.).
53. Ibid. Foreclosure and other collection activities are not restricted during the 60-day period.
54. NCLC *Fair Credit Reporting* § 3.3.4.4 (5th ed. 2002 and 2005 Supp.); 12 U.S.C. § 2605(d); RESPA has its own rules concerning noncompliance, which provide for $1,000 in statutory damages for each individual or up to $500,000 or 1 percent of the servicer's net worth in a class action, 12 U.S.C. § 2605(d); NCLC *Fair Credit Reporting* § 3.3.4.4 (5th ed. 2002 and 2005 Supp.).
55. 15 U.S.C. § 2605(f).

until the debt collector provides verification to the consumer.[56] And if the collection agency has already reported the account to a credit bureau, the FDCPA requires any subsequent reporting to indicate the item as disputed indefinitely.[57]

As such, it's a good idea to pull all reports 30 days after receiving an initial collection notice so that you have a record of any collection activity. (Validation letters are fully discussed in Chapter 7.)

Items Disputed with the Furnisher

Under the FCRA, if any entry is disputed directly with a furnisher, then it must be noted as disputed when furnished to a credit reporting agency, or not reported at all.[58] This holds true for all furnishers, including debt collectors—again, great for FICO scoring.

Any furnisher that fails to follow the rules regarding the furnishing of delinquent accounts and/or the requirements for disputed information is in breach of law, and you should deal with this appropriately by notifying the proper enforcer as listed in Table 2 (Chapter 2) and/or seeking a legal remedy if you're so inclined. And remember—always use any breach of law as negotiating leverage if you're seeking improved terms with a creditor or debt collector. (For more on this, refer to Chapter 9.)

---

56. 15 U.S.C. § 1692g(b); An informal FTC staff opinion states that reporting a charge-off is collection activity and, as such, is prohibited during this time, NCLC *Fair Credit Reporting* § 3.3.4.2 (5th ed. 2002 and 2005 Supp.).
57. 15 U.S.C. § 1682e(8); see *Brady v. Credit Recovery Co.*, 160 F.3d 64 (1st Cir. 1998); *Sullivan v. Equifax, Inc.*, 2002 WL 799856 (E.D. Pa. Apr. 19, 2002).
58. 15 U.S.C. § 1681s-2(a)(3).

CHAPTER 5

THE GAME BEGINS

Now that you have some idea of what you're up against, you can begin
to roll up your sleeves and get busy repairing your credit. From here,
I've laid out a plan that is methodical and realistic. If you wish to
jump to a particular section, that's entirely up to you, but you'd be
remiss in doing so. If this is going to work for you, you've got to get
serious and learn everything there is to know. And since the lesson
plan is cumulative, each bit of knowledge will function as a building
block. As with learning math, you can't understand algebra until you
know basic addition, subtraction, and multiplication. Formulating
the best strategy for credit restoration involves understanding many
nuances, since each individual decision you make can affect the overall results. The whole thing can hinge on something seemingly inconsequential—which is why reading everything carefully can at least
save you a great deal of aggravation and at most affect the outcome of
any legal claim you may have.

You must be adequately prepared to make a good evaluation of
your individual situation, and such an evaluation will likely look very

different after you've finished this book. The situational and collective assessments you make (explained later) will enable you to examine your unique position and make sense of it. As you work through the material in this book, keep an open mind, pay close attention to the details, and be receptive to the many possibilities. Credit is a lifeline—your credit, your life.

LAY THE GROUNDWORK

Credit restoration is work. Sometimes it's even hard work. Among other things, it takes dedication and a commitment to changing something that does not readily avail itself to change, at least not until pressure is applied. It takes the knowledge and ability to apply the right kind of pressure and at the right time and place. And it takes a certain kind of will. By adhering to the following fundamental principles, you will more easily achieve your personal goals:

1. *Start paying your bills on time.* Never, under any circumstances, pay your bills late.
2. *Start paying your bills on time.* Do what you have to do. Even if you have to "borrow from Peter to pay Paul," never pay your bills late under any circumstances. Yes, even if you have to move debt around, this is preferable to having late payments show up on a credit report.
3. *Start paying your bills on time, period.* Bad credit is brutal, isn't it? The whole idea is to put as much distance as you can between you and your bad credit. The way you do this is to pay your bills on time, starting now! Once again, I recommend using online bill-pay. Auto-debit (where the creditor can automatically tap your bank account) is not recommended, since it exposes you to the possibility of fraud. Yet online bill-pay can be set up to make recurring automatic payments from your checking account. Such an approach is super for those wishing to avoid late payments as a result of simple forgetfulness.
4. *If you blame anyone else for your situation, stop it now.* Forget the nasty boss, the bitter spouse who wouldn't pay the bills,

the unforeseen medical problems, and so on. It doesn't matter why; it's past, and you need to take responsibility for now to move forward. A friend once gave me some good advice that I'll now impart to you: get over it.

5. *Stop feeling bad.* While the feelings that often accompany bad credit—hopelessness, guilt, stress, and worse—are painful, the first step to feeling better is to do something about it. You're doing that right now, so you'll begin to feel better as you take control. Often I receive e-mails from people who have read my materials and tried my techniques. Many of them say that they discovered very quickly that things weren't nearly as bad as they thought.

6. *Get organized.* Pick up several file folders with two-hole paper fasteners at the top, a highlighter, and Post-it notes at an office supply store. Label three of the folders Experian, Trans Union, and Equifax. You're going to order your credit reports soon, and when you get them you'll fasten them in their respective folders on the left side, and any future correspondence with the bureaus will be fastened on the right. Once you've reviewed your credit files, you'll create a folder for every creditor (furnisher) that is reporting adverse information. Use the highlighter and Post-it notes as you read this book, marking important information to reference later.

7. *Be prepared to be bold.* Some credit improvement tactics will take some *cojones* and a strong will. If you're shy, come out of your shell. If nervous and averse to taking some risks, take a deep breath and show some backbone. Sound brash? Maybe so, but there's a psychology to credit restoration that requires mental toughness. Dealing with creditors and collectors can be difficult, and negotiating under stressful circumstances is likely to be a part of your future. I'd be remiss if I didn't explain this up front and at least begin to prepare you adequately for the challenges ahead. On the upside, just remember that with knowledge comes a certain degree of confidence.

8. *Take it one step at a time.* There's nothing that says it all has to be done at once. If you begin to feel overwhelmed, slow down. With each success your confidence will grow.

ORDER YOUR CREDIT REPORTS

FACTA requires that credit bureaus provide a free credit report to consumers once a year. The bureaus have set up a Web site for this purpose: www.annualcreditreport.com.

In addition, there are five special circumstances under which you may obtain a free credit report from the bureaus:

1. If you are currently unemployed and intend to apply for unemployment in the next 60 days
2. If you are on public welfare assistance
3. If you have reason to believe your file contains inaccurate information due to fraud
4. If you have been the subject of an adverse decision, such as denial of credit, insurance, or employment, within the past 60 days
5. If you have been the victim of identity theft

Even if you've already obtained your free annual credit report, you can still get additional reports free under the above circumstances. You must write the bureaus and substantiate your reason for requesting such a report.

Although credit reports are available for free, it's best to pay for them. Note that with FACTA's passage, bureaus were able to work a twist into the free credit report clause. In particular, if you obtain your credit reports for free, the bureaus now have 45 days to perform a reinvestigation of disputed entries, rather than the previously mandated 30 days. Permitting credit bureaus more time to perform their reinvestigations is counterproductive. The less time they have to verify the accuracy of disputed adverse data, the better.

In addition to FACTA's provisions for free credit reports, if you live in the following states, there are also laws in place concerning the maximum charge for a credit report (without a score) as of January 2004:[1]

---

1. Notice that Colorado and Georgia survived FACTA and are not preempted by federal law. (They had laws in place before the passage of FACTA and subsequently can offer additional reports, unlike other states, which must adhere to the federal law.)

- California: $8
- Colorado: $8; get a free copy if you've had eight or more inquiries in the past 12 months or if you've had any negative information added to your report
- Connecticut: $5 for the first disclosure and $7.50 thereafter
- Georgia: $9; two free per calendar year
- Maine: $5
- Maryland: $5
- Massachusetts: $8
- Minnesota: $3; $9.50 if the next one is within 12 months
- Montana: $8
- New Jersey: $8
- Vermont: $7
- All other states: $9.50

The FTC is permitted to modify this annually, based proportionally on changes in the consumer price index, with fractional changes rounded to the nearest 50 cents.

The bureaus are notorious for changing their addresses so that they don't have to deal with consumer disputes. They figure if they present

BUREAU CONTACT INFORMATION*		
Equifax	**Trans Union**	**Experian**
PO Box 740241	PO Box 1000	PO Box 2104
Atlanta, GA 30374-0241	Chester, PA 19022-2000	Allen, TX 75013-2104
www.equifax.com	www.transunion.com	www.experian.com

* The Big Three compile personal reports. For business reports, contact the credit reporting agency Dun & Bradstreet at www.dnb.com or Innovis at www.innovis.com. The repair of business credit can be performed in the same manner as that of personal credit, though not with regard to bureau disputes, only through negotiating with the creditor in accordance withe Chapter 9. (The FCRA only applies to consumer credit.)

Table 3.

enough hurdles, consumers will just get tired and go away. Always check with their Web sites to ensure that you have the most current address. And when ordering by mail, be sure to include the following in your request:

- Full name (including Jr., Sr., II, etc.).
- SSN.
- Current address, previous addresses in the last 24 months.
- Date of birth.
- Signature.
- Copy of utility bill mailed to you at the PO Box to which you are requesting that the report be sent. (Avoid sending a utility bill with the address of service on it, since you could be telling the world, including bill collectors, where you live.)
- A check or money order for the amount charged for the report, if applicable.

Warning: I used to recommend that people obtain their reports online but have since reversed that recommendation. I was informed by a FCRA attorney that the online reports will often now come with arbitration agreements and will also limit liability to the credit reporting agencies to the cost of the report! Can they get away with this? In response to this question, the FCRA attorney said, "I don't want to find out. Who knows what a judge will do?" This is yet another reason to avoid obtaining a report from annualcreditreport.com, freecreditreport.com, and the like. Always order your reports by mail unless ordering FICO reports.

If you opt to obtain your reports online, be sure to have all your previous account history available, since the bureaus (and FICO) will ask for all sorts of information to verify your identity, including account numbers, balances, employment history, and even previous address information. If you have old credit reports, this is often the best place to obtain historical account information.

Bureaus are notorious for stalling and will use whatever means necessary to avoid having to do something. The most common delay tactic in response to your letter is to ask you to verify that "you are who you say you are" by sending them another request and including a copy of a utility bill to verify your address. They do because of the rise of identity theft. In your first correspondence, always include a copy of a bill (one with the address of the location to which you want the file sent). For those wishing to avoid bill collectors, use a bill that has been sent to your PO Box, not to your home address. If you use your home address, it will end up on your report, and the creditor will have found you. (Consider that utility bills sent to PO Boxes will also often contain the address of service. Cell phone bills will only contain the billing address.) For more about staying lost, refer to the section on barriers and insulation in Chapter 6.

Tip: If you opt to follow my advice and instead purchase your reports online at the credit bureaus' respective Web sites, be careful. Some of the credit bureaus' Web sites only permit you to view your report once, so be sure to print it out. You can also select "printable view" and then hit file/save on your Web browser, saving the Web page to your hard drive for later viewing. The bureaus also will permit you to specify if you want your SSN truncated. This can be good for security, particularly if you're using someone else's computer. If that's the case, then perhaps it's best to save the file to a floppy disk or CD.

Be Wary of Free Offers from Resellers and Affiliates

You may see the phrases "credit reporting agency" and "credit bureau" used interchangeably in reference to all sorts of credit report suppliers, yet the only suppliers that you should be concerned about are the Big Three. Many firms that call themselves credit reporting agencies or credit bureaus actually get their information from one or more of the Big Three, and they are technically known as "resellers" by the FCRA definition. The Credit Bureau of Connecticut and Credit Bureau Systems are examples of credit bureau resellers. They buy large volumes of credit reports at discount rates from the Big Three and resell the data to lower-volume buyers, such as you and me, or mortgage lenders. Some resellers also compile data from the Big Three and merge it into a single report, often referred to as a "trimerge," or 3-in-1 credit report. Mortgage brokers often use these merged reports. Resellers may or may not actually collect data from furnishers, but since they provide credit reports to third parties, they are classified as credit reporting agencies and must therefore comply with the FCRA.

Beyond the FCRA definition, the term "reseller" is often used interchangeably with "affiliate," though it often has a broader meaning, at least colloquially. The Big Three sometimes set up arrangements with businesses that simply hawk the data directly to consumers. Since they don't compile data, merge reports, or sell to third parties, affiliates technically aren't resellers, at least not by the legal definition, though in effect that's what they appear—at least to a consumer. For this reason, I'll use the term affiliate to refer to businesses that resell reports exclusively to consumers, in order to avoid confusion.

FICO's unique position in the credit reporting industry throws yet another wrench into the works. The de facto standard among lenders, FICO has built a solid business-to-business partnership with the credit bureaus as a provider of their scoring software. It has also created a consumer division, known as myFICO, which acts as an affiliate of the bureaus, selling credit reports (with a FICO score) directly to consumers. Just as resellers often pull data from one or more of the Big Three databases and then deliver it to third parties in their own format, affiliates and resellers alike may use their own formats in presenting consumers with information culled from the bureaus. FICO does this and includes its credit score based on the data it collects. This enables consumers to obtain all three reports along with the score that matters with one-stop shopping.

Still other affiliates are licensed by the bureaus to provide bureau products on the Web, though some are far more closely integrated than others. You see, while FICO and certain other affiliates or partners are tied directly to the bureaus' databases, many aren't connected at all and simply provide an interface to a primary bureau. That is, the Web page of an affiliate may look different than that of the bureau, but it's really just a different graphic overlay. And still others are affiliates by virtue of simply providing hyperlinks to one of the bureaus or to even another affiliate! Such click-affiliates will receive a flat fee from the bureau it has a relationship with for every user who clicks on the hyperlink and submits an online credit bureau form.

Affiliates give away credit reports in addition to selling them. However, the ones that offer free credit reports aren't really giving them away, since consumers must agree to let them sell their personal information to the world in return (not worth it in my opinion). Even worse, 90 percent of affiliates now sell you some type of service with your "free" report, using the report as the bait to lure you into a "free 30-day trial" membership. (Before you know it, your credit card is being charged a fee month after month, and it won't stop no matter how hard you scream. Good luck in getting this one resolved.) They also sell consolidated credit reports, also known as 3-in-1 credit reports. There's no such thing as a free 3-in-1 report, but many affiliates will offer these with a "free trial membership" to something as well. Bear in mind that these companies are also notorious for selling your information for marketing purposes.

Consumers should also be wary of any offers for a "free" credit report from the Big Three. They too often package it with something else, such as Trans Union's ID-Fraud Watch, Experian's Credit Manager, Equifax's Credit Watch Gold, or some similar program. In other words, while you may be getting your credit report for free, it's in return for buying something, usually a monthly subscription you may not really want. Be careful what you agree to and read the fine print.

Get Credit Reports with a FICO Score

This is all very confusing to the average consumer who needs to order credit reports for the purpose of credit restoration. It can be a real challenge to decipher exactly what you need and where to find it. Simply put, to repair your credit you'll need your to track your progress by virtue of your score. The score that matters most is the FICO score, and only Fair Isaac, its affiliates, and Equifax currently offer all the Big Three credit reports *and* a FICO score.

Equifax will provide a FICO score, which it refers to as Score Power, along with its Equifax credit report for an additional charge of $5.45. Equifax also provides consumers with a 3-in-1 report for $37.90

or one that has Score Power for $47.90. Trans Union used to offer "credit profile plus FICO score" as an option on its Web site, but not anymore. If you order a free report from Trans Union online, you'll have the option of getting its proprietary TrueCredit score only, at a cost of $5.95. Likewise, Experian provides its scoring model, the "Plus Score," exclusively, offering it as an option for $6.95 when someone requests a free report. The bureaus make more money by selling their own proprietary scores, so why not? The fact that there are no standards in place makes things difficult for consumers, since creditors' use of different scoring models can sometimes mean the difference between getting approved for a loan or not. But as stated, focus on FICO.

Although Equifax appears to have the best solution for obtaining the Big Three reports with FICO score (Score Power), it is highly discouraged, since its online terms of service agreement contain arbitration, limitation of liability, and venue (where a lawsuit can be filed) provisions that are unconscionable.

There isn't a perfect solution for obtaining the Big Three credit reports, but at this time I recommend buying all three from myFICO (www.myfico.com) or one of its affiliates, such as All 3 Reports (www.all3reports.com). (**Disclosure**: All 3 Reports is also a BestCredit affiliate, and I maintain a promotional coupon code at www.bestcredit.com/ficopromotionalcode/ so you can save a few bucks over the cost of myFICO.)

Having sung the praises of FICO, I must point out that there is a downside. FICO's database integration with the bureaus isn't perfect, and myFICO reports will often lack important information, such as account numbers for certain tradelines (which you will need when researching items and disputing entries). The Big Three bureaus, on the other hand, almost always leave all the account numbers intact in their reports, so it's a good idea to purchase your reports directly from them as well. Another—and possibly more important—reason to order your credit reports directly from the bureaus is that doing so will produce inquiry-generated snapshots, or frozen scans, of the reports, and these duplicate records will remain in the bureaus' archives. As mentioned in Chapter 1, snapshots are particularly useful when you suspect identity theft or some other serious problems with your report. They can also assist you in any legal battle that may develop with the bureaus. FICO-generated reports don't create snapshots with the bureaus. And, again, ordering by mail will enable you to avoid any unfavorable online terms-of-service agreements.

For these reasons, I recommend that anyone who is serious about credit restoration purchase credit reports by mail (without scores) directly from Trans Union, Experian, and Equifax, in addition to buying all three directly from myFICO or All3Reports.com. The total cost is about $70 as of this writing.

HOW TO DECIPHER YOUR REPORT

There's no need to be intimidated by all the information on a report. Just focus on the status field (explained shortly) for each entry; look to see if the account was ever reported late (e.g., "3 times 90 days"). Also look at the balance, high credit, date of last activity, and remarks (e.g., collection account, included in bankruptcy, bad debt).

Formatting

It used to be that credit bureaus always used letter-number identifiers to indicate type of account and status on their reports, but this is changing. Online reports don't have them any longer, though some printed reports still do. When you see a two- to three-character (letter-number or letter-number-number) identifier included in each tradeline entry, the letter indicates the type of account (e.g., revolving, installment), and the number indicates the status. See Chart 1 on page 106 for an explaination of letter-number identifiers.

Not only do the bureaus often change their formatting, the online reports often have other differences from hard copies, which is why it pays to simply get the respective bureau's current explanation sheet and become familiar with it. These accompany mailed reports and are also available on the bureaus' respective Web sites.

Credit reporting agencies break their reports down into five main categories: personal information, such as date of birth, address, etc.; tradeline fields; public record entries; collection accounts; and inquiries. Sometimes tradeline entries are broken down further, by grouping accounts in good standing, for example. Categories can be displayed in any order, and each of the Big Three does them differently.

Credit Report Letter and Number Identifiers	
Letter Identifiers	
R	Revolving (payment amount variable, credit card account)
UR	Revolving, unrated (approved but unused or too new to rate)
O	Open account (entire balance due each month)
I	Installment (personal loan, fixed number of payments)
M	Mortgage
Number Identifiers	
R00	Revolving, unrated (approved but unused or too new to rate)
I01	Installment, paid as agreed
M02	Mortgage, 30+ days late
I03	Installment, 60+ days late
O04	Open, 90+ days late
I05	Installment, 120+ days late; or collection account
R06	Revolving, 150+ days late; or collection account
R07	Revolving; making regular payments under wage earner plan or similar arrangement
I08	Installment; repossession
R09	Revolving; charge-off

Chart 1.

Tradeline Fields (Credit Account)

Creditors will report their tradelines with several fields. The fields are the individual entries, such as "date opened," "date closed," and so on. Creditors will most often include the following fields in their Metro 2 dump to the bureaus, and the bureaus can lay them out any way they choose. See Chart 2 for tradeline fields.

Tradeline Fields Summary

- Creditor name
- Account number
- Open date
- Close date
- Reported since (date the creditor began reporting)
- Date of last activity
- High balance/high credit (the highest amount charged)
- Credit limit
- Account/loan type (revolving or installment)
- Responsibility (individual or joint)
- Terms (length of monthly installments)
- Monthly payment (minimum for revolving; set amount for installment)
- Number of months reviewed (same as "reported since," but shown as months)
- Last reported
- Balance
- Balance history (used to determine if debt is being moved around)
- Date paid
- Current/pay status
- Date placed for collection
- Balloon payment amount/date (amount/date when a lump payment is due; for installments only)
- Deferred payment start date (date for accounts in deferment to resume)
- Terms frequency (how often a payment is due, such as monthly)

Chart 2.

Public Record Fields

Public records that affect a score consist of judgments, foreclosures, repossessions, liens, tax liens, bankruptcies, and collection lawsuits. Public record entries are listed in a separate section from accounts on a credit report. These entries are covered in Chart 3.

Public Record Fields Summary

- Source (court name)
- Court address
- Court type
- Case number
- Individual/joint (whether individual or joint)
- Individual/business (whether individual or business)
- Bankruptcy disposition (if bankruptcy, type and pending/dismissed/discharged)
- Date paid/resolved (or discharged if bankruptcy)
- Date verified
- Date filed
- Plaintiff
- Plaintiff attorney
- Liabilities/liability amount
- Assets
- Estimated date of removal

Chart 3.

Collection Account Fields

Although a tradeline entry can contain the term "collection account," collection accounts that are reported by debt collectors are listed separately and in their own category. They will often contain the fields found in Chart 4.

Collection Account Fields Summary
• Agency address • Date reported • Date assigned • Creditor classification • Creditor name • Account number • Account owner (individual or joint) • Original amount owned • Date of first delinquency • Balance date (date balance reported) • Balance owed • Date of last activity • Status date (date status confirmed) • Status (D means default or unpaid; P means paid) • Comments

Chart 4.

Inquiry Fields

Inquiries are generated when a request is made for your credit report. They contain the name of the company that pulled the report, the date of the inquiry, and the type. The type can be PRM (promotional inquiry made for marketing purposes), AM/AR (account monitoring or review from a current creditor), or ACIS (internal account review by the credit bureau, generated by a consumer pulling his or her own report).

> **Tip:** Think very hard before you respond to that "six months same as cash" or similar offer. Every such response will result in an inquiry appearing on your credit report and could lower your score, raising your interest rate on a new car or home loan or even getting you denied!

Status Entries

Status entries contain information such as account open or closed, but potential lenders are primarily interested in one thing: do you pay your bills on time? The answer to this question also lies in the status, and it's also in this area where the FICO scoring model obtains the information for use in its payment history scorecard. Payment history can be viewed in one of three ways: neutral, positive, or adverse.

Neutral entries don't affect a score one way or another as far as payment history goes. Yet their presence may benefit a score in other ways, such as aging a credit profile. Positive entries will help raise a FICO score. Of course, these entries can be accomplished by always paying your bills on time!

Ah, the fun part; the reason you're reading this book: adverse entries. The list is a very long one, and I find it's far easier to remember positive and neutral status entries and then identify anything that's not one of them as adverse. Chart 5 contains all of the types of status entries that may be found on a credit report.

Status Entries Field Summary
Neutral Entries
• Paid • Refinanced • Credit Card Lost • Unrated • Account Closed by Credit Grantor (won't affect score; human eyes may not like it) • Account Closed by Consumer • Soft Inquiry (not performed for extension of credit; includes prescreened offers)
Positive Entries
• Paid Never Late • Paid (Pays) as Agreed • Account Current

(cont.)

Adverse Entries
• Paid Never Late
• Current/Paid was 30/60/90/120 (days late)
• 30/60/90/120 (days late)
• Charge-off (creditor doesn't expect to collect and has probably filed for a tax deduction)
• Paid Charge-off (same as charge-off, but balance paid)
• Bad Debt
• Delinquent (past due)
• Included in Bankruptcy (account included in a bankruptcy petition)
• Collection Account (placed for collections)
• Paid Collection (paid collection account)
• Paid Settlement (creditor settled for less than what was owed)
• SCNL (subscriber cannot locate, meaning you skipped)
• Settled (you were late and paid a portion; weighted less if it wasn't recent)
• Hard Inquiry (three or more in the preceding 12 months)
• Bankruptcy
• Judgment Paid or Unpaid (you were sued by the creditor and lost)
• Foreclosure (home was taken back by the lender)
• Repossession (auto/item was taken back by the creditor)
• Bankruptcy
• Collection Lawsuit
• Wage Garnishment
• Lien (attached to property in an attempt to collect unpaid debt)
• Tax Lien (unpaid back taxes)

Chart 5.

Things That Will Often Get You Denied

As explained previously, factors other than scoring and payment history can influence a potential lender in determining whether to extend credit or not. Often your credit can be perfect, but you will still be denied if you have excessive inquires or have been extended a large amount of credit relative to your income. When you are applying for credit, the following items will often cause your application to be denied when they appear on your report (or credit application):

- Past 30 days late two or more times or past 60 days late in the last 12 months or worse
- A bankruptcy in the last 24 months with no new credit
- Judgment against you in the last two years (any length of time is bad if it's unpaid)
- Excessive number of inquiries (more than three in previous year)
- No hard address (PO Box only)
- No telephone
- No credit references
- Fewer than six months at your current job
- High debt-to-income ratio (exceeds 45 percent)
- Large number of revolving accounts (i.e., credit cards, overdraft protection, and home equity line of credit; each has a minimum payment, and the credit can be accessed repeatedly)
- No bank accounts (checking or savings)
- Self-employed with unsubstantiated income (usually they want to see tax returns for the last two years), especially for a mortgage loan

HOW TO ANALYZE AND PRIORITIZE

An analysis of a credit report is not to be confused with a situational assessment (see Chapter 8). It's a sterile exercise to look at a report and make assumptions about how it's impacting you on its face, whereas viewing it in a situational context—that is, observing it in a real-world situation—will most often reshape your credit restoration (and possibly debt-reduction) strategy. And yet this initial examination is useful as a primer, because it will get you to thinking about priorities.

Analyze

Get some blank sheets of paper and begin writing down the following notes for each of your three reports:

1. Adverse information that is inaccurate (usually the easiest to repair)
2. Positive information that should be included but isn't
3. Adverse information that is accurate

Each credit report will often contain different items. In some cases, a negative item may be found on one report but not on the others, and likewise with positive information. Don't worry about this, since you will treat each report as separate in many respects. This exercise gives you a sense of what you're dealing with by helping to pinpoint exactly what needs to be addressed while disregarding all of the confusing ancillary data that accompanies the reports, and thus it becomes easier to analyze, prioritize, and *grasp*.

Tip: Joint accounts (i.e., credit extended in the name of two or more parties) create the potential for all sorts of problems. Where people and relationships are involved, unforeseen complications often arise. Therefore, it's best to keep all of your credit cards separate—even from your mate. Ever heard a divorcee say, "My ex ruined my credit . . . damn it." Of course you have, and having joint accounts is the number-one reason this happens. (The exception to this rule is when serious financial problems exist and bankruptcy is in the offing, as explained in Chapters 8 and 12.) Getting added as a user to an account is OK if it meets the criteria explained in Chapter 3 under "Establish Years of Good Credit Where None Existed Before."

Prioritize

This is where you "make your money," so to speak. Both time and energy are required to improve things, so you must focus your efforts where you can make the most headway in the shortest amount of time. Begin by attacking those things that will have the highest degree of success and can be accomplished the fastest. Usually, the order in which credit restoration strategy should be approached is as follows:

1. *Reestablish your credit.* This can be done in two ways. The first is by always paying your current open accounts on time. The second is by opening up one or two new accounts in order to create accounts with a perfect history. (See "Reestablish Credit" in Chapter 3.)

2. *Add positive information that should be reported but isn't to your report.* (See "Make Sure Positive Information Gets Reported" in Chapter 3.)

3. *Establish years of good credit where none existed.* This technique will enable you to create an account on your credit file that wasn't there before. It's useful for people with little or no credit and those with very few good account entries on their credit report. (See "Establish Years of Good Credit Where None Existed Before" in Chapter 3.)

4. *Remove erroneous adverse information from your report.* **Caution:** As the chapter on scoring shows, some duplicate positive entries can be a good thing. Moreover, because of the way in which credit bureaus will delete entire tradelines on accounts that can't be verified by the furnisher, the age of an account in a file may be helping more than any old adverse information is hurting. (See Chapter 11.)

5. *Remove accurate public record entries, such as judgments and liens. Bankruptcies are the exception here.* All accounts that have a reference to bankruptcy, such as "Included in Bankruptcy," must be removed before the bankruptcy entry. (For more information on how to remove bankruptcies and other public records, see Chapter 10.)

6 *Repair or remove accurate adverse tradeline entries that have an unpaid balance.* Those tradelines that have a balance hurt a score more than others, all things remaining equal. (See Chapter 9.)

7. *Repair accurate adverse tradeline entries that are less than three years old.* (See Chapter 9.)

8. *Remove accurate third-party (debt collector) collection account entries.* (See Chapters 7, 9, and 10.)

9. *Repair accurate adverse tradeline entries that are more than three years old.* (See Chapter 9.)
10. *Remove hard inquiries.* (See Chapter 10.)

This order may seem strange at first, but there are two primary factors to consider when prioritizing. The first is what is easiest to get changed or added, and the second is what will have the greatest impact on your score. For example, it's really easy to open another account, so that's a high priority. And since original-creditor entries carry more weight than third-party collection accounts, they are a generally a higher priority. Inquiries don't affect your score very much and drop off in two years, so they're always last. In truth, once the other adverse items are deleted or repaired, you likely won't even care about the inquiries, because your FICO score will likely be well above what you require.

Keep in mind that there may be some overlap as well. For example, although the priority for removing a collection account entry is below that for a tradeline entry less than three years old (as original creditor entries carry more weight on a FICO score), going after the adverse tradeline entry will often cause the collection account entry to come off as well, providing it's a related account. (See Chapters 9 and 10.)

Note that there's a difference between repair and remove. Tradelines are made up of many fields, and due to the nature of credit scoring it pays to repair some fields while leaving the tradeline intact wherever possible. The average age of an account makes a very big difference, and any positive tradelines will help a score directly as well as indirectly by reducing the impact of other adverse entries.

Keep in mind that this is a guide, not a set of hard-and-fast rules. Only you can determine your priorities, because only you know your circumstances. Which problems are the most pressing? More recent public record entries or late payments will hurt a score more than something older. What would positively impact *your* score the most? Are you about to lose a house or car? Are you about to get sued for failed credit card payments? All of us are busy, and surely you won't spend time opening new accounts when you're about to lose your car.

Think about it very carefully, and while weighing the impact of each individual mark on your overall score, take action relevant to your situation that will produce the largest improvement to your report in the shortest possible time. Go for the worst first. For example, if your report shows an unpaid collection account, this is more harmful than a "Paid Was 30 x 2." So go after the former first. Another example: if you have two different accounts that are equally negative and one is reported with only one bureau whereas the other is reported with two or three, go after the latter. If you have unpaid negative items that vary widely in dollar amounts, you may want to go after the ones that are the smallest if you're short on capital. A more recent lateness is more harmful than an older one, so go for improving the reporting on the newer account.

Also consider that if you're going for a mortgage loan, the lender will use the middle score. Perhaps this will affect priority, depending on where the top two scores are and what types of adverse information is weighting down each individual score.

Consider ahead of time that it may take some cash to get you out of one or more of your circumstances. But, fortunately, in the case of unsecured debt, you can usually get the amount you owe reduced by as much as 75 percent, with a deal that includes bad credit removal. Perhaps debt reduction is your main goal. Only you can decide, but you'll have a better idea once you fully understand your report and have studied all your options. And yet this early-stage exercise should get you to thinking in the right direction. As stated at the beginning, this section is intended as a primer only, and you will need to make a situational assessment (Chapter 8), viewing the sterile contents of your credit report in a real-world context, before you can make the very best decisions about priority.

6

LEGAL EXPOSURE—
WHERE DO YOU STAND?

Although credit reporting isn't exactly legal exposure, furnishing adverse information is the method of enforcement creditors use to get people to pay their bills. This tends to be effective, since many people—even law-abiding citizens—fear bad credit. It's common to fear something that's not understood. Yet the law can work for you as well as against you, which is why it's important to know your rights.

But the law can be used for more than just adverse reporting. It can be used to take things. People often ask: "Can they take my house? Can they garnish my wages? Can I avoid the collectors? A judgment is still on my credit report; isn't it supposed to drop off after seven years?"

Unfortunately, since there are many variables, the answers to such questions are usually not so simple. However, once you understand a few fundamentals, then you can begin to answer the important questions as they apply to you. These include the statute of limitations for credit reporting (how long something can remain on your credit report), the statute of limitations for debt collection (how long a collector can collect using a lawsuit), and techniques to insulate yourself from debt collectors.

CREDIT REPORTING STATUTE OF LIMITATIONS

Credit reporting agencies keep favorable information for 10 years, yet by law they can delete the information anytime they wish, even before seven years.[1] However, the FTC believes that agencies should not purge favorable information sooner than adverse information.[2] Although favorable information is generally retained in a credit bureau's repository for 10 years, the length of time that adverse information is retained is far more complicated. It's the credit reporting statute of limitations that governs adverse information, and this can vary greatly depending on the type of information (e.g., a judgment has a different statute of limitations than a late payment). Understanding the statute of limitations for reporting adverse information is very useful for developing priorities for credit restoration and resolving unpaid debts.

Adverse Information

Adverse information is that which will reduce a score or otherwise damage a consumer's creditworthiness or reputation (affecting employment, for example). All the following are considered adverse, and there are laws that restrict the retention of adverse information by the credit bureaus.

- **Bankruptcies.** Chapter 7, 11, and 12 bankruptcies remain on a credit report for 10 years. Chapter 13 bankruptcies will remain for seven years from the filing date if successfully completed, or 10 years if not completed.[3]
- **Collection accounts.** Collections accounts and charge-offs (those the creditor writes off as uncollectible, aka "charged to profit and loss") remain on file for seven years; reporting commences no later than 180 days from the beginning of the delinquency rather than on the date of any subsequent action.

---

1. FTC Official Staff Commentary § 605 item 4.
2. Trans Union Credit Info. Co., 102 FTC 1109; 1983; consent order.
3. 15 U.S.C. § 1681c(a)(1).

So if there are multiple delinquency dates (i.e., a consumer went delinquent, went current, and then went delinquent again), the date of the first delinquency is the one that will apply. The running time (reporting period) cannot be reset by subsequent payment or for any other reason, in any state, except with certain student loans, listed below.

• **Judgments.** Unpaid judgments remain for seven years or until the governing (i.e., state) statute of limitations has expired, whichever is the longer period.[4] The FTC believes paid judgments cannot be reported for more than seven years from the filing date (date of entry), as payment eliminates any governing statute of limitation that might lengthen this period.[5]

• **Tax liens.** Paid tax liens may not be reported more than seven years after the date of payment.[6] Unpaid ones may be reported as long as they're filed and in effect.[7]

• **Civil suits.** Civil suits show up on court records, and defendants (the objects of the lawsuits) in such actions are reported to the credit reporting agencies through the use of service bureaus. They're reported seven years from the date of entry or until the governing statute of limitations has expired, whichever is the longer period. For lawsuits, the date of entry is the date the suit is initiated (i.e., filed by the plaintiff). Incidentally, if a person files suit against another, then even if the defending party countersues, the countersuit cannot be reported on the plaintiff's credit report (though a judgment can be, regardless of who filed suit first).

---

4. 15 U.S.C. § 1681c(a)(2). See also *Beaver v. TRW Corp.*, 1988 WL 123636 (W.D.N.Y. 1988) (a satisfied judgment less than seven years may be reported); *Mulkey v. Credit Bureau, Inc.*, [1980-1989 Decision Transfer Binder], Consumer Cred. Guide (CCH) k 96,739 (D.D.C. Feb. 18, 1983), aff'd, 729 F.2d 863 (D.C. Cir. 1984).

5. FTC Official Staff Commentary § 605(a)(2) item 2. Cf. *Grays v. TransUnion Credit Info. Co.*, 759 F. Supp. 390 (N.D. Ohio 1990).

6. 15 U.S.C. § 1681c(a)(3).

7. FTC Official Staff Commentary § 605(a)(3) item 1.

- **Child support.** Overdue child support payments can only remain for seven years from the date it is overdue.[8]
- **Criminal records.** Certain public records (such as arrests, indictments, misdemeanor complaints, and convictions of crimes) aren't computed in a score. Nevertheless, many people wish to know when these drop off, since they can affect employment. It's seven years from the date of disposition, release, or parole, or until the governing statute of limitations has expired, whichever is the longer period. In the case of a conviction, the entry is removed if a full pardon is granted. In the case of an arrest, indictment, or misdemeanor complaint, the entry is removed if a conviction does not result. Criminal convictions remain indefinitely.[9]
- **Inquiries.** Inquiries remain for two years, or one year for pre-screened offers. Prescreened offer inquiries are not disclosed, other than to the consumer.[10] Prescreened offer inquiries don't affect a credit score.
- **Student loans.** There are two different sets of rules, depending on whether the student loan is a Federal Family Education Loan (FFEL) or a Perkins Loan. FFELs include Guaranteed Student or Stafford Loans, Supplemental Loans for Students (SLSs), and PLUS (Parent) Loans. They are obligations to a lender that are guaranteed by a guaranty agency and insured by the U.S. government. Another type is a Perkins Loan (formerly a National Direct Student Loan) and is an obligation owed to a school, but that obligation may be assigned to the U.S. government if the student defaults. FFEL loans are reported for seven years from the latest of three dates: the date the secretary of education or

---

8. 15 U.S.C. § 1681s-1. Since January 1, 2004, states are able to legislate when they can require child support agencies to provide this information to credit reporting agencies, and the notification requirements to the debtor in the event such information is furnished.
9. 15 U.S.C. § 1681c was amended in 1998 to exempt indictments and convictions of crimes from the seven-year limit, retroactive to September 30, 1997.
10. 15 U.S.C. § 1681b (c)(3).

the guarantee agency pays a claim to the loan holder on the guarantee (this is the same date the guaranty agency of the United States takes over the loan); the date the secretary of education, guaranty agency, lender, or any other loan holder first reports the account to the reporting agency; or the date when a borrower defaults on the loan a second time in the event that he or she resumed repayment after defaulting on the loan the first time.[11] Perkins Loans, on the other hand, are not subject to any limit on reporting. Furnishers of Perkins Loan information are required to update the account information to the bureaus if the debtor makes six consecutive monthly payments.[12]

- **All other adverse.** All other entries may remain no longer than seven years. Examples would include paid tax liens and other liens whether paid or unpaid. Another example includes tradeline entries (account entries by creditors). Adverse account entries that aren't categorized as collection or charge-off accounts will show on a report for seven years from the date of last activity (DLA). Examples include late payments and accounts marked as "included in bankruptcy," if there was no prior charge-off or collection event. For example, the collection account FCRA provision is explicit, so a delinquent debt included in bankruptcy would still be reported for seven years plus 180 days from the date of delinquency. However, if the debt was included in bankruptcy but was never delinquent (which rarely happens but sometimes does), then the statute of limitation would begin from the date it was included in bankruptcy and remain for seven years instead of seven years plus 180 days.

---

11. 20 U.S.C. § 1080a, as amended by Pub. Law 102-325, § 424, 106, Stat. 543 (July 23, 1992).
12. The Higher Education Act of 1965, section 430(a)(f); NCLC *Fair Credit Reporting* § 8.3.9 (5th ed. 2002 and 2005 Supp.). Special thanks to the NCLC for making the statute intelligible. See Chapter 10 for special methods for removal of adverse student loan entries.

Seven-Year-Rule Exceptions

There are exceptions to the seven-year reporting rule, which most people are completely unaware of. Lenders will notify the bureaus if the consumer's credit request meets certain criteria, and in such cases the bureaus will report negative items that are more than seven years old.

1. When a consumer attempts to get a loan for $150,000 or more, there's no time limit. (For those wanting to own a home in the future, this is yet another reason to get those adverse items removed.)
2. When a consumer attempts to obtain a job with a salary of more than $75,000, there is no time limit.
3. When a consumer applies for a life insurance policy worth more than $150,000, there is no time limit.

> **Note:** Since there are exceptions to the seven-year credit reporting statute, it makes the removal of any adverse data all that much more important.

Data retention by the bureaus of obsolete information is permitted for the purposes of providing information under the seven-year-rule exemptions. Reporting agencies are not required to retain obsolete information in their databases, but they are permitted to do so.

It's important to understand how these reporting rules affect your individual report, since your priorities for removal may change as accounts approach their drop-off date. (This is discussed further later on.)

> **Note:** The revised FCRA (FACTA, December 2003) has a provision mandating that items placed for collection or charged off must be removed from the credit report after three years, but the following caveats apply: (a) such removal can only be performed one time per consumer, (b) the debt cannot be greater than $100, and (c) the consumer (debtor) must have attended a credit and financial manage-

ment class during the three-year period. Although this may look attractive at first glance, much more powerful (and less troublesome) methods of bad credit removal can be employed, making this practically useless.

Obsolete Information

Adverse information that has expired due to a credit reporting statute of limitations is considered obsolete. Reporting of obsolete information is prohibited under 15 U.S.C. § 1681c(a). (All 1681 references are from the FCRA.) Further, credit reporting agencies may not indicate that obsolete adverse information exists.[13] For example, a reporting agency may not report that a creditor (whose debt is now obsolete) cannot locate the debtor.[14] Nothing in the Act prevents a user from using obsolete information should it be wrongfully included in a consumer's credit report; agencies and furnishers are held accountable for that, through the FCRA. Users bear no liability when they rely on obsolete information for their decision-making.[15]

Credit Reporting and Statute of Limitation Variations

The statutes of limitations on credit reporting can be a very confusing for most people, but it can be broken down as follows:

1. Federal law trumps state law. The Constitution contains a supremacy clause.[16] Federal law will always rule, unless a state law offers more protection to the consumer and it is not in conflict with federal law. This holds unless a federal law specifically preempts state law. (Many state credit reporting laws are

---

13. FTC Official Staff Commentary § 605 item 5.
14. FTC Official Staff Commentary § 605 item 6.
15. NCLC *Fair Credit Reporting* § 8.2 (5th ed. 2002 and 2005 Supp.).
16. The Supremacy Clause, Article VI: "This Constitution, and the Laws of the United States which shall be made in Pursuance thereof; and all Treaties made, or which shall be made, under the Authority of the United States, shall be the supreme Law of the Land; and the Judges in every State shall be bound thereby, any Thing in the Constitution or Laws of any State to the Contrary notwithstanding."

preempted by federal law by the FCRA.) A compiled list of many such exceptions will be provided shortly.

2. Since state laws can vary, it's a good idea to check your state's laws, which may offer you additional consumer protections not found in the FCRA.

3. Public record furnishing can vary by state, particularly where judgments and liens are concerned. This is really more a function of the public record entry itself, not the credit reporting statute. For example, a judgment in Ohio is only collectible for five years and then it expires as a court record. Once it expires, it is no longer collectible, as it technically does not exist. However, the judgment holder can have it renewed every five years indefinitely. It will report for seven years from the filing date whether paid or unpaid. In addition, every time a judgment holder renews an unpaid judgment with the court, it counts as a new public record filing—which resets the seven-year clock.

4. State laws concerning public record entries will not stand if they offer more protection to the consumer than the federal law, since the FCRA decrees that the longer period of reporting will rule, § 605 (a)(2). For a compiled reference list of state laws concerning public records, check the BestCredit Web site (www.bestcredit.com/creditreporting/) or consult an attorney.

5. The seven-year statute for collection and charge-off accounts cannot be reset by payment. Only certain student loans can be reset by payment, as specified above.

Credit Reporting of Civil Actions

Another state variation to credit reporting is the way civil actions are reported. As explained earlier, state laws vary with regard to the way in which they permit judgments to be refiled with the court. I mentioned Ohio, where there is a five-year limit on the collection of judgments, but judgments are renewable indefinitely. Oregon's limit is 10 years, and judgments are renewable one time. However, there are also rules regarding dormancy. For instance, in Ohio a judgment is renewable indefinitely, yet if it sits dormant (isn't reentered) for 21 years, then the creditor (the party to whom the judgment is owed) cannot refile. This is a problem for judgment debtors who think they've dodged a bullet when a judgment drops off their report after the time limit expires, only to have the same judgment show up on their credit report—a brand-new entry—a decade later. Individual judgment creditors usually forget about refiling, whereas companies often do not, and judgments are subject to interest accumulation for the period they remain unpaid. Moreover, judgments can be sold to a third party under certain circumstances. An individual holding a judgment may not be so astute as to refile, yet if he or she sells the judgment to someone in the business of purchasing debts, such a buyer would be more inclined to refile the judgment. State laws vary on whether judgments can be sold or transferred.

Always be cognizant of these pitfalls and avoid unpaid judgments when practical. Even a Chapter 7 bankruptcy can be preferable to unpaid judgments, since the former drops off your credit reports in 10 years, and you can obtain new, desirable credit after just two!

And although a judgment may seem a very troublesome prospect, a lien is even more so. It's essentially a judgment taken to another level, since it reflects unwillingness on the part of a judgment debtor to voluntarily comply with a court judgment. Unpaid tax liens are particularly nasty, as they may be reported indefinitely.

Judgment creditors can use the judgment to place a charge, security, or encumbrance on a piece of property, which is usually real property (e.g., a home). However, some states permit liens to be placed on personal property, such as jewelry or artwork. A lien on a home is an encumbrance, for example, one which requires that the holder of the lien be paid at the time the home is sold.

The ways in which judgments may be attached to property is explained in detail shortly, under "Collections and Civil Action," but for the purposes of how they apply to credit reporting statutes, liens work much the same way as judgments: they are filed and then expire in a certain period. Unpaid ones can be renewed in accordance with the governing statute (and each time one is renewed, it shows up as a fresh, unpaid lien on a credit report). This can be tricky, since some states that permit liens on personal property will have a different expiration date for liens placed on real property. For example, a real property lien in Florida is filed with the county clerk and lasts for 10 years and is renewable for 10 more, while a personal property lien is filed with the Florida Department of State and is good for five years and renewable for five more.

Once again, credit reporting statute of limitations can get confusing. To summarize, just remember that the credit reporting statute of limitations for most adverse information is seven years, with the exception of seven things: (1) criminal convictions are indefinite; other criminal entries are seven years or until the governing statute of limitations has expired, whichever is the longer period; (2) bankruptcies are 10 years; (3) unpaid tax liens can remain indefinitely; (4) accounts placed for collection or charged for profit and loss are seven years plus 180 days; (5) suits and judgments are seven years from the date of entry or until the governing statute of limitations has expired, whichever is longer; (6) student loans can vary based on type and other factors—some may be reported indefinitely; and (7) exceptions exist for three specific types of situations: (a) when applying for a loan, (b) when seeking life insurance of $150,000 or more, or (c) when seeking employment where the salary is $75,000 or more. Also remember that state laws can vary widely concerning the time permitted between refiling of unpaid claims. This would enable the reporting period for judgments, for example, to be reset every time the entry is renewed with the court and shows up as a new public record.

Credit Reporting Running Time Reset

It's been widely perpetuated by the collection industry that any payment can reset the seven-year credit reporting statute. Collection agencies will often unlawfully furnish account information beyond what is allowable by the FCRA. They can do this by either taking the delinquency date and rolling it forward to a future date or reporting the date of last activity (DLA) as the delinquency date, thereby having the entry report beyond the allowable statute of limitations. They do this to force payment, believing that those who don't understand the rules will pay the bill in order to resolve the adverse credit reporting issue. This is also known as "re-aging," and though it is against the law, collection agencies that do it believe the amount of money gained by doing so will outweigh any potential detriment. It's only when enough people file suit and contact the FTC regarding such a practice that a collection agency discovers that the penalties are not worth the risk.

Knowingly furnishing erroneous adverse information is considered a "deceptive debt collection practice." Moreover, if a consumer disputes it and a furnisher subsequently affirms it, their affirmation constitutes four additional causes of action for money damages: violations of 15 U.S.C. § 1681 (c), § 1681 (e)(b), § 1681 (i), and § 1681 (s-2)(b). Any bureau that affirms such an entry from a furnisher becomes liable and can become a party to any civil action.

Again, the statute of limitations for delinquent accounts is seven years plus 180 days. However, the FTC claims that accounts placed for collection prior to December 1997 are not subject to the additional 180 days. (When the FCRA was amended in 1996, it changed the requirement, adding 180 days.) The FCRA strictly prohibits accounts placed for collection or charge-off to be reported longer than seven years.[17]

At any rate, case law rules. For anyone who believes that re-aging is permissible with payment, take a look at *Edwin Gregory Urrego v. Citibank, NA, et al.*: U.S. Dist. Ct. – Texas – No. H-02-1471. Another one is *Andrew Cole Sr. v. Sherman Financial Group, et al.*: U.S. Dist. Ct. – Texas – No. 1:03CV-00271. (Sherman Financial is a collection agency.) In both cases, the furnishers were sued for using rolling dates in the reporting of their collection accounts, by substituting the "date of last activity" or "last payment" for the date of first delinquency, in effect recalculating the seven-year data-retention period in a manner that conflicts with the statute of limitations imposed by the FCRA. The bureaus were defendants in these cases as well, since they permitted the continued reporting after the consumer disputed it.

Why do the bureaus permit this to happen? Well, collection activity is good for business, since it generates the sale of more credit reports to consumers and collectors.

People often ask, "So, if states can have their own laws, then why can't the running time of an account be changed?" Let's take a closer look at the FCRA:

§ 605. Requirements relating to information contained in consumer reports [15 U.S.C. § 1681 c]

- (a)(2) Civil suits, civil judgments, and records of arrest that from date of entry, antedate the report by more than

---

17. 15 U.S.C. § 1681c(a)(4). Student loans are exempt, as well as the exemptions listed above. Check with an attorney.

seven years or until the governing statute of limitations has expired, whichever is the longer period.

- (a)(4) Accounts placed for collection or charged to profit and loss which antedate the report by more than seven years.
- (c) Running of the Reporting Period (1) In general. The seven-year period referred to in paragraphs (4) and (6) 3 of subsection (a) shall begin, with respect to any delinquent account that is placed for collection (internally or by referral to a third party, whichever is earlier), charged to profit and loss, or subjected to any similar action, upon the expiration of the 180-day period beginning on the date of the commencement of the delinquency which immediately preceded the collection activity, charge to profit and loss, or similar action.

Notice that federal statute of seven years plus 180 days begins *from delinquency* for collection accounts and charge-offs. Delinquency isn't date of last activity or last payment. And as you can see, there isn't any provision for states to change this as they can with civil actions and criminal entries: § 605 (a)(2): ". . . seven years or until the governing statute of limitations has expired, whichever is the longer period." So while states, by employing statutes of limitations of their own, can affect the reporting period for some things, no such provision exists for collection accounts or the like (e.g., accounts tagged "Included in Bankruptcy").

The FCRA amendments of 2003 (FACTA) addressed this further in order to prevent the use of rolling dates and other shenanigans on the part of collectors. Furnishers must provide the dates of delinquency to the credit reporting agency in order to assist in determining the seven-year obsolescence period and proper tolling (running time). This must be performed within 90 days from the date the item is furnished.[18]

The only way credit reporting of delinquent accounts can be extended is through legal action, where the creditor sues you and

---

18. 15 U.S.C. § 1681s-2(a).

wins—obtaining a judgment—thereby converting it to a public record and reporting it as such. From there it takes on new life, and the reporting period will depend on federal law (as described above) or a state's laws governing judgments, liens, wage garnishment, and the like.

STATE PECULIARITIES AND PREEMPTION

Although some states may offer consumers greater protection than that afforded by the FCRA, federal law preempts state law for the following types of subject matter:[19]

- Relating to the creation and use of prescreened reports.[20]
- Relating to the users of prescreened reports, limited to the duties of creditors and insurance companies that use reports for solicitations of such, where the consumer didn't initiate the transaction and involve a firm offer.[21]
- Relating to the time requirements in which an agency must respond to consumer disputes and reinvestigations, including notices. This does not apply to states that had laws in effect prior to September 30, 1996.[22] Any laws enacted after that are preempted.[23]

---

19. Does not apply to business credit reports or business insurance reports. NCLC *Fair Credit Reporting* § 10.4.4 (5th ed. 2002 and 2005 Supp.).
20. 15 U.S.C. § 1681t(b)(1)(A). See 15 U.S.C. §§ 1681b(c), (e). *Kennedy v. Chase Manhattan Bank*, 2003 WL 21181427 (E.D. La. May 19, 2003).
21. 15 U.S.C. § 1681t(b)(1)(D); § 1681m(d).
22. The following states prohibit a 15-day extension to perform reinvestigations: Arizona, Maryland, Massachusetts, Nevada, New Hampshire, Rhode Island, Vermont, and Washington. Maine has a 21-day cap to perform reinvestigations and immediate notification that a dispute is deemed frivolous. Maryland requires notification within seven days if information is considered accurate or inaccurate and seven days if determined to be frivolous. Texas requires items disputed and found inaccurate or incomplete investigations to be corrected within five business days; it also requires that consumers receive notice if there is insufficient time to conduct a reinvestigation within 30 days. Washington and California permit reinvestigations to be completed within 30 *business* days, though the FCRA cap of 30 days should trump any state laws that offer less consumer protection.
23. 15 U.S.C. § 1681t(b)(1)(B); § 1681i.

STATE LAWS: CONTENTS NOT PREEMPTED[1]

California	Criminal records capped at seven years; prohibited where no conviction obtained or if pardoned. The seven-year limit for reporting delinquencies begins exactly 180 days after delinquency.[2]
Colorado	Prohibits the reporting of both the names and the number of inquiries to users. Criminal records capped at seven years.[3]
Kentucky	Reporting criminal charges that did not result in a conviction is prohibited.[4]
Maine	Requires lenders to indicate to consumers when they're denied based on lack of credit history.[5]
Maryland	Criminal records capped at seven years after disposition, release, or parole.[6]
Massachusetts	Bankruptcy capped at 14 years. Criminal records capped at seven years after disposition, release, or parole. No cap on length of consumer statement.[7]
Montana	Bankruptcy capped at 14 years. Criminal records capped at seven years after disposition, release, or parole.[8]
Nevada	Agencies forbidden to report criminal proceedings more than seven years old and medical information.[9]
New Hampshire	Bankruptcy capped at 14 years. Criminal records capped at seven years after disposition, release, or parole.[10]
New Mexico	Bankruptcy capped at 14 years. Bureaus cannot merge specialized information applicable only to personnel

New Mexico, cont.	investigations. Criminal records capped at seven years; reporting prohibited if pardoned. Arrests and indictments prohibited if no conviction.[11]
New York	Five-year cap on paid judgments. Information relative to an arrest or criminal charge must be pending or result in a conviction to be reported. Seven-year cap on criminal convictions from release, disposition, or parole. Prohibition of information regarding race, color, religion, or ethnic origin. Drug or alcohol addiction or mental institution confinement capped at seven years. No polygraph information (for investigative reports). For employment purposes only, agencies may divulge uncoerced admissions of wrongdoing in the event of detention by a retail establishment if the consumer is notified of such reporting and that it may be disputed.[12]

NOTES

1. Additional rules exist concerning investigative reports. States that have such laws are Maine, Massachusetts, Maryland, and New Hampshire. Many other governing statutes exist concerning insurance-related usage. Check your state laws.
2. Cal. Civ. Code §§ 1785.1 to 1787.3.
3. Although this law wasn't enacted until after September 30, 1996, it isn't regarding "contents" per se, so it isn't preempted. Colo. Rev Stat. §§ 12-14.3-101 to 12.14.3-109.
4. Ky. Rev. Stat. Ann. §§ 367.310 and 367.990(16).
5. Me. Rev. Stat. Ann. tit. 10, §§ 131 to 1329.
6. Md. Code Ann. Com. Law §§ 14-1201 to 14-1218; see also Md. Regs. Code tit. 9, §§ 09.03.07.01 to 09.03.07.04.
7. Mass. Gen. Laws Ann. Ch. 93, §§ 50-68.
8. Mont. Code Ann. §§ 31-3-101 to 31-3-153. See also Mont. Admin. R. 2.61.301.
9. Nev. Rev. Stat. §§ 598C.010 to 598C.200.
10. N.H. Rev. Stat. §§ 598C.010 to 598C.200.
11. N.M. Stat. Ann. §§ 56-3-1 to 556-3-8.
12. N.Y. Gen. Bus. Law §§ 380 to 380-s.

Table 4.

- Relating to the duties of persons who take adverse actions against consumers based on reports or information provided by third parties (not credit reporting agencies).[24]
- Relating to subject matter of FCRA § 605 (§ 1681c), contents of consumer reports, e.g., obsolescence standards, reports of account closings, and those transactions not covered due to the size or amount (seven-year rule exemptions listed earlier). This doesn't apply to states that had laws in effect prior to September 30, 1996. Any laws enacted after that are preempted.[25]
- Relating to furnishers of information; preemption rules for all states except Massachusetts and California. Massachusetts requires furnishers to report voluntary account closures and must include consumer disputes and commencement dates of any delinquencies when reporting them. Though California requires creditors to notify the consumer before reporting adverse information to a reporting agency,[26] this now includes all states under FACTA.[27]

---

24. 15 U.S.C. § 1681t(b)(1)(C); §§ 1681m(a), (b).
25. 15 U.S.C. § 1681t(b)(1)(E). See 15 U.S.C. § 1681c.
26. Some California laws are preempted, while others are not. Even though the California law that prohibits reporting of information the furnisher "knows or should know" is inaccurate is not preempted, "the California law providing for a private right of action to enforce the prohibition is preempted" (*Lin v. Universal Card Services Corp.*, 238 F. Supp. 2d 1147 [N.D. Cal. 2002]). See also *Riley v. General Motors Acceptance Corp.*, 226 F. Supp. 2d 1316 (S.D. Ala. 2002) (cannot assert state law claims for violation of § 1681s-2(a)); NCLC *Fair Credit Reporting* § 10.4.4 (5th ed. 2002 and 2005 Supp.).
27. 15 U.S.C. § 1681s-2(a)(7)(A)(i), "If any financial institution that extends credit and regularly and in the ordinary course of business furnishes information to a consumer reporting agency described in section 603(p) furnishes negative information to such an agency regarding credit extended to a customer, the financial institution shall provide a notice of such furnishing of negative information, in writing, to the customer." 15 U.S.C. § 1681s-2(a)(7)(B)(i), "The notice required under subparagraph (A) shall be provided to the customer prior to, or no later than 30 days after, furnishing the negative information to a consumer reporting agency described in section 603(p)."

- Relating to affiliate sharing of information. Vermont is not preempted in this regard.[28]
- The summary of consumer rights that must be provided to consumers by credit reporting agencies,[29] and under FACTA:

  ❑ The obligation for a business to provide identity theft victims with transaction information upon request.[30]

  ❑ The right to opt out of certain types of solicitations.[31]

  ❑ The requirement for users to disclose to credit applicants when they are offering credit on "material terms that are materially less favorable" than what's offered to other consumers.[32]

Many states have laws on the books regarding furnishing to bureaus that were enacted after September 30, 1996. Such laws are all arguably preempted by federal law. Examples are state laws that require cosigners to be notified before adverse information is reported, such as in Illinois and Michigan. A Utah law requires notification to consumers before adverse information is reported to a bureau, just like California, but it came after 1996. Colorado requires furnishers to use SSNs when reporting information (to prevent or mitigate file mergers),

---

28. 15 U.S.C. § 1681t(b)(2). See 15 U.S.C. § 1681a(d); NCLC *Fair Credit Reporting* § 2.4.2 (5th ed. 2002 and 2005 Supp.). The Vermont law is referred to as § (a) and (c)(1) of § 2480e of title 9, Vermont Statute Annotated; *Bank of Am., N.A. v. City of Daly City, Cal.*, 279 F. Supp. 2d 1118 (N.D. Cal. 2003) (preempting information-sharing ordinance).

29. 15 U.S.C. § 1681t(b)(3). See, e.g., Connecticut (possibly as relates to summary of federal rights). See 15 U.S.C. § 1681g(c).

30. 15 U.S.C. § 1681g(e), added by Pub. L. No. 108-159, § 151 (2003). See also NCLC *Fair Credit Reporting* § 16.6.1a.1.2 (5th ed. 2002 and 2005 Supp.).

31. 15 U.S.C. § 1681t(b)(3) (citing § 1681g(c)). See also NCLC *Fair Credit Reporting* § 16.6.1a (5th ed. 2002 and 2005 Supp.).

32. 15 U.S.C. § 1682t(b)(1)(H), added by Pub. L. No. 108-159, § 214d(2)(B) (2003). See also NCLC *Fair Credit Reporting* § 16.6.1a (5th ed. 2002 and 2005 Supp.).

yet this too is preempted. Other states have laws concerning furnishing by public agencies to bureaus regarding child support, and those laws are also preempted.[33]

The NCLC's *Fair Credit Reporting* manual states that the preemption laws are broad, and their reach goes beyond state FCRA laws, extending to state laws in general. However, the preemptions are temporary to a point, since as of January 2004 states can enact new laws that give consumers greater protection. Those will not be superseded.[34]

In addition to subject matter preemption, FACTA added "conduct required by" preemptions as well. This includes the free annual report provision, the blocking of accounts based on identity theft, obligations of merchants to truncate credit and debit card numbers, fraud alerts, military alerts, and more. They can be found in FCRA § 625(b) and 15 U.S.C. § 1681t. Furthermore, FACTA added other preemptions, such as those regarding summary of rights to obtain reports and scores, fraud victim disclosures, and required disclosure of credit scores by lenders and bureaus.

COLLECTIONS AND CIVIL ACTION

From what I've seen, all states permit judgments to be obtained either in the state in which the contract was signed or where the debtor lives, at the discretion of the creditor. A creditor can obtain a judgment in one or the other but not both. Of course I can't confirm this for all 50 states, so check your state laws.

Debts are categorized as secured or unsecured, and the distinction is an important one:

- For unsecured debts, if a defendant can't be served with a summons, then the party suing can't obtain a judgment. When a

---

33. Connecticut, Georgia, Hawaii, Kansas, Michigan, Missouri, Montana, New Jersey, Ohio, Pennsylvania, Rhode Island, South Carolina, Tennessee, West Virginia, and Wisconsin. See NCLC *Fair Credit Reporting* §§ 10.4.4, 13.2.8.4 (5th ed. 2002 and 2005 Supp.).

34. 15 U.S.C. § 1681t(d).

summons is delivered, it's called "service of process." (For more on service of process, see Chapter 14.)

- For secured debts (e.g., home and auto loans), the property can be obtained without service of process by using foreclosure and repossession actions. Service will be attempted if required by law, but failed attempts won't stop the action.

If the debt you owe is secured, this often makes your job more difficult; the creditor can simply come and take the collateral away if the terms and conditions of the loan aren't met. However, banks are not in the real estate or auto business; they just loan money and want it back plus their interest. Reducing the amount owed on an auto or home is probably not something a creditor will do, but you can sometimes renegotiate the terms even on secured debt if the creditor feels it's cheaper than taking legal action against you. Foreclosures and repossessions are costly to creditors, averaging around $1,500. Of course, they can claim legal fees on top of the cost of their actual loss and recoup this as part of any sale, but they must be fairly certain of the odds of collecting in order to take such steps. Debtor property is often in need of repair and is sold at a discount anyway (usually at a sheriff's auction), so foreclosures are often risky for creditors, since people in financial trouble tend to have little equity in their homes.

It's usually much easier to negotiate a settlement for unsecured debt, particularly if the creditor can't find you and serve you with a summons. Moreover, unsecured credit has some additional features that are advantageous to debtors, since even creditors that have obtained judgments still have to find a way to collect on it, and that can often be made very difficult. (This is covered in "Creating Barriers and Insulation" later in this chapter.)

Judgment holders will never collect unless you have something that they can take, such as real estate, an auto, a bank account, or wages. Using a judgment, liens are placed placed on property, while levies are used to tap bank accounts and garnish wages. Liens are very inexpensive in most cases, and since a judgment creditor took the time to obtain a judgment, the cost of a lien is a nonissue.

> **Note:** Social Security income, VA pensions, pension bene-
> fits, unemployment benefits, welfare, and child support (to
> the extent it is actually needed for basic living expenses) are
> exempt from garnishment.

If you don't own any property (that the creditor knows of) on which liens may be placed, have wages (that the creditor knows of) to garnish, or have bank accounts (that the creditor knows of) that may be levied, you can really have unsecured creditors over a barrel, especially if they can't serve you and obtain a judgment in the first place. Creditors know how difficult it can be to collect on unsecured debt, so they're usually much more flexible with debtors.

It's important to note that liens are secured by the property to which they are attached, so even if the original debt was a credit card account and a lien is placed on property (using a judgment), the creditor may or may not need to serve you again to force a sale of the property, depending on your state's laws governing liens. Moreover, consider the following:

- Some states permit the forced sale of real estate for lien hold-ers, while others don't. In Ohio, for example, even if a credi-tor doesn't hold an actual mortgage, a creditor holding a judg-ment can place a lien on real estate and force a sale. But in other states, the laws prevent foreclosure unless the party is an actual mortgage holder. (Even if a state doesn't permit the forced sale of real estate and autos, the debt must be paid in full at the time the property is sold.)
- Some states permit the forced sale of autos for lien holders, while others don't. In Oregon, for example, some types of creditors can place a lien on a car, but they can't force the sale of it. (And yet even if a state permits the forced sale of an auto, a judgment holder would have to find out where the auto is registered/titled first.)
- Some states have exceptions for the principal place of resi-dence, making such a home impenetrable to most creditors. Florida is one such state, though it requires that both a

Homestead Property Tax Exemption and Homestead Asset Protection be filed with Florida Homestead Services. That filing must be in place before any judgment lien or levy. Some debts are not subject to the barrier, such as (a) mortgages, (b) real estate back taxes, (c) obligations contracted for the purchase (e.g., line of credit used for the purchase), and (d) improvement or repair of the home (e.g., where a contractor performed work on the home, such as adding a skylight). Homeowner's association liens may not be covered under the Homestead Protection Law, and foreclosure can occur based on contract law. Florida also requires that the debtor be a resident of Florida and reside on the property, and any homestead claim must be legal and proper. This example serves to illustrate how complex this can be.

- In states where exemptions exist for real estate, real estate that is not the personal residence of the judgment debtor is not exempt from liens.

- Some states will permit the forced sale of property owned by more than one party, even if there's a nondebtor owner. Yet the lien holder would not be entitled to the share of the nondebtor's interest in the property.

- Some states permit the forced sale of personal property for judgment holders. Personal property can be artwork and other items of value. California and Florida are among those that permit this; a judgment holder can file a writ of execution and then show up with a police officer at the judgment debtor's doorstep and seize the property. There are exceptions, however, depending on the statute. (Incidentally, credit card companies aren't interested in your personal property, and I've yet to hear of any doing this. It's usually done by individuals who have obtained a judgment in small-claims court.)

- Some states will permit the garnishment of the wages of a debtor's spouse if a judgment exists.

To summarize, to successfully use civil action to collect unsecured debt—assuming that the debt is within the collection statute of limitations (explained shortly)—the collector must

1. find you to serve you with a summons, and
2. obtain a judgment, and
3. find property to place a lien on it or know of wages that can be garnished or know of a bank account that can be tapped; and if property or a job is discovered, then
4. the state's laws must permit the garnishment of wages or the forced sale of an auto if the property is such, or the forced sale of a home if the property is such, or the forced sale of other personal property if the property is such.

You see, even if a judgment is obtained, there are additional hurdles that the creditor must overcome in most cases.[35] Smart debtors can often make those obstacles insurmountable, or nearly so, if they know their state laws and create barriers. Later, I'll go into some interesting ways to apply this knowledge for devising a strategy that strengthens your negotiating position. If you didn't initially, surely you are beginning to understand why in the Preface I strongly recommended reading the entire book carefully before taking any action.

And yet you won't be a major force until you understand your state's laws. Heck, many of them are available online or at your local legal library. Better yet, write down all your questions concerning state law, and consult an attorney.[36] It will usually only take about an hour or so. Providing you ask the right questions (and get the right answers), you should be armed to the teeth by the time you walk out of there.

When people learn how debts are collected through the use of civil action, many find that they're in better shape than they previously thought. Those who find themselves exposed can often take actions to insulate themselves from some types of legal recourse that creditors may have, thereby strengthening any negotiations.

---

35. A judgment can be executed in a different state from the one it was issued in by filing it in the state of execution. Also, some states may consider service complete when a debtor's residence is unknown and notice is made in a publication in the county in which the complaint is filed (e.g., Ohio Civ. R. 4.4, 4.6—if service is refused, then regular mail is permitted. Restrictions exist if the debtor is out of state, as the types of claims subject to these rule are limited).

36. Consulting doesn't mean retaining. Attorneys can be very helpful as consultants; retain only when necessary and in accordance with Chapter 14.

If you are negotiating with bill collectors, they will likely threaten legal action whether they intend to take it or not. From the creditor's perspective, even if you have property and wages, the debt usually must be high enough relative to what can be seized. However, there are no hard-and-fast rules as to what a creditor will and will not do, and you should judge every threat on its own merits. Personally, I only become concerned if I'm served court papers. And even then, I can avoid a judgment by settling before trial. The way I see it, I have 30 days to answer any complaint (some small-claims courts are 14 days), which gives me time to settle (roughly three weeks) before I have to retain an attorney. Of course, what you do is completely up to you.

Cross-Collateral Clauses

Often people will have several different contracts with the same creditor, some secured and others unsecured. Banks and credit unions often work cross-collateral clauses (CCC) into their agreements, enabling them to secure unsecured debts they have extended to a consumer by attaching them to secured debts, such as an auto loan. Some people who file bankruptcy wish to keep and continue to pay on certain assets (known as *reaffirming*). If an auto is reaffirmed under such circumstances, a creditor can demand the same of unsecured credit it has extended.[37]

Are the Lawyers Coming?

OK, so the next question is, when will creditors take civil action to collect a debt? There's no way to know for certain, of course, but there are some general guidelines:

- Generally, few creditors will attempt to obtain judgments on unsecured debts less than $1,000. It costs creditors money to get a judgment, and they will likely only do so if they think it can help them get their money (with legal fees) back.
- Creditors may not sue for large amounts if they do not ever

---

37. Cannot be used with certain accounts, such as credit cards, due to prohibition under 12 C.F.R. Part 226. Creditors cannot use a CCC with a mortgage, since they'll lose all future rights to offset the mortgage.

expect to collect. An example of this would be a debt of $15,000 where it is well documented that the debtor is disabled and will likely never be able to pay. Why spend money on legal fees if the likelihood is that the money is wasted? Creditors generally don't want to get even; they just want their money. Obtaining a judgment costs money, and why add to the bleeding? If you are not working and haven't worked (or the creditor doesn't know you are working), then clearly the creditor can't garnish income that isn't there. If, in addition to the lack of income, there are no assets to seize, then litigation is even less likely. However, since judgments are usually good for many years and are often renewable, this is a strong incentive to go after a judgment for any debt over $4,500 even if there's no chance to collect in the near term.

- Many third-party companies that purchase debt have a system, and it doesn't matter what the circumstances are concerning your individual debt. Their cookie-cutter approach is to acquire debt at pennies on the dollar, attempt to collect for 90 days, and then try to obtain a judgment. This is especially true if the debtor has a job and wage garnishment is permissible in the debtor's state. They figure they can work in any costs associated with tapping the account, so why not?

- Generally, collectors will begin searching for a debtor's assets for debts of $4,500 or more.

- Many states forbid lawsuits by collection agencies, so you should check your state laws. And if a collector threatens legal action when a state forbids it, then he or she is in breach of the FDCPA. (For more information on breaches of the FDCPA, see Chapter 7.)

Remember, there's no way to predict what a creditor will or won't do, so the best thing is to stay hidden if you wish to avoid being served.

COLLECTION STATUTES OF LIMITATION

In addition to credit reporting statutes of limitation, there are statutes of limitation that apply to debt collections, in terms of how long a creditor has to collect on a debt *using a lawsuit*. State laws will vary on debt collection, depending on the type of account. There are four types:

1. *Oral contract:* Verbal agreement. This can include your word, the creditor's word, or anyone who witnessed it. Harder to prove but is legally binding in most states.
2. *Written contract:* Signed document promising to pay.
3. *Promissory note:* A written contract with additional provisions; usually used for the purchase of real property. Notes can be sold to a third party.
4. *Open-ended account:* Revolving lines of credit and credit cards. May be sold to a third party.

Most states fall within a three- to six-year statute of limitations range for collection, and if a debt is outside of the state's limit, then it is no longer collectible and is considered junk debt. Would a debtor still owe the money? Yes, but it isn't collectible through civil action. Once a debt is no longer reported on a credit report and is outside the collection statute of limitations, the debtor is off the hook unless the debt is for a tax lien, student loan, or child support. Some states may even have additional categories of debts that can be collected indefinitely.

For examples of variations in collection statutes, one doesn't have to look very hard. In Oregon the statute of limitation is six years for all four types of debt, while in California it's four for all types of contracts except oral, for which it's two. Other states have additional quirks in the law. For instance, whereas Ohio and Kentucky both deem credit card contracts as written, some states view them as oral.[38]

A creditor may attempt to collect a debt that's beyond the statute of limitations. If you're served a summons under those circumstances, don't ignore it. File an answer (or show up to court if it's small claims) and present proof that the period for collection on the debt has expired.

---

38. See Appendix A for a complete list of the collection statutes by state.

COLLECTION RESET STATUTES FOR UNSECURED CREDIT CARD DEBT[1]

STATE	STATUTE (Open/Written)	BEGIN DATE (Clock Begins)	EXTENDERS (Clock Reset)
Alabama	3/6	• date of last payment if BK[2] filed	• date of BK dismissal
Colorado	6/6	• date of last payment	• payment or debtor out of state or skipped
Connecticut	6/6	• date of default or • date of last payment	• payment or • new note
Delaware	3/3	• date of last charge or • date of last payment or • written acknowledgment	• payment or • written acknowledgment
Georgia	4/6	• date of default or • written acknowledgment	• payment or • if BK dismissed, creditor has 30 days to file suit
Indiana	6/10	• date of last payment	• payment or • if BK dismissed, creditor has 30 days to file suit
Maryland	3/3	• date of last payment or • written acknowledgment	• payment or • written acknowledgment
Michigan	6/6	• date of last payment	• payment
Minnesota	6/6	• date of last payment	• payment
Missouri	5/10	• date of last payment or • written acknowledgment[3]	• payment or • written acknowledgment
New Jersey	6/6	• date of last payment or date of default; whichever is later	• payment or • if debtor leaves state to avoid service of process
New York	6/6	• date of last payment or date of default; the later	• payment or • if debtor leaves state to avoid service of process

STATE	STATUTE	BEGIN DATE	EXTENDERS
	(Open/Written)	(Clock Begins)	(Clock Reset)
Ohio	6/15	• date of default or missed obligation under agreement • date of last payment	• payment or • if debtor leaves the state then tolled[4] until return
Oklahoma	3/5	• date of default or last payment; the later	• payment or • written acknowledgment
Pennsylvania	4/4	• date of last payment	• payment
Tennessee	6/6	• date of last charge or • date of contract	• payment

NOTES

1. Check your local statutes. For some written contracts and in some states, if a contract is signed under seal, then the collection statutes are often longer. Such a document would have a seal next to the signature block. Being signed under seal is very rare with credit cards, but it may be the case with some of them. Check your state laws.
2. BK is bankruptcy.
3. Only applies to the one acknowledging if co-debtor.
4. Tolling is when the running time goes into temporary stasis.

Table 5.

Collection Action Running Time Reset

While state laws specify time frames for collection actions, some can actually be reset in some states. The collection running period can be *reset by payment* or even by a simple acknowledgment that a debt is owed, among other things. Table 5 lists reset collection provisions for unsecured credit cards by state (there may be others).

Paying can hurt. Running can hurt. Failing to obtain a bankruptcy discharge[39] after filing can hurt. Acknowledging that the money is

---

39. Bankruptcy dismissal is not the same as discharge. If a bankruptcy is dismissed, the debtor failed to complete it.

owed can hurt. This is a tricky business, since in many cases you're damned if you do and damned if you don't. And yet there are some ways around these extension pitfalls, which I'll explain shortly.[40]

Tip: Even if a debt collection statute is reset, the credit reporting running time cannot be reset.

BARRIERS AND INSULATION

All this information regarding judgments and the like may seem like a little much. Yet public records are an integral part of a credit report, and any such entry can not only devastate a score but also directly impact a person's way of life. This is why it's important to understand how to avoid such entries on a report in the first place. Of course, the best way is to pay bills on time. Yet many people are unable to do that, or they are now able but previously weren't.

Avoiding civil action is crucial, and there are measures—and then *there are measures*. Prevention measures not only serve to avoid public record entries, but they also greatly boost a debtor's negotiating position. If a creditor believes there isn't anything to take (whether there is or not), the leverage a debtor gains cannot be overstated.

When creditors cannot locate debtors, they will often attempt to find them by skip tracing (research conducted in an attempt to locate someone who cannot be located or has skipped). In addition, they'll try to find out what you own and either use that information against you in the negotiations or attempt to take it if the communication breaks down. There are many means available for them to locate the debtor and his or her assets, including the following:

- Contacting the post office and requesting any change of address information. If you rent a PO Box, the USPS is

---

40. Some claim that restrictively endorsed checks may be a way around debt collection reset in some circumstances, yet their employment can be very tricky. (See "Restrictively Endorsed Checks" in Chapter 10.)

required to give out your address if the box is registered in the name of a business. If registered in your name, then the USPS is required to give out the hard address if the request indicates that there are legal papers to be served on the box holder.

- Checking public records.
- Checking with the department of motor vehicles (DMV).
- Calling old neighbors and relatives.
- Contacting the secretary of state for any business activity and attached addresses. A collector can search a business registry to find out if a debtor has a business. The name of the business, even if a corporation, doesn't have to be known.[41]
- Calling the tax assessor's office to see if any property is owned and where the tax statements are mailed.
- Performing a crisscross search[42] against any phone numbers they have on file. This enables them to get an address attached to the phone number.
- Checking the Internet, using sites dedicated to finding people or performing search engine searches.
- Checking voter registration records.
- Obtaining directories of unlisted numbers from bill collectors that compile them.
- Though it's illegal, posing as you or someone else and then calling anyone they think may have information about your whereabouts. This includes old employers, utility companies, and even banks with which you've been known to do business. In the latter case, collectors will often have your SSN, your date of birth, your mother's maiden name, and your place of birth. They may even have your account number (if you've ever paid with a check). That's often enough.
- Reviewing credit report inquiries to find out where you do your banking or what other recent creditors extended credit to you.
- Reviewing credit reports to find out where you work.
- Reviewing credit reports for address information.

---

41. Many states charge a fee for a nonstandard search, often considered a special or advanced search.
42. Crisscross directories (also known as reverse directories) are widely available.

- Reviewing credit reports for anything that will give them a clue as to where you are.

Collection Avoidance

I suggest taking the cautious approach to collection avoidance. That is, if you're lost, then stay that way. If you're not lost, get lost. Why? Because most collectors are scum, and they will make your life hell without regard to the rules, even if you make it clear that you know the rules. In many cases you must be prepared to sue them, so keep very good records of whom you spoke with, when, who called whom, and what was said. In taking the cautious approach, it is better if collectors don't know

- where you are and can't find out;
- your telephone number and can't find out;
- where you work and can't find out;
- whether you own property (auto or home) and can't find out;
- where you do your banking and can't find out;
- what you're worth and can't find out.

Standard Measures

Standard measures are those taken to avoid mistreatment from debt collectors and to give them some difficulty in their research efforts. They wish to know everything they can about you, but mostly what they can *take* if all else fails.

Tip: Dodging your creditors isn't what collection avoidance is about. *BestCredit* is about tackling issues and dealing with the problems at hand. However, using a frontal attack against a superior force is suicide. A flank attack is smart and will often prevent debtors from having to file bankruptcy. Although your best results will likely come from making a deal with creditors, stay in the hills, meeting them on your terms.

The following standard measures are not only good for dealing with collectors on your terms, but they will also protect you from unwanted intrusions, which can take many forms, and by combining them with the identity theft prevention techniques in Chapter 11, it is also good for your overall safety and sanity.

- Get a PO Box. This prevents collectors from knowing your hard address. Bear in mind, however, that the USPS will reveal a true address if a written request indicates that legal papers are to be served on the box holder.

- When you move, don't file a change of address form with the post office, or if you must, list a PO Box or private mailbox. If you get a PO Box, don't list a business name. You can also provide an old hard address, which is illegal but not a hanging offense. Simply claim "negative habit transfer" if caught. ("Oops, I'm sorry! How silly of me.") In many states post offices will simply require two forms of ID when you apply for a box, whereas states such as California will perform a full-on rectal exam, requiring IDs, a rental agreement, and other documents. Sometimes Mail Boxes Etc., The UPS Store, or similar businesses will have less stringent requirements for opening a mailbox.

- Get an unlisted phone number. If you can, get rid of your landline and use a cellular phone.

- When you call collectors, be sure to use caller ID block (start your call by dialing *67) so they can't get your number. Understand that if you are calling a toll-free number, caller ID block doesn't work. In this case, you might want to get the collector's toll number with area code (this may be printed on a collection letter you've received, or you can try information by dialing (area code + 555-1212) or searching www.411.org.[43]

- Get anonymous call blocking, which is available from your phone company for a nominal charge. Many collectors use a caller ID blocker so that their number does not show up on

---

43. To get an area code, look in the front of any phone book for a nationwide area code table or log on to www.intrepidsoft.com/acjava.html and use the site's area code utility.

the caller ID box of the person they are calling. Anonymous call blocking is a countermeasure that prevents all callers to your number from using a caller ID blocker.

- When you send mail to collectors, don't use a return address on the envelope (or get a PO Box and use that). Also consider that they'll have the city you're in once they see the postmark. Yes, they look at everything!
- When you have utilities installed, use an alias first name (middle name works as a substitute) and password-protect the accounts. If you can get away with it, refuse to divulge your SSN. Sometimes utility companies won't insist.
- Password-protect all other accounts so that someone who obtains your SSN (collectors have that) can't pose as you and get your address, phone number, or other information from other creditors and various third parties.
- Give your relatives a cellular phone number if you can and inform them that they are not to give out your number to anyone.
- When you register to vote, you can use an old address (illegal in some states but not a hanging offense).
- If you have e-mail and want to use it to communicate with collectors, don't give use an e-mail address that is traceable (e.g., if it's harry@microsoft.com, the collector will know that you work for Microsoft). If it's a company e-mail address, all the collector has to do is check to see who owns the domain name, and he's found you. Also consider that the broadband provided by cable companies can clue in any recipient. For example, e-mail from homersimpson@columbus.rr.com is clearly from someone in Columbus. (Any broadband provider can tell you which city and state the e-mail address serves.) Get a Web-based free account from Hotmail, Gmail, or Yahoo. (Use e-mail to communicate, not negotiate. Negotiating is to be done over the telephone, unless you're nearing the end of the negotiations and already have a deal in principle. Once you have a verbal deal, you can use e-mail to finalize details or send and receive documents.)
- Never sign for anything that's sent to you by Return Receipt

Mail (RRM) unless you know specifically whom it's from. If you have roommates, make sure they know not to sign for anything addressed to you.

- Assume that a collector can get your phone number in spite of your precautions. Screen your phone calls using caller ID and an answering system. If your caller ID does not identify the caller, have the answering machine pick up the call. Use a generic message on your machine, such as, "I'm not in; please leave a message." Do not use your name.

- Keep a checking account separate from the one you pay your bills with, since someone with a judgment (whom you've paid using that checking account) will know where you do your banking and can tap that account by using a levy. Even for people who aren't in arrears, it's good practice to keep a separate account, just in case something unforeseen happens, such as a job loss.

- If you own a dog, consider providing an old address to the license bureau. More of that darn negative habit transfer . . .

- If you run a Web site, make sure the contact information listed on any Web site or domain name registry is a PO Box, and be careful about other contact information. Do the same for any Web site host.

- Don't talk with solicitors.

- When communicating with bureaus, provide them with a PO Box only. If they insist on a utility bill, make sure it doesn't contain your hard address. Cell phone bills that are billed to PO Boxes don't have other addresses on them.

- Never provide your driver's license number (or a copy of your license) to the credit bureaus.

- Some companies, such as fitness centers and medical offices, allow new clients to provide either an SSN or a driver's license when filling out their application or account paperwork. When given the choice, provide a driver's license number. The Privacy Act of 1997 forbids DMVs from providing information to third parties regarding the licensed party, and any attempt by collectors to use the driver's license number for collection purposes is useless unless a credit reporting agency already has the number and it can be used as an identifier. (Never send a copy of a driver's license or provide driver's license information to a credit bureau.)

- Don't open new accounts unless you have to. For any new credit, the inquiry will show on your report, and the collector may discover what bank you're doing business with. If a creditor has a judgment against you, it can attempt a levy at any bank it suspects has your account, for a small fee. Further, any application for new credit will contain your hard address information, which the creditor can use to serve you with court papers! (The new creditor will pass along any address placed on the application to the bureaus. Banks don't verify hard addresses, and they permit consumers to specify a PO Box for a mailing address. Failing to provide certain accurate information on a loan application may be a violation of the law. This usually applies to attempts to defraud the lender; listing an old address does not qualify and would not likely be provable as such. Check your state laws, and break any laws at your own risk.)

Tip: Consider that creditors provide your address to the bureaus. So if you have accounts that are in good standing and want those good-standing creditors to have your address, give them a PO Box. Otherwise, you will have collectors calling your neighbors and telling them all about what you owe and to whom. Further, if you are applying for credit and wish to avoid using a PO Box (since it might hurt your chances of being approved), consider providing the address of a relative or a close friend. When you apply for credit, the address you give the prospective lender will be provided to the bureaus. It's the world we live in, right or wrong.

Extreme Measures

Very few debtors will ever have to go to these lengths, particularly if their debt is unsecured and/or negotiations with creditors are proceeding well. However, there are some circumstances so extreme that a person is near bankruptcy. In that case, the following methods may be employed with caution:

- You may consider registering your auto in a different state than the one you live in. Although illegal, it's not a hanging offense.[44] If you're ever pulled over, the first thing a cop asks is, "Is this your current address?" He's referring to your driver's license, and if the answer no, then the follow-up question is, "What is your new address?" followed by "How long have you lived at your new address?" Most states require anyone who's moved into the state to contact the DMV and get that state's registration (and thus your vehicle will be titled in that state so debt collectors can either find you and/or place a lien on it if they have a judgment).[45] States also require that the DMV notify them within 30 days of any change of address. Incidentally, I like states that offer long-term driver's licenses (e.g., eight years in both Arizona and Oregon). The auto registration requirement is every two years in Oregon, unless a veteran is 60 percent or more disabled (as rated by the VA), in which case permanent plates are available.[46]
- If you own property, consider positioning it so that it can't be located using the tax assessor's records, either by using a corporate business entity or selling it and placing the money in a safe account. Transferring it to someone else is also an option, but I strongly discourage this.
- If you own a business, consider taking steps to avoid being found, either by providing an old address to the secretary of state or by registering your business in another state. Any collector obtain-

---

44. Failure to register in the state in which you live is much like walking a dog without a leash. Speeding is worse, as it carries a heftier fine and will get you points against your driving record. Yet state laws vary; check your state laws.

45. Any auto lender will have the title and can repossess. Even if a debtor has the auto, registration renewal cannot occur if the title holder prevents it. There are also insurance requirements and notification rules to lenders.

46. All states have disabled veteran plates, but the disability requirement varies. California and Ohio, for example, require a rating of 100 percent.

ing a business name can search for business assets and other information and then cross-reference. Most states require that you register in the state which you conduct business.

There are numerous ways to put real estate and autos beyond the reach of creditors. However, there are some types of transfers that can be considered fraudulent. Fraudulent transfers are difficult to prove, but it does happen. When an asset is transferred, usually three things are viewed as suspect: if the transferor is insolvent, is left with unreasonably small capital, or is about to incur debts beyond his or her ability to pay. As long as this isn't the case, then there are eight ways that I know of to protect assets: (1) gifting, (2) offshore trusts, (3) family limited partnerships (FLPs), (4) domestic trusts, (5) creation of a corporation or LLC, (6) bankruptcy, (7) retitling of property, and (8) insurance (life insurance policies are exempt assets under state and federal bankruptcy law, as are medical insurance policies that cover long-term care).

The proper employment of asset protection goes beyond the scope of this book, and it's highly recommended that you contact an attorney when attempting to insulate assets.

Find Out if You Can Be Tracked

Once you've taken precautions, check every couple of months to see if you're indeed invisible. Take a look at the ways in which you can be tracked and then, using those methods, see what you can discover about yourself.

Internet People and Pubic Record Searches

- www.555-1212.com—phone directory search.
- www.argali.com—White and Yellow Pages, reverse directory (if you know the number), e-mail address, and more. Requires a downloadable program, available free.
- www.411.org—White and Yellow Page directory and reverse lookup.
- www.anywho.com—White and Yellow pages, toll-free directories, and reverse directories, for those who have a telephone number.

- www.bigfoot.com—White and Yellow pages and e-mail addresses.
- www.411locate.com—White and Yellow Pages, e-mail addresses, and public records.
- www.searchsystems.net—A variety of public records on the Internet.

Paid Searches

- www.informus.com—Employment screening, driving records, criminal records, and credit reports.
- www.peoplesearch.com—Public records, criminal records, and more.
- www.peoplefind.com—Criminal records, public records, credit reports, PO Boxes, and more.
- www.knowx.com—Liens, bankruptcies and assets, public records, licenses, addresses, and telephone numbers.
- www.usinterlink.com—Unlisted numbers, including cell phone numbers and addresses.

A smart skip tracer can take one piece of information and use it to get the next. For example, if he or she can obtain an e-mail address that reveals the city (or company), that information will provide some direction on where to look next. If you're really serious about being lost, hire a professional skip tracer to see what he or she can find. (Though most people with credit problems may not be in a position to do this, I've found that many are.)

Does this seem like a lot of trouble to go to? Maybe, but if you've ever dealt with collectors, you'll understand why it's necessary.

In some cases you can't move or disappear because you have a house or because of other circumstances. If so, you can use any variation of the methods I describe in order to mitigate the problem.

Don't Skip

You don't need to skip; you need only to make the playing field favorable to you. As I explained at the beginning of this chapter, the less collectors know the better; keeping them in the dark will only serve to increase your bargaining position.

Don't confuse getting lost with running. Always keep in mind that collectors hate debtors who run and those with whom they have trouble establishing communications. So contact them on a regular basis if you are making progress and simply say that you don't own a phone.

Additional Privacy Measures

Although not necessary for avoiding bill collectors, the following measures can increase privacy and sanity:

- Ghost your movements on the 'Net by using a simulated proxy server, software that will insulate you from being tracked and remove footprints. Anonymizer (www.anonymizer.com) is a good one but requires a software download and costs $29.99 per year. A simple but effective one is Mezzy (www.mezzy.com), and not only is it free, but there's nothing to download and install. Mezzy either functions as an anonymous search engine or a simple proxy when you enter the URL of a site directly into the search bar.
- Stop unwanted telemarketers by registering with the FTC's do-not-call database at www.ftc.gov.
- Contact the Direct Marketing Association's Mail Preference Service (PO Box 643, Carmel, NY 10512) to stop unwanted junk mail.
- Many people prefer not to receive preapproved offers from credit card companies and prevent it by calling 1-888-5-OPTOUT. I prefer to stay on the list, since I may want to accept an offer that's good. After all, if it's preapproved, I'm guaranteed approval. If you do the same, make sure you have a PO Box, since thieves can steal your preapproved credit card applications.
- Avoid using browser plug-ins, such as those from eBay. Such plug-ins track movement and then "call home." If you wish to know which plug-ins are safe and which are not, perform a Web search. There's plenty of information available regarding plug-ins, and if you're unsure about a software program you've installed, run PestPatrol software (www.pestpatrol.com) to see what the software actually does.

- Be careful about using Google's tools and software. If you read the fine print, Google stores any information about your online habits. The company has also done some treacherous things, including claiming copyright ownership of Web pages that are attached using its Web Accelerator software and claiming ownership of all content posted to its Usenet archive, Deja News. Google is to be used for e-mail only, if anything. Google's slogan is "Do no evil." It should be "Do no evil; we will do it for you."

Always protect your privacy by employing prudent measures that are commensurate with your desire to avoid unwanted intrusions, and not just those from debt collectors. And when in doubt, better safe than sorry.

7

STOP BILL COLLECTORS— DEAL ON YOUR TERMS

One of the core elements of successful credit restoration is your ability to deal with all types of collectors. After all, they are the ones who will be making many of the decisions regarding you and your account. Considering this, your success will mostly depend on how you handle them. The information in this section is therefore among the most crucial in your quest for exemplary credit.

THE FAIR DEBT COLLECTION PRACTICES ACT

The term "collectors" generally refers to those who are collecting for themselves (i.e., original creditors), whereas the term "debt collectors" refers to those who are in the business of collecting for third parties, such as collection agencies and lawyers. This distinction is important where laws about how collectors and debt collectors conduct themselves are concerned, because the FDCPA applies only to debt collectors, not in-house (creditor) collectors. There are exceptions, however, as certain conduct by creditor collectors can actually bring them under the FDCPA when it would not otherwise apply (see Chapter 14).

A debt collector's contacts with a debtor are known as "duns," regardless of the method of contact. Even debt collectors' dunning letters are governed by the FDCPA, which places tight restrictions on the language they can use. As such, it's extremely important to know your rights before communicating with debt collectors. Such knowledge will provide the basis for the approach you will take and will give you confidence so that you will not allow yourself to be intimidated.

There are two general tests to determine whether a debt collector falls under the FDCPA. One involves the type of collector, and the other involves the type of transaction.

Collectors Covered by the FDCPA

Debt collectors that fall under the FDCPA include the following:[1]

- Collection agencies
- Attorneys who regularly collect debts
- Creditors using a false name
- Creditors collecting for another person
- Repossession and foreclosure companies (if made unlawfully)
- Suppliers or designers of deceptive forms (forms used in collection)
- Purchasers of debt after default
- Credit counselors (for profit)
- Check guarantee services
- Third-party collectors collecting for landlords, including attorneys, realty companies, and servicing companies that are collecting rent debts.[2] Deceptive eviction notices are also covered by the FDCPA. Many state UDAP laws also apply to abusive landlords and their rent-collection conduct.[3]

1. NCLC *Fair Debt Collection* § 4.1 (5th ed. 2004 and 2005 Supp.)
2. *Romea v. Heiberger & Associates*, 163 F.3d 111 (2d Cir. 1998); *Wenrich v. Robert E. Cole, P.C.*, 2000 U.S. Dist. LEXIS 18687 (E.D. Pa. Dec. 22, 2000); *Travieso v. Gutman, Mintz, Baker, & Sonnefeldt, P.C.*, 1995 U.S. Dist. LEXIS (E.D.N.Y. 1995).
3. NCLC *Fair Debt Collection* § 1.5.2.1 (5th ed. 2004 and 2005 Supp.). See NCLC *Unfair and Deceptive Acts and Practices* §§ 2.2.2, 2.2.5 (6th ed. 2004).

Collectors Excluded from the FDCPA

The following types of collectors are generally excluded from the FDCPA:[4]

- Creditors who are collecting their own debts
- Assignees (i.e., service companies, such as car finance companies, that take on the collection role prior to default on mortgages, student loans, rental agreements, utility bills, medical debts, and other consumer transactions)
- Government employees
- Business (aka commercial) creditors
- Nonprofit credit counselors

Transactions Covered by the FDCPA

Debts that fall under the FDCPA include consumer debts where the transaction was for personal, family, or household purposes, whether or not such obligation has been reduced to judgment. The Act does not apply to commercial debts.[5] The following are covered by the FDCPA:[6]

- Dishonored checks
- Rent
- Medical bills
- Utility bills
- Insurance bills and claims
- Student loans
- Credit cards
- Condominium fees
- Attorney fees
- Judgments
- Obligations discharged in bankruptcy
- Other personal debts (e.g., parking tickets, auto loans)

---

4. NCLC *Fair Debt Collection* § 4.1 (5th ed. 2004 and 2005 Supp.)
5. 15 U.S.C. § 1692a(5).
6. NCLC Fair *Debt Collection* § 4.4.2.2 (5th ed. 2004 and 2005 Supp.).

Prohibited Practices

The FDCPA defines a debt collector as any person (1) whose principle business is collecting debts, (2) who regularly collects debt owed to a third party, or (3) who uses a false name in the course of debt-collection activities or efforts.[7] The FDCPA prohibits debt collectors from engaging in unfair, deceptive, or abusive practices while collecting debts. The following are the rules under which collection agencies must operate:

- Debt collectors may contact you only between 8 A.M. and 9 P.M.
- Debt collectors may not contact you at work if they know your employer disapproves.
- Debt collectors may not harass, oppress, or abuse you.
- Debt collectors may not lie when collecting debts, such as falsely implying that you have committed a crime.
- Debt collectors must identify themselves to you on the phone.
- Debt collectors must stop contacting you if you ask them to stop in writing (known as a cease-communication letter).
- Debt collectors may call your neighbors, but only to determine where you are and only once.
- Debt collectors may not discuss your debts with any third party unless it's your attorney, the creditor's attorney, a credit reporting agency, co-debtor, guardian (administrator/executor), or parent (if the debtor is a minor).[8]

In a nutshell, bill collectors from collection agencies cannot harass you by calling late, calling your neighbors repeatedly (or talking to

---

7. 15 U.S.C. § 1692a(6). Use of a false name would indicate that a third-party collector is involved in the collection efforts, and, as such, the creditor would be subject to the FDCPA where he or she wouldn't have been otherwise. Even an in-house attorney (for the creditor) using his or her own name on stationery when communicating with a debtor would make the creditor subject to the FDCPA. See *Nielsen v. Dickerson*, 307 F.3d 623 (7th Cir. 2002); *Taylor v. Perrin, Landry, deLaunay & Durand*, 103 F.3d 1232 (5th Cir. 1997). Also see NCLC *Fair Debt Collection* § 4.2.5 (5th ed. 2004 and 2005 Supp.).

8. See NCLC *Fair Debt Collection* § 5.3.5.3 (5th ed. 2004 and 2005 Supp.).

them about your debts), calling your work, or at all! This means that you don't have to be a victim, and you can take action to see that the harassment stops or doesn't occur at all. A cease-communication letter is a way to get debt collectors to stop contacting you. This is explained in detail later in this chapter.

Threats

One of the most common illegal actions by debt collectors is to threaten legal action. Debt collectors believe they can get away with such threats because debtors often fear a lawsuit. Few debtors understand that the threat of legal action by debt collectors can actually be spun against them, since any such threat is a violation of the FDCPA. A very broad range of legal threats are a breach, including those that are (1) not intended to be carried out when made, (2) not as imminent as presented, (3) beyond the purview of the debt collector's authority (i.e., those the creditor didn't authorize), or (4) beyond the debt collector's legal authority (e.g., the state forbids lawsuits by collection agencies).[9]

Further, even oblique or disguised threats of a lawsuit on the part of debt collectors are classified as threats under the FDCPA. Examples include claiming that they will agree to settle debts "out of court," saying they "can" sue you, stating that the debt will be referred to a lawyer for debt collection, claiming that they are authorized to proceed with legal action against you, sending a complaint (lawsuit) to a debtor before actually filing it with the court, claiming that "action will be taken" to secure payment in full, listing available creditor remedies (inclusive of legal action), saying "every step will be taken," and marking an envelope with "legal matter enclosed" or the like.[10]

Dunning Letter Requirements

An initial letter from a debt collector must comply with the FDCPA rule requiring that a letter contain the following:[11]

---

9. NCLC *Fair Debt Collection* § 5.3.5.3 (5th ed. 2004 and 2005 Supp.).
10. Numerous other types of deceptive statements are also violations of the FDCPA. For a complete list and hundreds of case citations, see NCLC *Fair Debt Collection* § 5.5.2.8 (5th ed. 2004 and 2005 Supp.).
11. 15 U.S.C. § 1692g(a).

(a) Within five days after the initial communication with a consumer in connection with the collection of any debt, a debt collector shall, unless the following information is contained in the initial communication or the consumer has paid the debt, send the consumer a written notice containing—

    (1) the amount of the debt;

    (2) the name of the creditor to whom the debt is owed;

    (3) a statement that unless the consumer, within thirty days after receipt of the notice, disputes the validity of the debt, or any portion thereof, the debt will be assumed to be valid by the debt collector;

    (4) a statement that if the consumer notifies the debt collector in writing within the thirty-day period that the debt, or any portion thereof, is disputed, the debt collector will obtain verification of the debt or a copy of a judgment against the consumer and a copy of such verification or judgment will be mailed to the consumer by the debt collector; and

    (5) a statement that, upon the consumer's written request within the thirty-day period, the debt collector will provide the consumer with the name and address of the original creditor, if different from the current creditor.

(b) If the consumer notifies the debt collector in writing within the thirty-day period described in subsection (a) that the debt, or any portion thereof, is disputed, or that the consumer requests the name and address of the original creditor, the debt collector shall cease collection of the debt, or any disputed portion thereof, until the debt collector obtains verification of the debt or any copy of a judgment, or the name and address of the original creditor, and a copy of such verification or judgment, or name and address of the original creditor, is mailed to the consumer by the debt collector.

(c) The failure of a consumer to dispute the validity of a debt under this section may not be construed by any court as an admission of liability by the consumer.

The rules concerning a debt collector's communication are very strict, and even the validation rights notice (paragraph b above) must be placed in such a manner as to avoid confusion to the "least sophisticated consumer." "The law was not made for the protection of experts but for the public—that vast multitude of which includes the ignorant, the unthinking, and the credulous."[12] Not only must a validation notice be present, but it also cannot be obscured by other language, contradict the content of the validation rights, or serve to confuse a debtor. This includes making the font of the validation paragraph smaller than that of the rest of the notice, capitalizing nonvalidation content, or placing the validation notice on the back of the notice. Demanding payment within 10 days would also serve to confuse or contradict the validation rights by causing a debtor to perceive that he or she actually doesn't have 30 days to dispute a debt under validation.[13] Likewise, threatening lawsuit within 10 days is contradictory.[14]

And there's more. The letter must also contain the name of the creditor, state that the debt is assumed to be valid if it is not disputed, and disclose the exact amount of the debt, not just a principal balance "plus late fees, attorney fees, and interest."[15]

Re-Aging of Accounts

One of the most sinister tactics employed by collection agencies is the re-aging of account entries. Remember, the FCRA prohibits delinquent accounts that are charged off or placed for collection from being reported to bureaus after seven years plus 180 days from the date of

---

12. *Jeter v. Credit Bureau, Inc.*, 760 F.2d 1168 (11th Cir. 1985).

13. U.S.C. § 1692g and 1692e(10). *Graziano v. Harrison*, 950 F.2d 107, 111 (3rd Cir. 1991); *Johnson v. Revenue Management Corp.*, 169 F.3d 1057 (7th Cir. 1999). The 4th Circuit found likewise.

14. 15 U.S.C. § 1692g and 1692e(10). *Graziano v. Harrison*, 950 F.2d 107, 111 (3rd Cir. 1991). See also Bartlett v. Heibl, 128 F.3d 497 (7th Cir. 1997).

15. 15 U.S.C. § 1692g; *Miller v. McCalla, Raymer, Padrick, Cobb, Nichols, and Clark, L.L.C.*, 214 F.3d 872 (7th Cir. June 5, 2000); see also *Zaborac v. Phillips and Cohen Assocs., Ltd.*, 330 F. Supp. 2d 962 (N.D. Ill 2004) (section 1692g(a)(1) requires statement of the amount the consumer allegedly owes, not just the unpaid principal balance). See NCLC *Fair Debt Collection* § 5.7 (5th ed. 2004 and 2005 Supp.).

first delinquency. Collection agencies are notorious for changing this cutoff date to serve their ends and reporting information fraudulently to put pressure on consumers to pay their debts. Sound like science fiction? Guess again. Here's a partial press release from the FTC concerning a collection agency that does this:

FTC
For Release: May 13, 2004

NCO Group to Pay Largest FCRA Civil Penalty to Date

One of the nation's largest debt-collection firms will pay $1.5 million to settle Federal Trade Commission charges that it violated the Fair Credit Reporting Act (FCRA) by reporting inaccurate information about consumer accounts to credit bureaus. The civil penalty against Pennsylvania-based NCO Group, Inc. is the largest civil penalty ever obtained in a FCRA case.

According to the FTC's complaint, defendants NCO Group, Inc.; NCO Financial Systems, Inc.; and NCO Portfolio Management, Inc. violated Section 623(a)(5) of the FCRA, which specifies that any entity that reports information to credit bureaus about a delinquent consumer account that has been placed for collection or written off must report the actual month and year the account first became delinquent. In turn, this date is used by the credit bureaus to measure the maximum seven-year reporting period the FCRA mandates. The provision helps ensure that outdated debts—debts that are beyond this seven-year reporting period—do not appear on a consumer's credit report. Violations of this provision of the FCRA are subject to civil penalties of $2,500 per violation.

The FTC charges that NCO reported accounts using later-than-actual delinquency dates. Reporting later-than-actual dates may cause negative information to remain in a consumer's credit file beyond the seven-year reporting period permitted by the FCRA for most information. When this occurs, consumers' credit scores may be lowered, possibly resulting in their rejection for credit or their having to pay a higher interest rate.

The proposed consent decree orders the defendants to pay civil penalties of $1.5 million and permanently bars them from reporting later-than-actual delinquency dates to credit bureaus in the future. Additionally, NCO is required to implement a program to monitor all complaints received to ensure that reporting errors are corrected quickly. The consent agreement also contains standard recordkeeping and other requirements to assist the FTC in monitoring the defendants' compliance.

Most debt collectors are truly vicious. I suppose they also do this in order to get around not only the FCRA but also other state laws, like ones that forbid any collection activity for accounts older than a certain number of years. Yes, a consumer may still owe the debt until it is either paid or written off in bankruptcy, but collectors are forbidden to even attempt collection after a certain number of years.

And if NCO Group's shenanigans sound like an isolated incident, they're not. Michael Weed, a former employee of the collection agency Asset Acceptance, filed a suit against that company for wrongful termination. An employee for eight years, he claims that he went to upper management to report re-aging and was subsequently terminated. In addition to his claims of re-aging, he reported the following breaches:

- "In order for a consumer to clear their name, they have to pay the debt. They made a lot of money off of this. There were 500 mistakes that I know of.
- "Asset violated disclosure laws by giving out debt information to third parties, such as relatives.
- "Asset would intentionally delay settlement of debt disputes to force debtors to pay the claim, and even if they didn't even owe the debt, they would pay it in order to get a mortgage."

Be forewarned, this is not an isolated incident but the modus operandi of many collection agencies.

Finagling Subscriber Numbers and Account Identifiers

As you now know, bureaus use subscriber numbers to distinguish between furnishers, preventing duplication and reinsertion. Collection agencies know this and will often submit accounts to the bureaus using a new subscriber number for accounts that are outside the seven-year limit for credit reporting. This is especially true for sinister agencies that buy old junk debt for pennies. Since collection agencies understand the credit reporting agency's use of queries and filters within their repository, they'll use new or modified account identifiers to get the item to show up on the report when it otherwise wouldn't.

Through this and other illegal methods, the accounts are listed as new on someone's credit file, and then collection attempts resume. Many debtors become frustrated and pay the debts to save their credit, simply because they don't understand that they cannot only sue for money damages when this happens, but also they can have the collection agencies shut down by notifying the FTC and their state's attorney general.[16]

It's important that consumers dispute any bogus entries with the bureaus, since any affirmation creates huge liability on the part of the furnisher as additional causes of action under the FCRA become available. It can open up the bureau to civil liability as well, so dispute such entries in accordance with Chapter 11.

Violations of Bank Withdrawals

There are two types of bank withdrawals that can be performed by a debt collector. One is a preauthorized draft (demand draft), governed by the Uniform Commercial Code (UCC), and the other is an electronic fund transfer, governed by the Electronic Funds Transfer Act (EFTA). A preauthorized draft is simply a check that a collector prepares and endorses in the account holder's name. This is legal as long as the debtor authorizes it; if not, it is considered fraud, and the collector is liable under the FDCPA and state UDAP or state debt collection laws. And even if the debtor permits a series of preauthorized drafts, the collector must notify the debtor at least three days (and no more than 10 days) before submitting each draft.[17]

The UCC permits the account holder debtor to dispute the bank

---

16. Numerous breaches of law can exist, including multiple violations of the FCRA and the FDCPA.
17. 15 U.S.C. § 1692f(2).

check as long as the bank is notified "promptly." If the account holder doesn't dispute the initial check, then subsequent checks will be honored, and no remedy is available under the UCC.

In some cases a debtor will authorize a collector to withdraw money directly from a bank account. However, collectors cannot sign a debtor's name for a series of electronic funds transfers (EFTs), as they can with a preauthorized draft. If a collector taps an account without permission, the account holder has 60 days from the statement date (date of a billing statement that includes the transaction) to dispute the transaction and avoid liability for the withdrawal.

If there's no access device (e.g., automated teller machine or debit card) used in the withdrawal, an institution that fails to complete its investigation of a consumer dispute within 10 days and recredit the account can take 45 days to complete its investigation. This increases to 90 days if an access device was involved.[18] Consumers can also stop payment on EFTs by notifying the financial institution within three business days prior to the scheduled transfer. Banks are liable under the EFTA for failing to perform their duties under the Act.

Regardless of what type of unauthorized withdrawal takes place, a debt collector should also be liable under state UDAPs as well as the FDCPA.

Most banking institutions are also members of the Automated Clearing House (ACH) network and therefore subject to rules that govern electronic transactions, called the National Automated Clearing House Association (NACHA) rules. For more information on this, see the NCLC *Consumer Banking and Payments Law* (2d ed. 2002 and Supp.).

Telephone Company Violations

For violations of certain provisions by interstate phone companies of the Federal Communications Act (FCA) and Federal Communication Commission (FCC) tariffs (rules and regulations), a consumer can seek a private lawsuit for negligence and breach of telephone contract. This includes a phone company's failure to properly address a

---

18. Reg. E, §§ 205.6(b), 205.11(c)(2), 206.11(c)(3)(ii)(B).

complaint made to a telephone company by a consumer against a debt collector. Complaints made to the FCC can be made using its Web site: www.fcc.gov.

In-state breaches are more complicated, depending on state law. Contact the FCC or state Public Utilities Commission (PUC) to find out the enforcer in your state.

THE LIFE OF A DEBT

When any debt goes past 90 days late, it goes into collections. For secured debt, legal action will likely commence very shortly thereafter. Once a repossession or foreclosure has occurred, any deficit is treated as unsecured debt.

For unsecured debt, the average collection rate is 15 to 20 percent of the total debt when a debtor is 90 days late or more. Since creditors know this, they will do everything they can to settle the debt at this crucial point. At this juncture, they'll try to collect for 90 more days and may elect to use an outside collection agency.

If they are unsuccessful after 90 additional days, then they will likely turn the debt over to a collection agency and/or sell it to a third party. They really don't want this, since their chances of collecting at this point are minimal and whatever is collected must be shared with the agency; often 50 percent will go to the collector. Your chances of negotiating a good settlement just before the debt goes to an agency are quite good, but don't be alarmed if you can't settle before this happens.

Bank credit cards are the most common form of unsecured debt, and after six months these creditors will charge off (write off) the debt in order to obtain a tax credit on the loss. They'll continue trying to collect thereafter and hope that negative credit reporting will eventually force a debtor to pay up. Such debts are more likely to be sold to a third party after six months of delinquency.

Many "credit repair experts" claim that collection agencies are far easier to deal with than original creditors, since they're far more accustomed to reducing debt and wheeling and dealing. I don't find this to be true at all, and if there are any notable differences in what one will do over another, I believe it's more a function of time and simple economics. Creditors can charge off debt and recover part of it in the form of a tax write-off. Debts often get sold after six months, and buyers will purchase it for pennies on the dollar. As time passes and a debt approaches the statute of limitations for collections, any debt holder will become more flexible. And, besides, collectors from agencies are usually far more unruly anyway, which can make them more difficult to deal with.

COMMUNICATING WITH COLLECTORS

Collection agencies are in the business of collecting money, period. It's what they do, and they are good at it, which is why they are in business and creditors use them. Collectors from these organizations are even more abusive and loathsome. (Yes, I worked for a collection agency. Ugh!) The agency doesn't get any money if it doesn't collect, and the collector doesn't have a job for long if he or she doesn't collect money. This is quite a motivator, and so collectors will do anything in order to collect, including lying, cheating, badgering, and so on.

Collectors can't *ever* be trusted, which is why any renegotiated terms are handled in writing, no exceptions, and new terms include removal of any negative history on your credit report.[19] Now that you know how sinister collectors can be, you'll be better equipped to invoke your rights as you deal with them. Equally important in your quest to attain your ultimate goal of repairing your credit is the art of negotiation.

Master the Art of Negotiation

The most important and fundamental element of the credit restoration process is the art of negotiation. If you can learn this reasonably well, it will serve you in all things in life. An entire book can easily be devoted to the subject (and many have been). Negotiating is truly an art, and it involves understanding the following key points:

- *Everyone wants something.*

---

19. See Chapter 13 for information on settlement agreements.

- *Everyone is willing to do something for that something.*
- *You need to be able to, with reasonable accuracy, predict what that something is.*
- *Sometimes you should just listen.* Often people will just come out and say what they will do, or they will tell you in certain nonverbal ways (e.g., excitement level, tone). Besides, listening goes a long way toward building rapport.
- *You must be good at hiding certain cards.* That is, the something you want and what you're willing to do for it must sometimes be hidden. Put on your poker face.
- *Never reveal all your cards up front.* Once you're good at hiding your cards, learn how to reveal them at a pace that serves you. Only reveal that which is necessary at first and then more if needed. A prospective buyer of your car doesn't need to know that you'll sell it for $8,000. It's fine if he thinks you'll only take $9,000 if you think he'll pay it. (This is where predicting comes in—perceiving such signs as excitement or a hurried disposition.)
- *Engage in negotiations from a perspective of knowing what you want but giving up something only in little bits and stages.* Never be in a hurry. If you want something for something, don't offer your best deal. Offer far less. If far less doesn't work, offer a little more than far less. And if that doesn't work, tell the person you want to think about it for a few days. Try a little bit more. Go slowly.
- *Ensure that the person with whom you are negotiating has the power to give you what you want.* You can spend months negotiating a deal, only to find that the person has no power to help you. (Yes, it happens!) The person you need to speak with doesn't answer phones for the company. In fact, he or she probably doesn't even manage the people who answer phones! The people who can help you are too important for that and are usually found in the corporate offices of the creditor. As you make your way past the many people you'll talk with in trying to find the right person, remember to be nice. You will want to pull your hair out at times, but stay calm and be persistent.

- *Don't tell anyone who isn't in a position to help you what you are trying to do.* These people will hamper you and waste your time if you engage in specifics, and you'll usually be met with negativity. Simply explain that you wish to contact someone to discuss a problem with your report—someone with power to make changes. Indicate (nicely) that you don't wish to tell the whole story over and over again, that you wish to speak with the person who is in a position to make urgent changes. Stick to your guns, but be nice! (Most people you talk with won't even know who to send you to! Be prepared to go in circles, but start at corporate headquarters, the head of the collection department, or credit control. The right person is there; you just have to find him or her.) Remember, small minds and tender egos will do nothing but try to derail your efforts, since that's what small minds and tender egos do.

- *In attempting credit restoration, negotiate with creditors from the position of victim* (i.e., before you have exercised any of your legal options). The term "victim" isn't to be confused with weakness, nor is it to be confused with "a victim of the creditor." The term is used to describe an approach to negotiating wherein you are the "victim" of some unfortunate occurrence. In most other types of negotiating, you negotiate from a position of power and use logic; that is, you let the person you're negotiating with know that you have something he or she wants and use an analytical framework. But with credit restoration, I recommend this only as a last resort. I've found that negotiating from the position of victim works much better. Sure, you may even have their money in many cases, but they have what may amount to your new car or home loan! You will be playing on or appealing to a person's compassion. Good people have it; you just need to find the wedge to bring it out. Don't whine; just explain to the person what happened to cause the mistake (e.g., you lost your job, your house got flooded, your spouse put the screws to you) and then take responsibility by stating that you want to make it right! Use tempered emotion, where you display a heartfelt concern but are in control at all times.

Tip: There are no hard-and-fast rules on whether to use logic or appeal to emotions when negotiating. Usually you'll use a mix of both, but the situational approach is best—that is, using a tactic that's in direct relation to the personality and demeanor of the other party. This is another area where listening can be very helpful. And if you have begun legal action against a creditor as a *pro se* plaintiff (representing yourself), that's when you will likely change tactics—negotiating from a position of strength.

- *Make it clear that you are at fault and you are willing to take responsibility for what happened.* Never forget this and make it plain in your negotiations. Explain this repeatedly and mean it! Even if your spouse ruined your credit, you married him or her, right? Sorry if this sounds harsh, but that's reality. Bad things happen, but it's up to you to make things right.
- *An ounce of perseverance is worth a pound of talent.* You're going to hear it over and over: "You can't, you can't, you can't; that's not possible; no, won't happen; you can't." Nonsense. I was told numerous times that I'd never be an officer while enlisted in the service, never go to flight school, never fly an advanced aircraft like the Blackhawk helicopter, never fly airplanes because the army only trains about 100 pilots per year, never get published, and on and on. I did all of those things! Forget about the naysayers. There will be many obstacles, but be persistent in your negotiations. Focus and you will prevail!
- *Be nonchalant but not indifferent.* Yes, it's important to you to get your credit fixed, but don't get too exited or you'll make the person you are talking with nervous. You'll also tip your hand. Being nonchalant is the cornerstone of most negotiating. However, when dealing with creditors always show that you're concerned and you care, using tempered emotion. It's a balancing act.
- *Every person is different, and tactics must be changed accordingly.* Perceptions run the gamut, and this is where listening will

enable you to understand the other party and modify your methods accordingly.

- *Don't get greedy.* The quickest way to turn off the other party is to get greedy.
- *Everything is negotiable.* This, of course, assumes that the person you're negotiating with is reasonable.

Just a few more thoughts on negotiating: reasonable people will always negotiate matters of dollars and "sense." If you find that you aren't making any headway when you're negotiating and someone is intransigent, then you're not likely dealing with a reasonable person. After all, we aren't talking about heirlooms here. You'll either need to (a) change your tactics and/or (b) change the players and/or (c) go to a higher authority. You can also wait a while, and sometimes people change their minds—which is why it's important not to completely walk or burn bridges if it can be avoided. *Smart people work things out.*

This is true in all things—especially relationships. But understand what you're up against. The types you will encounter will likely be both educated and uneducated derelicts; some of them may even be very intelligent. Notice that I didn't say smart. Intelligent people are those who can memorize things, perform well in school, and even understand sterile concepts that are very complex. They are "good on paper," "good in a cubical," or "good with a pencil and numbers." Being smart is something very different. Smart people are cunning, clever, or creative in a practical sense, and they use these qualities to achieve real-world, desirable results. Reasonable people are often smart, and you need to be able to determine very quickly who is and who isn't reasonable so as not to waste too much time with frontline cronies with little common sense and even less sense of fair play and reason.

In the world of collection agencies and lawyers, you must prepare for the worst. I share this with you in an effort to prepare you for what will likely be very unpleasant, as discussions will invariably run afoul. Mental toughness is a necessary element of credit restoration, since collectors and lawyers have a penchant for abuse. They will make it personal, yell, and do everything they can to bait you into a verbal pissing contest.

Don't fall for it. You can't win this type of exchange, and it will do nothing to further your goals. Don't ever lose your cool, raise your voice, or say anything to stoop to that level. If you don't like what is being said, then say so clearly and succinctly, and then take it to a higher authority. Remember, harassment is illegal, but the law in and of itself is not a deterrent. If your skin is thin, you'd better toughen it up and right now.

Think very hard about the art of negotiation. Ponder it. It's a very powerful thing and will serve you in your quest for clean credit and in many other endeavors in your life. Try it out on simple things like negotiating a price for a pair of slacks or anything else. You want to learn and polish this skill to the highest degree possible.

In Chapter 9, I provide a real-world example of how to negotiate with a creditor using a real conversation. By the time you've made your way to that chapter, you'll likely feel knowledgeable enough to handle any collector.

Begin to Deal

Once you contact the collector or collection agency on your terms, politely make it clear that you understand the rules and will not tolerate any breach of the law. Once you have established some ground rules, you can begin negotiating, and you must take a conciliatory approach. Remember, you are negotiating a settlement, and you have to get the person to come around to your way of thinking.

Tip: Often a collector will try to get you to send any money at all, which may reset the debt collection statute, depending on the state. Although the credit reporting statute cannot be reset, sending money is an affirmation that the debt is owed and is not recommended.

Don't get personal, and don't argue. Simply state the facts and don't allow yourself to be abused on any level. Avoid ultimatums whenever possible when communicating with collectors, especially in-house collectors for creditors. In the case of unruly collection agencies, have the matter referred back to the original creditor if possible (see "Taking the Collection Agency Out of Play" later in this chapter).

When negotiating, be sure to tell the truth and stay real. Don't insult or belittle collectors (even if they *are* stupid). Don't take a deal you don't want or cannot live up to. Remember to just hang in there. Collectors will keep trying to beat you down, but you will beat them down!

Here are some additional things to keep in mind when dealing with collectors:

- When a collector—or any stranger—telephones you, immediately ask for the caller's full name, company affiliation, location, and phone number. Say that you're in the middle of something at the moment but you'll call right back. This is not only a good practice to prevent harassment and promote safety, but it's also a good way to take notes on what collectors have called and when, and it puts them on a little different footing. Collectors are required to identify themselves, and if any collector fails to provide the information you ask for, then you know right then and there that (a) this isn't someone you can deal with on any level (after all, if he or she can't provide this simple bit of information, then how can you ever expect to negotiate on any issues that really matter?), and (b) you'll have a legal claim against this collector for failure to follow the FDCPA and perhaps breaches of state laws as well. You do have caller ID and anonymous caller block, don't you? Of course, if the collector does provide the information and then turns abusive, you'll have all his or her information if you decide to pursue a legal remedy.
- If you contact collectors regularly, then they're far less likely to call neighbors. However, for bills over $4,500, they often perform research to find out what they can take if negotiations are going poorly for them.
- When dealing with collectors, don't say you're uncollectible—show it. Only say it when the negotiations have reached an impasse and you wish to let them know that you know you're uncollectible. Uncollectible means that you're "judgment proof." That means that you don't have anything a collector can take. Even some income is immune from seizure, such as Social Security, welfare, and VA checks. If an account contains

"commingled" funds (from both collectible and immune deposits), only the collectible deposits are available for seizure. It's best to place all uncollectible funds in a separate account, so you don't have to prove anything later.

Never Tell on Yourself

Always use common sense when communicating with collectors. If you want them to believe you're unemployed, contacting them only in the evening will cause them to think you have a day job. Don't tell them you're on unemployment, because they'll request proof; if proof is provided, they'll use the information against you where possible.

Collectors will often want you to fill out forms that list your income and obligations (i.e., financial statements). Don't do it. Why supply ammunition? They will just use this information against you later—maybe even in court. Furthermore, if you are disabled and collecting Social Security, you must decide whether or not to admit it (if asked). There's no harm in a little white lie; it's none of their business anyway.

Warning: Often collectors will say one thing on the phone and then send you something to sign that doesn't resemble what they agreed to. Their agreement will often say things like "Paid Account" or "Paid Settlement" or similar. This is not the same as removing the item (tradeline) from the report or "Paid as Agreed" because it is still derogatory information that will lower your credit score. Further, as explained previously, the recency of the negative entry will badly impact a score even more.

They shouldn't be asking such questions. There's nothing in your contract with them that says you consented to a rectal exam. Don't tell them anything that will hinder your negotiations for debt reduction or credit restoration. You can play the pauper; this is always believable, since few debtors have money. Or you can say that you have many more obligations than just what you owe them. Just remember, don't ever tell a white lie that you will get caught in, and be sure to take copious notes of discussions with creditors and review them before each conversation. Steer clear of flat-out lies; only white lies are acceptable in my opinion, even if the collector happens to be a scumbag. (White lies are simply untrue answers to questions that shouldn't be asked in the first place, or niceties used to spare someone's feelings.)

Have Credit History Changed or Deleted

As explained in "Ground Rules," there is no requirement that reporting agencies report information for the full seven years—they can delete adverse information whenever they choose before the seven-year period.[20]

Often collectors will say that credit history cannot be changed. Simply inform them that you know they are mistaken and that you are willing to make a deal, but it's up to them to remove the derogatory history as part of any settlement. Don't make ultimatums. Keep the dialogue open for as long as it advances your goals. If you aren't getting anywhere with a collection agency, have the matter referred back to the creditor or go higher up the food chain if you're dealing with the creditor directly. As a matter of settlement, any negative item can be changed or deleted altogether.

Record Phone Conversations

You might consider recording phone conversations with collectors using a small minicassette recorder (approximately $25) and telephone listening adapter (approximately $5) from Radio Shack. You may also record using your computer, a microphone, the telephone listening adapter, and recording software like Adobe Audition (www.adobe.com) or a decent freeware program called Audacity (http://bestcredit.com/audacity/). Another option for computer users is a product known as Personal Call Logger, which is simply placed on the phone line and connects to the PC's sound card (available for $69.99 from Hello Direct, www.hellodirect.com.) This is a good solution for those who don't have a telephone with a flat headset surface. The standard telephone listen-

---

20. FTC Official Staff Commentary § 605 item 4.

ing adapter, with its suction-cup end, is finicky about the surface to which it is attached.

Be advised that in some states you must inform the other party that you are recording the conversation, and the person must agree to being recorded. If you live in such a state and feel that you must record and the person won't agree, simply tell him or her that you're sorry, but you won't discuss the matter until you are permitted to tape the conversation. Be polite but firm.

In many states, only one party has to know that recording is taking place. Table 6 shows a summary of state laws concerning taping (correct as of this writing).

Recording phone conversations can go a long way toward making sure that you aren't mistreated. When recording, be sure to say the date and the name of the person you are speaking with and which collection agency he or she represents. This kind of evidence could also go a long way in court should you decide to sue. The downside to this tactic is that it often puts the person you're speaking with on the defensive. You may want to use this technique only after a conversation has gone badly and the collector has broken the law.

Note that this is primarily a technique for dealing with collection agencies, not for collectors in general. (Creditors will also have in-house collectors, who can be quite nasty but often not to the same extent.) Never be afraid to legally record conversations with agencies, since they are the most likely to be abusive. However, all collectors have the potential to be abusive, and you must never let anyone get away with breaking the rules. Representing myself, I successfully sued a collection agency, Risk Management Alternatives, for calling outside of allowable hours and harassment (i.e., calling repeatedly in the same day; see Chapter 15).

As you will soon learn, you don't need collection agencies and can often take them out of the loop entirely. One exception to this is if the agency has purchased the debt from the original creditor, in which case you may or may not need the agency, depending on (a) what you are willing to put up with, (b) whether the amount is so small that legal action isn't a concern, (c) whether you have assets that can be seized through legal action, and so on. Personally, if a collector from an agency that didn't own the debt was abusive to me, I'd tell him or her to "stick it" and then send a cease-communication letter.

SUMMARY OF STATE TAPING LAWS[1]

ONE-PARTY TAPING		CONSENT OF ALL PARTIES
Alabama	New Jersey	California
Alaska	New Mexico	Connecticut
Arizona	New York	Florida
Arkansas	North Carolina	Illinois
Colorado	North Dakota	Maryland
Delaware	Ohio	Massachusetts
D.C.	Oregon[2]	Michigan
Georgia	Oklahoma	Montana
Hawaii	Rhode Island	Nevada
Idaho	South Carolina	New Hampshire
Indiana	South Dakota	Pennsylvania
Iowa	Tennessee	Washington
Kansas	Texas	
Kentucky	Utah	
Louisiana	Vermont	
Maine	Virginia	
Minnesota	West Virginia	
Mississippi	Wisconsin	
Missouri	Wyoming	
Nebraska		

NOTES

1. This information was obtained from the Reporters Committee for Freedom of the Press, www.rcfp.org/taping/. And if you're recording a party in another state, then federal laws may apply as well. The safest bet, of course, is to notify the other party, since taping in some states violates criminal eavesdropping laws. Further, just because something is legal doesn't mean it's admissible in court. Check your state laws before recording.
2. If taping is from home. Or. Rev. Stat. § 165.540.

Table 6.

Dealing with Third Party Debt Owners

As explained previously, many creditors—especially bank card creditors—will sell debts to third parties after 180 days have elapsed. These third parties are companies that believe they can collect more money from a debtor than the price they paid to acquire the debt. The price varies but can typically range from 5 to 15 percent of the debt.

This situation often creates significant problems when attempting bad credit removal. You're still in a good position for a reduced settlement, but removing the bad marks from your credit report can be more problematic; the original creditor has sold the debt and thus no longer has a motivation to remove the bad history. The company that purchased the debt, on the other hand, has no control over what the original creditor reports. And far more insidious is a propensity for the current owner of the debt to report the account as a collection account under its company name (and a different subscriber and/or account number). When this happens, the same account will often show up as two or more different ones on your report.

A delinquent debt can be reported by the original creditor and be "technically accurate," since it will show adverse information *for a specific date*.[21] If the debt is sold when delinquent but before charge-off, then the new creditor will list it as a tradeline entry (and not just a collection account). The new owner can hire a collection agency to collect on the debt, which is then listed a *third time* as a collection account entry. Any subsequent purchaser after charge-off can also report the debt as a collection account.

When a debt is sold, the original owner is required to zero out the current balance field and inform the purchaser of the date the account first became delinquent, but they often don't.[22]

---

21. Some courts have held that technical accuracy is not a breach of the FCRA, while others have taken a different view. Many factors can influence this defense, such as additional laws that require an account included in bankruptcy to show a zero balance.

22. This is required as a part of the *Credit Reporting Resources Guide*, Associated Credit Bureaus 2000 (Metro Manual), pp. 10–14. NCLC *Fair Credit Reporting* § 3.3.3.7 (5th ed. 2002 and 2005 Supp.).

This hideous scenario is very common, especially for delinquent student loan debts, where the same delinquent student loan gets passed from buyer to buyer and each fails to code the balance field as zero.

Even more troublesome is the possibility of the third-party buyer's attempting to obtain a judgment against the debtor, particularly on larger debts. Often third-party buyers—ones that purchased from the original creditor—will do this after 90 days of attempting to settle the account, so often you can negotiate a good settlement before this happens. Just remember that the settlement agreement must specify that the owner of the debt will remove derogatory credit history that it is reporting.

If a judgment is obtained by the third party, there are still some options for getting this information taken off your report (more on this in Chapter 10). Keep in mind that judgments will remain on your report for many years, so it is important that you avoid them if possible. This still doesn't solve the problem of the original creditor, however, which will often just stop reporting where it left off (e.g., bad debt, collection account, charge-off, balance owed).

For example, the original creditor may have a reporting date that precedes any payment to the third party and report a balance and/or lateness on an account that you've paid. In this case, the original creditor is often unwilling to change it, and that leaves you in a position where (a) a potential lender will decline you until that account is "paid," and/or (b) your score is negatively impacted, which prevents you from getting approval or causes you to pay a higher interest rate.

Since it is often to your benefit for the original creditor to retain a debt (rather than selling it to a third party), it's important that you try to find out as much information as you can about your creditor's intentions. If you can, find out what the creditor does with debts after charging them off. Often the creditor will tell you, and keep in mind that what one person won't reveal, another will. If charged-off accounts are turned over to third-party buyers, this can affect your tactics for settlement and negotiation. To every extent possible, you want to avoid a debt's being sold, even if it means paying more than you thought or settling for terms that are somewhat less desirable.

Of course, removal of any adverse entries is paramount, and anything less will almost never do. A debt's being sold to a third party isn't the end of the world by a long shot; it just means that there will likely be additional hurdles when it comes to getting multiple adverse items removed from different sources. Since you can only pay one of them—the owner of the debt—there will be no leverage from which to negotiate on any reporting by the original creditor.

Yet there are four additional options for having the adverse information removed by the original creditor if the debt has been sold to a third party:

1. Original creditors are often willing to remove the bad history under some conditions, such as when you have a new account with them—perhaps a secured account—that is in good standing. Often people change jobs, and you may find someone more agreeable in the credit reporting/collection department who wasn't there when you were attempting to negotiate before.
2. Sellers of a debt sometimes won't affirm it to a bureau when there's a dispute filed, since they don't have anything to gain from doing so. Try disputing any sold debt with a bureau in accordance with Chapter 9.
3. If there's an aspect of the account that is erroneous, a declaratory judgment action can be performed to remove the tradeline entirely.[23]
4. If the original creditor has done something egregious, then any appropriate legal action can be taken. Such action will often strengthen negotiations.

For more information on how to handle third-party and multiple reporting, see Chapter 10.

---

23. See Chapter 14.

TAKING THE COLLECTION AGENCY OUT OF PLAY

There are some extremely powerful ways to deal with debt collectors, and collection agencies in particular. One is called validation, and the other is the cease-communication letter, often referred to as a cease-and-desist letter.

Validation: Create a Hurdle

If a debt collector receives a written dispute from a consumer within 30 days of its first notifying that consumer of a debt, the collector must cease all collection efforts. Those efforts must cease until the collector provides verification to the debtor.[24]

The FTC classifies any reporting of a charged-off debt as collection activity, and thus the debt may not be reported during this validation period (between when a debt collector receives a validation letter and when the verification is provided to the debtor).[25] If the debt collector ceases collection efforts entirely during this period, it still may not report the debt. If the debt collector had already reported the debt (before the written dispute was received), any further reporting of the debt must indicate that the debt is in dispute.[26]

Although the debt can be disputed verbally, as you well know I advise against getting into a he-said, she-said routine. As such, you should send a letter RRM, which simply says, "I dispute this debt," and lists the account number and name of the original creditor. Avoid any excuses as to why it hasn't been paid or why it's not owed.

---

24. 15 U.S.C. § 1692g(b). "Disputed debts. If the consumer notifies the debt collector in writing within the 30-day period described in subsection (a) of this section that the debt, or any portion thereof, is disputed, or that the consumer requests the name and address of the original creditor, the debt collector shall cease collection of the debt, or any disputed portion thereof, until the debt collector obtains verification of the debt or a copy of a judgment, or the name and address of the original creditor, and a copy of such verification or judgment, or name and address of the original creditor, is mailed to the consumer by the debt collector."
25. LeFevre, FTC informal staff opinion letter, Dec. 23, 1997.
26. 15 U.S.C. § 1682e(8); see *Brady v. Credit Recovery Co.*, 160 F.3d 64 (1st Cir. 1998); *Sullivan v. Equifax, Inc.*, 2002 WL 799856 (E.D. Pa. Apr. 19, 2002).

The debt collector must offer proof of the debt as owed by providing copies of the signed instrument or judgment *from the original creditor.*[27]

Clearly, validation offers some unique benefits and can be performed whether a collection agency (or any debt collector) owns the debt or is just acting as a proxy for a creditor. It's something that any debtor can employ and is often the most effective after a debt is sold or transferred for collection. And the older a debt becomes, the more likely that validation can work.[28]

Parties subject to the FDCPA that ignore the validation request are in violation of the Act. (Any failure to respond is a failure to assert the debt as owed, so therefore a debtor has the right to conclude it is not owed; known as "estoppel.")[29] Remember, if they first-time furnish before providing verification, they're in breach of the FCRA. And if they've already furnished and then receive a validation letter, any subsequent refurnishing must show the debt as in dispute, or they're also in violation of the FCRA. If unlawful furnishing occurs, it's best to send them a letter indicating that they're in breach of the FDCPA, the FCRA, and possibly other state laws. You may also demand that they stop reporting or face legal action.

---

27. "The statute requires that the debt collector obtain verification of the debt and mail it to the consumer. Because one of the principal purposes of this Section is to help consumers who have been misidentified by the debt collector or who dispute the amount of the debt, it is important that the verification of the identity of the consumer and the amount of the debt be obtained directly from the creditor. Mere itemization of what the debt collector already has does not accomplish this purpose. As stated above, the statute requires the debt collector, not the creditor, to mail the verification to the consumer." LeFevre, FTC informal staff opinion letter, May 17, 1993. See *Ost v. Collection Bureau, Inc.*, 493 F. Supp. 701 (D.N.D. 1980); *Graziano v. Harrison*, 950 F.2d 107 (3d Cir. 1991); *Miller v. Payco General American Credits, Inc.*, 943 F.2d 482 (4th Cir. 1991), et seq.

28. Be aware that there may be state laws concerning validation as well. Check your state laws.

29. Ignoring a validation is considered estoppel by silence. Estoppel is "a bar to the use of contradictory words or acts in asserting a claim or right against another." Estoppel by silence is "an estoppel preventing a person from making an assertion to another's disadvantage when the person previously had the opportunity and duty to speak but failed to do so." FindLaw definitions, www.findlaw.com.

Since adverse reporting by a debt collector during the first 30 days after initial notice (and before a dispute is received) would require him or her to report any account information subsequent to that as in dispute, it's a good idea to pull all reports 30 days after receiving an initial collection notice so that you have a record of any collection activity. As explained in Chapter 3, a debt reported as in dispute is good for FICO scoring, since it does not take into consideration debts reported as in dispute.

Cease-Communication Letter

If validation doesn't work (or it's too late to perform as an option) and/or you wish to try to negotiate with the third-party collection agency (or debt collector), then there are still other options available for taking it out of the loop later if you find that you're not making any headway.

Collection agencies are notorious for being very wicked and demanding all the money at once without delay. But you have them by the *cojones*. If your negotiations are getting nowhere, you can send a "cease-communication" letter demanding that the agency no longer contact you and cease communication in accordance with the FDCPA.

When I do this, if the collection agency doesn't own the debt, then I also demand that it refer the matter back to the original creditor. Though the agency is not required to do this, it often does anyway. You can stipulate in the letter that the agency has one more chance to settle and spell out the exact terms, but if your terms are not accepted (e.g., within 10 days), then you no longer wish to be contacted. (Of course, even if the agency does own the debt, you can also send it a conditional offer.)

This can work in your favor in one of two ways, either (a) the debt collector will wish to settle in order to get paid, or (b) if the account does go back to the original creditor, that creditor will be more likely to be flexible with you. But be advised, the creditor (or its proxy) can sue if it appears that it is worthwhile to do so. That is, if it can serve you with court papers.

Note: Usually creditors will not talk to you about an account while it's still in the hands of an agency. But if they do, and you've agreed to settle with the original creditor while the matter is still in the hands of the agency, make sure that you word any agreement in such a manner as to include the stipulation that (a) credit reporting agencies (Trans Union, Equifax, and Experian) will be notified to "remove any adverse reference" and (b) "the relevant collection agency" will be notified to delete the account from its database and stop reporting the account to the bureaus. A collection agency, if it doesn't own an account, will report it as indicated by the creditor. If a collection agency has purchased it, then the original creditor has no control over what the agency will report. (See Chapter 10.)

As explained, you'll often have more success dealing with the original creditor than a collection agency. So when an account is handed over to an agency, your best bet is to try once for an acceptable deal and then try to have the matter referred back to the original creditor using the cease-communication letter. (Sometimes debts are even referred back to the creditor when they receive a Validation letter.)

If your account has gone to a third-party debt collector and it hasn't purchased the debt (i.e., it is collecting on behalf of the creditor), sending the debt collector a cease-communication letter (and getting the debt referred back to the creditor, if possible) can also be good for your credit. Collection agency debt collectors in particular report bad credit with far more regularity and, again, often create new account numbers for the same account so as to compound the damage to your credit. Restrict your negotiations with them to days, not weeks. If you send a cease-communication letter and get the matter referred back quickly enough, you can possibly avoid a further tattering of your report. *Collection agencies often will not report an account at all if they receive a cease-communication letter before they've reported to the bureaus.*

Just remember that when negotiating with a third-party collection agency (or any debt collector) that doesn't own the debt, any deal you make will have to be approved by the original creditor. This "going back to the well" can extend the negotiations, but, again, limit the negotiating to days, not weeks.

Note: The FDCPA only applies to collection agencies (or third parties), so a debt collector that is "in house" for a bank does not have to abide by a cease-communication letter. However, most creditors either don't know this or, if they do, will abide by it anyway to avoid a lawsuit.

The cease-communication letter may help you retain your sanity, since any phone conversations will likely be abusive. Just remember that (a) if the debt collector doesn't own the debt, he or she must cease communication; (b) if the debt collector does own the debt, he or she will have to cease anyway, as bona fide debt collectors are required to abide by the cease-communication provision of the FDCPA; (c) a debt collector doesn't have to refer the matter back to the original creditor, but an agency often will anyway if it doesn't own the debt; and (d) the debt collector can sue, providing your state permits lawsuits by that particular type of debt collector (some states forbid lawsuit by collection agencies). Lawyer debt collectors can always sue, providing they're not representing a collection agency in a state that forbids lawsuits by debt collectors. Lawyer debt collectors will almost never refer a matter back to an original creditor when a debtor requests it, unless they have broken certain FDCPA laws and are leaned on very hard over such breaches. Most lawyers don't want to be sued . . . or disbarred.

COLLECTION LAWYERS

There are two types of lawyers that will attempt to collect debts— in-house and contract. In-house lawyers are payroll employees of the creditor or collection agency. Contract lawyers don't work directly for the creditor and often have other clients as well. In collection matters, contract lawyers often will not get paid unless they collect money, but in-house lawyers will usually get paid a salary and perhaps even a bonus based on debts collected. In either case, they are highly motivated.

Large banks usually have in-house attorneys, while smaller credit unions often do not. Collection agencies also likely will have payroll attorneys (some collection agencies are owned and operated by attorneys). Of course, an attorney representing a doctor with a small practice will likely be a contract attorney. The size of the organization will often dictate what type of lawyer it has.

Regardless of which kind of lawyer you come across, they all have the same basic criterion for deciding whether to sue: whether there's money in it for them and their clients (in the case of contract lawyers) or the creditor they work for (in the case of in-house lawyers).

A lawyer will assess the situation based on how much is owed and what he or she can take. It's just that simple. If you have wages to garnish or assets to seize and the amount is worth the trouble, they will sue if they can. However, settling is always preferable, since litigation costs money and there's always a chance that the creditor will get a judgment but still never collect. Debtors frequently have numerous obligations, and creditors that have obtained judgments have to wait in line behind other creditors with higher priority (e.g., the IRS or a mortgage lender). If creditors sense that they may have to "take a number," then this will impact their decision as well.

Keep in mind that this rule is not hard-and-fast, since people generally make bad decisions no matter what their education and intelligence quotient. In fact, some lawyers and creditors are downright stupid, and I've seen them make bad decisions with regularity. This is why you have to bring them around to a more prudent line of thinking, primarily using your negotiation skills and positioning yourself so that the hurdles become insurmountable, or at least *appear* to be so.

If a creditor's attorney is handling your account, as with all negotiations, be nice. Explain that you wish to do the best you can to resolve the issue—just as you would say to any other creditor. Don't panic. Your negotiations will be the same. However, if legal action is imminent *and* you get a notice to appear in court, by all means get a lawyer without delay. Remember, attorneys always threaten legal action, and it's not a huge issue unless they actually do. Again, this often hinges on what they can take, what your state's laws are concerning property and liens, and so on.

Even if you're served, you can most often settle before the court date, and a good attorney can assist in negotiating if you think you need one. In fact, answers usually aren't even required for 30 days from service, which leaves you lots of time to contact the attorney and reach an out-of-court settlement.

If you owe more than just a few dollars, you have to assume that the opposing lawyer has researched you to find out your place of employment, salary, assets, and obligations. The lawyer may have some or all of the facts, and you must try to discover what has been uncovered if possible by letting him or her speak. (Remember the art of negotiation.)

As in all negotiations, don't tell on yourself. If you make a good salary, own property, and have money to burn, why supply the motivation to sue you by saying so? Stick to the facts about the debt and explain that times could be better. (This is not a lie, since times can always be better.) You want to make the attorney think that there is nothing to be gained from suing and it is in everyone's best interest to settle. If lawyers (or the creditor who is paying them) believe it's more cost-effective to settle, they often will; appeal to the sensible part of their nature. As always, get any settlement agreement with an attorney in writing and view any agreement that's been drafted with caution. It will surely favor the creditor; I've yet to see a settlement agreement drafted by an opposing attorney—or an opposing creditor for that matter—contain language I would ever agree to.

DEFENSES TO DEBTS

There are circumstances under which a consumer may take issue with a debt. In other words, when a debtor has legitimate claims against owing a debt, he or she can claim that all or a portion of the debt is not owed, using defenses to debts (a) as a way to strengthen negotiations prior to legal action, (b) to file suit when negotiations have failed, or (c) to countersue. Here are some examples of defenses to debts:

- Incorrect calculation of amount due, amount paid, and other assessed charges
- Refusal on the part of the creditor to live up to an oral agreement, such as one involving a repayment plan
- Seller-related claims, such as defective merchandise, unfulfilled or incomplete services, slow delivery, fraud, deception, violation

of the Truth in Lending Act, usury (interest charges exceeding the rate allowed by law), and credit discrimination[30]
• Unlawful collection practices on the part of the creditor

Consumers may raise the seller-related defenses described above even if the debt has been sold to a third party, "even as to a purchase-money loan if the seller referred the consumer to the lender or there is some other special relationship between the lender and the seller."[31] An example of a special relationship could be a home electronics company's using a third-party lender to finance the purchase of its goods (e.g., Best Buy is the seller of a product, yet a third party, Household Finance, does the financing). Of course, any lender in this scenario will deny any such claim on the part of a consumer; claiming that, for example, "A defective television is between you and Best Buy. Pay up." Yet an informed consumer can make the lender a party to any dispute over the goods or services—and would be wise to do so.

According to the NCLC, "a classic example of potential disputes is a creditor's claim for a deficiency amount after an auto repossession. The consumer could have disputes concerning the car sale, warranty repairs, credit terms, the calculation of the amount owed prior to repossession, the method of seizure, the type of notice and disposition of the collateral, and the calculation of the delinquency amount."[32]

If you feel that any of these apply to your situation, you should raise these defenses in your negotiations. If you aren't making any headway on your own, consider your legal options.

Don't Pay Debts You Don't Owe

Often consumers will pay small debts they don't owe to get collection action to stop. The problem is that such a move will still leave a bad mark for years, bringing down a score. And it further emboldens collectors, enticing them to do things to innocent people in order to get money. Never pay a debt you don't owe, no matter how small. Use available consumer-protection laws to set the record straight.

---

30. NCLC *Fair Credit Reporting* § 13.15.1 (5th ed. 2002 and 2205 Supp.).
31. See NCLC *Unfair and Deceptive Acts and Practices* § 6.6 (6th ed. 2005).
32. NCLC *Fair Credit Reporting* § 13.15.1 (5th ed. 2002 and 2004 Supp.).

WHEN COLLECTORS BREAK THE RULES

As a bill collector, I witnessed abuse of biblical proportions, and rarely did debtors ever do anything about it. Collectors will likely abuse you if you let them, so make sure that you are clear on the front end that you won't stand for any of that.

I once had a bill collector call me and abuse me at all hours in an effort to locate a neighbor debtor. That was before the age of caller ID, and the bastard wouldn't identify himself. Good thing it ended, since I was nearly forced to change my phone number. In another instance, a bill collector called me and accused me of being someone else while refusing to give out his name or company name. If I'd had an unlisted number, perhaps these things could have been avoided.

Even the ones who don't abuse you will lie about the rules. The worst abusers are the ones from collection agencies. But don't be alarmed; using validation, cease communication, recordings of phone conversations, and the application of legal remedies, you can rid yourself of them for good. Creditor collectors typically lie as well but not to the same extent. Overall, the cruelty of these unsavory characters is without equal. Even minor infractions by exemplary customers (e.g., a payment that's one month late) will often yield the most poisonous venom that can be spoken from human lips. It's all smiles until you miss a payment, regardless of the circumstance, and then it's no-holds-barred abuse.

I once missed a single payment after having a perfect record for eight years with First USA Bank (a Bank One company, subsequently purchased by Chase). The check was returned by the Post Office for failure to provide postage, which of course can happen to anyone. When I provided the returned envelope with the postmark to the creditor and explained the circumstances (it was even date-stamped with the USPS "returned for postage"), all I got was verbal abuse and indifference. Even worse, I was not even speaking with someone in the collection department of the creditor but customer service. *Customer service!* Sadly, this is the rule rather than the exception. Believe me when I tell you that even if you were to lose all your limbs serving your country, collectors would still treat you like dirt. This same bank also did some other nasty things a few years later, and I jumped all over it when it breached the FCRA, successfully suing it for money damages.

Most collectors will not heed your verbal warnings and will continue to break the rules, since (a) few people actually sue, and (b) the penalty is so small under the FDCPA that it's not enough of a deterrent. Statutory damages carry a maximum of $1,000. Actual damages are permissible and can include emotional distress, but this can be difficult to prove. Although the FDCPA doesn't have a provision for punitive damages, FCRA does for violations involving credit reporting, and a collection agency may be in breach of both Acts. If a debt collector has done something particularly malicious, often state laws can be applied that carry punitive damages. The FTC will go after collection agencies with enough complaints filed against them, which is why it's important that you report every violation of the FDCPA or any other laws to the FTC and to your state's attorney general. The FTC, for example, fined collection agency Performance Capital Management, Inc., of Irvine, California, $2 million.[33] It likewise filed suit against collection agency DC Credit Services, Inc., fining it $300,000.[34]

Also notify the debt collector in writing of the specific breach and the recourse you intend to take. Note that if you seek a legal remedy, action must be taken within one year of the violation.[35] After that, the FDCPA statute of limitations will have passed. (Though other breaches of law, such as a breach of a state UDAP, may carry longer statutes of limitations. Check your state laws.)

---

33. Performance Capital Management, Inc., 2:01cv1047 (C.D. Cal. 2000) providing inaccurate delinquency dates, failure to properly investigate disputes, failure to report accounts as "disputed" to consumer reporting agencies; $2 million civil penalty. Prepared statement of Howard Beales, director of the Bureau of Consumer Protection, FTC, to the Senate Committee on Banking, Housing, and Urban Affairs (May 15, 2003).

34. DC Credit Services, Inc., No. 02-5115 (C.D. Cal. 2002) furnishing information to a consumer reporting agency knowing or consciously avoiding knowing that the information is inaccurate, failure to notify consumer reporting agencies when previously reported information is found to be inaccurate and to provide corrections, failure to provide accurate delinquency dates, failure to report accounts as "disputed" to consumer reporting agencies; $300,000 civil penalty. Prepared statement of Howard Beales, director of the Bureau of Consumer Protection, FTC, to the Senate Committee on Banking, Housing, and Urban Affairs (May 15, 2003).

35. 15 U.S.C. § 1692k(d).

As discussed at the beginning of this chapter, collectors will often make threats in order to get a debtor to pay, which violates the FDCPA. A common tactic is to threaten to report the debt to a credit reporting agency. When such a threat is made, I encourage debtors to immediately pull their credit reports for the record. If a debtor has still not paid after 60 days, he or she should pull another credit report. If the collector (or collection attorney) has not followed through with the threat, he or she has probably violated the FDCPA.[36] Furthermore, if during the 30-day validation period a debt collector threatens to furnish adverse information to a credit reporting agency, it is probably a violation if the threat is done strongly enough to suggest the debtor's validation request would not be honored.[37]

Use any violations of law as a way to gain leverage in your negotiations. Collectors who know they're in breach often won't believe a lawsuit is in the offing, yet they aren't certain that you won't follow though, and you can use this. Inform them you'll notify the FTC and the attorney general of any breaches; that will give them a clue that you understand your rights and know who can enforce them. If the collector is an attorney, it would also be wise to notify the state bar, since an egregious breach or a pattern of misconduct can get him or her disbarred.

If a collector has broken any laws with me, then I'll consider opening the negotiations with a lawsuit. That way there can be no doubt as to my sincerity and where the lines are drawn. This is extremely useful in negotiating a more favorable settlement. (Under certain conditions, a collector can't countersue for money owed; see Chapter 14.)

Remember, although the FDCPA only applies to certain types of collectors and debts, there may be other legal remedies available. (See Chapter 14.)

---

36. 15 U.S.C. § 1692. See also NCLC *Fair Debt Collection* § 5.5.8.1 (5th ed. 2004 and 2005 Supp.).
37. See *Swanson v. Southern Oregon Credit Serv.*, 869 F.2d 1222 (9th Cir. 1998); *Wells v. Thomas McDonough*, 1999 U.S. Dist. LEXIS 15535 (N.D. Ill. Sept. 29, 1999); *Creighton v. Emporia Credit Serv., Inc.*, 981 F. Supp. 411 (E.D. Va. 1997); See NCLC *Fair Debt Collection* § 5.7.2.7.4 (5th ed. 2004 and 2005 Supp.).

USING RESTRICTIVELY ENDORSED CHECKS

There are books that tout using restrictively endorsed checks as a way to get out of paying credit card bills. The recommended tactic goes like this: Send a letter to the creditor that spells out the terms of your proposed settlement, along with a check. On the back of the check, be sure to include the phrase, "This constitutes payment in full for . . . [whatever the goods/services are] due to [our dispute over] . . ." In the memo block on the front of the check, write: "Restrictively Endorsed." The amount of the check can be for whatever you feel is reasonable. If the creditor cashes the check, send the bureaus a copy of the letter you sent the creditor along with a copy of the check (once it has cleared your bank).

The book in which I read about this technique says that bureaus are then required by law to remove the derogatory item from your report, since the check represents a contract between two parties. Well, I tried this technique a few years back—in my more gullible days—and the bureaus would not remove the item. In addition, just to be sure, I had my lawyer send them a demand letter, which did not work either.

Now I fully understand that bureaus don't have to honor a contract between a creditor and a consumer. All they're required to do under the FCRA is notify the furnisher of the consumer dispute and request verification of the entry. If it isn't verified (or the reinvestigation cannot be performed within the time allowable by law, usually 30 days), then it must be deleted. As such, any dispute over restrictively endorsed checks would have to be taken up with the party that cashed the check. In the case of a creditor-furnisher, legal action would most likely be the only recourse when such an agreement is not honored. And this isn't the only problem: laws concerning such a transaction are very tricky. An entire book could be written on the complexities of restrictively endorsed checks and the numerous conflicting state laws that govern them.

In my research to get to the heart of matter, I discovered that it boils down to "accord and satisfaction." That is, when you spell out the terms of your proposed settlement in your written correspondence and on the back of the check, you effectively presented the other party with an accord.

Satisfaction of the accord occurs when the other party cashes the check. However, mitigating factors come into play from a legal standpoint. First of all, you already have a contract with the creditor to pay the balance as agreed in your original terms and conditions. Second, by rule, restrictively endorsed checks are only applicable if there's a bona fide dispute already in place over the value/price of the goods or services.

But what's a bona fide dispute? It's where the parties disagree on some issue in the contract, and thus the amount of consideration (dollars/services/goods) given by each side is called into question. Of course, the parties can have a dispute that isn't in writing, but those in writing give you more support for a legal case, which is why you should always put your disputes in writing and request a response.

To what extent is a dispute applicable to a dollar figure that is unambiguous? You borrowed a certain amount by use of the credit card, and so the value is pretty much without question. There's another rule called a "legal duty rule," which means that you have an obligation to perform on the contract. There's always a possibility that the other party breached the contract, but how is this applicable to credit cards? In some rare, odd cases it could happen, but in the normal course of credit card business it's extremely unlikely. What if everyone did this with his or her credit card payments? If it held up in court, then everyone would be doing it, and creditors wouldn't get paid.

There are other factors. For instance, every state has its own laws regarding restrictively endorsed checks. And some, like those in California, contradict each other, managing to confound judges on which statute rules. An analysis from *Loyola of Los Angeles Law Review* concluded the following with regard to California Civil Code 1526 saying one thing and then California Commercial Code 1331 saying something completely different:[38]

> In other words, it allows the creditor to accept the benefit while rejecting the condition. Until Civil Code section 1526 is repealed, our advice to debtors is that they cannot be certain that the issuance of a payment in full check to a creditor—and the

---

38. *Loyola of Los Angeles Law Review*, Vol. 33:1.

creditor's subsequent acceptance of that check—will render an effective accord and satisfaction, thus relinquishing the balance of the claim. Therefore, in order for a debtor to protect itself, the debtor should demand a formal release of the claim from the creditor in exchange for the debtor's partial payment.

Yet many other states have specific and nonconflicting laws on this issue. It's generally accepted that a bona fide dispute must be in play, that the terms must be spelled out conspicuously, and that "payment in full" or similar language must be used. It's also widely accepted that any amount must be a good-faith amount and that the addressee cannot be a PO Box or a third party.

Another problem is third-party rules about the acceptance of restrictively endorsed checks, which can also vary by state. What if the debt was in the hands of a collection agency? What if the consumer didn't actually own the debt? Could the collector then agree to terms on behalf of the creditor, terms the creditor did not actually agree to abide by? This is all very troublesome.

Surely the creditor could sue even if the check was "validly" restrictively endorsed (according to a state's rules), but the debtor in such a case should be able to file a motion to dismiss (attaching a copy of the canceled check) and get the suit squashed if the check was indeed valid. It's been my experience that such checks are not to be used with large creditors, since they'll likely continue to pursue collection regardless of whether such a check was valid or not.

However, if the creditor (or the collection agency that represents it) continues collection activity even after cashing a restrictively endorsed check (assuming it is validly employed, in accordance with state laws), then it would seem the debtor could get monetary damages for unlawful damage to his or her credit report. But again, in every state I've looked at, a "bona fide dispute" has to be in play, as well as other unique factors that relate to each state's laws.

Where credit cards are concerned, this technique is very problematic, especially considering that debts can be negotiated down and bad credit removed anyway. And while some "credit repair experts" claim that restrictively endorsed checks may be a way around debt collection reset in some circumstances, it's plain that using them for that purpose is fraught with peril, and the risk is needless given the many terrific alternatives.

Apply with Caution

Assuming it is executed properly and valid by a state's laws, a restrictively endorsed check can be employed in some situations with a likelihood of good results.

In the case of bodywork performed on a car, for example, the value of the work relative to the dollar amount charged might be called into question, and this is where a bona fide dispute is far more palpable. Was the work actually completed? Did the work performed actually cause a reduction in value of the car? Did the car sit in the shop for an unreasonable period? Did the other party breach the contract in some way? Complicating things even further, in some states, such as Ohio, there's a rule called "substantial performance," where if a contractor's performance departs from the contract in only minor respects, then the contractor is still entitled to get paid.

If you purchased a dealer-financed auto and then the auto failed to perform within reasonable expectations, compounded by the dealer's refusal to properly repair it, you may have a case of questionable value with the dealer-creditor. And remember seller-related defenses? Even if the auto was financed by a third party that had a special relationship with the dealer (e.g., one the dealer steered you to), the lender is still liable for the defective automobile. Could you send a valid restrictively endorsed check to the lender? Probably. But it's likely that the lender would cash it and continue to bill you unless you were to take legal action against it.

Taking another scenario, let's say you send the restrictively endorsed check to the party with whom you have a contract dispute and the other party cashes it yet still continues taking collection action and reporting it to the credit bureaus. In a case where you have good grounds for your bona fide dispute and can substantiate it, the restrictively endorsed check may prove somewhat useful.

If you can demonstrate a bona fide contract dispute over anything that involves goods or services, such as auto repair, contract work, medical bills, or faulty goods, and the other party has actually cashed your restrictively endorsed check, you've just added weight to any legal case that may develop (assuming you've properly employed such a check under the law). In fact, with the canceled check in hand you could file suit requesting a declaratory judgment (see Chapter 14) and provide all of the supporting evidence, including the original contract, receipts for any payments you've made, correspondence showing a bona fide dispute, and a copy of the canceled check. This way, you've either pre-empted collection action or stopped it, and possibly prevented a lawsuit from showing up on your credit report. (Your filing first precludes the suit from showing up, even if the other party countersues.)

Just remember, as I stated earlier, this is a very tricky business and must be employed in accordance with state laws. Ohio, for example, requires that the amount of the check be "reasonable" for the goods or services provided. If the creditor that cashed the check deemed the amount unreasonable, then it may still have a claim. (For a real-world example of a restrictively endorsed check, see Chapter 11.)

It's clear that using restrictively endorsed checks after collection action has occurred is probably not a good idea. Yet in my opinion, the safest and most effective way to employ such a check is when a new dispute exists with another party over the goods or services rendered and it is being used in an effort to prevent collection activity or legal action in the first place. When disputes first occur, the receiver of the check is not likely to be an attorney or collection agency and won't have the wherewithal to question the legalities of such a check and will likely simply accept it at face value. Furthermore, proper employment early on can also prevent adverse information from showing up on your credit report. This is discussed more fully in Chapter 11.

THE DUSTY PILE:
COLLECTION STATUTES AND RENEWED PURSUIT

Bill collectors have to eat. As such, they'll go after debts that they feel have a high probability of collection. Collectors are even issued accounts based on how much favor they have with the powers that be. As a young collector, I saw how politics played a role in the quality of accounts given to a particular employee. Quality accounts are ones that have a high chance of collection, such as those acquired recently. (I always got the crappy accounts; don't know what that says about me.)

Anyway, after about three to six months of trying to collect, collectors begin to get discouraged, and such accounts go into a dusty pile—that is, of course, until they are sold off and someone wants to try again fresh, or some bonehead debtor calls and wants to talk about it. Get my drift?

Renewed interest could even cause fresh skip tracing and legal activity, so it's important to weigh your options carefully when you consider contacting collectors about old debts. Even challenging such an entry with a bureau could cause renewed pursuit, since the bureaus will contact the collector in an attempt to verify the data as accurate. Of course, you have to weigh this against other factors, such as collection statutes. For example, delinquent credit card debt can be collected in California for four years from the date of delinquency. If this time has passed, then a furnisher is less likely to respond to a bureau's attempt to verify a debt's accuracy. (This assumes that the contract was signed in California and you reside there.) Collectors have thousands of accounts, and those known to be outside of the debt collection statutes are often filtered out of the system by those running legitimate, high-volume operations, which could work to your advantage.

If you do live in a state that has a reset provision (where a debt collection statute can be reset with payment) and you're unsure about an account belonging to you (and see a need to straighten out any potential file merger or identity theft mistake on your report), it's best to perform a credit bureau dispute instead of contacting the furnisher. If the bureau verifies it as accurate, then of course it may still not be yours (such as in the case of identity theft). If you're still unsure, then and only then should you contact the furnisher in an effort to discover the source of entry; do so only in writing, denying owing the debt and requesting proof that you owe it.

TAX CONSEQUENCES OF SETTLEMENTS AND CHARGE-OFFS

Let's face it—most great things come with a downside. Many people, even collectors, fail to realize this, but when a bank settles with a debtor or does a charge-off, the information is sent to the IRS via a Form 1099 for the year in which it occurred. Therefore, whatever amount you don't pay the creditor will be treated as income. Thus, you will be taxed at whatever your rate was for that year. For example, if you make $25,000 at your job and have a standard deduction of $4,550, then you normally end up being taxed on $20,450. However, if you owed a bank or banks a total of $20,000 and only paid them $5,000, then your taxable income goes up to $35,450 ($20,450 plus the $15,000 you didn't pay).

What does this mean exactly? Well, normally you would pay $3,071 in total tax, but since your taxable income went up by $15,000, you will owe $6,374.[39] The difference is $3,303, and this is the amount the IRS is going to want from you when it discovers the charge-off. It often takes three years before things catch up to the IRS, but it could be sooner. If you get a 1099 from a bank you settled with, be sure to report the income. If it was for a previous year, simply file a form 1040X (amended return) and, if necessary, contact the IRS to schedule payment arrangements.

So what's the net difference of your settlement in this example? The bank forgave $15,000, but the IRS wants $3,303. Still not a bad deal, but keep in mind that there will be state taxes as well.

Still another consideration may be the way a settlement contract is worded. For example, many people who have filed bankruptcy find that a creditor will continue to report a balance and that an account is in arrears. When filing suit against a creditor for such erroneous reporting, be aware that the creditor may indicate in any settlement agreement something like ". . . forgives the balance of $13,436 in exchange for dismissal of the suit . . ." The creditor uses this tactic to screw you—i.e., he sends you a 1099 at the end of the year so you'll have to pay taxes on that amount. You have to watch everything you do. (For more on settlement agreements, see Chapter 13.)

---

39. This author is neither an attorney nor an accountant.

CHAPTER

8

GAME PLANNING

Since each situation is unique and there is no one-size-fits-all game plan, you must begin by performing both a situational and a collective assessment of your circumstances and then overlaying the results onto a workable plan.

This is even more critical when you are knee-deep in debt with several creditors and/or have lots of unpaid adverse entries on your credit report. The collective assessment section of this chapter will address that scenario in depth. In cases where you don't owe money or have only a couple of debts and aren't in financial trouble, prioritizing is often quite simple. Thus, those who are swimming in debt and/or have lots of unpaid adverse entries will likely get the most out of this section.

PERFORM A SITUATIONAL ASSESSMENT

The contents of a credit report only tell one aspect of the whole story. Although it's an aspect that matters a great deal (after all, it's the mechanism by which you're being denied credit), there are many other real-world factors that will play into it, affecting the overall plan of attack.

Since there are many different scenarios around which negative credit can exist, you must ask yourself the following questions:

- When will the entry become obsolete (meet the credit reporting statute of limitations and fall off your credit report)?
- How long does your state permit collection of debts by lawsuit?
- What are your state's laws concerning statute of limitations reset for debt collection (i.e., when payment restarts the period within which a collector can collect a debt using a lawsuit)?
- Is legal action of some kind expected, or has it occurred? Has it been threatened?
- Does your state permit lawsuits by collection agencies?
- Is the debt secured or unsecured?
- How long ago were you late?
- How much do you owe?
- What kind of creditor is involved—a bank . . . a doctor?
- When was the last time you made a payment?
- How often were you late? (What's the severity of the bad mark?)
- Is the account open or closed?
- Is your debt folder sitting in a collector's dusty pile?
- Do you have wages that can be garnished or property that can be seized?
- Do you have bank accounts that can be tapped? Can they be found?
- If you're married, do you have community property that can be seized? Does your state permit that?
- How much money do you (or will you) have?
- Are you hard to find? Can you be served (summoned) by the court?
- What are your state's laws concerning property liens? Are forced sales permitted (i.e., can the lien holder force the sale of property)?
- What measures can you take (e.g., avoiding a summons, hiding assets) to create barriers for the collector?
- What are the creditors willing to do?

- Is adverse checking account reporting keeping you from having a checking account?
- What are the tax ramifications of any settlements?
- Has a debt collector, bureau, or furnisher broken any laws?

You must answer each of these questions in order to determine the proper course of action. Look at each adverse item and take notes, answering all the above questions for each item. Once you have all the answers, you can begin to come up with the best remedy.

Answers to some of the above questions will emerge as more important than others based on your particular circumstances. For example, from the standpoint of statute of limitations for debt collections and credit reporting, the age of a debt is often paramount, since those debts falling outside the scope of both reporting and lawsuit collection (or nearing the statutes of limitation) will surely influence your strategy. Such an entry may be resolved by using a simple credit bureau dispute, or ignored entirely under certain circumstances. Yet, an entry that involves a pending lawsuit will take precedence over all others. Even a collector's breaking of the law can cause a shift in priorities if such an occurrence is nearing its statute of limitations (the FDCPA requires that a lawsuit be filed within one year of a breach). Weigh these types of considerations when answering the questions, bearing in mind that the order in which the questions are posed here is not relevant; what's important is determining for yourself what the larger issues are in your case.

I advise that you first look at the age of the debt and consider its debt collection and reporting statutes of limitations. A debt that is old and will fall off your credit report relatively soon (or soon enough for your needs) is not worth wasting your time on; put it at the bottom of your priority list unless legal action has already commenced on it. However, as explained, just because a debt will fall off a credit report after seven years doesn't mean it isn't collectible by lawsuit, and vice versa. For example, in Ohio a collector can collect by lawsuit on a delinquent credit card account for 15 years but can only furnish information to a credit reporting agency for seven years plus 180 days from the time the account went delinquent (a bureau can only retain the information for seven years plus 180 days, and then it is obsolete and must be deleted). By contrast, a collector in Oregon can only collect by lawsuit on a delinquent credit card account for four years yet can furnish the delinquency information the bureaus for seven years plus 180 days.

Once you have determined that it's worthwhile to pursue a debt based on the statutes of limitations involved, ask yourself whether the debt is secured or unsecured. (Again, secured debt requires you to put up collateral for the money, such as a car or home. Unsecured debt is backed up only by your promise to pay and doesn't require any collateral.) Why is this important in removing negative credit? With unsecured debt, such as credit card balances, you are in a much better position to negotiate, since the creditor has little or no power, other than the ability to ruin your credit and/or obtain a judgment. Ruining your credit doesn't get creditors their money back, nor does obtaining a judgment guarantee that they will get paid.

Are the lawyers coming? If you expect legal action of some kind, you must consider whether you can be served (for unsecured debt). If a judgment is already in place against you, you need to determine what assets can be taken according to your state laws. As explained in Chapter 6, there must be assets to take (e.g., a house, car, bank account) or wages to garnish. There's no way to know what a collector will or won't do, but collectors generally won't start looking for assets unless a debt is $4,500 or more. However, many will sue if the debtor has a job, no matter what the amount owed.

Another important consideration is the threat of legal action against you. Collectors will almost always threaten it, and debtors with property are often scared into paying and agreeing to bad terms. Remember that most threats of legal action, even if implied, are against the law (see Chapter 7). And even if legal action commences, you can still strike a good deal! My rule is this: If legal action hasn't commenced on unsecured debt, then I'm under no pressure. And if it has commenced, then I still usually have 30 days in which to file an answer, which gives me roughly three weeks to negotiate a settlement before retaining an attorney if I feel I need one. Of course, you must decide for yourself how to handle legal matters. But always ask, does the creditor know where you are; that is, can you be served? As you know, for unsecured debt, hiding will prevent a judgment from ever being rendered.

Tip: Automobiles can be repossessed for nonpayment of an auto loan. Many consumers are duped into thinking that if they give the car back voluntarily then it's paid off. Not so. The car will be sold at auction and the amount applied to your loan, and then you will owe the repossession fee, the difference between what you owe and what the car sold for, plus late fees and interest. This will still show as a repossession on your credit report as well. If this hasn't yet happened, you can always contact the creditor/agency and state that you have financial problems but do intend to pay. Ask for an extension or new terms. Was the auto unreliable? If so, there may be other debtor defenses under the law, as explained in Chapter 7.

To whom do you owe money? This affects your chances of removal. If the creditor is an individual, such as a doctor, then it's often easier to negotiate with him or her than with a large bank. With large banks, you often have to make your way through an array of cronies before you can even speak with a decision-maker. And even they have specific guidelines and must answer to others. Doctors, on the other hand, are usually easy to contact and easy to negotiate with. This is because they don't have large collection divisions and will simply refer debts that are more than 90 days late to a collection agency (giving up half of the debt owed in exchange). Unlike large creditors with the resources to chase endlessly, most doctors just want to get whatever payment they can and be done with it. And if you had a medical issue, you can use that as leverage, appealing to the creditor's emotions.[1] Many health or medical-related creditors will be very flexible, as will those to whom you owe debts that are likewise unsecured. If it's a department store, you're likely to encounter a certain amount of flexibility, since the store wants your business and the debt is unsecured. If

---

1. It's estimated that 50 percent of collection accounts are for unpaid medical bills. Evan Hendricks, *Credit Scores & Credit Reports.*

it's a credit card company, chances are good that you can negotiate a settlement and get the item removed. Secured debt is often another story. If you owe on an auto loan, the creditor can always repossess the car if it hasn't already. Likewise, it can be difficult to negotiate with a mortgage holder, since the bank can simply take your house for non-payment through foreclosure (though enticing the bank with payment can give you some leverage). Bear in mind that all creditors are likely to deal if there is something in it for them.

How often were you late? Was it patterned lateness or scattered? If patterned (adjacent in time), then your chances are better, since you can easily demonstrate that the lateness occurred during a particular rough period (e.g., you lost your job or got a divorce). If scattered, then it may appear to the creditor that you are a little flaky or unreliable in general. Creditors are always assessing you, sizing you up: Can you be trusted? Can they make money from you in the future? Is the account still open? If so, the creditor is making money off you, likely charging exorbitant interest rates, and will want to continue to do so.

When pressured, the creditor will often do what it takes to keep you as a customer because you are profitable. Pressure can take many forms, such as threatening to close the account and find another creditor. Threatening not to pay can sometimes gain you leverage, but refusing to pay (due to lack of funds is the best reason) is likely to have more success. Although this may seem like a strong-arm tactic and carries with it the risk of additional adverse reporting—and perhaps collection action—it usually causes an intransigent creditor to become more agreeable. (It should be noted here that this is exactly what debt settlement companies do to get creditors to capitulate. They instruct the debtor not to pay, until finally the creditor gives in to their demands. This has been very lucrative for debt settlement companies, which take a slice of whatever discount is negotiated on the debt.)

How long ago were you late? If it's been more than two years, your chances of removal are better. In the case of more recent lateness, it's a little bit harder. If the debt is older, you can use that in your negotiations (so and so happened during that time . . . blah, blah, blah).

Do you lack a checking account because of bounced checks or unpaid overdrafts? If so, you need to place the offending account near the top of your priority list, since reputable lenders will most often deny credit to those without a checking account. (For more information on repairing such an account, use the checking account repair techniques spelled out in Chapter 10.)

Tip: The credit report will indicate whether the lender or the consumer closed an account, and it looks better if you closed it. If you know you are going to become late (and stay late and default) on an open account, then close it. Revolving accounts can be closed even if there's an outstanding balance. Close accounts in writing only, using certified mail with a request for return receipt. American Express is notorious for reporting that it closed an account even when it was the consumer who did it. I sued it for this very thing, causing the entire tradeline to be deleted (see Chapters 14 and 15).

You must ask all these questions and more, and prioritize accordingly. There are no hard-and-fast rules for prioritizing; the weight given any single adverse entry will shift according to individual circumstances. Again, you must look at the larger questions as they relate to your specific situation in order to determine the best course of action. Once you've fully examined each adverse entry in terms of the relevant questions, the order of priority will jump right out at you, and your situational assessment will be complete.

PERFORM A COLLECTIVE ASSESSMENT

From what you've read—and hopefully done—so far, you can take all that you know about your report and your situation and make some educated decisions about individual accounts. Yet in the final analysis, it also pays to look at your situation from a holistic perspective. In a case where you owe money to many different creditors, you must determine these two things: Do you have the money to settle with all of them? If so, will *all* of those creditors remove the adverse history? If not, what are acceptable terms when taken on the whole? This is where a collective assessment comes in.

Of course, the second question cannot be answered until you've spoken with all your creditors. Go fishing first; see what they will agree to by using the art of negotiation and the techniques for repairing accurate adverse credit that are spelled out in the next chapter. This exploratory work will enable you to discover what they are all willing to do, making it far easier to decide whom to pay how much—or whether to pay any of them at all. If your situation is such that five of seven creditors agree to your terms, while the other two are on the brink of obtaining a judgment, perhaps it's better not to pay any of them. Maybe it's better to pay them only if you can make the *entire plan* work to your satisfaction.

As stated previously, states differ. In Oregon, for example, judgments remain on your credit report for 10 years, and if the attorney for the creditor takes the time, a 10-year renewal is an option, making it 20. In Ohio a judgment stays on your report for five years, renewable indefinitely. Of course, there are paid and unpaid judgments, paid ones having a less severe effect on a score and being less worrisome to an underwriter. They are severe nonetheless. Unsatisfied charge-offs (ones that you still owe money on) are also quite severe. If your credit is picture-perfect except for a combination of two judgments or unsatisfied charge-offs, you will likely have significant trouble obtaining any credit at all.

If you cannot get all your creditors to agree to terms that are favorable, that doesn't necessarily mean you shouldn't pay any of them. It just means that you must look at your particular circumstances and carefully decide. If you find that "hold-outs" to your proposals are making the entire plan unworkable, think carefully before you pay any of the debts. Some scenarios are so extreme that it doesn't make sense to pay any of your creditors. These are situations where the total debt is so high and the number of unyielding creditors so great that settling with a few won't help at all. In these rare circumstances, bankruptcy is certainly an option (see Chapter 12).

You may find yourself in a situation where you owe far more than you have—for example, you owe $250,000 but can only come up with $40,000 after liquidating assets. Are there many creditors? Have any of them filed suit yet? How long can you stay afloat with a lot of debt and an income stream that doesn't meet the demand or a job with questionable future stability? Perhaps a business failure has hurt you. All these issues and more can make your financial situation untenable, and a single creditor that fails to meet your repair framework may throw the whole thing into doubt.

Usually, unless all the creditors agree to favorable terms (i.e., to reduce not the monthly payment but the total amounts owed *and* remove the bad credit), then bankruptcy could be the better option. Why? Look at it this way: if you have to liquidate all your assets to pay off creditors, only to end up with "paid collection account" reported on some or all your accounts, then how is this better than a bankruptcy? Yes, if you do the bankruptcy wrong, then it might be better than bankruptcy, but if you do it right—by planning ahead and putting your money into assets that are immune to seizure (this differs from state to state), you could come out ahead. Of course, bankruptcy can brutalize a credit score and impinge your ability to get credit in the near term, whereas a paid judgment that's old won't have nearly the same impact.

Always look into the future. In 24 months, what will the situation be, based on the actions you take today? Often the choice is (bad credit + no money) vs. (bad credit + money). Which would you rather have? On the other hand, how will your future credit opportunities be impinged? Though it's more difficult, even bankruptcies can sometimes be removed from credit reports, so you may be able to have your cake and eat it too. Yes, bankruptcies can often be deleted (see Chapter 10); married couples can often benefit from a Chapter 13 bankruptcy (see Chapter 12).

See what creditors see, and think about how they'll view your *future* report. Another example of an unworkable credit restoration plan is one that would leave you with an unpaid judgment(s) on your report or a bad debt(s) that is unsatisfied (unpaid). Think about it: if you were a potential lender, would you rather lend to someone with a bankruptcy that is two years old or someone with one or two unsatisfied judgments that are seven years old? Lenders simply won't lend to you until you have paid your existing debts, even if you are looking for secured money for a house or car. Those unpaid bills haunt you for seven years (longer in some cases, such as some student loans and unpaid tax liens), and the unpaid judgments will likely haunt you for many more. Although a bankruptcy will haunt you for 10, you may get to keep some money/assets when you file, and you can obtain conventional financing to buy a house or anything else after two years (if you've reestablished good credit in accordance with Chapter 3). Choose the lesser of the evils relevant to your particular situation so that you can get on with your life.

Can you buy time? Usually only the previous 180 days of your financial activity must be disclosed to the court in a bankruptcy petition, so buying time may enable you to insulate some assets.

Moving to another state may help, though not as much as before. For example, prior to the Bankruptcy Reform Bill of 2005, moving to a "homestead" state such as Florida (where a debtor's home is exempt from liability, preventing creditors from obtaining satisfaction on the home) before declaring bankruptcy could enable you to keep your home, no matter what the equity or the value. (This is why O.J. Simpson moved to Florida when the families of Nicole Brown Simpson and Ronald Goldman went after him in a civil suit.) But now, the maximum exemption is $150,000—no matter what state you're in. This is still a powerful method of asset protection, since it enables someone with cash to protect it from creditors, keeping money—in the form of home equity—even in the event of bankruptcy. But another change in the law is the requirement that the home must have been purchased three years and four months prior to filing bankruptcy. Since a bankruptcy must be filed in the state where the filer spent the bulk of the previous six months, people seeking the homestead exemption used to move to a homestead state, buy a home, and then file bankruptcy six months later. The "three years and four months" provision was included in the Bankruptcy Reform Bill in order to close this loophole.

Most states have a relatively low home exemption for bankruptcy filers, capping the equity at an average of $25,000. Bankruptcy filers can therefore keep their homes if they have equity that does not exceed this amount. With a $150,000 cap in Florida, Texas, Iowa, Kansas, and South Dakota, residents of those states who file bankruptcy will still have an attractive home exemption. Texas also has a nice provision for automobiles, allowing a $30,000 exemption (i.e., someone with up to $30,000 in equity can keep it if he or she files bankruptcy).[2]

Other ways that buying time can help include concluding a pending divorce beforehand while segregating property/debts, and possibly even creating a business (corporation) to insulate some things. Incidentally, a business entity such as a corporation or limited liability company is a great way to insulate from disasters anyway, by creating an umbrella that keeps either you or your business from getting "wet."[3]

This type of thing is very tricky, and a good attorney is best suited to explain your options. He or she can help you maneuver your way into keeping some or all of what you own by simply liquidating your assets before you file and moving the cash into exempt positions. In some cases, IRAs, real estate, and other types of assets have high dollar exemptions in certain states, allowing bankruptcy filers to keep a substantial part of that wealth. Always talk to an attorney in your state before you do anything, but keep in mind attorneys make money if you file bankruptcy—a conflict of interest.[4]

Don't be disheartened by my references to bankruptcy; your chances for credit removal and debt reduction are good in nearly all cases, and very few people will ever have to take that route. In fact, many people believe that bankruptcy is their only option, yet in most cases it's not a viable option at all—especially since the Bankruptcy Reform Bill took effect. Since you have several courses of action in virtually every scenario, if one thing doesn't work, you will be able to try another. This puts you in a good position for getting the results you want.

---

2. If a petitioner is to keep his or her home or auto, the asset must be able to withstand a claim by any lien holder. Check your state laws.

3. "The use of a corporation does not protect professionals from liability for their own professional errors and omissions or for those under their direct supervision. The same is true for closely-held business owners." *Financial Planning Management*, June 1999.

4. NACA attorneys are best; see Chapter 14. The state in which you file will be the state where you spent the majority of the previous 180 days prior to the filing date. There are also disclosure laws regarding the sale of assets prior to filing, usually six months prior.

DEVELOP A PLAN FOR DEBT REDUCTION
AND CREDIT RESTORATION

When there are numerous creditors and limited funds, you have to come up with the best scenario that fits your situation. For debt reduction and credit restoration, Table 7 (pages 214–215) contains general rules about what creditors will agree to do when a debtor is late.

Here are some additional things to keep in mind:

- A close inspection of the table will reveal that creditors are looking to collect half of what is owed. Anything paid above and beyond that will significantly strengthen the chances for bad credit removal.
- Since creditors can get roughly 25 cents on the dollar from a charge-off by getting a tax credit, they won't likely ever go below 25 cents.[5]
- Since state laws vary as to what creditors can do with judgments and liens, this can change the equation and will affect a creditor's decision making. You can do better or worse depending on these factors.
- Most debtors owe a lot of money after repossession in order to make up any deficit from the auction sale, plus the added cost of the repossession. For example, an auto worth $12,000 will be sold at auction for $9,000. The repossession will add at least another $1,000, plus interest and late fees, so if you originally owed $12,000, then the total bill deficit would likely exceed $4,000.
- Once a home is taken back and sold at auction, the debtor will be required to make up any deficit. Some states have additional statutes of limitations concerning the collection of this deficit. Although the debt collection statute of limitations on written

---

5. Tax-exempt credit unions do not get a tax credit for charge-offs and similar losses. As such, they're usually the most flexible. Creditors that have already charged off (received the tax deduction) will take less over time. There may be other exceptions, of course.

contracts for Ohio is 15 years, for example, there's another Ohio statute that prohibits the collection of any foreclosure deficit after two years (a Depression-era law). In these types of shortened debt collection statutes, creditors will take as little as 10 cents on the dollar or 45 cents with bad credit removal.

- If the collector/creditor has breached any law, terms can be more favorable. Use such a breach as leverage in negotiating a settlement. This can be any breach, including violations of state law, the FCRA, FCBA, FDCPA, and UDAP (see Chapter 14).

- Collectors are more flexible as time passes, particularly as debt collection nears its statute of limitations. For anything older than two years from delinquency, you should find the creditor very agreeable.

- The lowest ranges are often obtainable for (a) medical bills, (b) credit card debt approaching charge-off and after charge-off, (c) debts nearing the statute of limitations for collection, (d) debts owed to tax-exempt credit unions, and (e) when payoff of the agreed-upon amount is performed within 30 days.

- Some creditors will permit a lower payoff on real estate upon a bona fide sale to a third party. This is known as a "short sale." If the debtor can find a buyer (with third-party financing) before foreclosure action, then creditors have been known to reduce a debt by 10 percent or so. If the property goes through foreclosure and fails to sell at the sheriff's auction, then a creditor will take even less, often agreeing to a 20 percent or greater reduction. Creditors are very unlikely to remove any derogatory credit reference in the event of a short sale, however. You can always ask.

- Debts that are old or charged off are often sold to third parties (mostly collection agencies) as part of a portfolio (with thousands of other accounts) for 10 cents on the dollar. Moreover, the buyers of such debts cannot get a tax deduction (write-off) as the original creditor can. As such, these debts can often be bargained at the lowest ranges.[6]

---

6. As explained in Chapter 7, once a debt is sold, the consumer often has to contend with the reporting by multiple sources, with no leverage over the original creditor.

CREDITOR'S GENERAL FLEXIBILITY (DEBTOR IS 90+ DAYS LATE)[1]	
UNSECURED DEBT—Debtor Disabled or Unemployed, No Real Property	
Low	• .25 (N) (N = Creditor will not remove adverse.) • .25 (R) (R = Creditor will remove adverse.)
Average	• .45 (N) • .70 (R)
UNSECURED DEBT UNDER $1,000—Debtor Owns Property	
Low	• .25 (N) • .45 (R)
Average	• .50 (N) • .70 (R)
UNSECURED DEBT OVER $1,000—Debtor Owns Property	
Low	• .35 (N) • .60 (R)
Average	• .50 (N) • .70 (R)
UNSECURED DEBT OVER $4,500—Debtor Owns Property	
Low	• .45 (N) • .60 (R)
Average	• .50 (N) • .70 (R)

SECURED DEBT—Autos[2]
Creditors will not take less than what is owed but may offer new terms. They will frequently remove bad credit in exchange for full payment if a debtor is 60 days late or more. Usually can be performed only once.

REPOSSESSED AUTOS
Refer to the unsecured debt above.

SECURED DEBT—Real Estate
Creditors will usually not accept anything short of full payment but will often remove the bad credit in exchange for bringing a debt current if a debtor is late by 60 days or more. Many prefer this over foreclosure. Usually can only be performed once. (An exception is a short sale, explained on page 213.)

AFTER FORECLOSURE
Refer to the unsecured debt above.

JUDGMENTS
Judgment creditors will almost always agree to set aside a judgment when payment is made in full. Many will also set aside for less, depending on the particular issues surrounding how it was obtained in the first place.

NOTES
1. Amounts shown are in cents on the dollar, or percentage of what a creditor will accept (e.g., a debtor that is disabled with a $3,000 debt can expect to pay 70 cents for every dollar owed, $2,100 on average, which includes bad credit removal).
2. Any auto lender will have the title and can repossess without serving court papers.

Table 7.

Table 7 contains general guidelines and is not to be construed as gospel. There's no way to predict what a creditor will or won't do.

So the next question is, when will a creditor generally agree to reduce a person's debt and remove derogatory entries from a credit report? I've found that creditors won't agree to do anything unless people are late—usually 60 days. When a debt is approaching 90 days and beyond, they become even more flexible.

Often, people will ask me if they should stop paying their creditors in order to gain leverage in getting their payments/balances reduced. My answer is always the same: that's your decision.

Get the Best Deal

A few years back, a good friend and his wife invited me over for a shindig with his family. His brother was there, along with his painfully pretentious wife. Anyway, my friend was very happy, beaming over his new television and taking pride in his amazing ability to strike a great bargain. His sister-in-law remarked, "I can't believe you haggled over that. I work hard so that I can pay retail for everything."

At least she's consistent.

She's as short-sighted as she is snooty, I thought. Paying retail for something on sale is just dumb. Paying a bill—especially in full—without having any bad credit removed in exchange is like paying retail for something on sale.

In addition to getting derogatory credit removed, you can always request that creditors remove inquiries as well, but don't get hung up on this. Remember to look at the whole picture. The important thing is the bad mark; everything else is secondary. Inquiries will only stay on your report for two years and affect a score very little—even less over a short time. Don't get greedy in all things, since you could lose your credibility and the whole thing will blow up in your face. After you make a deal with the creditor, you can always go back later and attempt to get the bureau to remove the inquiry, as prescribed in the section of Chapter 10 that addresses removing inquiries. Think about your options and your methods while using a methodical approach. And remember: *don't get greedy.*

Insulate Your Credit from Business Activities

Many banks offer credit cards under a business name but have the name of an employee or officer on the card. There are two types of business credit: recourse and nonrecourse. Recourse means that the signer is personally liable for the credit, and nonrecourse means that only the company is liable. Be aware that most business credit cards are recourse, which means that if a business goes under, the bank can come and collect from anyone who signed the credit card agreement.

Oddly though, few banks will report business credit card late payments to the signer's personal credit report, with the exception of American Express. However, bear in mind that if an account is purchased by an aggressive creditor who's in the business of buying bad notes at pennies on the dollar (in the hopes of turning a profit by collecting debts that others failed to collect) or turned over to a collection agency, that creditor can surely report the derogatory credit.

This is another area where timing is critical. Either work out arrangements with the creditor before things go too far or file personal bankruptcy (last resort; see Chapter 12) before the account ends up on your personal credit report. If you file bankruptcy, the account can't be sold, and collection efforts must cease. If it's not on your personal report the day you file, then it likely won't ever make it to the report—one less account to be repaired after the bankruptcy is discharged. (Business debts that a consumer is liable for can be included in personal bankruptcy.)

DEBT FUSION™

By now, you should be gaining a clearer picture of Debt Fusion™. At the beginning of the book I defined it as the fusing of credit restoration and debt reduction. That was oversimplifying it—now you can see that there's much more involved. Debt Fusion™ is taking very possible angle and going nuclear on your debt *and* your credit report. If you're excited about the possibilities now, wait until you see it work for you. When it does, log on to bestcredit.com and tell your story.

Using all the knowledge you've gathered so far, take your individual circumstance, overlay it with the possibilities, and then piece together the very best outcome. Always remember, bad credit removal is paramount in any deal in my opinion, and going for anything less in an attempt to keep money in your pocket is a *very bad idea*. It goes against the very purpose of *BestCredit*. Moreover, any adverse settlement information will be reported as a new, recent credit report entry and will hurt a score—particularly if it's being reported by an original creditor.

The only scenario where anything less than bad credit removal is acceptable is when your entire plan hinges on a single holdout, which is very unlikely, or when you just don't have the funds to make it all work at or near ideal. Having anything adverse on your credit report that's unpaid is unacceptable, even if you've deleted the bulk of adverse entries, since such a mark will usually get you denied by any reputable lender. So what's the point in paying any of them under such circumstances?

It's a personal decision, of course. Perhaps paying all but one intransigent creditor would make sense if that one holdout is nearing the statute of limitations for reporting or if the information can be deleted using a credit bureau dispute. If you feel morally obligated to pay even under such circumstances, by all means do. Most people go delinquent because they couldn't pay in the first place and then feel compelled to make good when their financial outlook improves. But carefully consider that one holdout can ruin everything by creating a situation where you've expended considerable resources to improve your credit only to find that prospective lenders will *still deny you.*

Yet even after a paid settlement has been agreed to and satisfied, keep in mind that, using a credit reporting agency dispute, you can even try for a removal of the entry *after* you've settled with the creditor. And if the creditor reports an aspect wrongly after settlement, which creditors will often do, even a declaratory judgment (nonmonetary) action is an option to remove it (see Chapter 14).

Of course, you can seek numerous variations of deals involving payment terms and debt reduction, and you can even get new payment terms that are greatly modified or extended, especially on open accounts or accounts not yet in collections. If you go for reducing the debt on a payment plan, then having the interest rate placed below 10 percent on credit cards will help as well. I would shoot for 6 percent on unsecured credit. On autos, 6 percent is also a good rate. Just ensure that in any deal this is worded as a *permanent* lowering, or a *fixed* interest rate.

Caution: If you can get a home equity loan or second mortgage, place the money in your bank account and then use the money as leverage to get bad marks removed, this is acceptable. If this isn't possible, then forgo any "debt consolidation loan," since such a loan will only be possible if the lender can pay off your existing creditors directly, which will defeat the purpose altogether; you've done nothing for overall debt reduction or credit restoration. Your lack of leverage in this scenario will make getting the bad credit removed far more difficult. With the money in the bank, you can negotiate the best terms for each individual account, getting your debt reduced and getting the bad credit removed. Once you've gotten your debt reduced on each individual account and have your credit file cleared up, then if there are remaining creditors you may opt for a debt consolidation loan if it will substantially lower your interest rate and the closing costs are nominal to zero. Further, waiting until your credit report is squeaky clean to obtain such a loan will yield the best interest rates. Now that's having your cake and eating it too!

NINE RULES TO REMEMBER

As stated at the beginning of this chapter, sometimes things can get overwhelming, especially when you have numerous creditors and entries to deal with. Therefore, I've created a list of rules that I believe provide a solid foundation for anyone performing credit restoration. Some of them you've seen already and will serve as important reminders, whereas others are new.

1. *Carefully prioritize the removal of entries and follow the fundamental guidelines.* This includes things like always removing adverse entries with unpaid balances, giving credit restoration priority over debt reduction, and always factoring in the FICO score in your decision-making.
2. *Learn and study the art of negotiation before speaking with creditors.*
3. *In all of your verbal negotiations with creditors, be nice!* It will go a long, long way. Even if you get the wrong answer, be nice. Trust me. I know what I'm talking about. I recommend a fabulous book, which has sold millions of copies: *How to Win Friends and Influence People* by Dale Carnegie. It will serve you well for this project and for all future endeavors.
4. *If you can, take action that will trip up furnishers of adverse history.* Create a situation where furnishers are either restricted

from reporting or must report an entry as in dispute, using methods outlined in Chapter 4.

5. *Always use the insurance method in your dealings with creditors, collectors, and bureaus.* This means that you get things in writing, and when you send something to them, request a return receipt from the Post Office. This prevents their backpedaling or ignoring you entirely when it's time for them to do something that they promised or are required by law to do. It's also useful when filing suit. Make sure that in all your telephone contacts, you keep a log (full name of whom you spoke with, phone number and extension, the time, and the date). Begin every conversation by politely asking for a name (first and last). If you can't get a last name, get the last initial or operator number and geographical location. It can also be useful to get an e-mail address, since people are apt to say things via e-mail they wouldn't normally say, and e-mail provides you with a record of the correspondence. (Yes, e-mails have been shown to be admissible in many courts!)

6. *Know ahead of time what you're going to do if a creditor goes back on a deal.* What do you do if a creditor goes back on written agreements? Well, that's your business, but if the creditor won't live up to written agreements, the only way to force him or her is through legal action. Don't make agreements that you aren't willing to enforce.

7. *Make sure that you get corrected copies of your credit report each time something is improved* (corrected copies are free). As you go along, you'll find that the bureaus will make changes to your report. Put the old files in another folder labeled "Credit Bureau Archives" to avoid confusion. (If you ever have a legal claim, these will come in handy.)

8. *Carefully track correspondence with creditors/furnishers.* Place any written communication and notes in their respective folder, and take copious notes on any verbal communications.

9. *Always pay your bills on time!*

Now that you've performed meaningful assessments, you're ready to devise your strategy. Take a deep breath and let 'er rip.

RESTORE ACCURATE BAD CREDIT

This chapter is of the most interest to many people, because it's the accurate bad credit that usually takes the most time and effort to fix. Some of you may have jumped to this chapter. If you're among them, you should examine your sincerity and give greater attention to your overall plan. I guarantee that's there's a crucial piece of information that you've missed—some neglected morsel that can make all the difference in your success. You will need the combined knowledge of the preceding chapters to make the best decisions. Only from a position of knowing all the rules can you apply the right strategy.

When removing adverse accurate information from a credit report, you have three tactics available to you: (1) get the credit bureau to remove the entry, (2) get the furnisher/creditor to remove/change it using effective negotiating strategies, or (3) in cases where money isn't owed, use the courts in accordance with Chapter 14.

Personally, I don't like using credit bureau disputes—a method that credit repair agencies use exclusively. Few disputes ever work on accurate information, and when they do work, they most often do so on one or two of the Big Three, often leaving the overall credit reporting picture spotty. And although the method may be successful in raising a score on one or two reports, mortgage and most auto lenders pull all three reports and may deny anyway, depending on the offending entries. Moreover, as you will learn shortly, care must be taken when removing adverse tradelines, as FICO scoring components (such as age of the credit entry and overall file age) may be helping more than the adverse entry is hurting. Negotiating with a creditor permits targeted removal of adverse entries, while retaining the most favorable parts. Bureau disputes are more like a broadsword and can sometimes have undesirable consequences.

On the other hand, when doing an auto loan, some credit unions will often pull only the credit report from the bureau to which they subscribe. If a dispute happens to work on that particular bureau, then some benefit may be gained from such a tactic. In addition, if the venerable middle score can be raised by causing an adverse entry to be removed using a credit bureau dispute, then it often doesn't matter if the offending remark is left on one or the other two bureaus. If it's a paid entry, then it's no big deal. If unpaid, then the lender will simply require the debt to be satisfied at or before closing the loan. If the score was raised and a better interest rate obtained using bureau dispute, then surely it can be worth the effort.

Having said all this, I much prefer going to the creditor to resolve bad credit entries, even if that means I have to deal with people I probably won't like and will have to pay—in some way—to get the creditor to come around. After all, if the bad credit is accurate, then it's because I was the one who screwed up.

Understand also that there's a certain amount of satisfaction and pride that comes with getting on the same page with a creditor. And knowing a debt is satisfied is priceless.

Since this book is about teaching every single credit restoration tool available, I'll explain the best methods that I know for crafting credit bureau disputes. What you do with the information is your business.

DISPUTING CREDIT BUREAU ENTRIES

Bureaus have taken measures to counter the barrage of disputes they receive from credit repair agencies, since it's anecdotally estimated that these account for 25 to 35 percent of their total disputes.[1] As such, repeated disputes from the same customer may be counterproductive. In addition, there are many other reasons to take great care in corresponding with the bureaus, as you will soon discover.

---

1. Evan Hendricks, *Credit Scores & Credit Reports*, 189.

This doesn't mean you shouldn't attempt to have items removed by contacting the bureaus. Even when an item is accurate, dispute the information (if this your course), since it costs almost nothing. There's always a chance that disputing entries can work, especially if you employ tactics that take advantage of little quirks in the system (though, as explained in Chapter 7, the dusty pile is something you should always consider before disputing information with the bureaus, since doing so can reinvigorate collection efforts when money is still owed).

Credit Bureau Letter Handling

When a bureau receives a simple dispute letter, it is converted to a consumer dispute verification (CDV) form, entered into the computer, and sent to the furnisher for verification. If the furnisher and the consumer claim different things, then the bureau will always report what the furnisher wishes.

However, bureaus consider letters to fall into two basic categories: standard and elevated. The standard handling occurs just as I described in Chapter 1—the hamburger flippers do their thing. But if the letter includes language that threatens legal action, it gets elevated and goes to a higher authority for handling. This can work in your favor if you have erroneous information that you wish to have deleted, but it may work against you if you are trying to have accurate information removed.

In either case, I recommend starting with a standard letter (see "Crafting a Dispute" below), and if that fails, send one with language that will cause the letter to be elevated. Usually any threat of legal action accompanied by "You are in violation of the FCRA" will suffice.

Magic Number

When I wrote the first edition in 1999, I recommended that people never dispute more than two to three items at one time with a bureau, to avoid raising red flags. I've since changed that view slightly, since I've been recommending a maximum of four or five for a while now and have yet to hear of anyone having a problem with this. Remember, each bureau will task an individual with reviewing each dispute and entering it into the computer. Although it's unclear what happens in the event that a consumer disputes many entries simultaneously, it seems reasonable to assume that bureaus are on the lookout for those performing credit repair. Thus, you should exercise reasonable caution to avoid drawing attention. Anyone with eight negative marks who disputes all them at the same time, for example, is probably going to raise red flags. Bureaus will often consider the frequency of disputes in addition to the number of disputed items in a single dispute letter. It's a balancing act, and all contact with the bureaus must be performed in a manner that has the least likelihood of creating suspicion. My recommendations are as follows: If you have up to a total of four accurate adverse entries, you should dispute them together. If you have a total of five to nine, you should dispute five first, and then the remaining one to four. Ten or more accurate adverse entries should be disputed in blocks of five (and then any remaining number). This will likely keep suspicion to a minimum by keeping the number of disputed items reasonable. It will also place most people in a position of limiting the total number of dispute letters to two, since in my experience most people have between five and ten adverse accurate entries.

Crafting a Dispute

A well-planned dispute of accurate adverse information will employ the following guidelines to make the system work to the highest degree possible:

- Do not obtain free reports. Remember that under FACTA, if you receive a credit report for free, the bureaus will have 45 days instead of 30 to verify the data as accurate, which can often work against you.[2] If you've already ordered free ones, simply purchase new ones.

---

2. 15 U.S.C. § 1681j(a)(3). The following states prohibit a 15-day extension to perform reinvestigations: Arizona, Maryland, Massachusetts, Nevada, New Hampshire, Rhode Island, Vermont, and Washington. Maine has a 21-day cap to perform reinvestigations and requires immediate notification that a dispute is deemed frivolous. Maryland requires notification within seven days if information is considered accurate or inaccurate and seven days if it's determined to be frivolous. Texas requires items disputed found inaccurate or incomplete investigations to be corrected within five business days; it also requires that consumers receive notice if there is insufficient time to conduct a reinvestigation within 30 days. Washington and California permit reinvestigations to be completed within 30 *business* days.

- Bureaus will often ask you for clarification of a negative item or proof of bankruptcy. Never provide them with information concerning any account, as it will only assist them in making sure the information stays. It's up to them to prove it's correct, not the other way around.
- Contact the bureaus only by certified mail with a return receipt request; never contact them by telephone.
- Don't use the bureaus' online dispute system.
- Don't use the bureaus' dispute forms.
- Don't provide a credit report ID number with your dispute.
- Don't provide a copy of your credit report highlighting the disputed information.
- Don't dispute more than four to five items at the same time.
- Don't provide your driver's license or a copy of your driver's license.

Caution: Never reveal your current employment or driver's license number to the credit bureaus. Keep in mind that when you're applying for new credit, the address and employment information you provide on the application will be sent to the credit reporting agencies.

- Be specific with regard to your personal identity information. That is, provide your name, SSN, date of birth, previous employer, current address, addresses in the previous 24 months, and perhaps a credit card or utility bill (with an address on it that you claim is your address).
- Be vague in your dispute information. Provide only an account number and the furnisher, and simply dispute the entry as "not mine," with the exception of some multiple entries.
- For multiple entries of the same account, such as accounts that are sold and reported by different furnishers, you can state that "this is the same account as . . ." An example would be a student loan that was reported by three different owners of the debt. If two of the entries are adverse, then dispute them with

the bureaus by stating that they are duplicates of the third account (the one that's in good standing). If all the accounts are reported with adverse entries, generally go for removal of the one showing money owed, followed by the most recent adverse, followed by severity of the mark. Going after one (in the case of two entries, or two in the case of three entries) in any initial dispute, and using the "duplicate entry" as a bureau dispute pretext will often work. Target any remaining entries in a subsequent dispute.

Note: Appendix C contains sample letters that you can use to help you craft your own letters to creditors, debt collectors, and credit bureaus. But be aware that reporting agencies are on the lookout for "form letters" from credit repair agencies, and they might deem such letters frivolous and refuse to perform a reinvestigation. So use your own words and avoid using industry words (e.g., tradeline, snapshot).

- State in your letters that you understand the bureaus have 30 days to complete the investigation (unless your state is not preempted by the FCRA; see footnote 2).
- Leave 45 days between separate disputes.
- Don't contact the bureaus during the reinvestigation period for any reason, since this will extend the period by 15 days (with the exception of the states not preempted by the FCRA).
- Avoid using any legal language in your initial correspondence, though you may do so in further attempts at removal. When working with accurate information, I believe it's better to stay under the radar of trained human eyes. Although the higher priority given a letter containing legal language may actually slow down the process, perhaps precluding the bureau from meeting the 30-day deadline, it also increases the potential for discovering problems with your dispute. Therefore, I recommend first using a request

letter that's cordial and matter-of-fact and, if that fails, sending a demand letter stating that you understand your rights under the FCRA and may seek a legal remedy if the bureau doesn't comply with your demands. This way, you are using both of the bureau's letter-handling avenues, and that can't hurt.

- If you have both inaccurate and accurate entries, dispute the erroneous ones first. Dispute the accurate entries only after the investigation for the first dispute is concluded (unless you're in emergency mode and need to raise your FICO score in less than 60 days).

- Because of FICO scoring, you must be careful about disputing entries that are adverse, yet paid and old, particularly if the credit file itself is new (less than five years old), as age helps scoring.

- If you have public record entries, follow the guidelines here, but look to Chapter 10 for additional information.

- When a bureau affirms that an adverse entry is accurate, a subsequent letter should include (1) a demand for the description of the reinvestigation procedure and (2) a sentence disrupting the entry again.[3]

- In all disputes, include a statement of how the entry is hurting you (e.g., denied credit, lost sleep).

Remember, FACTA states that a reinvestigation must be reasonable and also clarifies the agency conduct requirement.[4] If the bureaus cannot demonstrate that the item is legitimate, then the law requires

---

3. 15 U.S.C. § 1681i(6)(B)(iii), a notice that, if requested by the consumer, a description of the procedure used to determine the accuracy and completeness of the information shall be provided to the consumer by the agency, including the business name and address of any furnisher of information contacted in connection with such information and the telephone number of such furnisher, if reasonably available; 15 U.S.C. § 1681i(7), a description of reinvestigation procedure. A consumer reporting agency shall provide to a consumer a description referred to in paragraph (6)(B)(iii) by not later than 15 days after receiving a request from the consumer for that description.

4. 15 U.S.C. § 1681i(a), amended by Pub. L. 108-159, § 317 (2003); 16 C.F.R. § 602.1(c)(3)(xviii), added by 69 Fed. Reg. 6526-31 (Feb. 5, 2004).

that it be removed. They usually have 30 days to investigate, and then they must either affirm it or remove it from your file. Often, when they contact the furnisher, it will simply be too busy to respond! Yes, even the worst of credit can be removed this way. This is often the best course for public records, since it only costs you the price of a stamp. You have nothing to lose.

Your chances will depend on how old the entry is, what type it is (auto loan, credit card, etc.), and whether it is paid. Creditors are more likely to ignore requests from bureaus if the item is paid, since it costs them time and money to respond. But they often get busy, and things will fall through the cracks! Disputing with the bureaus is low-cost and low-risk. Your chances with public record removal are usually better after two years, since records will often get archived (see Chapter 10).

I've heard reports that initiating disputes in mid-December works best, since many people go on vacation, and lean staffs get over-whelmed. (Equifax processes disputes in Jamaica, but Christmas and New Year's Day are both celebrated there. Check the BestCredit Web site to determine whether the other bureaus have moved their opera-tions offshore. When and if they do, I'll post holiday information for those countries on my Web site.)

Use Caution When Removing Adverse Items

Due to FICO's use of scorecards, it's not always a good idea to remove adverse entries. Old accounts that are paid and yet reporting a few late payments don't hurt much, and their contribution to the longevity of your credit history may be helping more than the late payments are hurting. My general rules are as follows: if the average age of all accounts is 15 years or older, then remove anything nega-tive; if it's less than 15 years, then remove (1) any public record entries, (2) anything adverse that's reporting as unpaid, (3) anything adverse less than three years old, and (4) any adverse entries that are 90 days late or worse.

For all ages of credit history, I also tend to keep adverse credit on accounts that are open, providing the account was never past 90 days and the account is at least five years old. Now, when I say, "keep," I mean keep the accounts reporting and don't dispute the account with the bureaus. Care must be taken when disputing information with the bureaus in particular. This is especially true with closed accounts, since furnishers will often not respond to a bureau's query. If they can't verify the accuracy of a specific field (entry within a tradeline, such as amount owed, credit limit, or payment history), then they nuke the whole tradeline. Credit reporting agencies are not in the business of modifying individual entries and will not do so unless a furnisher instructs them to. If a furnisher fails to verify information as accurate when queried by a bureau as a result of a consumer dispute, then the bureau always deletes the entire tradeline. Such action may end up hurting more than helping if the account is older, particularly for those with a shorter credit history. Of course, you can attempt to have the creditor remove individual derogatory entries, thereby keeping the account reporting and benefiting your FICO score by virtue of its age (more on this technique shortly).

DISPUTING ENTRIES WITH A FURNISHER

If a credit reporting agency fails to remove an adverse entry, disputing it directly with the furnisher, even if it's accurate, can prove fruitful.

As explained previously, accounts in dispute are not included in a FICO score. When an account is disputed with a furnisher, the furnisher is prohibited from reporting the account in the future unless it reports it as in dispute.[5] This applies to all furnishers of information, and it doesn't matter if the creditor believes the dispute is frivolous or the matter is resolved. All future reporting to the bureaus to which the furnisher reports must be tagged as in dispute. As such, if an account has gone into arrears, it's a good idea to formally dispute the account directly with the furnisher. Using validation in the case of debt collectors will also cause a debt to be reported as in dispute indefinitely. (Validation is possible under some circumstances; see Chapter 7.)

Not only does this affect scoring, but it may also set up a legal claim against the furnisher. Since any future reporting must be

---

5. 15 U.S.C. § 1681s-2(a)(3).

tagged as in dispute, any failure to do so on the part of the furnisher is a violation of the FCRA. The likelihood of a furnisher's screwing this up is 90 percent in my opinion, and such a breach can serve to strengthen negotiations.

NEGOTIATING DIRECTLY WITH THE CREDITOR/FURNISHER

Negotiating directly with the creditor/furnisher is, hands down, the best method of bad credit removal available. Everything else pales in comparison, since getting on the same page with a creditor/furnisher can bring results very quickly, tackling the issues of credit reporting, debt collection, and debt reduction simultaneously.

It's amazing what a credit bureau is willing to do when the request comes from a furnisher. It's also a tremendous relief knowing that your debts are settled and there's no fear of their ever coming back to bite you. In my opinion, 99 percent of all bad credit can be removed this way.

Of course, you can start by disputing entries with the bureaus, but if any credit reporting agency fails to respond in your favor, the next step is negotiating directly with the furnisher.

There are many stages of lateness, but if a debt is more than 90 days late, the creditor will often turn it over to a collection agency if it's unsecured. (Of course, creditors will take foreclosure action in the case of real property or repossession action in the case of an auto.) Once a collection agency has the debt, it will try to collect whatever it can, since it gets a commission on what is paid. If the collection agency doesn't collect anything from you, it doesn't get paid. At this stage of the game, the collection agency is only expecting to collect 15 to 20 percent of whatever is owed—the national average. Keep this in mind when negotiating with collection agencies.

Continuing to review old ground, there is nothing at all wrong with dealing with a collection agency, on the off chance that it behaves properly and you are making progress. If not, you can often have the matter referred back to the creditor if the agency doesn't own the debt, as detailed in Chapter 7.

Tip: Many books and Internet sites tout a credit repair method known as file segregation, whereby you create a new identity through the use of an employee identification number (EIN). This number is issued by the IRS to businesses and has nine digits, just like your SSN. You apply for one by starting a business and then calling the IRS to request the number. Once the EIN has been issued, you go into a bank, open an account, and provide the EIN on your application just like you would your SSN, and wham—now you have a new identity and fresh credit. The problem is that it's a felony, and you can go to prison if caught.[6]

As you already know, some marks on your report are worse than others. In addition, certain situations will give you higher leverage than others. For example, if you have a rating of R9, which is considered a bad debt (the worst), you might think that would be the hardest to remove. Sometimes it is, but sometimes not. Why? Because if it's this bad, then you probably still owe money, which gives you leverage in negotiating a deal. You see, you have their money, which they want, and when someone wants something, it gives you some power. You can negotiate this off, and I have personally done so, not once but twice! Your goal is negotiating a deal with the creditor (or collection agency) that will accomplish one of the following, listed in order of desirability:

1. The account is changed from a negative to a positive rating, thereby raising the tradeline on the report and benefiting your credit score by its age.
2. The current rating is replaced with one based on future performance.

---

6. It is a federal crime to make any false statements on a loan or credit application. Why would anyone take such a risk, especially given the fact that there are perfectly legally techniques to repair credit that work just fine? Furthermore, consider how much time it takes to build up new credit; the adverse information from the "true" credit file would probably have dropped off by that time anyway.

3. The account is changed from negative to neutral.
4. The account is removed from your credit report entirely.

When negotiating, always ask for the best deal first, so you can have a place in the middle to meet should you encounter resistance. That is, ask that the rating be changed to positive from negative, since the creditor/furnisher might say yes right away. If you get no for an answer at first, keep trying for that high point, going up the chain of command if you feel you need to. (Don't ask to go higher if the negotiations are going well, since this can squelch your chances at getting a good deal and delay any settlement at all. Don't get too greedy!) In any case, by aiming high in the beginning, you still have middle ground where you can meet, which is still very desirable. Your goal is to elevate your score, so what you really want is to remove the bad credit. Each of the four things listed above does exactly that.

Cases Where Money Is Owed

When I was in college, I drove a 1976 Oldsmobile Cutlass. Sometimes it needed repair, as do most cars that students own. On one occasion a tire needed changed, and the lug nut was rusted on so incredibly tight that it seemed nothing I could do would get it off. There I sat in my buddy's garage, frustrated. Then he looked at me and said, "Try this," while handing me a hollow pipe that was roughly five feet in length.

The lug nut had become stripped, and at this point I was using a small craftsman ratchet no longer than five inches in length. I placed the pipe over the handle of the ratchet, inserting it all the way down to the base of the socket, and then began to press my weight on the other end. It wouldn't budge.

I began to put all my weight onto the pipe, my feet leaving the ground. As I did so, the small ratchet was under so much strain that it flexed. *This damn thing is going to break*, I thought. Something was surely going to break . . .

But it didn't break. The small ratchet held up, and I began to hear a loud, high-pitched creaking . . . something was going to give . . . slowly my feet were approaching the floor . . . and the immovable lug nut was somehow moving. The lug nut was free. How in the world did that ratchet hold up? To this day, I still wonder about that.

This is leverage. Many things respond to it, and it's the most powerful thing available in credit restoration. All you have to do is take a pseudo pipe, wrap it around the right tool, and then stand on that sucker until the immovable is moved.

Owing money is the best scenario, since you have leverage. Contact the creditor/furnisher, and simply state that you want to pay off the debt, but you need to get the amount reduced, since times are tough. Appeal to the person's emotions, but also make it clear that you are willing to make good. If you want, depending on the stage the debt is in, you can negotiate a settlement lower than the full amount in addition to the removal of the bad credit. What kind of settlement? Usually it will range from 70 to 80 cents on the dollar. Again, this will depend on the stage that the debt is in and to whom it is owed. At the collection stage (on closed accounts, past 90 days) you will get good results, since the agency is expecting only 15 to 20 cents on the dollar anyway. Most will simply want money; they don't care what your report looks like if they can get their money. Would they like to see your report hinder you ad infinitum? Sure, some people are that vindictive, but not always at the expense of their money!

Always remember, once you pay a creditor then you have used your chips. Don't pay until you have what you want. You must get the terms writing—the creditor will "remove all derogatory information regarding the account from your credit report" once the account is paid in full. If the creditor agrees to the terms and sends you a letter, make sure you read it carefully. Often you'll reach an agreement over the phone, and then the letter outlining the terms won't resemble what you agreed to. The letter will often say something about reporting the item as a "Paid Account," "Paid Settlement," or similar. Such reporting, though paid, is adverse and will lower your credit score. It is not the same as *removing* the adverse entry/tradeline from your report.

When negotiating, start by going for the reduction in debt if you have limited resources, and then ask for the bad credit removal as a part of the agreement in exchange for payment. One approach is to offer up front to pay off the debt in full in exchange for removal of any derogatory history. Remember, you're appealing to the creditor to allow you to "get on with your life."

When you look at the debt-reduction table in Chapter 8, it's easy to get excited. But don't lick your chops just yet. When negotiating, things have to be revealed *in their due course*. For example, if you have the money to pay all of your creditors and simply wish to have the bad credit removed, you may want to start from the other direction. That is, start with debt reduction.

Why do that if you have the money to pay? Well, there's a bit of psychology to negotiating. People want to feel as if they've won or made the other party give up something. Don't ask me why this is, but it is. Having said that, even if you can pay 100 percent of the debt, begin by negotiating debt reduction and start at 50 percent. When you have a minimum dollar amount that the creditor will agree to, ask for the bad credit removal. The creditor will likely ask for more money to do that—making you pay a premium for it—mainly for the sense of having accomplished something.

This approach is tricky, since you might make a claim in the initial debt-reduction stage of the negotiating, such as, "80 percent is all I have." If you've already made such a claim, then it's hard to go back and say there's more money. Always be careful, as it's best to say something like, "I have other creditors that also want money, and this is all I can come up with right at the moment." If the creditor won't agree to delete the adverse information unless more money is paid, then say something like, "I really need to get that bad information off. If I can borrow some money from someone and pay you more, can you have it taken off?" Or something like, "My other creditor wouldn't agree to remove the bad credit, so I'm going to pay you with the money I was going to pay it with if you will agree." This way you don't look disingenuous, and the creditor will be very happy to get all the money it can.

This is just a technique. I've done perfectly well with saying up front, "I'll pay you 100 percent of what I owe you tomorrow if you'll remove any bad credit." That often works well too.

Prepare Your Words

How you speak or otherwise communicate with creditors is very important. You must think carefully before you talk to anyone about fixing your credit. Don't ever let on that you are using a credit restoration course or technique. You are just an ordinary person with a need to get that car, home loan, or whatever. If creditors find out or even suspect you are using a credit repair technique, you are likely finished, because they are not going to empathize with you at that point.

Do you have poor social skills? If so, you will have a much harder time of it. These skills are paramount in all your life endeavors. They require a lot of work and thought, and I believe that people aren't born with them but rather learn them. The more you work on them, the better they become, and I recommend that you constantly work to improve them. Many of us had less than stellar parents; they didn't do much to help us in the social skills department. But you can work on developing them everywhere you go—at the Post Office when talking with clerks, by shooting the breeze with the wait staff in restaurants, at home with your kids and spouse, at work, and so on.

Every time you have an encounter with a creditor, you will learn from the experience. In each successive encounter you will gain confidence and be better able to negotiate and cope with the "wrong" answers or the unexpected. Whatever happens, keep your cool and use reason with the person. Always remember that you are appealing to his or her emotions in most cases and logic to a lesser degree.

Tip: Lenders will require that collection accounts be paid before granting a mortgage. This money is often dispersed at closing. Any homebuyer in this situation would be foolish not to negotiate the removal of bad credit in exchange for payment. (Don't tell the creditor that a home loan is in the offing.) Furthermore, any attorney representing a debtor who doesn't negotiate bad credit removal in exchange for payment does his or her client a disservice.[7]

Finally, if you're in a bad mood, don't communicate with creditors. Wait another day, so you can present yourself in the best possible light.

---

7. Assumes the state permits attorneys to perform credit repair; see Credit Repair Organizations Act (CROA); www.bestcredit.com/creditrepairorganizationact/.

Inspiration and Motivation

Here are a couple of real-life examples of how negative information was removed while money was still owed.

EXAMPLE A:
CREDIT CARD, 150 DAYS LATE, R6

I was issued a major credit card from a large national bank while in college, when I didn't yet understand the value of good credit. Sound familiar? My report entry was an R6, which is pretty bad. I contacted the creditor, managed to talk to the right person, and made a deal: I'd pay the creditor what I owed ($600) if it removed the negative credit rating. The creditor agreed, and it was that simple. I got the deal in writing, of course.

EXAMPLE B:
CREDIT CARD, CHARGE-OFF, R9

I had another major credit card on which I still owed $900, reported as R9. I negotiated a deal where I would pay the balance, and in exchange the bank would report it as unrated. This is a little-known tactic in negotiating credit restoration, since most people don't know about it, including creditors!

When I negotiated this, I didn't have the faintest clue about FICO scoring. I believed that this unrated rating was actually worse than removing it entirely and did not realize the scoring benefit of having the account remain (by increasing length of credit history). For the purpose of this example, understand that I was aiming for what *I thought* was a better deal: the deletion of the tradeline entirely. I settled for less, which was unrated, and it turned out even better in terms of FICO scoring.

The lesson is that I never made the minimum I would accept the starting point. Instead, I aimed higher, and the account remained on my credit report as a neutral payment history. (It's very unlikely that a potential lender will call and try to find out the exact history.) Always start by asking for a lot when you negotiate and make deletion of the tradeline your last resort. (See Figure 8 for my unrated settlement letter.)

As explained previously, you can seek any number of variations in payment terms, and you can even get new payment terms that are

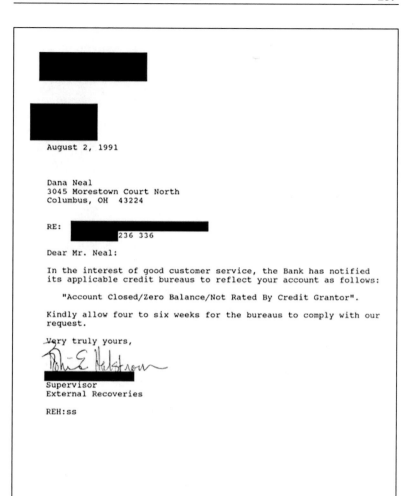

August 2, 1991

Dana Neal
3045 Morestown Court North
Columbus, OH   43224

RE: ███████████████ 236 336

Dear Mr. Neal:

In the interest of good customer service, the Bank has notified
its applicable credit bureaus to reflect your account as follows:

"Account Closed/Zero Balance/Not Rated By Credit Grantor".

Kindly allow four to six weeks for the bureaus to comply with our
request.

Very truly yours,

Supervisor
External Recoveries

REH:ss

Figure 8.

greatly modified or extended, especially on open accounts or accounts that are not yet in collections.

Cases Where Money Is Not Owed

Since there's no real leverage when you don't owe money, it's trickier to get bad credit removed, short of legal options (see Chapter 14). In actuality, the legal route is extremely powerful, and I happen to like it a lot, as I'll describe later. But for now, here are some real-life examples of how bad credit was removed voluntarily by a creditor without the use of the courts when money was not owed.

EXAMPLE C:
CREDIT CARD, COLLECTION ACCOUNT, R7

A credit card issuer reported an R7, and since I didn't owe any money, I had no leverage. It took me a year to find the right person (the vice president of credit management) and negotiate a deal. The deal? I agreed to open a secured card with a $300 limit, didn't miss a payment on the card for 12 months, and, in return, the company deleted the tradeline of the old account. Don't believe it? See Figure 9.

Note: This major bank also tried to bust the deal after the year expired and I had lived up to my end. Had I not had the deal in writing and forced the issue, I would have been out of luck. The person who made the deal was very cold and avoided my calls, but I kept calling every three or four days, leaving messages explaining that I wasn't going to go away and I expected him to live up to his agreement. Just when I had finished drafting a letter threatening legal action (after about 30 days of the runaround), he finally answered my call and agreed to send a letter requesting removal to the credit bureaus. That's why you use the insurance method!

I simply convinced the vice president of the bank that removal of the bad credit was in the bank's best interest, since it got a new, long-term customer who had learned his lesson, and everyone was a winner.

October 16, 1992

Dana Neal
3045 Morsetown Ct., N.
Columbus, OH 43224

Dear Mr. Neal:

As per our phone conversation last month and prior conversations you have had with ███ in South Dakota, we have agreed to the following:

1. Open a $300 Secured Card account (To be opened by 10/19/92) in your name.

2. If you make timely payments and otherwise meet our criteria for conversion to our Unsecured account I will issue written requests to Equifax, Transunion and TRW and the Credit Bureau of Columbus to delete all information that pertains to account number ███274-583.

I would like to stress that deleting accurate information from the credit bureau is not a usual and customary practice in this business. However, we will make this exception.

This agreement will constitute a full settlement and release of any claim you may now have, or hereafter assert, by reason of any matter,cause or thing against ███ in respect of card-related matters.

If you should have any further questions, please contact me at ███5482.

Sincerely,

Vice President
Credit Management

MLC/eyg

Figure 9.

Pitch it as good customer service—you're going to be around for a while, and the bank can benefit from having you as a customer. Using this tactic gives you a happy meeting ground. Was a year of negotiating worth it? You'd better believe it! That bad mark would have stayed on for another four years, seven total years, and would have prevented me from doing all sorts of things during that time.

EXAMPLE D:
CREDIT CARD, 150 DAYS LATE, R6

Another large credit card issuer reported an R6 rating, and I again didn't owe any money and therefore lacked leverage. Would you believe that I got no for an answer about 10 times before I talked with someone who said yes? In fact, I got even more than I asked for! I asked to open a secured card for six months in return for the bank's removing the old negative information from my report as long as I paid on time. The guy said, "That won't be necessary; we'll open you up a new account right now and remove any reference to the old account right away." No kidding. Can you believe it? It really happened: see Figure 10.

A Real-World Example of the Art of Negotiation

Many lessons can be learned from a single encounter. I advise you to read this example carefully and glean whatever lessons you can from it. It's an actual conversation (summarized) that I had with a creditor (a bank, not a collection agency). This type of verbal exchange is the rule, not the exception. The names are changed to protect the guilty:

I telephoned, and a man answered.
"Hello," I said. "How are you today?"
"I'm fine. What can I do for you?"
"My name is Dana Neal, and I wish to discuss my account." I gave him my account number and learned that his name was Mr. Smith. I said, "Yes, sir. Well, I'm calling to talk with you about my account and wish to come up with a way in which we can settle it amicably."
"Sounds good. I see here that you previously offered a 25 percent settlement on your debt. We are prepared to take 50 percent, but no less. Your account will charge off unless you pay the bill by the end of next month." He was very cold.

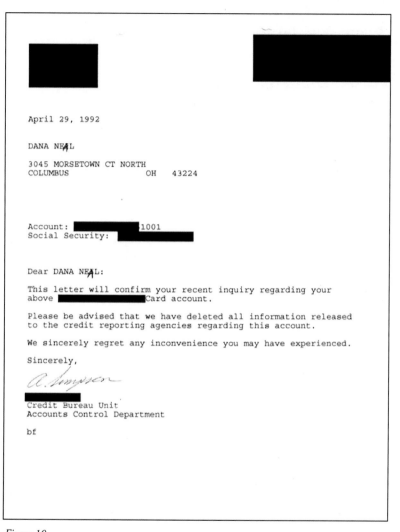

April 29, 1992

DANA NEAL

3045 MORSETOWN CT NORTH
COLUMBUS   OH   43224

Account: █████████ 1001
Social Security: ████████████

Dear DANA NEAL:

This letter will confirm your recent inquiry regarding your
above █████████████ Card account.

Please be advised that we have deleted all information released
to the credit reporting agencies regarding this account.

We sincerely regret any inconvenience you may have experienced.

Sincerely,

A. Simpson

████████
Credit Bureau Unit
Accounts Control Department

bf

Figure 10.

Note: To review, a charge-off usually occurs after six months of nonpayment. The creditor no longer expects to receive money for the debt and charges it off on the books. The creditor, in turn, receives a tax deduction from the government for the loss. (I don't know what this amount is, but it must be at or below 25 percent of the debt, since prior to charging off a creditor will take a 25 percent settlement. If a creditor thought the charge-off would be more profitable than taking $2,500 on a $10,000 debt, then it would never take 25 percent or any amount less than a tax benefit. Keep in mind that this does not apply to tax-exempt credit unions.) The creditor no longer expects to ever receive any money for the debt, so whatever it receives above the amount of the tax deduction is welcome. Have no fear of the common tactic of a collector: "A charge-off is imminent." Your position is not really hampered by a charge-off.

I replied, "I understand. But I have other creditors who are also demanding money, and I can only afford to pay some of them. Therefore, I must pay those who give me the best settlement deal. There are others willing to settle for 25 percent, and I'm sorry for this situation, but if it comes down to paying 50 percent or 25 percent, I'm going to have to choose the 25 percent deal."

"Then we will send it to our legal department, and they will take action against you."

"With all due respect, Mr. Smith, I'd like to take this matter up the chain of command. I understand that you are just doing your job, but I'd like to take the matter up with your supervisor. What is his name?"

"His name is Mr. Brindle," he replied, "but he will not tell you anything different than what I just told you." He was clearly agitated.

"I understand. Just the same, I'd like to speak with him if you don't mind. I understand that you are trying to do your job, and it's nothing personal."

Now he became terse. "What for? He is going to tell you the exact same thing that I just told you. You are wasting our time here. We will not take less than 50 percent under any circumstances."

See what happened here? This person wouldn't budge, and besides, he was a simpleton who didn't have the power to give me what I asked for. Furthermore, he was an ass in spite of my cordial demeanor.

Maintaining my calm, I said, "Look, I've asked nicely to speak with your supervisor, and there is nothing wrong with that request."

He hung up on me.

Get the picture? These people are jerks. However, you have to buckle down and be persistent, because you aren't going to get what you want unless you make it happen. Nobody will settle your problems for you, and nobody cares. I repeat: nobody cares. It's all up to you. Perseverance.

I called back with a plan to ask for the head of the department. In this case, the department I was dealing with is actually separate from the collection department. How do I know this? I had already spent several hours talking with various people in the collection department, asking them who could approve settlements. Can you imagine what it took to get the number for that department? It takes work, and you just keep calling and asking until you get the answer you want. Remember, you have to talk directly with a decision-maker; nobody else will do. Nobody!

A woman answered.

"With whom am I speaking please?" I asked.

"Jennifer."

"Can I get your last name please?"

"I'm sorry, I don't give that out," she replied. This is typical.

"I understand; how about a last initial or your operator number?"

"L."

"Thank you. Now, miss, could you please tell me who is the head of your division?"

"Well, we have several supervisors here." She was unsure what to do.

"I would like to know who the head of the department is."

"I don't quite know how to answer that."

"Let me put it this way: what is the position, or title, of Mr. Brindle?"

"He is a supervisor."

"OK. Who is his supervisor?"

"Supervisors work for team leaders. His team leader is Paula."

"Paula who?"

"If she wants to tell you that she can herself."

"All right. Is she available to speak with please?" Notice that I stayed calm and polite.

"What is your name and account number?"

I gave her my account number, knowing full well that it would send me to a place I didn't want to go. However, I had received some information so far from Jennifer and knew I might need her again later.

"Hold on," she replied.

Three minutes passed. There was some gnashing of teeth going on for sure. A gruff voice came on the line.

"Hello, this is Mr. Brindle. How can I help you?"

"Yes, hello. My name is Neal, and I've asked to speak with team leader Paula."

"Well, I know who you are, and you are talking to me. How can I help you?"

"With all due respect, I did not ask for you. Please transfer me to Paula."

"That isn't going to happen. If you want a settlement, you are going to have to deal with me."

"I asked to speak to Paula, and you refuse to transfer me?"

"That's right. I'm making the decisions around here." This vitriolic demeanor is the rule, not the exception. But I wasn't about to stop.

"I've asked to speak to your supervisor, and that is a reasonable request."

"I don't care," he said. "Now what do you want to do about your account?"

"I tell you what. I will agree to speak with you about my account, but I reserve the right to speak with Paula if we cannot come to an amicable arrangement."

"No! It's not going to happen."

"Look, I telephoned your bank in order to make settlement arrangements, and I get treated like this? We are finished."

I hung up. I called back and asked to speak with Paula. I explained to the person who answered the phone that I didn't wish to be transferred to anyone else unless he or she was senior to Paula or a team leader. I was adamant about my request. A few minutes passed, and a woman answered.

"Hello, Mr. Neal, my name is Miss Casic. How can I help you?"

"Well, I don't know if you can or not. I asked to speak with Paula or someone with her authority. Would you be that person?"

"I can approve any decision that comes through this office."

"Good. Let me first start by saying that I'm unhappy with my treatment by your colleagues." I ran the gamut of my conversations with Brindle and Smith. Then I said, "It's not unreasonable for me to ask for a superior if I don't get the answer I am looking for. This treatment is uncalled for, and it is I who called your department in an attempt to settle this matter. If someone asks to speak with a supervisor, the policy should be clear that the caller should be placed on hold and the superior found immediately."

"I agree," she said calmly.

"Very good. Now, here is my situation . . ."

I briefly explained my circumstances . . . taking responsibility for the problem, stating why I became late (you use whatever good reason, or combination of reasons, you can come up with here, e.g., losing a job, becoming disabled, or whatever), and explaining that I had other debts and could not pay them all (but would pay the ones on which I was able to get the best settlement), and so on.

Tip: Remember, there is a stark difference between reasons and excuses, between whining and explaining. Stay real, and remain professional.

I informed her that I'd been offered a 50 percent settlement by her bank, but that it just wasn't possible for me to accept that, especially considering that I'd been offered 25 percent settlements from others. When she asked who they were, I explained that I could not tell her due to confidentiality agreements I had with the creditors. She pressed and tried (using my credit report, which no doubt was in front of her) to get me to tell her, but I argued that for the purposes of the settlement with her bank, what occurred with other creditors was not relevant and would not help the bank's bottom line.

She told me she would review the case and asked if she could have my telephone number. I explained that because I was inundated with calls from collectors, I'd had to change my number. I asked her to not take offense but said that I could not give it out. I told her I'd be glad to call her back at the time of her choosing. We agreed that I would call her back in two hours.

When I called her back, she offered a 40 percent settlement. I explained that I appreciated her working with me and said I knew she was trying. However, I said I could not justify settling with her bank for 40 percent when I could settle with others for 25 percent. She tried again to find out with whom I'd settled on those terms, and I used the same excuse as to why I could not.

I apologized for not being able to settle with her bank, especially considering the special attention she had given my case. I said that if I could pay all my creditors the balance owed, I would gladly do it, but that I just was not in a position to do it because the total amount owed was far more than I had. Furthermore, I explained, the money I was using to settle with was borrowed money, and I would have to pay that back as well.

When I attempted to close the conversation and get off the phone, she said that she would like to look at my situation more closely and asked if I would call her back the next day.

When I called her back, she agreed to accept 25 percent. This amounted to roughly $6,000. (Yes, the original balance was $24,000!) The deal stipulated that I would be required to pay the balance within 30 days. Great? Well, almost. Remember, there was still that little matter of the poor credit. If I settled with the bank, it would automatically show up on my credit report as a "Paid Settlement," a derogatory item (better than a charge-off, but derogatory).

I thanked Ms. Casic for working with me and told her how much this would help me to get out from under this debt. Now I'm going to take you back to Chapter 5. Remember my statement, "Be prepared to be bold"?

Very naively, I asked, "What would happen to my credit report?"

"It will show paid settlement," she replied.

"That's bad, isn't it?"

"It's not good, but better than a charge-off."

I sighed, paused a moment, and then said, "I see. Is there something that could be done about that?"

"No," she replied.

Tip: Never mention that you are using a credit restoration technique. If you do, you will surely fail no matter what you say after that. Put on your poker face: you are a novice at credit but are a fast learner and are very concerned about it.

"Hmmm," I said. "It seems to me that we have a settlement here, one that is acceptable to both of us." I continued, "Would you consider removing the derogatory information in this account?"

"No. We can't change it."

"I see. Well, this concerns me. It doesn't seem to benefit the bank in any way to keep the derogatory history on there, and it seems punitive. I don't want to seem ungrateful for all of your efforts, but I have to take all things into account when I settle with my various creditors."

Tip: Remember the situational approach from "The Art of Negotiation?" The only thing that you can tell from the dialogue is that she was both logical and reasonable. The tone of her voice said the same, yet while she was mostly all business, she was interested in my story. Like most people, she wasn't going to respond to whining; I used equal doses of logic and tempered emotion to win her over.

She then said, "Banks use information to assess credit risk, and my bank cannot list your account as positive, since that would be seen as endorsing you as a risk."

I went on to explain that it would be good business for both of us if we could settle this account, deleting the derogatory credit as well.

And after listening carefully, she said, "I hear what you are saying. However, I have responsibilities to this bank, and when it comes time for our internal auditing, how will I be able to justify this action? The many settlement accounts that come through this office are all approved by me and are looked at by people higher than me, even though I make decisions."

I explained that I would need time to consider my options and talk to an attorney and then get back to her. I then sent her an e-mail later that day, which went something like this:

> I understand your comments about endorsing a credit risk. I do see your point, but there is something else that must be considered. I failed to pay, but it was beyond my control. Yes, I take responsibility, and that's why I contacted you. This bad credit is harming me, and it's not fair. On the subject of your internal audits, I understand that you have those. But auditors don't look at every single file, they only look at a few random files, and this is probably only performed quarterly. The chances of this becoming an issue are very small. Furthermore, even if it was discovered, you could justify the action based on my history and on the basis that you are doing what is in the best interest of the bank. It certainly wouldn't be the first time. Besides, you are paid to make those decisions.

Tip: Wait a couple of days between conversations. You don't want to seem pushy or too exited, and you want the person you're negotiating with to think about you as a person and your situation. By the same token, don't wait more than three days, since bank supervisors are busy people and will begin to forget about you.

This was the gist of my e-mail, and I closed it by pleading with her to understand. When I called her three days later, I explained that my lawyer told me removing the negative information was okay, and that this is often done in settlement agreements. (People with debts often have lawyers, so it should have come as no surprise that I was talking to one.)

She refused to budge. I told her that I'd gotten another creditor to agree to it remove it and added, "I understand that it's my fault that this has occurred; however, whom does it benefit to leave the bad mark on the report? It doesn't benefit the bank, and it only hurts me."

She said that the bank would not remove it, to which I responded, "I appreciate your willingness to take 25 percent on this account and your time in trying to settle the matter. The issue of the credit report disturbs me, and I have to consider all factors when settling with the various creditors. I want to settle with your bank, but there are others willing to go a little further by removing the derogatory mark. I still fail to see why I'm being penalized when we are settling." Notice the positive, unambiguous remark: we are settling. I continued, "I ask you to please reconsider, since the bad mark does not benefit the bank in any way, and removing it costs the bank nothing."

She still wouldn't budge, and then I offered her a compromise.

I said, "I have a compromise that my attorney told me about—one that may satisfy both our needs. I'll agree to pay the 25 percent settlement and, in exchange, the bank will report the account as nonrated (unrated), or R0. This, while not giving me a positive rating and increasing my credit score, does not reflect badly. It neither helps nor hinders my credit score, since it is neutral. The bank can get its money, and I don't get penalized for seven years for the mistake."

She said that she was unaware of such a rating (which is common), but she would check with her credit-reporting department. She asked if I would call her back on Monday so she could have time to research it, and I agreed (it was a Thursday).

I called her back, and she said that she could not change the reporting unless I paid the entire balance, which is quite common.

What did I do? That's not important; what's important is what *you* would do. It depends on your situation—how many accounts you have in arrears, what your credit report looks like otherwise, and how much money you have.

Remember Debt Fusion™? What are your real goals? You could settle with her for 25 percent with bad credit or 100 percent with no bad credit. You could thank her for her time and for her hard work and walk away, wait for the bank's attorney to contact you, and then try for a better settlement with the attorney. Does this bank sell its debts to collection agencies? If so, maybe you would be better off to take one of these two options right now. How is your sanity? If you've come this far, can you handle starting over with a third party who purchased the debt or a crony who works for a two-bit collection attorney? Only you can decide. But *BestCredit* is about bad credit removal, and doing anything outside this goal is unacceptable unless this one account makes an entire Debt Fusion™ plan unworkable in the larger scope. Furthermore, any "Paid Settlement" account will ravage a credit score, since it is a recent entry. (An example of accepting less than bad credit removal is when you have eight creditors and all agree to remove the adverse entry except one. If you lack the funds to pay 100 percent, better to take the 25 percent deal and have one remaining paid adverse entry, and then go for a credit bureau dispute to remove it. As explained in Chapter 3, one adverse paid entry is acceptable, but two is one too many. The first adverse entry doesn't affect a score as much as subsequent adverse entries.)

Note: As demonstrated in Chapter 8, creditors generally want 70 percent or more to remove bad credit. More often, a 25 percent deal plus bad credit removal with a creditor of this type will occur after legal proceedings have commenced and the discussions are with a lawyer. Even then, most creditors would rather try for a judgment if you have a job or own property, or they'll demand at least 50 percent for the bad credit to come off. But what one creditor won't do, another often will. As always, getting greedy probably won't help you.

For those just dying to know, I didn't take either deal I was offered. Even though I had expended a great deal of time and energy with this creditor, neither option was a good one for my situation.

When the Creditor Has Broken the Law

Now, let's add a twist to this scenario. If the creditor had broken any law, especially a FCRA or FDCPA regulation, then this would have given me leverage in my negotiating.

Let's say that one of the bank's collectors called me outside allowable hours, which is easy to prove. I could handle the discussions in the exact same manner, and once I decided that her best deal wasn't going to work for me and I was at the end of the line with this creditor, then I could afford to bring out my ace in the hole. After all, I would have nothing to lose at that point, having already decided that her best deal wasn't good enough.

At the point where we reached an impasse, I could say, "Ms. Casic, when I went to speak with my attorney about the bad credit removal, he informed me that your company was in breach of a federal law. He said that you broke the law when one of your collectors, Mr. Brindle, called me repeatedly at all hours. I didn't want to bring this up, but he says that's a violation of the Fair Debt Act or some such and that I shouldn't pay you anything—that I should sue you for damages."

Now the shoe is on the other foot.

I could continue, "Look, I don't really want to do that, and we have an agreement here, so why don't you agree to remove the bad credit in exchange for the amount we've agreed and I'll forget about it?" Then she would have to decide, based on this new information, what to do. (At her level, Ms. Casic would probably know that the FDCPA doesn't have a provision for punitive damages and caps out at $1,000 in statutory damages per occurrence, yet the cost of litigating makes the prospect unappealing. Furthermore, some states may have damage remedies that are unavailable under federal law.)

If she balked, I could continue, "You can always sue me, but I'm uncollectible anyway. I don't have anything you can take, and you know that. And if you sue, my attorney says I'll have to countersue, since your collector broke the law. Let's not go there. I'm offering to pay you what I can, and that should be enough for you. Leaving any bad mark is only being vindictive at this point, and it makes no sense."

I would continue to be matter-of-fact with Ms. Casic, letting her know that a deal without bad credit removal won't ever work under any circumstances. If she were to balk again, then I'd say, "Well, thank you for trying anyway. Have a nice day." Then I'd end the conversation.

Personally, I'd follow up any such conversation with a letter to Ms. Casic, sent RRM, spelling out the breach by her collector and threatening a civil suit for violations. She would be forced to respond in writing to such a letter, and it would also create a situation where she may begin to believe I'm serious—and perhaps offering me a better deal.

Of course, I could have *started* the negotiations this way, putting Ms. Casic completely on the defensive and making her concerned about my next move. But by starting with the money first, I discovered what dollar amount the bank was willing to accept, and that gave me leverage. As to whether you bring out your ace on the front end or on the back, there is no right or wrong; it's a matter of style. Scare them up front or flank them on the end. It's all a question of the severity of the breach—and, as always, the personality of the party you're negotiating with.

I also could have sued the bank for the breach on the front end and started the negotiating that way. Of course, it could have tried to countersue for the balance owed. But this probably would not have been a problem since I had a claim against the bank and it likely would have wanted to avoid any lengthy legal battle. This approach would likely lead to a better deal than 100 percent plus bad credit removal—probably something on the order of 40 percent plus removal. But each creditor is different, and there's no way to know for sure.

Incidentally, if I do bring a lawsuit in federal court under an FCDPA or FCRA breach, then the creditor couldn't file a counterclaim in such an action. It would have to start a new claim that was distinct and separate, with service of process and all.[8]

For Those Who Can't Buy Their Way Out

If you can't buy your way out of bad credit, there are still some options:

- Negotiate a deal where you pay it off in stages.
- Work hard and save your money, and then use it to pay your creditors off. You owe it, right?
- Borrow the money from someone else to pay the creditor, either a lending institution or friend/family member.

---

8. 28 U.S.C. § 1387, 28 U.S.C. § 1332. Any counterclaim in this case wouldn't meet the $75,000 minimum required by federal law. (See Chapter 14 for more on this issue.) A defendant could file a counterclaim if I initiate a state court action.

You could also go see the president of your local bank, explain the situation, tell him you have a job, that you've changed or the situation has changed, and that you want to get an installment loan to pay off these creditors. He or she can even send the money directly to the creditors you owe. Take a copy of your credit report with you; show that you're not afraid, that you're just trying to fulfill your obligations. Heck, try three or four banks. I once went to four banks before I got a car loan with bad credit! Sometimes small banks or credit unions work best. Agree to open a savings and a checking account with the bank and have direct deposit; whatever it takes.

Find Your Voice and Your Style

Back in the day when I was a young lieutenant in the army, I was flying for a medevac helicopter unit near Cleveland, Ohio. One afternoon while I was going over some details with two captains in the flight planning room, my crew chief came in and began to give me some bunk. Not getting upset, I told him succinctly what I expected of him and then sent him on his way.

About 10 minutes later, I was outside with one of the captains performing a preflight inspection on the helicopter. He said, "Lieutenant, I can't believe you let that sergeant get away with talking to you like that. I would have torn him a new one."

I just nodded and replied, "I see."

A few minutes later, I went back inside the building and as I was walking down the hall, the second captain stopped me, "Lieutenant, you were awfully hard on that sergeant. If you go a little easier, you may be able to get more out of your subordinates."

I just nodded. "I see."

This story is true. It illustrates the differences in style and technique as well as perception. Both captains were smart and well meaning. And yet everyone has an opinion, everyone has a style.

When negotiating, you just need to find your voice and play to your strengths. And, remember, the other person has his or her own perceptions, and you'll need to work off that by listening and learning what you can about this person. Whether your style is effective is best determined by one thing: the success or failure of your goals.

You see, it's all about negotiating. You start out giving a little here and there, and see what happens. You overcome objections by giving a little, appealing to the person's good nature, explaining your mistake, giving a little more, agreeing that you did wrong, giving a little more, and so on.

From 1991 through 1993, only once in my many attempts at getting a creditor to remove negative information did I fail, and that was with a very small bank in a small town. (The president of the bank was a very mean, vindictive old man; I wasn't going to change his mind.) Remember what I said about reasonable people? Since 1999, all readers of my material who have taken the time to contact me have reported similar results. In fact, as of this writing, I have yet to receive a single contact from anyone who claimed unfavorable results. And if I had known in 1993 what I know now, then my success rate would have been 100 percent.

You can make it work by believing and being steadfast. In every single interaction, I learned something. Then I used it in the next. Every person you contact will be different; some will be nice, others not. But in all cases, be nice, because that's what works. If you can't get the answer you want, take it to the person's supervisor. If that doesn't work, then take it to his or her supervisor, and so on. Be respectful and ask to speak with someone higher up the chain. Someone will say yes in most cases. Just be persistent, and don't give up!

Come up with a plan for what you're going to say before you ever make the first call. Take notes before you ever pick up the phone, and carefully jot down the name of the person with whom you spoke, what was said, and when. Get the person's direct extension as well as an address. Many companies have offices in multiple states, and you must be able to know where the other party is located should legal action ensue and also be able to send any decision-maker RRM. Be methodical. You see, there's no secret. It's all about knowing all the rules of the game, planning carefully, and then negotiating. That's it!

Get It in Writing

I'll say it over and over: get the deal in writing before providing the creditor with the settlement funds. Mark the check or money order with "paid in full" in the memo block, and be sure to follow up in 30 days by obtaining a copy of your report and verifying that the change in reporting has occurred.

Note: If you have agreed to settle with the original creditor while the matter is still in the hands of the agency, make sure that you word the settlement in such a manner as to include not only "all credit reporting agencies to be notified to remove negative marks" but also "the relevant collection agency to be notified to delete the marks from its database and stop reporting it to the credit reporting agencies." As with all agreements, if you get the deal and then a creditor goes back on it, hound that creditor for 30 days, and then consider a legal remedy. Remember, you've been harmed, and the best way to deal with it is to force the creditor into 'fessing up.

You may also consider using a restrictively endorsed check even after you have a written agreement in place. It is unnecessary when a formal agreement is in place, though may be useful when the agreement is simply a letter from a creditor.

What if You Can't Make a Deal?

You will not likely fail if you follow the guidelines in the book. If anyone has failed, I have yet to hear of it—and I'm accessible by e-mail. Sincerely, everyone I have spoken with who has used the negotiation methods outlined in this book has succeeded. But if for some reason you fail, don't worry; it's not the end of the world! Keep trying with all your creditors, and remember to put as much distance between you and the bad credit as you can, by paying your bills on time and reestablishing credit.

In the first edition, I recommended that people place a statement in their credit file concerning derogatory information. I've since changed that view, since it does nothing to help your score and only draws more attention to it. Besides, putting a statement there is an admission that you owe the money and may hurt your chances of removing it!

Finally, before losing all hope when a creditor is intransigent, you should know that there's another powerful method of removal that is used in cases where money isn't owed: a declaratory judgment. Fully explained in Chapter 14, this is where one false aspect of an entry is used as a pretext to file a lawsuit, resulting in removal of the whole entry.

10

UNIQUE CASES FOR REMOVING BAD CREDIT THAT IS ACCURATE

Most of the time, adverse credit entries are very straightforward; they simply involve tradelines reported by creditors and collection accounts reported by debt collectors. However, there are several types of entries that present unique problems for removal, including bankruptcies, judgments, liens, inquiries, student loans, checking account reporting, joint accounts, and residential leases.

BANKRUPTCIES

Since bankruptcies are a matter of public record, it's been widely reported and generally accepted that they can't be removed from credit reports. However, recent evidence shows that they can be deleted under certain circumstances.

Since public records cannot be "deleted" from the court records (save judgments, which can be "set aside" by a judge), the only possible remedy for a bankruptcy on your credit report is to challenge the bureaus as to the validity of the record. The key here is timing.

Most states didn't begin electronic filing of bankruptcies until the early 2000s. Also, prior to electronic filing, records were usually only kept on site for two years and then transferred to another location to be archived.

Case in point: the District Court of (Portland) Oregon's bankruptcies were all paper filed until November 7, 2003. Though petitions were still required to be filed manually, on paper, after that date, that's when the court began to scan in the bankruptcy records and convert them to electronic filings.

All bankruptcy petitions performed prior to that date were stored for two years and then sent to Seattle, Washington, for archival. With court records, service bureaus are the furnishers. They would have to contact the court in the event of a consumer dispute. Since credit bureaus have only 30 days (in most cases) to validate an entry and must remove it if they can't do so within this time frame, this becomes problematic for a credit bureau attempting to validate a bankruptcy, because the records are not readily available. Furthermore, service bureaus have no vested interests in the outcome of a consumer dispute. They have nothing to gain by furnishing adverse information and everything to lose if they're wrong in their affirmations.

In any case, I recommend that anyone who has filed for bankruptcy take the time to discover what his or her local court does with records and then challenge the entry with the bureaus accordingly. In fact, I believe it's a safe bet to wait two years and then dispute it regardless. What's there to lose?

Use disputes in accordance with Chapter 9, but here are some additional rules for dealing with bankruptcy entries:

- Before attempting to delete a bankruptcy, be sure to get all other references to it deleted first. That is, delete any accounts that show "included in bankruptcy" beforehand. That way, since credit bureaus will likely look at old snapshots, any recent previous scans won't show any reference to it.[1]
- Wait 60 days after all of the "included in bankruptcy" entries are deleted before disputing the bankruptcy. Purchase all three reports directly from the bureaus, and check them to make sure they don't contain reinsertion of previously deleted

---

1. A consumer who filed bankruptcy is expected to have accounts that are included in bankruptcy. The lack of any such accounts will only help, while the existence of them will raise eyebrows—perhaps creating interest.

"included in bankruptcy" entries. By doing this, not only do you ensure no reference to it, but you also create a snapshot for the bureau letter handler to see. You can bet the first thing the bureau will do is go back and look at the last couple of snapshots to see if there are any creditor references. Once you're certain that there are no reinsertions, wait 30 additional days before disputing. That way, you've not only created your own snapshot with the pulling of your report, but there will also be at least two additional monthly scans in the bureau's archives.

- Contact the bankruptcy court and find out where your file is. If it's still at the courthouse, ask if you can check it out for review. If so, check it out and then file a dispute with the bureaus; the file won't be there for them to verify the data in it. (I have yet to find a courthouse that will permit an original bankruptcy file to be checked out, permitting copies only. But try it anyway; there may be a new person on staff who doesn't know the rules.)

- Look for a pretext to dispute the bankruptcy entry. Look at the filing date, SSN, discharge date, bankruptcy type, docket number, asset liability, and anything else. Try to find anything wrong with accuracy and dispute it in combination with "not mine." In other words, if the court number is incorrect (it often is), dispute it by writing, "The bankruptcy entry with court entry #4567 is not mine."

- As with all accurate entries, be vague in your dispute. Don't provide a copy of a credit report, ID number, or anything. Simply dispute "the bankruptcy entry."

Again, follow the dispute procedures outlined in Chapter 9, including those involving follow-up disputes if the first one fails. There's a very good chance that a bankruptcy entry can be removed in this way.

JUDGMENTS

A money judgment is really just a piece of paper—a court document that says someone owes someone money. Having a judgment on your report can be a real showstopper, even with a substantial amount of good credit. If you think a judgment is unwarranted because of extenuating circumstances, your first course of action is to dispute the item with the bureau by sending formal dispute letter and, if that fails, a demand letter. For all bureau correspondence, use the techniques outlined in Chapter 9.

If the bureau cannot verify that the judgment is legitimate within the reinvestigation time frame set forth by the FCRA, then the law requires that it be removed from your report. You may or may not be aware of the circumstances surrounding the judgment, since it could have been awarded in absentia (e.g., you were not present at the hearing or failed to respond to a lawsuit, so you lost by default). In any case, when you begin disputing it with the bureaus, ask them to provide specific documentation to back up the legitimacy of the judgment, information you may find helpful when you are attempting to have it removed. Which court is it in? What's the case number? Perhaps you don't have a copy of the judgment. If not, get one from the court as soon as you can.

Note: As stated in the section on public records, service bureaus are notorious for making mistakes, including transcribing SSNs incorrectly. If you believe a judgment is on your report in error, simply send a letter to the bureaus requesting that they remove it, in accordance with Chapter 11. If they fail to comply, you'll likely find some useful information in Chapter 14.

Unpaid Judgments

Surely a judgment on which you still owe money will look worse on your credit file than one that has been paid. The former is called an unsatisfied (unpaid) judgment, but it's not a cause for alarm. Actually, the fact that you still owe money gives you leverage in negotiating the removal of the judgment. If the bureau continues to report the judgment after you have disputed it twice, then your next course of action is to contact the plaintiff (the party that sued you, also known as the judgment-creditor) and negotiate a partial or full settlement. Most people will take a partial payment, since they would rather have something than nothing. Remember to be nice. (As a last resort, explain that you wish to settle because the judgment is hurting you, and reason with the plaintiff: it will do him or her no good to have the derogatory information remain on your credit report once you both settle. This is a last resort because you don't want to give the plaintiff any ammunition in your negotiations.) Offer 20 percent of the judgment and work your way up in small bits from there. Maybe you can get off with paying 25 to 50 percent! In return, the plaintiff agrees to a stipulation to your payment, wherein he or she "sets aside" the judgment in exchange for your cash. Make sure you secure the deal in writing before you send any money. In fact, if possible it's better to meet with the other party and have the documents signed at the same time money changes hands.

Explain to the plaintiff that this will require his or her filing papers stipulating that the judgment is set aside, but that you know how to do it and will handle that part of it. Since each state's respective laws are different, I cannot provide you with a sample stipulation. A judge will not approve it anyway unless it is correct (i.e., adheres to your state laws). It's a good idea to go to your local courthouse and talk to the civil clerk. The clerk will probably send you to the file room, but ask for a sample of a stipulation to set aside judgment, and that way you will have a template to work from so you will get the format and the language right. If the clerk won't help, ask to peruse the court's files (they are open to the public) until you come across a stipulation document. Also, check the local court rules for information on the proper format.

Be sure the stipulation includes all the information necessary for a judge to sign it. For instance, you must include your name and address, identify yourself as the defendant, provide a signature block for yourself, and include all the same for the plaintiff. In addition, you'll need to include the original judgment's case number, court, and so on. Title this document "Stipulation to Set Aside Judgment" and place exactly what the settlement agreement is in the body copy. If you can't meet with the judgment-creditor, send it and let him or her know that it must be notarized at the time of signing. Provide a self-addressed, stamped envelope to make it easy to return it to you.

Make a certified true copy (an exact copy of a document with no alterations) of the document that is signed by the judgment-creditor, using a notary. This is just in case the court loses it and the judgment-creditor has a change of heart or dies! You then file the stipulation with the court, in person if possible. If not, supply a self-addressed, stamped envelope and request that it be used to provide you with a copy of the stipulation once the judge signs it. The settlement is not complete until the judge signs the stipulation!

Once you receive the stipulation with the judge's signature, make a copy for the bureaus and send it to them right away, demanding that the judgment be removed from your credit files. Keep the original for yourself, placing it in your permanent files.

If you're confused or unsure and need help, contact an attorney and explain what you're trying to do. An attorney can assist you in this process, usually for a nominal fee, since you've already negotiated a deal and simply need him or her to handle the paperwork.

Paid Judgments

If the judgment is paid, make sure that it is reported as such. Having an unpaid judgment on your credit report will certainly hurt your credit score, so provide proof to the bureaus that it was paid if you have it. Whether you have proof or not, you still want to get the plaintiff to provide a Stipulation to Set Aside Judgment (following the procedures outlined above). The plaintiff should be cooperative, since you already paid him or her. Be nice! It's your problem, and you have no leverage to make the other party sign anything.

If you meet a lot of resistance in getting a stipulation, settle for getting the plaintiff to report the judgment correctly if it's paid but reported unpaid. Explain that you simply want the facts presented on your credit report and that he or she is responsible for that happening.

Of course, if you do have proof that the judgment was paid, simply provide it to the reporting agencies and demand that the judgment be reported as satisfied. Just remember, this comes after you've tried to get it deleted by disputing the validity of the whole entry. By providing proof that it's been paid, you've just admitted that the entry is valid.

What if You Can't Get It Removed?

Don't worry; if you're unable to get a judgment removed, it's not the end of the world. Keep trying with all your creditors, and remember to put as much distance between you and the bad credit as you can by paying your bills on time and reestablishing credit. And, remember, you can always continue to dispute the judgment with the bureaus. If you fail using two disputes, wait six months and try again.

LIENS AND OTHER PUBLIC RECORDS

Most public records, including liens, are entered in court records and county files. If the lien is paid and shown that way, it's best to perform a reporting agency dispute in accordance with Chapter 9. If it's unpaid, you can contact the lien holder and cut a deal, much as you can with judgments, though a lien cannot be "set aside" by a judge. Once the lien is paid, dispute the entry in accordance with Chapter 9. Do likewise for other public record entries.

INQUIRIES

As explained in Chapter 3, certain types of inquiries can be harmful to a score, whereas others have no effect at all. Once you've determined which ones are hurting your score, you can devise a strategy to get them removed. Always bear in mind that having a low number of legitimate inquiries, a few within the proceeding 12 months, will have little impact on a score. If there are more pressing matters that are significantly weighing down a score, you should focus on removing those tradelines or public records first. In addition, since it usually takes several months to remove any offending data from a credit report, simply avoiding applying for new credit during this period will make any existing inquiries weigh even less.

Having said that, if the inquiries are hurting your score, then by all means attempt to get them removed. Since they stay on your report for two years, many inquiries (more than five in the preceding 24 months or more than three in the preceding 12 months) can be a thorn in the side of consumers who have otherwise flawless reports.

There are basically two types of inquiries on every report, sometimes referred to hard hits and soft hits. "Hard" hits get added whenever you apply for any credit extension, either new credit or a limit increase; these will affect your score. "Soft" hits will not affect your credit score. They get added as a result of any of the following:

- A promotional inquiry (coded PRM) in response to which only your name and address are provided. Basically, the reporting agencies sell your name and address to third parties, and you end up on a mailing list since you meet certain lending criteria. If you wish to avoid these types of inquiries, simply send a letter to the Big Three stating that you wish to OPT OUT of these solicitations. Use the insurance method in all things. (These inquiries remain for 12 months and don't affect a score.)
- Periodic reviews (coded AM or AR; aka account review), which occur when current creditors pull your credit file. (These inquiries remain for 12 months.)
- Requests you make to review your credit file.
- Requests you make to update or change your report and to receive a copy of the updated report.
- Multiple inquiries for an auto or mortgage loan that are within the same 14-day period. (These count as one inquiry.)

Remember, rate shopping has no impact as long as you restrict it to 30 days or less; a score doesn't calculate inquiries performed within the preceding 30 days.

When accounts enter collections, creditors will often continue to make periodic review inquiries to obtain information about you. They want to know as much as they can, and your credit report will often provide useful information, such as how much money you make, where you live, and what your other debts are. Unfortunately, such inquiries are legal; banks have made them part of their standard contracts. But, fortunately, they are coded AR/AM and don't affect a score.

Collection agencies will often perform inquiries, and these end up as hard inquiries, which is wrong. Another problem is with periodic reviews, since bureaus very often fail to properly categorize such inquiries as AR/AM, so they often end up on your hard inquiry list as well. Fortunately, there are three courses of action you can take to get them removed from your report. Simply try one, and if that doesn't work, try another.

1. Send a dispute letter to the bureau explaining that you did not authorize the inquiry and want it to be removed. If you know that the reporting agency made a mistake (e.g., the inquiry came from an existing creditor and was a periodic review, or a collection agency was using it for collection purposes), be sure to spell that out in your letter. As stated at the beginning of this chapter, bureaus are required to contact the furnisher to verify the legitimacy of an item per your request. This includes inquiries. Since furnishers often have other fish to fry, it is possible that they won't respond to the bureau's attempt to verify. Remember, reporting agencies must verify data within a time frame set by the FCRA, and if they cannot do so, the adverse entry must be deleted. When drafting inquiry disputes, use the dispute techniques spelled out in Chapter 9 for accurate inquiries.

2. If a bureau dispute doesn't work and the inquiry entry should have been coded soft, send a letter to the furnisher demanding that the inquiry be removed. Explain that the inquiry is not supposed to show up on your credit report without being coded as an account review, since you never requested an extension or an increase in credit. Follow the procedures for furnisher disputes in accordance with Chapter 11.

3. Seek a legal remedy. If all else fails and you know for a fact that the inquiry resulted from a periodic review (and can prove it by showing that an extension of credit was never requested) and should not be part of your hard inquiry list, consider legal action if there are other, related problems for which you have a claim against a furnisher or bureau.

Although inquiries will hardly affect your score, if you have other legitimate complaints against the same creditor or reporting agency, teaming up with a zealous FCRA attorney may be just what's needed to get the furnisher or bureau to change the way it conducts business.

Just remember, inquiries are small fry and for legal purposes should only ride existing beefs, adding weight to existing claims, for example.

Tip: Always be cognizant that applying for any type of new credit, even overdraft protection, generates an inquiry! So never apply for credit unless absolutely necessary, and only when you're assured approval.

STUDENT LOAN REMOVAL AND REHABILITATION

Student loans are tough, since they can't be dissolved in bankruptcy unless some extraordinary hardship exists. Furthermore, while many states will limit how long collection activity can occur on most debts, student loans have no limit. Collection agencies will wreak havoc on a credit report for years and years by performing inquiries and doggedly going after those in default. But there are ways of dealing with student loan entries, many of which may surprise you.

Discharge the Loan

The Higher Education Act (HEA) provides for student loans to be discharged under the following six circumstances:[2]

1. The school closed while the student was still enrolled. The school must have closed either when the student was enrolled or within 90 days of enrollment. This applies to FFELs, Federal Direct Loans, and Perkins Loans (aka National Direct Student Loans, or NDSLs) received at least in part on or after January 1, 1986. The secretary of education determines the closure date.[3]
2. The school falsely certified a student's eligibility. This applies to FFELs and Federal Direct Loans issued after January 1,

---

2. NCLC *Fair Credit Reporting* § 13.6.11 (5th ed. 2002 and 2005 Supp.).
3. See www.ed.gov/offices/osfap/students/closedschool/search.html. See NCLC *Student Loan Law* § 6.2.2.2 (2nd ed. 2002).

1986. Perkins Loans aren't covered, but any misconduct is a defense to debt (see Chapter 7). There are three types of falsification that qualify: (1) falsification of a non-high-school graduate's ability to benefit from the school's program, (2) enrollment of the student in a job training program for which the student cannot meet the minimum state employment requirements for the job he or she is being trained for, or (3) forgery or alteration of the student loan note or checks.

3. The school failed to pay a refund owed to a student. This applies to the following federal loans issued after January 1, 1986: Guaranteed Student (Stafford) Loans, Unsubsidized Stafford Loans, Supplemental Loans for Students (SLSs), PLUS Loans, and Federal Direct Loans. Perkins Loans aren't covered, but any misconduct is a defense to debt.
4. The borrower is permanently and totally disabled.
5. The borrower dies.
6. The borrower filed for bankruptcy. Certain conditions must be met, and it's not easy to get student loans included.

In the event of discharge, the loan holder is required to inform the bureaus to delete all adverse credit history assigned to the loan.[4] Any dispute in this area should be made in accordance with the guidelines for disputing inaccurate information in the next chapter.

Consolidation
As a method of bad credit removal, this is not recommended. Although accounts won't be listed as delinquent, any previous creditors will still report the accounts as adverse paid entries.

Consolidation is available to those in default if six consecutive loan payments are made. For available options in this regard, check the government's education Web site, www.loanconsolidation.ed.gov.

Rehabilitation
If you've fallen behind on your student loans, under Title IV of the

---

4.   34 C.F.R. §§ 682.402(d)(2)(iv), 682.402(e)(2)(iv).

HEA you can now clean up that credit by making payments on time for 12 consecutive months. If this is performed and followed by a resale of the loan, it will not only make you eligible for additional student loans but also remove the bad credit from your reports. This is a terrific opportunity for those who are in arrears, and it's a policy all creditors should adopt! For more information, contact the grantor of your loan. As always, get any deals in writing.

Rehabilitation can only be performed once in a lifetime, and this HEA amnesty program may not last. Further, if you wish to get back in the good graces of the guarantor so that you can consolidate student loans at lower interest rates, you'd better hurry. Since the passage of the College Access and Opportunity Act of 2005, FFELs (Stafford) issued after July 1, 2006, will no longer be available for consolidation on a fixed-rate basis with a cap of 6.8 percent. That will leave many with only variable-interest-rate options that move the cap up to 8.25 percent.

The opportunity for student loan consolidation is no small thing, since it may lower the payments significantly and, more importantly, bring the account current for the purposes of credit restoration. Laws are changing regarding consolidation as this book goes to print, so check current law carefully before doing anything.

Of course, anything that shows up on a credit report can be challenged with a credit reporting agency as well. But given the ability for those who are current on their payments to consolidate, the unlimited length of time that student loans can be collected, and the inability to write them off in bankruptcy, it's best to bring them current.

As gravy, any installment accounts that improve the average age of all accounts, as well as the average age of open accounts, can be terrific for a FICO score. It can also be significant if the loan happens to be the oldest tradeline entry, which student loans often are.

CHECKING ACCOUNT REPAIR

It's important that consumers maintain a checking account in good standing, since failure to do so will often result in a credit denial for many types of credit. When you go into a bank to open a new checking account, the bank will often perform an inquiry on your credit file, as well as contact the main clearinghouse for checking account reporting, ChexSystems. Banks are losing about $1.6 billion a year to bad checks as of this writing, so they've taken steps to ban what they consider abusers of the system. Furnishers report adverse consumer history to ChexSystems as a method of enforcement. Such information includes the following and can result in new-account denial:

- Forced closure of a consumer's account as a result of nonpayment, bounced checks, or overdrafts
- Multiple overdrafts
- Savings account, debit card, or ATM abuse
- Fraud
- Providing false information when opening an account
- The consumer's reporting of lost or stolen checks (shared with banks to prevent losses against a closed account)
- Attempts by consumers to open more than one account in less than three months (considered a red flag for account theft and money laundering)
- Outstanding debts, checks, and payment plans set up when the bank was unable to collect for an overdraft or a payment it honored on insufficient funds (the amount being insignificant)

ChexSystems is technically a credit reporting agency as defined by the FCRA, but it stores data related to checking account history. The de facto standard in checking account reporting performed by banks and credit unions, ChexSystems serves 80 percent of America's financial institutions.[5] The list remains active for five years.

If you've been reported to ChexSystems or a similar reporting agency, you'll approach it no differently than any other adverse data (see Chapter 9). That is, you can dispute it with the reporting agency or contact the furnisher and make a deal. If you still owe the bank money, use that as leverage to get any bad credit removed. If you don't

---

5. Bankrate, "ChexSystems: 'Big Brother' of Banking Is Watching," www.bankrate.com.

owe money, make a deal to either open up a savings account and have direct deposit in exchange for deletion or open a certificate of deposit in exchange for deletion. And if those offers don't work, ask the bank what will.

ChexSystems also offers a benefit that is unlike any other reporting agency—one that actually permits people who've had past problems and were subsequently banned to get back into the banking system. Known as Get Checking, it is an educational program designed to help consumers start over. Once a consumer completes an educational course approved by Get Checking, he or she can open up a new account at a participating local bank or credit union using a certificate earned by attending the class. The six-hour classes, which are open to consumers who aren't suspected of fraud and who make good on their outstanding checks and overdraft fees, costs about $40 to $50—a bargain in my opinion. For more information on what may be available in your area, contact www.aboutchecking.com; for updates, check www.bestcredit.com/getchecking/.

Since ChexSystems is bound by the FCRA, you are entitled to a free credit report from it once per annum. The following is a list of the other major check reporting agencies and their contact information:

- ChexSystems: www.consumerdebit.com
- CheckRite: (800) 766-2748
- TeleCheck: www.telecheck.com
- SCAN/DPPS: www.consumerdebit.com[6]
- CheckCenter/CrossCheck: www.crosscheck.com
- Certegy/Equifax: www.certegy.com
- International Check Services: (800) 631-9656; acquired by TeleCheck in 2002

TeleCheck and ChexSystems are the most widely used checking credit reporting agencies, but it's a good idea to check with all of them if you suspect anything adverse is being reported. Remember, they are considered bureaus by law, so anything on their reports can be disput-

---

6. Both SCAN/DPPS and ChexSystems are owned by eFunds Corporation.

ed and must be deleted if it cannot be verified within 30 days (or 45 if the report was obtained free).

JOINT ACCOUNTS AND DIVORCE

A joint account is one to which two or more people are party. Anyone considered an account holder is legally responsible for the account. Many people mistakenly believe that if a divorce decree states that one party is responsible for an account balance, the creditor cannot go after the other for the debt. In reality, creditors can rightfully go after any account holder who is contractually liable, regardless of the divorce decree.

If an ex-spouse fails to pay up on a joint account, the only remedies are to pay the account or to file suit against the ex-spouse. This is why joint accounts should be separated before divorce, not after.

I'm a firm believer that joint accounts should almost never be employed. Fifty percent of marriages end in divorce, and joint accounts are completely unnecessary anyway. There's only one exception to this—when a bankruptcy is in the offing, as explained in Chapter 12.

RESIDENTIAL CREDIT HISTORY

National tenant reporting agencies are bound by the FCRA, and consumers can dispute adverse information in the same manner as they can with the Big Three. Anytime you are disputing accurate information, use the techniques spelled out in Chapter 9. If the information you are disputing is inaccurate, see Chapter 11.

Be aware that residential leases are unique in that the contractual terms, tenant rights, and local proximity to the lessee (one who holds a lease) provide distinct advantages to a lease holder. By taking advantage of this knowledge, lease holders can employ powerful methods to avoid any incidents of adverse reporting in their files. For more information, see the section on erroneous billing and property lease disputes in Chapter 11.

Tenant Reporting Agencies
The following are some of the most prominent companies that specialize in tenant screening:

- Accufax: www.accufax-us.com
- American Tenant Screen: www.atshome.com
- Choicepoint Tenant History Reports: www.choicetrust.com (will provide a report if it provided your report to a landlord)
- UD Registry: www.udregistry.com
- National Tenant Network: www.ntnonline.com
- Tenant Data Services: www.tenantdata.com
- Tenant Screening Services: www.tenantscreening.com

These national tenant reporting agencies must also provide a free credit report once per annum to consumers, but like the Big Three, they are allowed 45 days to perform a reinvestigation instead of 30 when a consumer obtains a free report.

MULTIPLE REPORTING SCENARIOS

As explained, as debts get transferred and sold to parties other than the original creditor, the same adverse account may be reported more than once. This can be very troublesome to someone wishing to remove an adverse account, but there are effective ways of dealing with it. (Collectors will gladly tell you who owns a debt, so you should always ask if there's a third party involved in reporting or collecting on a debt.)

Third Party Doesn't Own the Debt
When a creditor reports an adverse tradeline, often a collection agency will report the same debt as a collection account as well. But if the collector doesn't own the debt, it will often refer the matter back to the original creditor if it receives a cease-communication letter from the debtor, no matter what the original debt was for. (If it receives such a letter before it has reported the adverse information, then it often never reports it.)

Once a debt is referred back to an original creditor, a third party that doesn't have a stake in it will have no incentive to tangle with a proactive debtor that sends letters and makes demands under the FDCPA and FCRA. As such, it will often (a) delete the account on the instruction of the original creditor (which you can have included in any settlement agreement language, though it will spell out that the original creditor doesn't actually control what a third party does), or (b) fail to affirm the account in the event of a credit bureau dispute. If a collection account remains on your report after you've pursued each of these avenues, and the original creditor has already agreed to remove its own adverse entry, then continued reporting of the collection account may be in violation of the FCRA. In that case, send a letter directly to the collection agency demanding removal, along with a copy of the entry as reported and a copy of original creditor instructions. Explain that the reporting is in violation of the FDCPA, FCRA, and state UDAPs. Demand a UDF and set a deadline of 10 days. This always seems to work. If it doesn't, consider seeking a legal remedy where appropriate. (See Chapter 14.)

Third Party Owns the Debt

When debts get sold, the previous owners are supposed to stop reporting it. Unfortunately, they believe this to mean that they can stop sending *additional* information to the bureaus; whatever they last reported will remain. As a result, even if an arrangement can be made with any current debt holder, the previous owner/original creditor has already furnished adverse information, and that won't change unless a) it agrees to change or delete the entry voluntarily, or b) it fails to affirm/agree to update the information in a credit bureau dispute, or c) it is ordered to stop reporting by a court. A court order is injunctive only, meaning the creditor can be ordered to stop future reporting. This works on information already furnished to the bureaus, as a formal credit bureau dispute of the offending entry (after such a court ruling is in place) will require the bureau to contact the furnisher, while the furnisher will not be permitted to affirm it; it should be deleted by the bureau for failure to verify in accordance with the FCRA.

I prefer going directly to the original owner after I've made a deal with the current debt holder. I explain that the debt is satisfied, keeping any terms confidential. You can say, "My settlement agreement says that I cannot speak of any terms of the deal. But it is satisfied and no longer reporting." Explain that you'd like to establish a new relationship by opening up an account or whatever in order to have the bad credit deleted. If this proves futile, I would go straight for a declaratory judgment in accordance with Chapter 14. It's cheap, and it works.

11

RESTORE INACCURATE BAD CREDIT

Although some adverse information on credit reports is accurate, of course some is often inaccurate. Furthermore, an adverse entry may be accurate in a technical sense but inaccurate by virtue of a legitimate dispute between a consumer and a furnisher. This is particularly common with residential lease and utility disputes, and there are very powerful methods of avoiding such reporting before it ever occurs. Though this chapter will address accurate adverse removal, a big part of winning the credit game is *prevention*.

And as a reminder, one thing you must always consider carefully when removing inaccurate information is your FICO credit score. Some inaccurate information may not be adverse at all, and its presence may be helping your score more than it's hurting it. Even certain inaccurate information that *is* adverse may be helping more than hurting by virtue of its age, credit limit, and so on.

ERRONEOUS REPORTING

Inaccurate data can get on your report in a number of ways: a service bureau can make a mistake, the credit bureau's unruly database and query system can cause a mistake, a furnisher can provide wrong or outdated information, or someone can steal your identity. The remedies for each scenario are generally the same, although identity theft is a special case for which some additional countermeasures must be taken.

Sometimes you won't even know how something ended up on your report until you do some investigating. New accounts under your SSN will often suggest identity theft, whereas correspondence with a bureau and a furnisher can indicate that a file merger has occurred.

You may have items on your report that are outright false that can be settled very quickly. For instance, an item was paid on time but shows "paid late." In many cases it's just a mistake. (They do happen!)

What to Remove? It's about the Score

While many would argue that removing anything that isn't accurate is the goal, I take issue with that approach. I use the following guidelines when determining which entries to target for removal:

- Remove duplicate accounts that are detrimental to your score. Often credit reporting agencies will report the same account multiple times on a single report. This can occur for many reasons. Perhaps a tradeline is being reported by two furnishers using different subscriber numbers, or there's a glitch in the credit bureau's database. Remove only the duplicate accounts that are adverse or carry large balances; good duplicate accounts will likely help a FICO score.
- Remove any invalid adverse accounts (e.g., accounts that aren't yours, are obsolete, or are part of an authorized user account that has adverse information attached to it).[1]
- Remove any invalid public record entries, such as judgments, bankruptcies, or liens.
- Dispute only adverse entries that are entirely inaccurate. In other words, if an account has both accurate and inaccurate

---

1. Upon request, credit reporting agencies are required to delete the tradeline of user accounts, whether or not the account contains adverse information. Reporting agencies will report cosigner and joint accounts, however.

adverse data, don't bother having the inaccurate portion corrected. Such scenarios should be handled differently, in accordance with Chapter 9. You see, the ultimate goal is removal or modification of adverse accounts that are reported accurately. Requesting credit bureau corrections to accounts that contain both accurate and inaccurate adverse entries instead of going for deletion of the entire tradeline (in accordance with Chapter 9) is counterproductive.

When erroneous adverse information exists, simultaneously contact the bureau(s) and the furnishers. Remember to handle all such correspondence in writing only, using the insurance method (see Appendix C for sample letters). Do not use the online forms the bureaus provide for any reason. By providing them with every possible bit of information, spelled out in writing and accompanied by supporting documentation, you preclude any possible claims on their part that the information you provided is incomplete. (Don't be confused with the use of vague disputes advised in Chapter 9; vague language is to be used in disputing accurate adverse information only.) Furthermore, should a legal battle ensue, any claims they make in defense of their actions will not help them. They'll be hog-tied, pinned, finished. Get it? It's *game over*. Protections are in place under the FCRA for your benefit, and your paper trail provides the necessary proof when they fail to follow the rules.

When you're disputing inaccurate information with the bureaus, it's important to be as specific as possible. Bureaus will often expedite the processing of your dispute if it contains your (1) full name with suffix, (2) current address (as reported by a current creditor) and previous addresses over the previous 24 months, (3) date of birth, (4) telephone number, (5) SSN, (6) spouse's name if married, (7) current employer, (8) description of the item in dispute accompanied by a copy of your credit report with the item highlighted in some fashion, (9) explanation as to why you are disputing the information (e.g., "doesn't belong to me"), and (10) request to delete or correct the erroneous information.[2]

---

2. NCLC *Fair Credit Reporting* § 7.3.2.3 (5th ed. 2002 and 2005 Supp.).

Again, your initial correspondence with bureaus and furnishers should not contain any threats or even mention of legal action. It should simply be clear and concise and list any ways in which the inaccurate entry is hurting you.

When contacting a furnisher, you must dispute specific information about the debt for the dispute to meet FCRA requirements. You may contact furnishers by phone when you're in a hurry, but only in conjunction with a written dispute sent RRM. Providing any supporting evidence (e.g., a canceled check or receipt of payment) is also helpful. Make sure your letter references any specific attached documentation. Also be sure to use the address a creditor provides for disputes (usually on its invoices); if one is not provided, send the dispute to a street address and not a PO Box if possible.

No private cause of action is available under the FCRA for disputing directly with furnishers, which means that consumers cannot sue furnishers for violations of the Act.[3] However, the lawsuit restriction is lifted when a formal dispute is filed with the bureau and a furnisher affirms the inaccurate data. The furnisher may, of course, rectify the error. But should it fail to correct or delete an inaccurate entry after reinvestigation, your combining a direct furnisher dispute with a bureau dispute will strengthen any legal case you may file against the furnisher.

If you're in a rush to get the offending data removed, telephone the furnisher simultaneously with sending your written dispute and explain the situation, going up the food chain until you find someone who is willing to help you. Often the furnisher will agree that the information is erroneous and correct it. Get the name of the person you spoke with, and have him or her send (fax is best) a copy of the correction to you and to the bureaus. Be sure and ask the furnisher for a copy of the UDF. When you get the letter and/or UDF, send copies to the bureaus as well (using the insurance method), along with a statement indicating what you expect them to do: fix your report immediately and send you a corrected copy.[4]

---

3. A properly presented dispute to the bureaus is required to subject the furnisher to liability for failure to conduct an adequate investigation. NCLC *Fair Credit Reporting* § 3.11.2 (5th Ed. 2002 and 2005 Supp.).

4. The correction may have occurred in the furnisher's database, but the bureaus likely won't get it until the monthly Metro 2 update is sent to them.

If you can't get the furnisher to agree by phone to remove the data, wait 14 days. If the furnisher either responds in the negative or doesn't respond at all to your written letter within 14 days, send another letter, this one mentioning that the furnisher is in violation of the FCRA. If you're so inclined, this second letter can state that you will take legal action for a FCRA breach if that's your plan. (Personally, I wouldn't make this threat if I didn't intend to follow through with legal action, but what you do is your business, of course.) Wait another 14 days, and then check any report(s) affected.

If the furnisher has not removed the offending data after two passes and the bureau fails to remove it in accordance with the FCRA reinvestigation requirements (usually within 30 days of receiving your dispute), send a second dispute letter to the bureaus reiterating how the inaccurate information is hurting you. Demand that the results of the reinvestigation are provided to you within 15 days, as required by FCRA. (Again, I always state that I'll take legal action and then follow through if the bureau doesn't remove it.) If the inaccurate information remains on your report after you have contacted the furnisher and the bureaus twice, you can do one of the following: (1) continue to battle with the furnisher and the bureaus using letters, (2) file a lawsuit for money damages, or (3) file a declaratory judgment lawsuit to get the entry deleted. (See Chapter 14 for legal recourse.) You are not required to suffer actual damages in order to obtain punitive money damages for willful failure to comply with the FCRA. Yet if you can show that you were adversely affected in terms of any credit extension or that the inaccurate reporting affected your emotional well-being, it will strengthen your claim.[5] If the information caused you to be denied credit or affected your interest rates on a home or auto loan, get letters to that effect from the lender(s). If the interest rates were affected, make sure any letter specifies to what extent.

---

5. A seasoned FCRA attorney once explained that creditors and bureaus alike will fight any lawsuit, taking it to trial, if the consumer didn't experience a denial of credit resulting from the entry. It's better to have a loan denial letter, thereby avoiding trial and obtaining a good settlement offer.

If you opt to continue to do battle using letters, ask for a "re-investigation." Again, indicate how the erroneous information is hurting you.

While each of these three courses of action may seem unattractive, the good thing is that there are legal remedies available. If it were me, I'd sue the bastards.

Paid Items Shown as Unpaid or Late

If you have proof (e.g., a canceled check or receipt of payment) that an item reported as unpaid or late was actually paid on time, then you can likely get the offending data removed by disputing it with the bureaus. In fact, if I had irrefutable proof of payment, then I might just send the proof to the bureaus and skip the furnisher altogether.

Caution: If you don't have proof that the account reported as unpaid or late was paid on time, don't reveal the fact that you've lost your receipt. This could open up Pandora's box if the creditor has the scruples of Enron executives. Simply ask that the creditor provide a letter to the bureaus correcting the error and send you a copy.

But if you elect to contact the furnisher by telephone and you fail to get a favorable response even after you've requested help nicely, ask to speak to the manager. Continue moving up the chain of command with your request until you believe you've exhausted your efforts. If your short-term efforts fail, make sure you initiate further correspondence with the creditor in writing, and use the insurance method.

If things get bad—i.e., neither the furnisher nor the bureaus have responded favorably to your dispute letters—then clearly and succinctly state in writing that you intend to seek a legal remedy if that's your plan. Don't make idle threats; simply describe whatever actions you intend to carry out. I assure you, creditors—and sometimes the bureaus at this point—will often deny any knowledge of your previous contact. Be nice nonetheless, and explain that this is your "last ditch effort" to resolve the matter amicably.

Erroneous Reporting of Student Loans

Many times, student loan accounts that are placed for collection will get sold repeatedly to different collection agencies. The buyers of such debt will report it under different subscriber numbers and other identifying account data. As a result, student loans are often reported multiple times.

Simply handle this as you would any other inaccurate data, by disputing the erroneous account entries with the bureaus. Only the current loan holder is permitted to report a student loan debt as owed, and ones who've furnished previous to selling the debt must furnish a zeroed-out balance to the bureaus. (For deleting accurate reporting of adverse student loan history, see Chapter 10.)

Other Erroneous Public Records Entries

Often a public record is reported and then a change in status occurs, such as an arrest that doesn't result in a conviction or a lien that's paid. Perhaps it's just a case of mistaken identity. In any case, it's best to go to the source of the problem: the county or court records. County and court clerks are used to dealing with mistakes and are often more than willing to help you resolve a problem if you can readily prove the error (e.g., of identity, transcription) through documentation. Once the error is cleared up at the source, a subsequent dispute with the bureaus should bring positive results.

File Merger Mistakes

As demonstrated in Chapter 1, credit reporting agencies commonly merge the file of one person with another due to the way they use identifiers when compiling credit reports. One way to counter this problem is through the use of a "do-not-confuse" statement.

When a credit bureau confuses you once with another party, the odds are high that it will happen again. Using a do-not-confuse statement, notify the bureau that you don't wish to be confused with the other party. In your letter provide all the information you can about the other party (e.g., name, address, phone number, place of employment).

The FCRA does not address do-not-confuse statements; it's something that the bureaus have instituted to deal with the high propensity for such errors. The bureaus require the statement to be filed by *both parties* for it to be effective. Thus it's best to contact the other party directly and request that he or she also file a do-not-confuse statement. If you are having trouble locating the other party, consider using the skip tracing methods outlined in Chapter 6.

Post-Bankruptcy Erroneous Reporting

Banks are notorious for continuing to report accounts in arrears after a consumer has filed bankruptcy. They even do so after the consumer disputes the items with the bureaus, reaffirming the debts as owed during the bureaus' investigation! This is nothing more than a malicious attempt to get even with the consumer for failure to satisfy the debt.

This presents a big problem for consumers, since the tradelines in question will often show unpaid balances, charge-offs, and collection accounts—worse than bankruptcy, since loan approval won't come until the debts are "satisfied" in the mind of a potential lender. Even if you can show the lender your bankruptcy petition, you will either (a) still be denied because your FICO score is too low or (b) be approved but at a higher interest rate. Lenders are bound by federal law to treat all consumers equally, and your score is the key—the method by which they meet that requirement.

The FCRA requires furnishers to indicate a zero balance when an account is included in bankruptcy.[6] They can report the account as included in bankruptcy, but they must also indicate a zero balance. It also requires that they indicate when a nonfiling spouse is not the primary obligator. In other words, if your spouse filed bankruptcy and wrapped joint debts into it, then the furnisher cannot report your account as "included in bankruptcy."[7] Moreover, the furnisher must indicate the bankruptcy chapter under which a consumer filed.[8]

---

6. FTC Official Staff Commentary § 607 item 6; see also *Learn v. Credit Bureau of Lancaster County*, 664 F. Supp. 962 (E.D. Pa. 1987), rev'd without opinion, 838 F2d 461 (3d Cir. 1987); Brinckerhoff, FTC informal staff opinion letters, Mar. 19, 1987, and Nov. 4, 1986.
7. FTC Official Staff Commentary § 607 item 3F(3).
8. 15 U.S.C. § 1681c(d).

Many states have their own laws concerning bankruptcy reporting, and it would be wise to check to see whether any such laws are being violated.[9]

If a creditor reported erroneously under any of the circumstances here, I would (a) dispute the entry with the bureaus and the furnisher (and then look at legal avenues if they fail to make the entry accurate), or (b) file a declaratory judgment lawsuit and have the whole tradeline removed.[10]

Personally, I like the second option a lot better. Having the tradeline removed will strengthen your chances of removing the bankruptcy entry altogether. (See Chapter 10.) Again, if the furnisher rectifies the situation as a result of a credit bureau dispute, then there's no cause of action available under the FCRA, but there may be other breaches of law.

Note: It's a bad idea to make payments on debts discharged in bankruptcy. If you ever become late again, creditors may report delinquencies subsequent to the bankruptcy.[11] If you run into some money and wish to pay such debts, only do so when they can be paid in full and there's no possible chance of future delinquency. Further, do so only when the furnisher agrees to remove all adverse references in exchange for payment.

High Damage Awards for Creditor and Bureau Negligence

Juries appear to be getting sick and tired of the bureaus and creditors running over people, and the damage awards for failing to perform "reasonable investigations" into consumer disputes are growing.

As mentioned earlier, Virginia-based NACA attorney Leonard Bennett represented Linda Johnson in a case against MBNA and the three bureaus and won a $90,000 actual damage award for an erro-

---

9. California and Maine require that a bankruptcy reporting include the type. Check your state laws.
10. See Chapter 14.
11. Foster, FTC Informal Staff Opinion Letter, Feb. 15, 2000.

neous item on her report, a credit card account belonging to her ex-husband. The defendants (MBNA and the bureaus) refused to delete the information, and the jury found that they didn't perform a reasonable investigation in accordance with the FCRA. Although MBNA appealed the jury award, the 4th Circuit Court of Appeals upheld the award in February 2004.[12]

I also mentioned the award of $5 million in punitive damages in Judy Thompson's suit against the bureaus, which a judge subsequently reduced to $1 million. If you're representing yourself, the odds of getting such an award are slim; so in these types of cases (and any credit reporting money damage claim), you should certainly seek an attorney—one who's a consumer advocate by nature and has experience litigating FCRA matters.

If you feel your case is strong, I'd advise you to seek out an attorney without delay, in accordance with Chapter 14.

ERRONEOUS BILLING:
PREVENTION AND AVOIDANCE

Often people will get billed (or overbilled) for products or services they didn't receive and then, to add insult to injury, will be harassed by bill collectors attempting to collect on the bogus debt.

If the erroneous billing involves a credit card, you may be in luck. Often credit card statements will include charges that don't belong to you, are for a dollar amount greater than you authorized, or are for goods or services you ordered but never received. In such cases, you have 60 days from the date of the billing statement to dispute the charge. (This is why the travel industry loves to bill far in advance of travel, since problems will often arise outside of this dispute period, leaving consumers with no recourse.) The technique for disputing a charge is known as a charge-back, and consumers are not responsible for items that the merchant cannot substantiate. Your bank will work on your behalf to resolve the issue, and the burden of proof will be on

---

12. Furnishers aren't liable for money damages unless the matter was formerly disputed with the credit bureaus (see Chapter 14).

the merchant's bank to back up the charge. Further, once disputed the charge goes in stasis, the charge won't incur interest charges or show up on your bill until the matter is resolved. As always, send disputes to your bank using the insurance method. If you're outside the time period allowed for a charge-back, then you'll likely need to use a court option to get the issue resolved, since the matter often will end up in collections and severely damage your credit.

As always, try to reason with the party who billed you (in person, if possible). If you are able to resolve the issue in a way that you find favorable, get the agreement in writing and make sure that you stipulate removal of bad credit, if any, as part of the deal. If the account has been turned over to a collection agency, try to have the matter referred back to the original creditor as described in Chapter 7. Of course, if the collection agency has already purchased the debt, this won't be possible.

You have two options in the case of erroneous billing. One is to pay the bill under protest and then sue in small claims court to recover the money. The other is filing a declaratory judgment lawsuit. I like the latter option better, because it offers many advantages. First, if you sue first, then a lawsuit can't end up on your credit report, even if the defendant countersues. Second, it puts the party that erroneously billed you on a defensive footing, made even worse by the expense that party incurs to defend its position in court. (Smaller creditors, such as doctors and small businesses, are billed by attorneys on an hourly basis in most cases.) Third, most erroneous billing cases are for small dollar amounts (less than $200), so they will likely go uncontested and you'll win by default.

Once you're billed improperly, the clock is ticking, and you'll face collection action if you don't do something right away. This erroneous debt will end up on your credit report and hurt your credit, which is why filing suit immediately after you've attempted to have the matter resolved amicably (give your negotiations three days) is a good thing—regardless of the dollar amount.

If a collection agency has purchased the debt, it won't cease its collection efforts (while it may be required to cease communication, it can still attempt to collect by lawsuit) until you either pay or file bankruptcy. The agency will jack up your report and ignore your pleas to stop what it's doing. You can always file for a declaratory judgment at this stage, but you might be better served by retaining a lawyer and filing a civil suit seeking punitive damages. A good FCRA/FDCPA attorney will list both the collection agency and the original creditor as defendants in the action. In the end, they'll get theirs—just make sure that you keep copies of all your credit reports and all correspondence as evidence. If your case is sound, many attorneys will take it on a contingency fee basis (i.e., they get paid if and when you win the lawsuit). (See Chapter 14.)

Note: When you win a judgment, send a copy to the bureaus and demand that they stop reporting the account (not report it as paid, but remove it from your file altogether—be explicit in your demand). Also, if you decide to sue, ask the judge to order the defendant(s) to stop reporting the adverse entry as part of your request for relief. With standard civil suits (not declaratory), if you get a monetary award, then you can turn the tables and make the judgment-debtor squirm as you damage its credit with a judgment, especially if the judgment-debtor is an individual! Justice is best served up with the cold taste of irony.

Sometimes when you file suit, a creditor will still refer the matter over to a collection agency. In this case, just send the agency a letter demanding that it cease its collection action; then you dispute the debt and attach a copy of the complaint (lawsuit) against the creditor. Inform the collection agency that it will be next if it doesn't comply. This is usually enough, but be prepared to sue the agency if it doesn't heed your warning.

USA Today published a report about a lawsuit (Case No. 02CC15162), involving Washington Mutual Bank and the Alonso family, who experienced a number of unforeseen difficulties and fell behind in their loan payments in the first half of 2002. They received a default notice, but in July they entered into a repayment agreement with the bank by which they would make monthly payments in the amount of $3,994.89, beginning in August. On August 30, Mrs. Alonso went in person to Washington Mutual to make the first payment but did not have a copy of the repayment agreement with her. She asked a teller to look up her home loan account and was told that the amount due was $3,943.33. Relying on that information, she wrote a check for that amount.

On September 10, the Alonsos received a letter from Washington Mutual, returning their check and informing them that, since partial payments were not acceptable, the loan was in foreclosure, effective immediately. Their efforts to pay the amount due fell through, since they were never able to connect with the bank's designated officer, despite their repeated attempts. Washington Mutual informed the plaintiffs that if they did not enter into a modification of their repayment plan, they would foreclose on the house on September 24. To their complete shock, the Alonsos learned that their home sold at foreclosure on September 20. Ultimately, the parties reached an out-of-court settlement, and the Alonsos were able to keep their home.

Apparently, class actions are being brought against Washington Mutual as well, and, if the allegations are true, it appears that this bank has been failing to post payments made by hundreds of consumers. (Some Web sites have compiled the numerous complaints against Washington Mutual, including www.wamufraud.com.)

The lesson is this: bad things can happen to good people at the hands of a trusted institution. Erroneous billing is quite common, and it's usually followed by collection action, so always keep your receipts of payment, and as soon as something begins to run amuck, take good notes and be prepared for a legal battle.

Property Lease Disputes

The property lease is unique in so many ways, not the least of which is the opportunity for you to specify the terms of the contract before signing it, unlike with preprinted contracts so often used by lenders. As such, you can greatly enhance your position as a tenant in the event that your situation changes after you move in or the place doesn't live up to your expectations.

Before you sign a lease, you can build in desirable terms, particularly exit terms. Some examples include the option to vacate with 60 days' notice (even though you signed for a year) with no penalty, the option to sublet, and the option to transfer the lease. Make sure that everything is agreed to in writing, especially pet policies (if you own a pet). For my dog, I always list his name, breed, and weight. That way, if there's ever a dispute and the landlords want to juice up any claim against me, they can never come back and say, "I agreed to a small dog, not a 120-pound malamute."

Once you have negotiated your terms and have signed the lease, you have another opportunity to document the condition of the unit and other potential problems. I strongly recommend using a camcorder to take video footage of the premises before you move in. Include a newspaper published from that day in the footage so there are no questions later, and state in the introduction of the video what you are doing and why. If you don't have a camcorder or can't borrow one, then take pictures at the very least. Landlords are notorious for cheating tenants, and these measures are invaluable in terms of protecting yourself.

If for some reason the unit doesn't work out and you need to vacate before the lease expires, give the landlord a call and explain the circumstances. Sometimes a landlord will be glad you're leaving and will let you out of the lease. If the unit didn't live up to your expectations (e.g., barking dog, bad neighbors, landlord's failure to make repairs), create a paper trail every time something goes wrong. That is, notify the landlord (or the landlord's proxy) in writing, using the insurance method. This avoids the he said/she said routine.

Tip: Never abandon a unit; not only will it look bad in front of a judge, but the landlord can say anything he or she wants about the condition of the unit and will likely be believed. After all, if you were a judge, would you believe someone who just left with no communication and no notice?

If the landlord is willing to let you out of the lease, of course you'll need to get the agreement in writing immediately, with all of the terms spelled out succinctly. In a case where the landlord is unwilling to let you out or agree to what you deem are reasonable terms, consider whether he lived up to his end of the contract (e.g., was the property safe, quiet, functional?). You may need to send a "notice of intent to vacate in 30 days" (30 days is always considered reasonable notice) and request a reasonable time for a walk-through to be completed and the keys/garage door openers turned in.

Whether or not the landlord agrees to meet to perform a walk-through, don't argue; have the place professionally cleaned, including carpets, and keep your receipts. Take more video (or pictures) on the day of departure, and include the landlord in the shots if possible.

Even though the landlord may still want a lease penalty, he or she may be willing to perform the walk-through and sign a statement saying he received the unit (and the keys) back in a satisfactory condition. Get this if you can. If he's unwilling to do this or has made himself unavailable, return the keys with a note explaining what your intentions are and stating that the keys are enclosed; use the insurance method, as always. What you're doing is mitigating the damage for what could be a legal battle. (Go to your local courthouse and ask the clerk what the most common complaint filed is . . . the answer will be landlord-tenant disputes.)

What are your intentions? Well, that depends on many factors, such as how much the landlord claims you owe, how far apart you are, whether he's being reasonable, and under what conditions you felt compelled to move in the first place. Your intentions may be to get out of the lease without paying any penalties, in spite of the fact that the contract calls for them; to litigate in order to get damages for unnecessary suffering (hard to prove, unless you are totally disabled); or simply to get your deposit back. Some of this may be attainable if you can demonstrate that the landlord didn't live up to his end of the bargain and that you were the reasonable one.

Again, your first course under adversarial conditions would be to send the notice of intent to vacate and explain the reasons. If you get a response that you're not happy with, stay as amicable as you can and, as stated before, get the landlord to sign a statement that he received the unit (and keys) in good order.

> **Tip:** If it can be avoided, don't lease a rental unit from a management company or agent of the owner. If you ever have a problem, then it will inevitably sink into the abyss, with each party blaming the other. The mess that will ensue will not only drive you mad, but litigation can become problematic due to the convoluted nature of it. Keep dealings simple and avoid third parties where possible.

Once you've vacated and still can't obtain a release from the contract, you can get more aggressive. Now you're in a time crunch, since doing nothing will inevitably lead to collection action, likely from a collection agency. Your credit will surely be damaged if you don't take preemptive action to stop it. That action can either be a restrictively endorsed check (explained later) or a lawsuit.

Before that happens, immediately send a follow-up letter (using the insurance method) stating that you tried to be amicable, but since the landlord is not, you'll take the following actions within 10 days if you don't hear back: (a) notify the health department of specific violations (if they exist), (b) Notify HUD of the same deficiencies, (c) notify the attorney general's office of the same. Is the landlord operating under a real estate license? Explain that you'll also notify the state agency that oversees such licenses. Moreover, I'd inform the landlord of my intention to file suit and seek damages, since he failed to live up to his end of the contract. Wait 14 days, and then go through with whatever you said you were going to do in your letter.

Litigation under landlord-tenant laws can be quite troublesome, which is why many lawyers don't take such cases, and the ones that do want a retainer up front and will only work on an hourly rate (no flat rates). And those hours can add up really fast.

Many states have laws stating that "irreparable damage" must have occurred before you can get damages from a landlord, and this standard is usually an insurmountable hurdle. While Americans with Disabilities Act (ADA) cases are the exception, these cases are tricky and are conducted in federal court. You'll need an attorney for sure, one who specializes in such cases. Federal court can be quite complicated (even for attorneys), and new laws are being written on ADA every day. It's the most progressive area of the law in America as of this writing.

Of course, some states have more favorable tenant laws, so it's up to you to learn what you can do and/or consult an attorney. Don't assume anything.

Any more, if the dollar amount is high enough, landlords (or their counsel) will simply file suit against you not long after they've attempted collection action. This suit will likely end up on your credit report and damage you immensely. (The collection action itself will damage your report as well.) Furthermore, they'll often sue for far more than the contract actually calls for or for damages that don't exist.

When I walk out of a lease for good reason (i.e., the landlord broke the lease) and the landlord won't agree to void the contract, then I will consider filing suit right away, requesting a declaratory judgment in accordance with Chapter 14.

This works well in many ways. First, if you retain a lawyer but only *threaten* a lawsuit, then the landlord could sue you first, in anticipation of your action. By rule, if you are the plaintiff, the lawsuit won't end up on your credit report—even if the other party countersues. If the other party sues you first, then it will likely end up on your credit report as a public record civil action. Of course, if the other party wins the suit and obtains a judgment, then the judgment will end up on your report no matter who filed first.

Keep in mind that a lawsuit on your credit report is not the same as a collection account, which brings me to my second point: even though you've sued first, the landlord can still hand the matter over to a collection agency and attempt to collect the debt—less likely, but possible. The debt will probably show up on your report as a collection action. Now you've potentially saved yourself two bad marks, and maybe even a third, a judgment.

Even if the debt is handed over to a collection agency while in litigation, a letter from your attorney demanding that it be removed will almost always lead to removal. The agency knows you're serious at that point, since you've filed suit once already.

Third, the debt surely can't be sold to a third party when it's in litigation, which is even better.

These are all compelling reasons why I don't waste too much time with threats—I file suit right when I know there's trouble.

If collection action has already begun and the landlord hasn't sued you yet, try to settle the matter in accordance with the methods spelled out earlier in the sections on dealing with debt collectors and negotiating. Through discussion, find out the status of the landlord's collection action and get a handle on where it's going. As I said, you might also consider suing first if you can demonstrate that the landlord breached the lease first.

You have the right to the quiet, peaceful enjoyment of the property, safety, and basic services. If any of these conditions was not met and if there are contractual provisions in the lease that the landlord has failed to meet, then your landlord is in breach of the lease.

There are so many possible scenarios and circumstances surrounding leases, and tenant-landlord laws vary widely from state to state. Carefully assess your situation; if you feel you aren't making any headway on your own, then contact an attorney.

With leases, the bottom line is this—you must act fast before your credit is damaged. It's a pain in the neck, but being proactive will save you a great deal of time and money in the long run.

Use of a Restrictively Endorsed Check: Real-World Example

I once used a restrictively endorsed check in a dispute over a one-year lease. When I moved into an apartment complex, there was a provision in the contract stating that I could cancel it at any time within 30 days of signing. Since there was nothing available on the first floor, I accepted a third-floor apartment with the understanding that I would be in the queue for one on the first floor when it became available.

Two weeks later, I moved into a first-floor apartment and agreed to pay a cleaning fee for the third-floor apartment that I had vacated. The property management company required me to sign a new lease for the first-floor apartment.

After a short time, I discovered that not one but two yapping dogs lived right above me. I reported this and found that neither dog was on the neighbor's lease. Yet they were permitted to stay, and I soon found this situation to be intolerable. In addition, the management company failed to provide services as required by the lease, namely (a) security services, and (b) parking permit controls. As a result, the complex was chaos at all hours.

When I notified the management company of my intent to move based on a 30-day option built into the contract, I was told that my lease began when I originally moved into the third-floor apartment. But if that were true, then why did I sign a new lease upon moving into the first-floor apartment and pay exit fees (cleaning) for the old? You get the picture: it was both an old lease and a new lease, depending on what particular situation suited the management company.

My logic was met with a vitriolic manager's refusal to listen to any reason. The conversation ended like this: I said, "You've shown that you are unreasonable and can't be trusted. All further communication with you shall be done in writing." And so it was.

I spelled out my concerns in writing, providing notice of my intent to exercise my 30-day right to cancel by vacating, while also explaining the ways in which the management company was in breach of the lease. I sent this letter using the insurance method, of course.

Notice that this started a paper trail—which proved that there was a "bona fide dispute" in play (see Chapter 7). Had I not done this, I can only imagine having to stand in front of a judge at some later date, listening to the property manager lie, "There was never a dispute . . . ."

The letter also stated that there was a restrictively endorsed check enclosed and that it covered rent (and cleaning fees) through my departure date. It also requested that someone meet me on the afternoon of my departure date to perform a walk-though inspection and stated that I would turn in the keys and the garage door opener at that time.

In the memo block of the check, I wrote, "Restrictively endorsed check." On the back, I wrote, "restrictively endorsed check," underlined it, and then added the following: "This check constitutes payment in full for tenancy of [address] through the period September 1, 2003, due to a bona fide dispute over 30-day cancellation terms, noise, and failure of [company] to provide parking and security services. Upon cashing, no cause of action may lie as to this contract dispute or tenancy, and this check is satisfactory payment, made in full settlement."

In my letter, I informed the manager of my intent to cancel the check in 10 days if it went uncashed and stated that there would be no further checks forthcoming; we could dance in court if she chose. The company did the smart thing and cashed the check and then performed a walk-through with me on my move-out date. Of course, I took video of the walk-through and made sure to show the company's agent in it.

I saved myself a lot of money and aggravation. Further, my credit report was spared some ugly collection activity. And if the management company had decided to collect anyway, I could have used the restrictively endorsed check to go for a declaratory judgment (Chapter 14), or perhaps even sought damages for breach of contract, wrongful collection action, and harm to my credit report. In any case, I was holding all the cards, and that's where you always want to be.

This real-world example shows how a landlord can be put over a barrel through the use of a restrictively endorsed check, since he could either cash the check in hand—an amount that I believed was fair, though it was less than he wanted—or get nothing at all. You see, even if I had paid the landlord what I felt I owed upon exit, he could have come back and sued for more. This way, I was ahead because *I had his money*. As I see it, if I'm going to get sued, then they'll have to come after me for the whole enchilada. Ever heard the old saying, "Possession is nine-tenths of the law"? It's just means that in law, it's a better position to be ahead than to come from behind. Just remember, laws vary from state to state. If you want to employ a restrictively endorsed check, I suggest you consult an attorney.

Utility Bills

Utility companies commonly make mistakes, including billing for services not rendered, overcharging for services, and failing to apply a credit that was promised. The latter is very common, which is why I always get the name and address of any utility customer service agent who agrees to adjust a bill.

This happened to me when I canceled my DirecTV service. DirecTV requires that customers agree to a one-year commitment. However, when customers move and cannot have service at the new address, this presents a problem. When I contacted the company and explained that I had moved and could not get service at the new location, the representative said that I could return the equipment and there would be no additional charges or fees. DirecTV sent me boxes for shipment of the electronics, which I returned immediately.

Shortly thereafter, I received a bill for a $100 cancellation fee. When I telephoned customer service, all I got was a nasty woman explaining that $112 was due (a $12 late fee was added), and that wouldn't change. When I asked to speak to her supervisor, she hung up on me.

That's not something I respond well to.

Knowing that a collection agency would soon be contacting me, I waited. Sure enough, within about 60 days, I received a bill from the agency. I immediately sent it a cease-communication letter and also requested that it refer the matter back to DirecTV. (Of course, I could have called back again right away after the DirecTV representative first hung up on me, but talking to someone when angry would not likely have had a positive result. Remember what I said in Chapter 9 regarding negotiating? It's best to wait until you can put your best foot forward. Besides, using techniques to inhibit their collection efforts is good practice for me and provides book material.)

Once again I contacted DirecTV. This time, I immediately asked to speak with the head of the customer service division and wouldn't take no for an answer. It wasn't long before we were speaking, and when I explained the situation to him, he said it was all a misunderstanding and that the $112 would be removed from my account. Of course, I received his name and requested a new invoice that was zeroed out, he agreed and I received it within a week. The case was resolved. Since I sent a cease-communication letter to the collection agency before it reported the erroneous debt (they often don't report it until after the 30-day validation period), adverse furnishing was averted.

But what if he hadn't agreed? Would I have paid the $112 to save my credit report? What else could I do?

A lot. The best bet in that scenario would have been to pay them by check, writing "under protest" on the front and back; attach a letter explaining my beef; and then file suit against them in small claims court to recover the $112 plus any court costs. (Although paying by credit card is always preferable when there's a dispute, since the charge can then be disputed with the issuing bank under a charge-back, the credit card receipt should also have "under protest" written on it, and this isn't possible when I am paying by phone. Writing "under protest" on the bill does nothing.)

Of course, the problem with paying the bill is that I could always lose the small claims lawsuit. Another option would be to file a declaratory judgment suit *pro se* and end up paying $200 to have a judge rule that I don't owe $112.[13] Sound silly? Perhaps, but I don't like being walked on; that suit could cost DirecTV a fair bit of cash to deal with. And I could write about it . . .

In any case, being proactive and vigilant can save you a lot of aggravation. Again, if you're ever wrongly billed for something, get right on the problem before it ends up on your credit report. If more people stood their ground instead of paying these types of bills, erroneous billing would be far less likely to occur in my opinion. As it stands, many people just pay in, emboldening utility companies to do more wrong.

Incidentally, DirecTV doesn't explain this when customers call and order, but upon installation, it requires that customers either pay by credit card immediately (before service is activated) or be billed later. For the latter, it requires a SSN. (How nice that it didn't explain this to me until after the Dish and electronics were installed.) Of course, I opted to pay by credit card, since I don't give my SSN to anyone who doesn't absolutely need it. DirecTV's subsequent erroneous billing effort seems to prove this guideline warranted, since its lack of my SSN would have hampered its collection efforts.

IDENTITY THEFT PREVENTION AND RECOVERY

Should a thief open new accounts using your identity and then fail to pay off the debts, your credit will be ruined, and unfortunately the mechanism for repairing the damage is spotty.

Identity theft is the fastest growing crime in America, and the reasons are simple: it's easy, and it pays. I guess criminals figure, why go through life with their crappy identity when they can just steal someone else's for little more than the cost of pizza and beer? You can buy

---

13. See Chapter 14 for declaratory actions.

an identity package online, complete with a SSN, for about $40. Yes, it's just that easy.

Of the 516,740 FTC complaints received in 2003, 301,835 were complaints about fraud, and 214,905 were identity theft reports. Identity theft reports represented 42 percent of all complaints, up from 40 percent in 2002.[14]

Of the 635,173 complaints received in 2004, 246,570 were identity theft reports, and 388,603 were fraud complaints. For the fifth year in a row, identity theft topped the list of complaints, accounting for 39 percent of the consumer fraud complaints filed with the agency. Internet-related complaints accounted for 53 percent of all reported fraud complaints.[15]

As mentioned earlier, the loss or theft of Bank One and Citibank computer tapes in 2005 resulted in the compromise of millions of account and SSNs. This is just one example of the many ways in which thieves can obtain personal data from businesses.

In February 2005, ChoicePoint disclosed that thieves opened up 50 accounts and received personal data on some 145,000 consumers. Incidentally, ChoicePoint analyzes insurance claims information; it's a clearinghouse for personal data on hundreds of millions of people. The thieves used fraudulent information to set up accounts, which granted them access to the database, and operated for a year before being discovered, defrauding some 750 people.

In April 2005, DSW Shoe Warehouse said that 1.4 million customers were affected by a cyber break-in of the company's database. In the same month, London-based Reed Elsevier (owner of LexisNexis) announced that there may have been a breach of the LexisNexis system and that criminals may have accessed computer files containing the personal information of 310,000 people since January 2003.

Identity Theft Prevention

The FTC numbers and the reports of stolen information are staggering, and most people now know of someone who's been a victim of

---

14. FTC, www.ftc.gov.
15. Ibid.

identity theft. Take it seriously. Although nobody is fully immune to it, a little vigilance can greatly reduce your chances of becoming a victim. Following are some proactive measures you can take:

- Never leave the carbon copies of your credit card transactions lying around, and don't throw them in the trash. Shred them and anything else with personal or account information on it (e.g., utility bills and any other bills or documents with personal data on them). A good shredder costs about $125 (I once bought one for $35, and it didn't last very long).
- Don't leave your automobile registration in your glove compartment. Place it in the trunk or carry it in your purse or wallet.
- If unauthorized charges appear on your billing statement(s), contact the creditor immediately.
- If billing statements stop reaching you, contact the creditor.
- Keep personal numbers (e.g., SSN) off your checks.
- If you have a local mailbox, place a lock on it. (Better yet, get a PO Box and file a change of address with the Post Office directing all mail to the PO Box.)
- Get an unlisted phone number.
- Credit card companies will often solicit you for preapproved credit cards. If you can't put a lock on your mailbox, you should opt out of these offers. You can do so by calling 888-567-8688. If you decide not to opt out and you do not respond to these offers, be sure to shred the applications.
- Check your credit reports at least every six months.
- If you use a computer, use a software firewall to provide some measure of intrusion protection. The one I recommend is Tiny Personal Firewall, available free for home users at www.tinysoftware.com. Not only will this program provide intrusion detection, but it will also catch programs on your computer trying to call out! Symantec also has a good firewall, Norton Internet Security, found at www.symantec.com. And for Windows users, Windows XP with Service Pack 2 (SP2) also offers decent protection. Hardware firewalls, basically just routers (some wireless) with firewalls built in, are also available and offer more reliable protection from inbound hackers. The

good ones are made by D-Link (www.dlink.com), Linksys (www.linksys.com), and Netgear (www.netgear.com). They run about $50–$150, depending on features. If you run a wireless router, be sure to turn on encryption.

- The abbreviation "https" should always precede any Web site address where you enter personal information. The "s" signifies that the transmission is encrypted for security. If you don't see "https," you're not in a secure Web session.

- Password-protect or encrypt when using wireless routers to prevent those nearby from tapping into your network.

- Run spyware detection software on your computer at least once a week. Spyware programs are nefarious software programs installed without your knowledge. They can perform tasks on your computer without your consent. This may include feeding you advertising or collecting personal information about you. The free spyware detection programs I recommend are Spybot and Ad-Aware, available at www.safer-networking.de and www.lavasoft.de respectively. The only problem with using these programs is that they don't prevent the installation of spyware; they can only detect (and delete) it when the programs are run. For those wishing to prevent the installation of spyware, a good free one is SpywareBlaster, available from Javacool Software (www.javacoolsoftware.com). SpywareBlaster doesn't actually run in the background of Windows, since it stores information about nefarious sites and must be updated regularly. The free version doesn't update automatically, but the paid version does and costs $9.95 as of this writing. Another good one is PestPatrol, found at www.pestpatrol.com. It runs in the background (protects continuously), costs $29.95, and is very powerful. For those running Windows XP, Microsoft also has a free tool available at www.microsoft.com/spyware.

- Instead of using the Internet Explorer (IE) Web browser, consider using Mozilla Firefox (www.mozilla.org). Firefox is considered more secure than IE primarily because it doesn't run ActiveX components or VB script. It's a far better browser in my opinion, not just for security reasons but because of its speed and stability. It's becoming very popular, to the point that Microsoft has reconstituted its IE development team to counter the commercial threat posed by Firefox.[16]

- When you have utilities installed, use an alias first name (middle name works as a substitute) and password-protect the accounts. If you can get away with it, refuse to divulge your SSN. Sometimes companies won't insist.
- Create a startup password for your computer so that when it boots up you are prompted for it. This works well for nosy baby-sitters, maids, or anyone who may just happen to break into your home while you're on vacation.
- Password-protect all your accounts. This means your credit card, bank, gas, electric, landline phone, cell phone, Internet service, cable, and satellite TV accounts, and any others you can think of. Make it clear to these companies that when anyone calls about your account, they are to ask for the password first thing. If they don't prompt you for it every time you call, then make it clear that you want to be prompted.
- Never carry your Social Security card—or anything else with your number it on it. Many states will even give you a driver's license without your SSN if you request it.
- Never give out your SSN to anyone unless absolutely necessary. Even rental car agencies request it, but I'll often ramble off a fake one, since it's none of their business. If a company such as a fitness club requires something for identity, then it often will accept a driver's license number.
- Don't give your SSN over the Internet for any reason, unless you're on a bank site.
- Send a "victim statement letter" to the three bureaus (explained shortly). You don't have to be a victim to send it. This will require that the potential lender notify you when someone requests credit extended in your name. Two downsides to this: (1) you will not be able to get credit approval as quickly as you would otherwise, making instant credit impossible, and (2) you will not be able to get your online credit report.

---

16. Firefox is open source software developed by Mozilla, available at www.mozilla.org.

- Take steps to prevent people from getting a driver's license under your name. The Driver's Protection Act (DDPA) of 2000 required that all state DMVs close records to the public. This stemmed from several well-publicized road-rage incidents where people were gunned down after raging maniacs simply went to the DMV and, using the victims' license plate numbers, obtained their addresses. This Act is a good start, but you can also provide a "request for verification letter" to the DMV, which requires that you be notified by phone or in writing before a driver's license can be issued in your name. Contact your state DMV for more information.

- Beware of "phishing," the latest scam used by ID thieves and account thieves. They will often send you phony e-mails that look like the real deal, posing as a bank, PayPal, or any other company to gain access to your personal data and/or money. Figure 11 shows a phishing example I just received as I was preparing this book:

The hyperlink to "Log On for Online Services" actually points to http://www.paypalcs.com/cgi/webscr.php?cmd=LogIn.

As you can see by the URL, this isn't PayPal.com. When people go to this fraudulent site, it is basically a clone of the real PayPal, and once the victim enters his or her user name and password onto the form, the scammer gains access to that account.

Keep in mind that many PayPal users have the service connected to several if not all their bank accounts and credit cards, which practically gives the scammer carte blanche power over financials.

Tip: Maintain a list of your credit card account numbers and issuing creditor phone numbers in a safe place, just in case you need to cancel them in a hurry.

I've seen even better phishing scams, where the links appear real and then redirect, among other things. And until Congress acts to do something about this, it will continue to be a major problem.

Although some high-profile arrests and convictions will certainly help curb the problem, many of the scammers are overseas and are well disguised and insulated from U.S. justice. They set the computer servers up in a remote location (in Asia, for example), then spoof (hide) their IP address (using a false computer number that makes it harder to track), and then take the phishing server down after a short time. By the time the authorities are notified, the scammer's Web site—and the ability to track the perpetrator—is long gone.

If you receive any e-mail from a company, be sure to check the URL to ensure that it is the correct company. Even www4.paypal.com can possibly be wrong, so it's up to you to type in the URL as www.paypal.com. (Scammers also like to use a URL with a PayPal in it, such as www.paypal.payup.com; the URL is actually for payup.com, the last entry before .com.) If you receive an e-mail from a site that contains some kind of offer or request, the safe bet is to avoid clicking anything, open a new Web browser window and type in the URL of the site directly.

Credit Monitoring Is Early Detection

In spite of the above precautions, anyone is susceptible to identity theft. There is no way to avoid it completely, yet the odds of its occurrence can be lowered and the damage reduced. A credit monitoring service doesn't prevent identity theft; it only puts an early warning system in place—alerting you to new entries and inquiries to your credit report—so that you can take action early and mitigate the damage in the event that identity theft does occur.

Credit monitoring is very confusing, as each of the Big Three has its own version available, as does FICO. Trans Union's ID-Fraud Watch is $10.95 per quarter ($43.80 per year) and provides weekly monitoring of Trans Union's credit report. For an additional $5.95 per quarter ($23.80 per year), it will also monitor Trans Union's proprietary TrueCredit Score. It permits consumers a free credit report each quarter. It does not offer monitoring of the other bureaus.

Trans Union also recently began offering 3-Bureau Credit Monitoring for $9.95 per month ($109.45 per year; one month free). However, it won't sell you this product unless you also purchase a 3-in-1 credit report for $29.95, making the total price $139.40). It will then

To:myemail@yahoo.com
Subject: PayPal eCare department. Unusual activity in your account !
From: service@paypal.com Add to Address Book Add to Address Book
Date: Sun, 1 May 2005 15:10:03 +0800 (HKT)

PayPal, an eBay company Encrypted Key: wm-101g/mgxa4fhv54nmzl

Dear PayPal, Inc. member,
PayPal, is committed to maintaining a safe environment for our customers. To protect the security of your account, PayPal, employs some of the most advanced security systems in the world and our anti-fraud teams regularly screen the PayPal payment system for unusual activity.

We are contacting you to remind you that on May 01, 2005 our Account Review Team identified some unusual activity in your account. In accordance with PayPal's User Agreement and to ensure that your account has not been compromised, access to your account was limited. Your account access will remain limited until this issue has been resolved. We encourage you to log in and perform the steps necessary to restore your account access as soon as possible. Allowing your account access to remain limited for an extended period of time may result in further limitations on the use of your account and possible account closure. Visit the login page and perform verification process:

Log On for Online Services

Thank you for your prompt attention to this matter. Please understand that this is a security measure meant to help protect you and your account. We apologize for any inconvenience.

Sincerely,

PayPal, Inc. Account Review Department
Copyright ?1999-2005 PayPal. All rights reserved.

Figure 11.

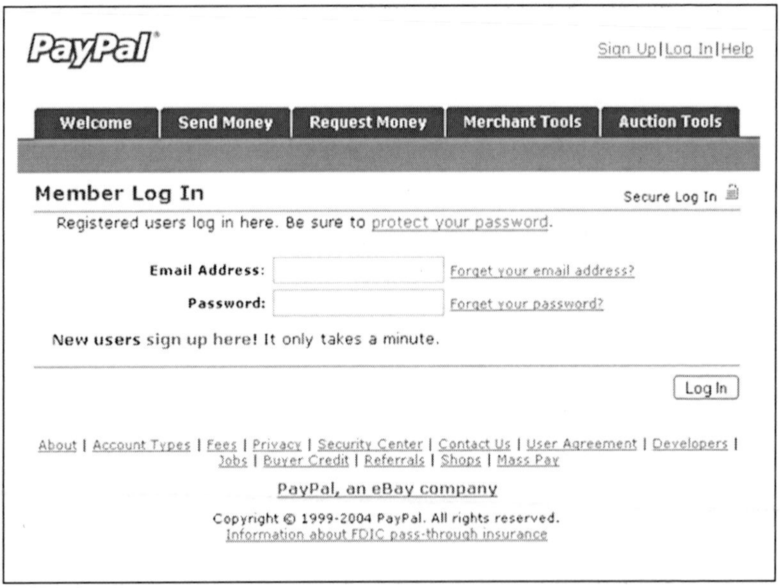

Figure 11a.

monitor all three reports and provide 24-hour notice when something changes on your report. In addition, you get unlimited access to the Trans Union credit report, enabling you to get a new report anytime you like.

Equifax's Credit Watch Gold monitors all of the Big Three reports daily (24-hour notification) at a cost of $9.95 per month ($119.40 per year), or $99.95 if a yearly subscription is purchased in advance. It offers unlimited Equifax credit report access. Equifax's Credit Watch Silver monitors the Equifax report daily and also notifies the user of key changes within 24 hours. It costs $4.95 per month ($59.40 per year) or is discounted for an annual payment of $49.95. It offers two free reports, one at enrollment and one anytime during the subscription period.

As the summary in Table 9 clearly shows, some options aren't options at all. Trans Union's ID-Fraud Watch is lackluster, as is Experian's Credit Manager. FICO's limited monitoring of one each of the Big Three also leaves a lot to be desired.

The monitoring of a FICO score may seem useful and nice to have, but this really isn't what monitoring is all about. It's about *early detection* of identity theft. Having said that, I believe that Equifax's Credit Watch Gold and Trans Union's 3-Bureau Credit Monitoring do exactly that, covering all three reports while providing daily monitoring and 24-hour notification. Both also offer unlimited access to new reports (for each), which can be useful for those who are earnestly tracking their credit restoration progress and wish to pull their reports frequently in order when creditors are reporting account information.[17] (See "Factors That Affect Your FICO Score" in Chapter 3.)

Each of the services offers insurance in the event of identity theft, but there are so many caveats that it's not worth considering.[18]

Once you repair your bad credit, you may want to consider protecting it by using credit monitoring or by taking another preventative measure, such as a security freeze.[19] (Although paying for credit monitoring from a credit reporting agency—an identity theft enabler—does seem a bit ridiculous.)

Always read the fine print when purchasing credit monitoring online from the Big Three. Remember that their online forms may have arbitration and other undesirable terms attached (see Chapter 1).

Active Duty Alert

Military personnel on active duty can place an active duty alert with the Big Three. This has the same effect as a fraud alert, where any business that sees the alert on your credit report must absolutely verify your identity before issuing any credit. The service member need only contact the bureaus and place a statement that he or she is on

---

17. Check the bureaus' Web sites (Equifax.com, TransUnion.com, and Experian.com) for the latest offers.
18. Equifax limits issues to ID theft arising out of the Internet, for example. Trans Union listed a summary of benefits, failing to provide the complete terms. Experian doesn't appear to provide any coverage, while FICO has coverage for the Identity Theft Security Deluxe, which mimics the insurance from Trans Union (third-party insurer is AIG eBusiness Risk Solutions).
19. The security freeze used to be available only to California residents, but a provision in FACTA has made it available to everyone.

SUMMARY OF CREDIT MONITORING SERVICES[20]	
Trans Union's ID-Fraud Watch $10.95/quarter ($43.80/year)	Provides weekly monitoring of Trans Union's credit report. For an additional fee of $23.80/year, it will monitor Trans Union's proprietary TrueCredit Score. It permits consumers a free credit report per quarter. It does not offer monitoring of the other bureaus.
Trans Union's 3-Bureau Credit Monitoring $9.95/month ($109.45/year; one month free). Requires the purchase of a 3-in-1 credit report for $29.95.	Monitors all three reports and provides 24-hour notice when something changes on your report. Enables unlimited access to the Trans Union credit report (users get a new report anytime they like).
Experian's Credit Manager $9.95/month ($119.40/year)	Monitors the Experian report and proprietary score daily, but permits unlimited access to the Experian report and score.
Equifax's Credit Watch Gold $12.95/month ($155.40/year) or $99.95 if paid annually.	Monitors all of the Big Three reports daily and alerts within 24 hours when key changes are detected. Offers unlimited Equifax credit report access.
Equifax's Credit Watch Silver $4.95/month ($59.40/year) or $49.95 if paid annually.	Monitors the Equifax report daily and sends a report of file key changes within 24 hours. It offers two free reports, one at enrollment and one anytime during the subscription period.
myFICO Identity Theft Security Deluxe $4.95/month ($59.95/year) or $49.95 if paid annually.	Monitors your FICO score for Trans Union and provides access to quarterly Trans Union reports. Monitoring and notification occur quarterly.
FICO's Score Watch $7.95/month ($95.40/year) or $79.95 if paid annually.	Monitors the Equifax credit report and FICO score daily and alerts when key changes are detected; includes two free Equifax reports for anytime during the subscription period.

Table 9.

---

20. As of July 10, 2005. Be sure to check the BestCredit Web site (www.bestcredit.com/identitytheftmonitoring/) periodically, since the offerings may change. Also be aware that creditors often offer their own credit report monitoring, and the prices and features vary wildly.

active duty in the credit file. The alert will remain for 12 months and can be renewed. Another effect of the active duty alert is the temporary suspension of prescreened offers for two years.

Security Freeze

When a security freeze is placed on a consumer's credit file, the credit bureaus will freeze credit reports. This prevents anyone from performing an inquiry while the freeze is in place.

For victims of identity theft and California residents, the freeze is provided at no charge. Otherwise, the fee is $10. Some states, such as Colorado, are enacting laws similar to California's as this book goes to print, so check your state laws.

Bureaus will provide the consumer with a security freeze PIN, which can be used to take the freeze off (usually five days). The PIN can remove the freeze temporarily for the purpose of obtaining credit, and it can even remove it "globally" for a specified period of time or a creditor-specific allowance. That is, the consumer will be given a unique code to provide the creditor, and the creditor will in turn provide it to the agency. The fee for a temporary lift of the freeze is $10, or free for identity theft victims and California residents.[21]

---

21. The following are exempted from a security freeze in California: companies with which the account holder has a current financial relationship; a prospective assignee of a financial obligation that is reviewing the account for maintenance, monitoring, increasing credit lines, account upgrades and enhancements, or collecting the financial obligation; state or local agencies, law enforcement, trial court, child support agencies or private collection agencies acting on a court order, warrant, or subpoena; the California Franchise Tax Board, if it is investigating or collecting delinquent taxes or unpaid court orders or fulfilling any statutory responsibilities; the California State Department of Health Services or its agents or assignees if they are investigating Medi-Cal fraud; uses falling under FCRA Section 608—Disclosures to Governmental Agencies; uses falling under FCRA Section 625—Disclosure to FBI for Counterintelligence Purposes; FCRA defined prescreening; any person or entity for the purpose of administering a credit file monitoring subscription service to which the consumer has subscribed providing a consumer with a copy of his or her credit report upon the consumer's request; any person or entity for the purpose of providing a consumer with a copy of his or her credit report upon the consumer's request.

Though this may slow the ability to obtain credit, it's a nearly iron-clad way to prevent identity theft. But be aware that the file is truly *frozen*, and not even address information provided by creditors can be updated while the security freeze is imposed. The security freeze remains in place until the consumer cancels it.

Identity Theft Recovery

Indications that identity theft has occurred include unfamiliar tradelines and inquiries.

Once identity theft has occurred, you will certainly fight an uphill battle to get things straightened out, particularly if you don't take action early and follow the FCRA guidelines. Innocent people can have their credit wrecked and even get sued. Again, the credit reporting and finance systems in this country are not well equipped to deal with identity theft, and you'll find that they are insensitive to your cause. In many cases, you will find them unwilling to help you at all. But by taking corrective measures that are built into the FCRA, you can greatly increase your chances of walking away unscathed.

- File a police report. Send a copy to all three bureaus and your creditors, including those that are not yet affected. Use the insurance method, of course.
- Contact the fraud departments of the Big Three (see Table 10 for contact information) and place a fraud alert on your file. When you contact one, it's supposed to contact the others (a process known as a "one call" alert). But I recommend contacting all three just to be safe. The alert will be in place

BUREAU FRAUD ALERT CONTACTS		
Equifax PO Box 740256 Atlanta, GA 30374 800-766-0088	**Trans Union** PO Box 1000 Chester, PA 19022 800-680-7289	**Experian** PO Box 2002 Allen, TX 75013 888-397-3742

Table 10.

for three months and can be extended to seven years, but only if a police report has been filed and provided to the bureaus. After placing an extended alert, consumers can obtain two free reports in the 12 months that follow.

- Block any item on your report that isn't yours with both the furnisher and the bureaus by providing them with a copy of a police report. When compiling a report, the bureaus are required to block any information relating to identity theft, including any inquiries made within four days after you notify them.[22] Be advised that disputing information is not the same as blocking. Consumers must specifically request a block and specify exactly what information they want blocked, including inquiries.

- Close any account that you suspect may have been tampered with or that the thief has opened. Fill out the FTC's ID Theft Affidavit form[23] and send it to any creditor affected and to the Big Three.

- File a complaint with the FTC.

- Be prepared to sue companies that spread false information about you. It's now federal law that you have two years from the occurrence to file suit, so don't delay if you've been a victim.

- Contact the USPS inspector and ensure that your mail hasn't been forwarded to another location.

- If your driver's license has been stolen, notify the DMV to cancel that license and have another one issued.

- If a checking account has been issued to the thief in your name, contact the bank and provide an ID Theft Affidavit. Also contact ChexSystems or the check reporting agency for that bank and provide it with an ID Theft Affidavit (see Chapter 10 for contact information for checking account reporting). Make sure it deletes any adverse entries related to the fraudulent account.

---

22. 15 U.S.C. §1681c-2(a).
23. Available at the BestCredit consumer Web site: bestcredit.com/ftcidaffidavitform/.

- Contact the Social Security Administration and notify it of the problem.
- If there's a judgment pending or entered based on the thief's activity, contact an attorney.
- Log your activities and keep track of time and money spent on the problem in case you need to sue.
- You may use the phone when contacting bureaus and creditors, but this is not a substitute for written communication. Do everything in writing as well, using the insurance method.
- Check with your local state unemployment and welfare office to see if benefits have been obtained by using your identity. Yes, I know a person whose identity was used to obtain unemployment benefits! Talk about a bold thief! If this happens to you, contact the Internal Revenue Service immediately so that you aren't taxed on those benefits.

When a credit reporting agency is notified of a fraud alert, it must notify the consumer of his or her right to a free report, and the report must be provided within three business days of the consumer request.[24]

The effect of an extended fraud alert is to prevent the bureaus from providing the victim's information on prescreened lists for a period of five years. If the victim desires, a fraud alert can prevent the issuance of new credit, an increase in credit on an existing account, or an additional card on an existing account. But the alert must specifically state what the limitations are.[25]

You may also add a victim statement letter to your report, which should simply state something like, "Fraud victim. Contact me at [phone numbers] before extending credit." Also consider placing a security freeze on all three bureau reports.

---

24. 15 U.S.C. § 1681j(d), *added by* Pub. L. No. 108-159, § 211(a)(4) (2003).
25. "Other than an extension under an existing open-end credit account, that is, a credit card. 15 U.S.C. §§ 1681c-1(h)(1)(A) (initial fraud and active duty military alerts), 1681c-1(h)(2)(A) (active military duty alerts)." NCLC *Fair Credit Reporting* § 16.6.1a.2.5.

Debt collectors are prohibited from selling, transferring, or placing for collection certain debts that are caused by identity theft. The notice to the debt collector must come from the credit reporting agency pursuant to section 1681c-2.[26]

If you're a victim of identity theft, act fast. Things deteriorate very quickly, and only you can set things straight, as creditors and bureaus alike will not perform the legwork that's required.

---

26. 15 U.S.C. § 1681m(f), as amended by Pub. L. No. 108-159, § 154 (2003); see also § NCLC *Fair Credit Reporting* § 16.6.1a.4.2.

CHAPTER

12

BANKRUPTCY—A MISUNDERSTOOD OPTION

When people find themselves swimming in debt, they often believe that their best recourse is bankruptcy. And with bankruptcy attorneys making fees for such filings, where is the impetus to steer consumers to alternatives?

Bankruptcy is misunderstood on two levels: first, people facing serious financial difficulties tend to see it as their only recourse; and, second, once they've filed, most people wrongly believe that their future credit opportunities are severely hampered.

With regard to the latter, credit recovery from bankruptcy can be achieved with time and work, as previously explained in Chapters 3 and 10. Bankruptcy entries can indeed be removed from a credit report, and even if bankruptcy remains, credit opportunities are very fruitful if the right steps are taken to rebuild credit. Nevertheless, it should be viewed as a last-resort option for those who find themselves in an untenable situation—their debt-to-income ratio and their total debt make a financial future unworkable. Many things have to be considered before filing bankruptcy, including the fact that some debts, such as student loans, are nearly impossible to discharge in bankruptcy. Other debts that aren't dischargeable in Chapter 7 bankruptcy include recent federal, state, and local taxes; child support and spousal maintenance (alimony); government-imposed restitution, fines, or penalties; court fees; debts resulting from driving while intoxicated; and debts not dischargeable in a previous bankruptcy because of the debtor's fraud.

In addition, the following debts are not discharged if the creditor objects during the case and proves that the debt fits one of these categories: debts from fraud, including certain debts for luxury goods or services incurred within 60 days prior to filing and certain cash advances taken within sixty days after filing; debts from willful and malicious acts; debts from embezzlement, larceny, or breach of fiduciary duty; and debts from a divorce settlement agreement or court decree if the debtor has the ability to pay and the detriment to the recipient would be greater than the benefit to the debtor.

THE BANKRUPTCY ABUSE PREVENTION AND CONSUMER PROTECTION ACT

In October 2005, the Bankruptcy Abuse Prevention and Consumer Protection Act took effect, changing existing law and making bankruptcy a far less attractive option. This is primarily due to the following:

- A "means test" is now be used to determine whether or not someone is eligible for a Chapter 7 bankruptcy, where assets are liquidated and all unsecured debt (including medical expenses) is dissolved. Those who fail the means test now fall under Chapter 13 bankruptcy, where they're forced to repay their debts (or a portion of them) on a payment schedule devised by the court. The means test employs several different measurements, but essentially those with more than $100 per month in expendable income (above the cost of necessary bills and reasonable living expenses, as determined by the IRS) are now forced to file Chapter 13. Another measurement is income. If it falls above the median for your state and you can afford to pay 25 percent of your "nonpriority, unsecured debt," you'll be forced into Chapter 13. Even if your income falls below the median, if you can pay 25 percent, the court can force you into Chapter 13.[1]

- There are provisions for the disabled in the new law, allowing them exceptions to the means test under certain circumstances.
- Attorneys incur far more liability for the bankruptcy petition, making it far less appealing to handle bankruptcies as an attorney.
- Tax debts that are at least three years old are no longer exempt.
- Petitioners (those who file bankruptcy) are required to attend bankruptcy credit counseling at their own expense.
- The petitioner's cost of bankruptcy is expected to double, to between $1,800 and $2,000 in most cases.
- Consumers used to be permitted to file bankruptcy every seven years, but now it's every eight.
- Homestead states (such as Florida and Texas) used to place no limit on how much equity a petitioner can exempt from creditors in a bankruptcy. Now there's a $150,000 cap on the equity in a home, and the petitioner must have owned the home for at least three years and four months.

As explained, if a bankruptcy is in the offing, choosing the correct type is important. Although Chapter 7 bankruptcy is usually more desirable, it can't be used to write off tax debt, child support, alimony, and more. For those with high levels of debt that can't be written off, Chapter 13 could be more feasible.

It's always been best to avoid bankruptcy where possible, but the new laws have made this even more true. As you now know, many debts can be significantly reduced anyway, and, on top of that, much (if not all) of bad credit can be removed. The changes to the bankruptcy law make the debt reduction and credit restoration lessons in this book all the more valuable.

If you do opt for bankruptcy, be sure to plan ahead to the extent that you are able by talking with a good bankruptcy attorney so that

---

1. For more information concerning bankruptcy, a good Web site is www.total-bankruptcy.com. But if you're in need of a bankruptcy attorney, see Chapter 14.

you can insulate yourself as much as possible prior to filing. And if you're married, take a close look at the Chapter 13 bankruptcy option, as explained in the next section.

CHAPTER 13 BANKRUPTCY: MARRIED COUPLES CAN BENEFIT

Although Chapter 13 bankruptcy is usually unattractive compared to Chapter 7, there are unique provisions within it that, if employed properly by married couples, can be extremely powerful.

In the event that one spouse files for Chapter 13 bankruptcy, any debts that person has, as well as any joint debts—both secured and unsecured—are wrapped into it. Yes, even the house and autos that are jointly owned! Any stay (a court order that prohibits the collection of debts as a result of bankruptcy) will apply to the nonfiling spouse as well.

Having said that, take the lowest wage earner and file Chapter 13 bankruptcy. Of course, the lowest wage earner would have to qualify for Chapter 13 and not be forced into Chapter 7, so this would only work if the petitioner's total debts and income fell with certain parameters. This almost always works, since the nonfiling spouse can make the house payment and such. This can be tuned by simply including some debts but not others. Here are some additional considerations:

*   If the intended filer doesn't have a job, he or she can get a job to make it work. The repayment plans last for six years, so technically the filer would have to remain employed for that period. However, if the filing spouse chooses, he or she can leave the job after a short period and simply make payments directly to the bankruptcy trustee using the income from the nonfiler. Although there isn't a provision for this in the law, as a matter of practicality the trustee will look the other way and distribute the payments to the creditors. That's because the trustee gets 8 percent of the total amount paid by a filer (under a wage-earner plan) for the full term of the repayment plan!

- If there's enough headroom (based on the filer's income) to add debts belonging to the nonfiling spouse to the bankruptcy petition, then those accounts can always be made joint accounts prior to filing. (Put another way, add as many debts into the bankruptcy as the wage-earner plan will allow.)
- The Chapter 13 bankruptcy plan can reduce debts a great deal, even to as little as five cents on the dollar, depending on the debts and income.

Now, before you get too exited, there is a downside to this approach. The nonfiling spouse will get some splash damage to a certain degree, since any joint accounts that are included in bankruptcy will end up on his or credit report. Bureaus often list the accounts accurately in all other aspects yet list them as "included in bankruptcy" or similar reference for the nonfiler. Chances are very high that they will, and any such entries should be disputed. If the adverse items are affirmed, then the bureau may be subject to civil liability under the FCRA.[2] Any such faulty reporting on the part of a furnisher in this case can be a good candidate for a declaratory judgment, which will get the whole entry removed.[3]

It may even be helpful to obtain a book on Chapter 13 bankruptcy and then run tests to determine your best course. A good one is *Chapter 13 Bankruptcy: Repay Your Debts* by Robin Leonard. You may be surprised at what you discover.[4]

---

2. *Spellman v. Experian*, 289 F.3d 600 (9th Cir. 2002) (failing to adequately and sufficiently identify that a mortgage was included in the bankruptcy of only one joint holder and failing to adequately and sufficiently identify that only the liability of the joint holder was discharged by bankruptcy created a misleading report); *C.F. Trundle v. Homeside Lending, Inc.*, 162 F. Supp. 2d 396 (D. Md. 2001) (in a state defamation action it is not a false statement to say that a mortgage loan was "included in bankruptcy" when co-obligor husband has filed for bankruptcy); *Heupel v. Trans Union, L.L.C.*, 193 F. Supp. 2d 1234 (N.D. Ala. 2002) ("included in bankruptcy" technically accurate; entry in single tradeline reduced credit score). NCLC *Fair Credit Reporting* § 7.8.4.10.2 (5th ed. 2002 and 2005 Supp.).
3. Consult an attorney (see Chapter 14).
4. As always, find a good bankruptcy attorney, in accordance with Chapter 14.

DISMISSED BANKRUPTCIES AND COLLECTIONS

Many people confuse the word "dismissed" with "discharged." Dismissed bankruptcies are those that were never completed (i.e., the petition was filed but the debts were not discharged). So what happens to the debts?

The debts still exist, of course, but tolling (time clock stasis) exists during the bankruptcy period, meaning that the statute of limitations for collection action is suspended while the debts are in bankruptcy.

For example, let's say a contractor performed work on August 30, 1998, and the customer failed to pay. By law, the contractor can file a lawsuit for contract breach for three years, at which time the statute of limitations runs out. However, if the debtor files for Chapter 13 bankruptcy on June 5, 2000, the three-year clock stops running. If the bankruptcy is dismissed (not discharged) on July 5, 2003, then the clock begins to run again. At this point, the contractor has until September 29, 2004, to file a complaint.

CREDIT AFTER BANKRUPTCY

People who file bankruptcy will often drop out of the credit reporting system altogether and go strictly cash. This is the worst thing they can do.

By following the methods outlined in Chapter 3, anyone who files bankruptcy can rebuild his or her credit rating very quickly and even get a home loan with favorable interest rates within 24 months of discharge (36 if there was home mortgage included in the bankruptcy). The best bet is to have at least three tradelines in good standing since the bankruptcy—two unsecured and one secured (installment)—because lenders like to see that you've been responsible with credit since you filed.

CHAPTER

13

WRITTEN
SETTLEMENT AGREEMENTS

It's very common for collectors to make deals and then fail to live up to their agreements. Collectors rarely live up to verbal agreements— never that I've heard of—and the only way to protect yourself against this is to put all your agreements in writing, clearly and succinctly spelling out the terms and outlining the responsibilities of both parties (e.g., payment amounts, dates of payment, deletion of a tradeline, late payments). This holds true regardless of the status of any dispute and whether or not legal action has already commenced between a collector and a debtor.

If legal action hasn't yet commenced, it's OK to simply have the creditor draft a letter that spells out the terms of any deal. An example of such a letter might be, "In exchange for full payment within 30 days of the date of this letter, we agree to instruct all credit reporting agencies to which we report to delete the tradeline of [account number]." Whatever the terms are, they can be included in the language of the letter, and I always require a signature on the part of the creditor-furnisher, as well as an original copy of the letter, prior to providing payment.

Even though a letter of this type is common when legal action hasn't commenced between two parties, it's better to have a formal settlement agreement (i.e., a written contract) in place if possible—especially if the other party is a collection agency, since they have a penchant for reneging on deals. (Personally, I won't accept a simple settlement letter from a collection agency.) Further, once legal action commences, it's imperative that a formal contract, known as a "mutual settlement agreement and general release," is put in place.

Being schooled in the ways of credit restoration, contracts, and the legal system has been a double-edged sword for me. Sometimes the other party will recognize the depth and breadth of my knowledge and get spooked. Even some opposing lawyers are taken aback, so I must be careful in how I choose my words. Of course, any *pro se* legal action that I initiate has to be well pled to the court, which is a catch-22.

You may have a similar problem as you improve your skills. Just consider that it's a fine line you have to walk, but it's best to play the neophyte who's "learning as you go." ("Oh, I see. Now I understand. Let me check into that, and I'll get back to you.")

No, this isn't a game. Its dual purpose is to ensure that the other party doesn't start asking questions about motives or methods and to keep the door open for negotiating the best possible written agreement.

Which brings me to my next point. The agreement itself will often open up a whole other set of negotiations, with each side jockeying for position. The language will change, going back and forth until each party is satisfied with the document.

BEFORE LEGAL ACTION

If you're to the point where you have a verbal agreement in place, then it stands to reason that you and the other party have spent a fair amount of time negotiating and hammering out the terms. In many cases, the other party will not be an attorney and could get spooked if you suddenly put a written, detailed contract in front of him or her. Since neither party has taken legal action, such an overt move could jeopardize any deal because it has the potential to scare away the other party. This is especially true for small creditors; larger ones (such as banks) are less likely to be surprised by the insistence upon a written contract. If you feel that a letter simply won't do, either because you're concerned the other party won't comply and/or you want to take advantage of some of the things that a settlement contract offers (e.g., venue; that is, where a party can file suit in the event of noncompliance), then your best bet is to state up front that you'll be speaking to an attorney about the settlement or that you've downloaded a settlement agreement from a consumer Web site. That way, the contract is not a big surprise when you present it, and you can then explain how it addresses your concerns.

Better yet, explain that you wish to have a written contract in place, and suggest that the other party present one to you. It will surely be a pile of crap, favoring the creditor immensely and leaving you holding the bag if it fails to comply. However, approaching the contract issue in this way often serves to soften the creditor up. Once you get the contract, simply state that you'll have an attorney look it over. Then you can come back with a version that suits your needs, having averted the spook factor that might have spoiled the deal had you presented your own contract initially.

I don't recommend using the settlement agreement later in this chapter for prelitigation settlements. If *BestCredit* students started using it, then many creditors would know that a credit restoration technique was being used—which could jeopardize a deal. Besides, my readers report that signed letters work fine. Just make sure that your letters are signed by the creditor.

AFTER LEGAL ACTION

Very few civil cases ever go to trial because most are settled out of court. A settlement agreement will enable a plaintiff to dismiss a lawsuit, and both parties can walk away knowing there is a legal remedy in the event that the other party fails to comply with the terms.

Caution: As with anything pertaining to legal action in this book, bear in mind that I'm not an attorney, and nothing contained herein is to be construed as a substitute for legal advice. When dealing with contracts, be aware that there are entire courses dedicated to the subject in law school.

Each state has laws that govern contracts, and they may differ widely. However, there are some basic things you should look for in any settlement agreement with a creditor. As stated before, venue and remedy are useful provisions, as are confidentiality and severance.

Originally I had planned to provide what I considered to be the ideal settlement contract, but after writing it, I still didn't feel comfortable including it, since I'm not an attorney. So I turned to the NCLC, which was kind enough to grant me permission to reprint the stellar settlement agreements its attorneys developed (below).[1]

There are two versions—one for deleting any mention of the debt, and the other for correcting/changing the account status while leaving the account to be reported.

Alternative One: Deleting All Mention of the Debt

The following is proposed settlement language that would require the creditor to request that the bureaus delete all reference to a disputed debt in a consumer's credit reporting file where complete deletion is preferable to amendment of the information:

> It is further agreed that [name of creditor] shall take all steps necessary to ensure that no credit report or credit reference that is unfavorable or that may be construed unfavorably to [name of consumer] shall be made by it or by any consumer reporting agency with regard to any debts or claims as between [creditor] and [consumer]. Without limiting the effect of the foregoing obligation, [creditor] shall also within ten days hereof send notice [in writing or electronically or both] [in the form attached hereto as Appendix A], to each consumer reporting agency to which the creditor has reported any information about [consumer], deleting from their files all references to the [alleged] debt which is the subject of this settlement agreement. To that end, [creditor] shall submit a [Metro II form coded with "DA" (delete account)] [and/or] [a Universal Data Form with the "Delete Tradeline" option box checked] to each consumer reporting agency to which

---

the creditor has reported any information about the consumer. Prior to any execution of any release of claims by [consumer], [creditor] shall submit to counsel for [consumer] clear and complete copies of these forms (with [creditor's] subscriber/password code redacted if [creditor] chooses) and proof that creditor has submitted these forms. Each required "Universal Data Form" or the equivalent must contain [creditor's] certification that it has modified its internal records so that the information to be deleted is not re-reported. In the event Plaintiffs discover, more than 45 days following [creditor's] submission of the [Metro II form] [Universal Data Form] as described, that any consumer reporting agency still reports the alleged debt, [consumer] may notify [creditor] in writing, and [creditor] will within ten business days resubmit a request for deletion of all reference to the debt.

[Creditor] shall adjust its relevant internal records in a manner that will permanently reflect the agreed-upon status of the debt. [Creditor] agrees to take all steps necessary or appropriate to prevent the re-reporting of any information about the [alleged] debt. In the event any such information is re-reported to any consumer reporting agency, [creditor] agrees to take all steps necessary or appropriate to ensure that the re-reported information is deleted from the files of every consumer reporting agency to which the information was re-reported. Further, should a consumer reporting agency ever notify [creditor] that [consumer] is disputing the tradeline, [creditor] will not verify the tradeline or will confirm that the tradeline should be deleted; in such an event [creditor] will also submit to counsel for [consumer], within forty-five days after receiving the notification of the dispute from the consumer reporting agency, clear and complete copies of the notification of the dispute and any and all forms (including electronic forms) by which it responds to such notification (with [creditor's] subscriber/password code redacted if [creditor] chooses). [Creditor] further agrees that it will not assign, hypothecate, or transfer the [alleged] debt to another creditor, a collection agency, or any other third party,[2] and that it will not alter the account number

---

2. The consumer may also want to include a paragraph in the settlement agreement in which the creditor certifies that it has not already assigned, hypothecated, or transferred the debt.

or otherwise relabel the account. The parties agree that time is of the essence of this contract. This release shall not extend to the obligations created by this Agreement or to any claim or cause of Action based in whole or in part upon a communication to a consumer reporting agency after the date of this agreement.[3]

Alternative Two: Correcting the Status of an Account but Retaining Information about the Account

The following is proposed settlement language that would require the creditor to request that the credit bureaus correct a disputed credit account but leave the account listed in the consumer's credit reporting file. This option is recommended only when there is significant benefit to the client [consumer] of maintaining information about the account, since it is far more likely to raise postsettlement problems.[4]

> It is further agreed that [creditor] shall take all steps necessary to ensure that no credit report or credit reference that is unfavorable or that may be construed unfavorably to [consumer] shall be made by it or by any consumer reporting agency with regard to any debts or claims as between [creditor] and [consumer]. Without limiting the foregoing obligation, the [creditor] shall, within ten days hereof, send written or electronic notice of the current status of the debt which is the subject of this settlement agreement to each consumer reporting agency to which the creditor has reported to be in a form [approved by counsel for consumer] [or, attached hereto as Appendix A], and shall cause the deletion of all information that is unfavorable or may be construed unfavorably to [name of consumer]. For this purpose, the parties agree that the current status of the debt is [describe]. [Creditor] shall submit a [Metro II form coded with [describe

---

3. This language is advisable in light of the lower court opinion that was reversed in *Young v. Equifax Credit Information Servs., Inc.*, 294 F.3d 631 (5th Cir. 2002).
4. The NCLC believes that deletion is preferable to leaving a tradeline reporting, since there's a greater likelihood for problems to develop with the creditor. This is a legitimate concern, yet it makes no difference if an account is open and will continue reporting anyway. Further, the potential problems that can arise have to be balanced against the benefits. If the account is old and it will assist in raising the average age of a consumer's accounts, then it will boost a FICO score.

codes] [and/or] [a Universal Data Form [describe marks to be made on the form]] to each credit reporting agency to which the creditor has reported any information about the consumer. Prior to any execution of any release of claims by [consumer], [creditor] shall submit to counsel for [consumer] clear and complete copies of these forms (with [creditor's] subscriber/password code redacted if [creditor] chooses) and proof that [creditor] has submitted these forms.

In the event Plaintiffs discover, more than 45 days following [creditor's] submission of the [Metro II form] [Universal Data Form] as described, that any consumer reporting agency still reports the [alleged] debt other than as described above, [consumer] may notify [creditor] in writing, and [creditor] will within ten business days re-submit a request for reporting of the [alleged] debt, as described above. Furthermore, should a consumer reporting agency ever notify [creditor] that [consumer] is disputing the [alleged] debt, [creditor] will re-report the [alleged] debt only as described above; in such an event, [creditor] will also submit to counsel for [consumer], within forty-five days after receiving the notification of the dispute from the consumer reporting agency, clear and complete copies of the notification of the dispute and any and all forms (including electronic forms) by which it responds to such notification (with [creditor's] subscriber password code redacted if [creditor] chooses).

[Creditor] shall further refrain from reporting any information that is unfavorable or may be construed unfavorably to [consumer] about said debt, so long as consumer] remains in compliance with [specify any paragraphs of the settlement deal with future payments].

[Creditor] shall adjust its relevant internal records in a manner that will permanently reflect the agreed-upon status of the debt. [Creditor] agrees to take all steps necessary or appropriate to prevent the re-reporting of any information about the debt that is inconsistent with the current status of the debt or the payment history from the date of this settlement agreement. In the event that any such information is re-reported to any consumer reporting agency, [creditor] agrees to take all steps necessary or appropriate to ensure that the reported information is deleted from the files of every consumer reporting agency to which the information was re-reported. [Creditor] further agrees that it will not

assign, hypothecate, or transfer the [alleged] debt to another creditor, a collection agency, or any other third party,[5] and that it will
not alter the account number or otherwise relabel the account.
The parties agree that time is of the essence of this contract. This
release shall not extend to the obligations created by this
Agreement or to any claim or cause of action based in whole or
in part upon a communication to a consumer reporting agency
after the date of this agreement.[6]

If [creditor] receives inquiries about said debt from anyone
not a party to this settlement agreement, [creditor] will report
only the current status of the debt as described above and the payment history from the date of this settlement. [Creditor] shall not
provide directly or indirectly, any information regarding the status if the debt before the date of this settlement, including [delin-
quencies] [repossessions] [deficiencies] [judgments] [foreclosures]
[collection efforts].

I like the language in the NCLC's contracts for many reasons,
not the least of which is the provision enabling the consumer to go
after the creditor for *future acts*. Most creditors will object to such
language, but simply tell them, "It's reasonable for me to dismiss my
claim for past deeds, but that dismissal does not extend to future
deeds. If you [your client] comply as you're supposed to, then there's
not going to be any problem. It would be silly of me to release you
from acts not yet committed."

They will often counter that you can sue for a contract breach in
the event of noncompliance on their part, which is true. Yet having a
general release agreement not extend to the acts not yet committed
(with the language, "This release shall not extend to the obligations
created by this Agreement or to any claim or cause of Action based in
whole or in part upon a communication to a consumer reporting
agency after the date of this agreement") opens them up to other caus-

---

5. The consumer may also want to include a paragraph in the settlement agreement
   in which the creditor certifies that it has not already assigned, hypothecated, or
   transferred the debt.
6. This language is advisable in light of the lower court opinion that was reversed in
   Young v. Equifax Credit Information Services, Inc., 294 F.3d 631 (5th Cir. 2002).

es of action other than a simple contract breach, a FCRA cause of action, for example.

I also really like the part that reads, "Further, should a consumer reporting agency ever notify [creditor] that [consumer] is disputing the tradeline, [creditor] will not verify the tradeline or will confirm that the tradeline should be deleted; in such an event [creditor] will also submit to counsel for [consumer], within forty-five days after receiving the notification of the dispute from the consumer reporting agency, clear and complete copies of the notification of the dispute and any and all forms (including electronic forms) by which it responds to such notification (with [creditor's] subscriber/password code redacted if [creditor] chooses)." This concerns the prevention of re-reporting and how the furnisher will have to provide notification to the debtor in the event that the furnisher is contacted by a credit reporting agency regarding a consumer reinvestigation. This not only keeps the creditor honest, but any notification evidence generated as a result of this requirement will absolutely destroy a credit reporting agency iin court f it breaches the FCRA.

The language in these contracts is "ideal language," and, in practice, most creditors will not agree to such strict language as that provided in the NCLC's ideal contracts, particularly regarding refurnishing and notification requirements in the event of reinvestigation. The refurnishing component opens them up to liability they don't want, while the notification provision puts a strict burden on them for very detailed future performance.

Regarding any refusal on their part as to the refurnishing clause, if they fail to comply with the terms of the contract where no such provision exists, you may be stuck with a simple contract breach when seeking a legal remedy. That's not a deal breaker; just make sure that there's a provision stating that any refurnishing of the account to the bureaus will constitute a breach of the contract.

As for the requirement for notification in the event of reinvestigation, they often refuse this clause outright but will offer other language that addresses the issue of a bureau's failure to delete/change, such as the following:

> Defendant shall take all necessary steps to ensure that the account is not re-reported and that the credit reporting agencies

follow its instruction to delete the tradeline for the account. If at any time following 60 days of the execution of this Agreement by all parties, Plaintiff determines that the tradeline for the account still appears at one or more of the credit reporting agencies to which Defendant reports, Plaintiff agrees to provide prompt written notice to Defendant and to provide copies of any credit bureau reports for which Plaintiff contends the tradelines were not updated. Notice shall be directed to [name and address of party]. In that event, Defendant will, within 10 business days following receipt of such notice and report, recontact the credit bureaus to which it reports that have not updated Plaintiff's credit reports and again request that the tradeline be deleted as set forth above.

Though not ideal, this is acceptable language in my layman opinion, since it addresses the issue of a bureau's failure to delete, requiring the creditor/furnisher to rectify any such occurrence under the contract.

Finally, whatever you do with regard to modifying language contained in the NCLC's settlement contracts, ensure that there is language spelling out time frames for which the furnisher will perform key actions and methods, such as when it will inform the credit reporting agencies and the method (e.g., UDF) by which it will do so. Personally, I always insist that a UDF be provided to the bureaus and a copy to me within 10 days of signing the agreement.

Venue and Other Provisions

The above settlement agreements don't speak to the issue of venue and other contract provisions, since it's assumed that users of the NCLC manual are attorneys, and such standard contract clauses are things that they would already know about. I'll summarize a few of those here.[7]

- *Venue:* Settlement agreements should always include a clause that enables you to come back at a furnisher no matter where you happen to live, so instead of having a venue of a specific state, you'll have a venue clause that reads, "Any civil action

---

7. Consult an attorney and check your state laws for proper wording of settlement agreements.

which arises out of a breach of this Agreement may be filed and adjudicated in the state of [state], or the place where Plaintiff resides at the time any complaint is filed. Such Action can be initiated in state or federal court, at the Plaintiff's discretion, and may not be removable in the event that it's a state court Action." This covers you just in case you move after a year or so and the furnisher breaches the terms—you won't have to travel to another state to file an action for a contract breach.

- *Fees:* Many agreements will be such that each party walks away without having to pay the court costs of the other. It's important to spell that out. "Each side is to bear its own attorney's fees and costs."

- *Authority:* "Party warrants that it has the right and authority to release the claims made in the Action and the other claims released herein and that it has not heretofore sold, assigned, or transferred any such claims to any third party." ("Other claims release herein" means it includes all releases, not just that of the court action.) The authority provision protects each party in a contract so that neither can claim it didn't have the authority to sign.

- *Entire agreement:* "This Agreement contains the entire agreement of the parties and shall be considered an integrated agreement that supersedes all negotiations and previous drafts. It may only be modified in writing, signed by all parties. All consideration and representations on which this Agreement is based are recited herein, and no party has relied on any other representation of another party or its counsel."

- *State-specific requirements:* Many states also have specific language that must be in all settlement agreements, such as California, which requires, "The parties hereby waive any rights they may have under California Civil Code section 1542 or any similar statute or rule of law of any other jurisdiction, but only as to claims, liabilities, and causes of Action based on or arising out of the Accounts. Said section provides as follows: 'A general release does not extend to claims which the creditor does not know or suspect to exist in his favor at the time of executing the release, which if known by him must have materially affected his settlement with the debtor.'" Check your state laws for such state-specific requirements.

- *Severance:* Many states require that certain provisions be included and can rule clauses invalid, as the state-specific requirement serves to demonstrate. That's why severance provision is useful. Not even veteran attorneys can know every clause that would or wouldn't be permissible, so they often use the following severance clause: "If any provision of this Agreement is held to be invalid by a court of competent jurisdiction, that provision shall be deemed to be severed and deleted, and neither that provision, nor its severance and deletion, shall affect the validity of the remaining provisions." Such a provision keeps the heart of the document intact.

- *Execution:* I like having both sides notarize the agreement so as to avoid any claims of forgery. "This Agreement may be executed simultaneously in two counterparts, each of which shall be deemed an original and all of which together shall constitute but one and the same instrument. Each Party's signature shall be authenticated by a notary public." Some creditors will insist on notarization, while others will insist on the lack of it. I prefer it, though I almost never insist. Insist if you feel you must.

- *Attorney's fees:* "In the event that a party shall fail to comply with or perform any condition or agreement hereof promptly at the time and manner specified herein, the defaulting party shall thereafter pay all costs and expenses, including reasonable attorney's fees and costs, incurred by the nondefaulting party in the enforcement of said nondefaulting party's rights." In America, generally each party pays its own way in a lawsuit in the event of a contract dispute, unless the contract specifically calls for attorney's fees. This clause permits the recovery of attorney's fees if one party breaches the contract and the other party must sue in order to remedy that breach.

- *Confidentiality:* This is simply a nondisclosure provision, whereby both parties agree not to disclose the terms of the settlement. Often creditors will try for this, and some will insist on it. I try to avoid it whenever possible, since I don't want the liability, and I enjoy being able to write about my exploits.

Such a provision may read something like, "The Parties agree that they will keep the terms of this Agreement completely confidential and that they will not disclose any information concerning this Agreement or its terms to anyone, except to their legal counsel, accountants, taxing authorities, or other persons to whom disclosure of this Agreement's terms is required by law, court order, or subpoena."

- *Mutual release:* The title of any settlement document should read, "Mutual Settlement and General Release." Any release should work both ways, for example: "Except as to the rights and liabilities as created by this Agreement, Plaintiff hereby releases, acquits, and discharges Defendant and its past, present, and future officers, directors, shareholders, employees, agents, attorneys, affiliates, parents, successors, assigns, heirs, subsidiaries, affiliates and parent entities, partners, insurers, and representatives of and from any and all claims, liabilities, causes of action, administrative violations, regulatory violations, actions, costs, and attorney's fees, either accrued or unaccrued, known or unknown, but limited to all claims made in the Action. Defendant likewise releases Plaintiff of all claims relating to the account or the Action. This Mutual Release shall not extend to the obligations created by this Agreement or to any claim or cause of action based in whole or in part upon a communication to a consumer reporting agency after the date of this agreement."

- *Notification to third parties:* If there are multiple parties reporting, then be sure to include in any agreement the stipulation that "the [other party]" will be notified to delete the account from its database and stop reporting the account to the bureaus. A collection agency, if it doesn't own an account, will report it as indicated by the creditor. If a third party (such as a collection agency) has purchased the debt, then the original creditor has no control over what the collection agency will report, however.

Problematic Language

Often creditors will try to sneak in language that is undesirable. Among the most common tactics is to say that the debt is "forgiven," or something similar. Such language creates tax liability for the consumer.

This is very common following a bankruptcy, where a creditor continues reporting—erroneously—that a balance is owed and that a debt is in arrears and/or is a collection account. In that case, any settlement agreement should clearly state that a debt was written off in bankruptcy. Any language implying that a debt is "forgiven" enables the creditor to generate a 1099 at the end of the year, which it will provide to the IRS. It's best to specify in the agreement how any settlement amount will be reported to the IRS; otherwise the creditor will likely report it as income paid to the debtor, and the debtor will be required to pay taxes on said income.

Other language that I would always object to is something that doesn't provide a full mutual release. Only a full, mutual release is acceptable, and one that will offer additional remedies for refurnishing to the bureaus.

The following additional language can be useful, since it extends the release a step further: "Release Effective notwithstanding Discovery of Additional Facts. The Parties fully intend that the aforementioned releases are valid, effective, binding, and enforceable in accordance with their terms and the other terms of this Agreement, notwithstanding the possibility that any Party may hereafter discover facts, which, if such facts had been known by it as of the [Closing Date of this Agreement], may have materially affected its decision to enter into this Agreement, and accordingly the Parties hereby waive the benefits of any state or federal statute, law, order, or rule that would provide to the contrary."

Court Endorsement

The NCLC also recommends that settlement agreements be signed by a judge whenever possible, yet this would depend on whether it is permissible in the jurisdiction and may also depend on the status of a case (this assumes that litigation has commenced). If any problems arise with the opposing party, the weight of a court-approved settlement would be helpful in convincing a credit reporting agency to comply with any terms contained within it.[8]

---

8. NCLC *Fair Credit Reporting* § 13.5.4.6 (5th ed. 2002 and 2005 Supp.).

Local Rules Concerning Dismissals

One of the tricky things regarding local state rules is how the entry of lawsuit dismissals is required to be handled. Once a contract is in place, a plaintiff will be required to dismiss a lawsuit with prejudice, meaning that the cause of action cannot be brought against the defendant again for the same thing. (Yet a future cause of action can be brought for something different, such as a breach of the contract.) For example, when the plaintiff files a dismissal with the court, the court's rules may require all parties to sign the dismissal, or perhaps only the plaintiff. Some courts even have different signature requirements, requiring a plaintiff's signature only if an answer hasn't yet been filed by a defendant to the court as required, or if filed it must have the signatures of both parties.

Federal district rules often differ as well, making things even more complex. This can even affect how any terms are specified in the contract by changing the responsibilities of either party. For example, one of the plaintiff's duties under the contract may be to "file a dismissal with prejudice with the Court within 10 days of executing this Agreement." Yet if the court requires both parties to sign the dismissal, then the settlement agreement could read something like, "Plaintiff will sign a dismissal and provide it to the Defendant within 10 days of executing this Agreement. The Defendant will then sign it and file it with the court within 5 days of receiving it." Check your local rules before you make contract provisions so as to ensure that any duties are performable under the court's rules.

Whatever you do, don't dismiss an action until both parties sign the agreement.

Noncompliance by a Creditor

Regardless of what an agreement says, creditors will sometimes refuse to remove adverse entries in accordance with the agreement, in which case you must consider an appropriate legal remedy. You can always provide proof of payment and the agreement to the bureau, and a settlement agreement signed by a judge will certainly help, yet the bureaus almost always report the item as prescribed by the furnisher anyway.

Although there may a legal claim for a contract breach against such a furnisher, civil liability under the FCRA may not exist unless your settlement release does not extend to refurnishing of information *and* there's been a formal dispute—a reinvestigation—lodged with the bureau (though other non-FCRA claims may be available, of course).[9] In any case, be sure to file a formal dispute with the bureaus. This will not only provide recourse in the event that it's the furnisher's fault but also cause the credit reporting agency to incur liability if it fails to change/delete it.

---

9. See Chapter 14; *Young v. Equifax Credit Information Services, Inc.*, 294 F3d 631 (5th Cir. 2002); *Yelder v. Credit Bureau of Montgomery, L.L.C.*, 131 F. Supp. 2d 356 (E.D. Pa. 2001); NCLC *Fair Credit Reporting* references many more, § 3.9 (5th ed. 2002 and 2005 Supp.).

14

COURT—A VIABLE OPTION

When I was young, my mother told me that it was wrong to sue people, regardless of the circumstances. She was steadfast in this view, which she based on her Christian values, all her life. If you hold this belief, I certainly respect that. After all, I don't have to eat your breakfast for you. But for those who feel that there are no absolutes and that justice can be served through the courts, a lawsuit can be a useful path.

If you find yourself in a situation where all other avenues have been exhausted in your attempts to resolve a credit-related dispute (e.g., a breach of contract, erroneous billing or credit reporting, a land-lord problem, or harassment by a collection agency), the courts can help. They are there for a reason, and let's face it: some things just don't happen unless they're made to happen.

If Ayn Rand was correct and money is the tool by which men deal with one another, then I believe the courts are the tool by which civilized people settle their differences. A hammer can be used for its intended purpose: to pound a nail. Or it can be used to break something or someone. The same can be said of anything with weight.

Courts have weight. And although many people are intimidated by the prospect, some of the best results can come from using a hammer.

A few years ago when I was in Ohio, I had a dispute with a landlord. I went to the local courthouse to file a complaint. Not having been there before, I first stood uncomfortably at the entrance to the file room while taking in the scene. The clerk, an older lady behind a long desk, seemed friendly enough. As I perused the computer records for similar cases to my own, I noticed a tall, older man standing at the other end of the counter. Well dressed, he appeared to be in his sixties and wore a long, brown trench coat and fine shoes. Judging from his gray hair and the lines in his face, I guessed he'd been 'round the block a time or two.

Knowing instinctively that he was an attorney, I struck up a conversation and politely asked him a question concerning Ohio law. He gladly gave the answer in a friendly tone and, and as he did so I could see the clerk's interest pique.

I said, "Well, thanks for helping with that question. I guess I'll move forward with this."

"Fire away," he replied, simultaneously slicing his arm high into the air—a tomahawk chop.

"Fire away," said the clerk in response.

"Fire away," I said, giving the exchange a sort of cheerleading quality.

Since then, that's what I always do when everything else fails— I fire away.

Of course, I'm not an attorney, but I've filed my fair share of lawsuits, both as a *pro se* plaintiff and with representation. *Represent Yourself in Court: How to Prepare and Try a Winning Case* by Paul Bergman, Sara J. Berman-Barrett, and Lisa Guerin is an excellent primer on going it alone. Armed with this book and a copy of your local court rules (the court clerk will provide you with this), you can be very effective. Be sure to go to the file room of the civil court as well, since those records are open to the public and you can see exactly how things are done.

Note: In the United States, each party to a suit pays its own legal costs, unless (a) a statute specifies otherwise (e.g., in cases involving copyright or trademark infringement, violations of the FCRA,[1] and violations of the FDCPA[2]) or (b) a contract calls for the loser to pay the prevailing party's attorney's fees. This might affect my decision about self-representation. For example, if someone breaches a contract with me and there's no provision within the contract for prevailing party legal fees and no statutory provision, then it would be silly for me to pay an attorney a $25,000 retainer if my damages are only $1,000. I must decide whether to risk proceeding alone or drop it.

For California residents, *Sue in California without a Lawyer* by Ron Duncan is another good reference.[3] By law, you have the right to represent yourself, and all the U.S. courts are accessible to you. Your local legal library is also a great source of information, and it will probably have access to such online services as LexisNexis and Westlaw. Useful for searching old case law, they can provide you with a framework for your arguments and background on how cases like yours have played out in the past. Public legal libraries will sometimes have classes on self-representation as well, particularly on the West Coast, where the legal climate is often friendlier toward laymen.[4]

Caution: I can't tell you what legal avenue to take in your particular situation, but I can give you real-world examples of what I've done. Consult an attorney in all matters concerning law; this book is no substitute for legal advice.

---

1. FCRA § 616 & 617, 15 U.S.C. § 1681n, 1681o.
2. FDCPA § 813, 15 U.S.C. § 1692k.
3. Both *Represent Yourself in Court* and *Sue in California without a Lawyer* are from Nolo Press (www.nolo.com), which specializes in legal how-to books.
4. Some very advanced consumer protection legal manuals available that were written to assist lawyers with their cases are also available. If you are serious about self-representation and hungry for more information, try the books from the NCLC at www.nclc.org.

I'm not necessarily advocating self-representation; you can always get an attorney to represent you. It's just what I normally do in many situations, since I have the time, the desire, and the thick skin to deal with it. And while prepared to accept the risks, I also learn a great deal and can write about it. With each case I learn something new, because every opposing attorney—whether intending to or not—teaches me something about the law. And I reason, "What's the worst that can happen to me? They can't put me on the block and stretch me out—although they may want to!" Worst case: I may owe money—or be made to look like a fool. So what? It wouldn't be the first time I owed money or looked like a fool, and it surely won't be the last. One thing is for sure: I'll walk away from that experience less of a fool then when I walked into it. And perhaps the next time I'll make the other party look like a fool because of it.

Also consider that I've had some bad experiences with attorneys who have either been incompetent or untrustworthy or both. Soured, I was often left feeling that I could have done a better job. Besides, since few civil suits ever go to trial anyway, I can usually just file a suit and that's enough to bring the defendant to the bargaining table—amazing how they're much more willing to listen after I've filed suit. All I need at that point is to put a good out-of-court settlement agreement in place, just in case they screw up after I've dismissed my complaint.

Having said this, *pro se* litigation concerning credit bureau and creditor issues can be very problematic. The bureaus and furnishers—banks in particular—will have high-powered lawyers. And though a lawsuit is often enough to bring people around to a more prudent line of thinking, sometimes it isn't. In fact, even when they know they're dead wrong, some banks and bureaus prefer to do battle against *pro se* litigants so that they can beat them up in court and get new case law on the books that's favorable to the industry. This only makes it more difficult for any litigants that come after. With their fancy lawyers, MBNA and the Big Three must have spent somewhere in the neighborhood of $350,000 to take the *Johnson v. MBNA* case to the federal appellate level. I couldn't for the life of me understand why they would do this—they knew were dead wrong. And then Michael Baxter, a FCRA attorney in Portland, cleared it up for me: they weren't trying to win *one case*; they were trying to set a precedent for future cases. They don't care what's right or whom they hurt. As such, don't sue a bureau without a FCRA attorney and don't sue a furnisher for money damages without stellar representation.

Another problem is how attorneys tend to view cases filed by *pro se* litigants. Even if the plaintiff's goal is to bring a defendant around to a settlement, sometimes this won't happen, and at that point many attorneys won't take cases filed by *pro se* litigants. They assume that there will be some defect in the complaint that will weaken the case, a hurdle that they'll have to overcome straightaway. Their concern is well-founded, since most *pro se* litigants don't understand the complexities of a FCRA complaint, or a simple contract breach for that matter. A complaint can fail on many levels, as I have learned firsthand.

For example, in California, a simple contract breach complaint must show (1) the existence of a contract (as well as a copy of it, contained either within the text of the complaint or attached), (2) the plaintiff's performance or excuse for nonperformance under the contract, (3) the defendant's breach of the contract, and (4) damage to the plaintiff caused by the breach. All these must be present and shown in a complaint, or the defendant can file a pleading, such as a demurrer or dismissal to get the case thrown out and/or slow the process.

And this is just for starters. A solid complaint must be well-drafted, and even non-FCRA attorneys don't understand the many nuances that can go into this (e.g., What issues are actionable against the furnisher? Against the bureau? When was the derogatory credit discovered?) A plaintiff only has 24 months to file a FCRA complaint after discovery of the errant entry, or five years after the date on which the violation that is the basis for such liability occurs.[5] That is, if the errant mark was discovered five years and one day after it was entered into a report, then there would be no FCRA

---

5. 15 U.S.C. § 1681p, amended by Pub. L. No. 108-159, § 156; FACTA overturned the Supreme Court's 2001 *Andrews vs. TRW* decision limiting the statute of limitations for suing credit bureaus to only two years following the date of an error, instead of two years after a consumer discovers an error.

cause of action.[6] Other claims, such as contract breaches, may have different statutory limits.[7]

How will such statutory limits impact a case or legal strategy? If you discover an errant mark on one report and then allow three years to pass without initiating legal action and it's still there, what then? Perhaps you can pull the other two Big Three reports and see if the item is there and then dispute it, and you may have a FCRA case against a furnisher, but only if the furnisher affirms the item during reinvestigation. And yet liability may exist with the other credit bureaus as well; regardless of whether it's determined what liability against a furnisher exists, liability may exist against bureaus for which the errant entry was newly discovered. And if not, there may be remedies outside the FCRA that permit civil action beyond 24 months.

And what about proper venue? Does jurisdiction exist for a state court action? What are the appropriate claims to make and how would that affect forum choice? Does my state have additional remedies? Is the item reported really unlawful? Some courts have ruled the reporting of certain items to be perfectly acceptable, whereas others have ruled it unlawful. For example, some courts have ruled that accounts included in bankruptcy that are reported as collection accounts constitute "illegal collection activity," while other courts have not. Why the inconsistencies? Perhaps a weak *pro se* litigant screwed up, or perhaps a judge was hell-bent on ruling for the industry in spite of the law. Clearly accounts included in bankruptcy should not be reported as collection accounts, since such reporting indicates money is owed and will have a far worse effect on a consumer's score over time, impinging future credit opportunities severely. But how many judges understand credit scoring?

Given the myriad of complexities, I keep my *pro se* actions restricted to a few garden-variety types. I always go it alone when filing for declaratory judgments (explained later) or in small-claims court. I'll sometimes go *pro se* on minor money-damage complaints, depending on who the defendant is and whether a provision exists for the prevailing party's attorney's fees to be paid by the losing party. (For example, if there's a provision for

---

6. States may have more favorable statutes of limitations.
7. This varies by state. See Appendix A for statute of limitations by state.

attorney's fees but the defendant has limited resources, it does me no good, since the attorney I hired will want his money regardless of whether I collect on the judgment—unless he or she has agreed to take the case on a contingency fee basis.) What you do is up to you, but certainly for high-damage awards where a creditor or bureau has wronged you, I recommend finding a good FCRA attorney on the front end (follow the guidelines for selecting and retaining a lawyer later in this chapter).

Tip: National Association of Consumer Advocates (NACA) attorney Leonard Bennett claims that his average award is $50,000 for FCRA cases. However, as his testimony to Congress shows,[8] a plaintiff has yet to win an award where he or she didn't first dispute the item with the bureaus.[9] In other words, if you haven't disputed an item with the bureau(s) then you have no case for FCRA damages![10] In cases where you've been harmed by erroneous reporting, always formally dispute the entry with the bureaus. Sometimes it's not clear whether it was the furnisher or the bureau that failed to conduct an adequate investigation. In such cases, both parties should be made defendants to any civil action.[11]

---

8. See Appendix B. When the formal dispute process is followed and a furnisher affirms adverse information, it opens up four additional causes of action for violations of 15 U.S.C. § 1681(c), § 1681e(b), § 1681i(b), and § 1681s-2(b).

9. This is confirmed by cases cited by the NCLC. A person who fails to initiate a dispute with a reporting agency under Section 1681i and instead only deals with the furnisher cannot invoke the remedies available under 1681s-2(b). *Young v. Equifax Credit Information Services, Inc.*, 294 F3d 631 (5th Cir. 2002); *Yelder v. Credit Bureau of Montgomery, L.L.C.*, 131 F. Supp. 2d 356 (E.D. Pa. 2001); NCLC *Fair Credit Reporting* references many more, § 3.9 (5th ed. 2002 and 2005 Supp.).

10. Other non-FCRA claims may have remedies that don't require a consumer to have first disputed the entry with the bureaus. Further, some states even have punitive damage awards for a contract breach. See *Punitive Damages Review* by Wilson, Elser, Moskowitz, Edelman, and Dicker LLP at www.wemed.com.

11. NCLC *Fair Credit Reporting* § 3.14.3 (5th ed. 2002 and 2005 Supp.).

PROTECTION FOR CONSUMERS FILING SUIT

Consumers are often afraid of filing a suit when they owe a debt, fearing that it will only hasten the debt collector's ability to obtain a judgment. However, there are consumer protections in place. "Defendant furnishers may attempt to bring a state law counterclaim against the consumer to collect an underlying debt. If the case is in federal court, the counterclaim raises a jurisdictional issue; it must either meet the statutory supplemental jurisdiction requirements[12] or fulfill the demands of diversity jurisdiction, including the requisite $75,000 amount in controversy."[13]

Courts use the "same transaction or occurrence test" to determine whether any counterclaim is "part of the same case or controversy." This is not often the case, as "federal courts generally refuse supplemental jurisdiction over a debt collector's counterclaim in Fair Debt Collection Practices Act cases;[14] establishing the underlying debt requires evidence of the existence, performance, validity and breach of a contract, none of which are necessary to prove a violation of the FDCPA."[15]

Protections are also provided for consumers exercising their rights in "good faith" for violations by furnishers. That is, furnishers may not report adverse information in response to a lawsuit.[16]

---

12. 28 U.S.C. § 1387 allows a federal court to exercise supplemental jurisdiction over counterclaims that are "so related to claims in the action within such original jurisdiction that they form part of the same case or controversy." Such claims that "arise out of the same transaction or occurrence that is the subject matter of the opposing party's claim" are compulsory counterclaims under federal Rule of Civil Procedure 13 and are entitled to supplemental jurisdiction. See James Moore, *Moore's Federal Practice* §§ 13.10, 13.30 (1999).
13. 28 U.S.C. § 1332. See NCLC *Fair Credit Reporting* § 10.9.2 (5th ed. 2002 and 2005 Supp.).
14. See NCLC *Fair Debt Collection* § 7.3 (5th ed. 2004 and 2005 Supp.).
15. See *Leatherwood v. Universal Business Serv. Co.*, 115 F.R.D. 48 (W.D.N.Y. 1987); NCLC *Fair Credit Reporting* § 10.9.2 (5th ed. 2002 and 2005 Supp.).
16. The federal Consumer Credit Protections Act. 12 C.F.R. § 202.2(m), (z). NCLC *Fair Credit Reporting* § 13.5.2.2 (5th ed. 2002 and 2005 Supp.).

ACTIONABLE CLAIMS AND VENUE

Plaintiffs who file in state court must be aware of removal (where the defendant transfers a case from state court to federal court), as 28 U.S.C § 1141 says, "The district courts shall have original jurisdiction of all civil actions arising under the Constitution, laws, or treaties of the United States." The FCRA is a law of the United States, and it states, "An action to enforce any liability created under this subchapter may be brought in any appropriate United States district court without regard to the amount in controversy, or in any other court of competent jurisdiction."

Consequently, if a suit for a FCRA violation is filed in state court, a defendant can have it "removed." That is, the case is removable to federal court, even if additional nonfederal claims accompany it. If a defendant does this, the plaintiff may end up in a venue (court forum) that wouldn't be as favorable as a state court, or perhaps have to travel to another city to have the case heard.

Although case law is split on remand (plaintiff request to return the matter to state court after removal), it seems unlikely that a FCRA or FDCPA case will be remanded.

I've successfully filed suit in state court seeking money damages using a FCRA cause of action. Evidently the defendant's attorney didn't feel the need to have it removed (or didn't know he could). I've also had one of my actions removed to federal court and then my motion to remand denied.

Federal courts are not as easy to navigate for the layman because the rules are different than in state courts and the judges seem less tolerant of *pro se* plaintiffs. The whole atmosphere is less consumer friendly in my limited experience. However, many attorneys have had very good success by operating solely in this forum for FCRA claims. At least such an action can be filed in "any federal district court," so forum shopping—seeking the most favorable district court—is possible.[17]

---

17. Personal jurisdiction must exist, which is generally a matter of state law. NCLC *Fair Credit Reporting* § 10.9.3 (5th ed. 2002 and 2005 Supp.).

Incidentally, all bureaus will remove actions to federal court, and many will have success. Any FCRA actions against the bureaus should be filed there.

As far as actionable claims, so many possibilities against furnishers, bureaus, and collectors exist that it goes well beyond the scope of this book. It's best to have a FCRA attorney look at your specific case to determine what claims are available and advise you as to what strategy to employ based on those claims. But for our purposes, suffice it to say that actionable claims would include violations of the FCRA, FDCPA, FCBA, state FCRAs, state UDAP statutes, common law torts, and so on. And then there are preemption considerations, where federal law would override state law on many issues.[18]

Furthermore, there are some issues surrounding correct action against furnishers and reporting agencies due to the existence of limited qualified immunity under the FCRA, which limits the actions that can be brought. However, limited qualified immunity does not extend to the furnishing of false information with malice or willful intent to injure.[19] Second, immunity only applies to actions and proceedings with the "nature of" defamation, invasion of privacy, or negligence.[20] And, third, qualified immunity does not apply to the furnishing of information to a party that is not a reporting agency.[21] For example, if the party is another creditor, then the furnisher is not immune.

Regarding causes of action in which the limited qualified immunity does not apply, the NCLC's *Fair Credit Reporting* says, "Examples might include intentional infliction of emotional distress, misrepre-

---

18. Unfair and Deceptive Acts and Practices. Some states require a demand letter before a UDAP claim can be filed.

19. See Chapter 6. Also see 15 U.S.C. § 1681h(e). See NCLC *Fair Credit Reporting* § 10.3.6 (5th ed. 2002 and 2005 Supp.); *Borner v. Zale Lipshy Univ. Hosp.*, 2002 WL 449576 (N.D. Tex. 2002) (false report quickly corrected shows lack of malice).

20. Many caveats exist. 15 U.S.C. § 1681h(e); states have their own views on defamation and privacy. California and Montana, for example, have state FCRAs that expressly permit the use of defamation and invasion of privacy claims— punitive damages and all for willful acts (though a federal FCRA action will bar a California state action for the same act or omission). Cal. Civ. Code § 1785.52. Check your state laws!

21. 15 U.S.C. § 1681h(e).

sentation, intentional interference with prospective contractual relations, or injurious falsehood.[22] Courts have refused to dismiss claims based on torts of interference with contract prima facie tort,[23] and injurious falsehood.[24] In another case, a state supreme court upheld a verdict for breach of contract.[25] Additional examples of tort actions not restricted by court decisions include tortuous interference with employment[26] and conspiracy to violate the FCRA or commit unlawful acts. Harassment and invasion of privacy claims unrelated to reporting of information are not preempted."[27]

"The immunity clearly does not apply to claims not based in tort at all. Examples include state credit reporting statutes,[28] state decep-

---

22. A tort is a wrongful act other than a contract breach. NCLC: "The tort requires intent (or likelihood) to harm the pecuniary interests of another, and knowledge or reckless disregard of falsity. It is usually applied to disparagement of property or intangible things. Restatement (Second) Torts § 623A *et seq*. (1979). E.g., reporting a lien or attachment on property could be disparagement of title, to which truth would be a defense. Another tort, malicious prosecution, could not be established under New York law by an allegation that a lawsuit caused a diminished credit rating. A diminished credit rating does not make the required showing of 'some interference with person or property.' *Diamond v. Strassberg*, 751 F. Supp. 1152 (S.D.N.Y. 1990)." Quote from NCLC *Fair Credit Reporting* § 10.3.4, footnote 191 (5th ed. 2002 and 2005 Supp.).

23. A prima facie tort is "the infliction of intentional harm, resulting in damage, without excuse or justification, by an act or a series of acts which would otherwise be lawful." *ATI, Inc. v. Ruder & Finn, Inc.*, 42 N.Y.2d 454, 458, 368 N.E.2d 1230, 1232, 398 N.Y.S.2d 864, 866 (1977) (quoting *Ruza v. Ruza*, 286 A.D. 767, 769, 146 N.Y.S.2d 808, 811 (1st Dep't. 1955)).

24. Injurious falsehood is a disparagement: the publication of false and injurious statements that are derogatory of another's property, business, or product (*Merriam-Webster's Dictionary of Law*); *Yeager v. TRW Inc.*, 984 F. Supp. 517 (E.D. Tex. 1997); *Maberry v. Said*, 911 F. Supp. 1393 (D. Kan. 1995) (applying Missouri law). Creditor had submitted a negative credit report after notification that consumer had legitimate reasons to withhold payments.

25. *Hoglan v. First Security Bank*, 120 Idaho 682, 819 P.2d 100 (1991). Plaintiff alleged that the bank wrongly listed and reported an account as a charge-off.

26. *Wiggins v. Phillip Morris, Inc.*, 853 F. Supp. 470 (D.D.C. 1994); *Wiggins v. District Cablevision, Inc.*, 853 F. Supp. 484 (D.D.C. 1994).

27. *Stafford v. Cross Country Bank*, 262 F. Supp. 2d 776 (W.D. Ky. 3003).

28. NCLC *Fair Credit Reporting* § 10.3.3 (5th ed. 2002 and 2005 Supp.).

tive practice statutes,[29] state and federal debt collection statutes,[30] and contract claims."[31]

Note: Whenever possible, I request a trial by jury. Juries will typically show more empathy toward consumers than judges will, especially in FCRA claims or claims against corporate America. As well they should, people get sick to their stomachs when they learn what goes on behind closed doors of the bureaus and furnishers.

Many states have their own FCRAs, which often mimic state UDAP violations.[32] Yet all states have UDAP statutes that prohibit

---

29. NCLC *Fair Credit Reporting* § 10.4 (5th ed. 2002 and 2005 Supp.).

30. NCLC: "But see *Greenwood Trust Co. v. Conley*, 938 P.2d 1141 (Colo. 1997) (allegation that creditor wrongly reported a debt to a reporting agency without disclosing that it was in the nature of defamation, and thereby 'preempted' by the FCRA's qualified immunity. The statute listed several factors for determining unconscionability; plaintiff relied upon only one factor—injury to reputation or economic status. The court indicated that had plaintiff also relied upon any other factor, the state claim would not have been preempted. At p.149. Although the court held that the FCRA qualified immunity applied, it remanded the case for further proceedings because a genuine dispute existed over whether the defendant acted with malice.)." Quote from NCLC *Fair Credit Reporting* § 10.3.4, footnote 198 (5th ed. 2002 and 2005 Supp.).

31. But see *McAnly v. Middleton & Rentlinger, P.S.C.*, 77 F. Supp. 2d 810 (W.D. Ky. 1999). (Consumer is not a third-party beneficiary of contract between reporting agency and user of report); quotes from NCLC *Fair Credit Reporting* § 10.3.4 (5th ed. 2002 and 2005 Supp.). "Effective in 1997, Congress adopted an additional immunity from state laws. The courts are having difficulty in reconciling the qualified immunity with seemingly broader state law immunity." 15 U.S.C. § 1681t; courts are split every which way, discussed in NCLC *Fair Credit Reporting* § 10.4.4 (5th ed. 2002 and 2005 Supp.).

32. *Cisneros v. U.D. Registry*, 39 Cal. App. 4th 548, 46 Cal. Rptr. 2d 233 (1995) (violation of state and federal fair credit reporting statutes is a violation of California's UDAP statute); NCLC *Fair Credit Reporting* § 10.4.2 (5th ed. 2002 and 2005 Supp.).

certain acts:[33] "The FCRA's limited tort immunity should not apply to deceptive practices claims because they are statutory causes of action not sounding in tort."[34]

It also appears that FACTA extended the exceptions to immunity to include four additional things, three of which apply to reporting agencies: (1) a reporting agency's failure to truncate the first five digits of the consumer's SSN at the consumer's request, (2) the agency's failure to notify the consumer of the FTC's summary of rights on consumer disputes and obtaining credit scores, (3) a bureau's requirement to provide identity theft victims with a statement of rights, and (4) (which applies to furnishers) the responsibility for businesses to provide—at the victim's request—transaction information in the event of identity theft.[35]

This information from the NCLC isn't intended to confuse the layman. It only serves to show that there are many remedies outside of the FCRA—remedies that can be very useful for those wishing to simply *have information deleted*, including information that is in part *accurate and adverse.*

For the purposes of this book, I wish to focus on the notion of using state claims against furnishers exclusively for the removal of adverse accurate information. (Exceptions include some types of FDCPA and FCRA claims where money is owed to a creditor, which can be useful in federal court if it would preclude a counterclaim. Check with an attorney.) Such an approach can be very attractive for

---

33. A preemption test must be made, both a general standard for inconsistent state provisions (the one offering more protections is not considered inconsistent) and a specific list of preempted laws must be looked at; see Chapter 6 and NCLC *Fair Credit Reporting* § 10.4.2 (5th ed. 2002 and 2005 Supp.).

34. Quote from NCLC *Fair Credit Reporting* § 10.4.2 (5th ed. 2002 and 2005 Supp.). *Jaramillo v. Experian Inf. Solution, Inc.*, 155 F. Supp. 2d 356 (E.D. Pa. 2001), vacated in part, 2001 U.S. Dist. LEXIS 10221 (June 20, 2001) (vacated as to § 1681t(b) preemption holding). See § 10.3.4 NCLC *Fair Credit Reporting*. But see *Polzer v. TRW, Inc.* 682 N.Y.S.2d 194 (N.Y. App. Div. 1998). *Agosta v. Inovision, Inc.*, 2003 WL 22999213 (E.D. Pa. Dec. 16, 2003) (UDAP claim for intentional failure to reinvestigate is preempted).

35. 15 U.S.C. § 1681g; NCLC *Fair Credit Reporting* § 10.3.2 (5th ed. 2002 and 2005 Supp.).

someone who only seeks relief from a creditor's adverse entries. The power of declaratory judgments cannot be overstated, particularly if the action can be crafted in such a way as to be nonremovable for those wishing to avoid federal court.

DECLARATORY JUDGMENTS

Three types of legal remedies are available in civil cases: money damages, injunctive relief, and declaratory relief. Money damages are self-explanatory. Injunctive relief is an equitable remedy in the form of a court order compelling a party to do or refrain from doing a specified act.[36] Declaratory relief or judgment is simply the declaring or interpretation of a legal right, declaring what is the existing law.[37]

Judges can exercise their powers to enjoin (prevent, prohibit) someone from doing something that will cause harm. In the case of credit reporting, a judge may order an injunction against a furnisher or bureau that simply tells it, "Stop reporting." This is both declaratory and injunctive relief. It's declaratory in that the judge will declare a right of the consumer based on law and injunctive in that it precludes further reporting. (Private litigants cannot seek injunctive relief against a credit reporting agency, only against furnishers.)[38] Declaratory relief should be accompanied by claims for other relief, such as injunctive or monetary. For the purpose of this text, I'll refer to them collectively as declaratory judgments.[39]

---

36. An injunction is available as a remedy for harm for which there is no adequate remedy at law. Thus it is used to prevent a future harmful action rather than to compensate for an injury that has already occurred. Violators of an injunction are subject to penalty for contempt of court.

37. Declaratory actions may be brought in federal or state court, yet each state may have its own laws as to what causes of action may be brought using a declaratory action.

38. *Washington v. CSC Credit Services, Inc.*, 199 F.3d 263, 265 (5th Cir. 2000), "Congress vested the power to obtain injunctive relief solely with the FTC."

39. Declaratory actions cannot be made for issues based solely on "pure torts" (e.g., an auto accident). Yet they can be used for state credit reporting statutes, state deceptive practice statutes, and state and federal debt collection statutes and contract claims. Check with an attorney.

This action is sometimes faster and easier to obtain than a money judgment, and creditors will not feel compelled to fight it in any way. Because the plaintiff isn't seeking money damages, it puts the defendant on a whole different footing. He thinks, "Should I defend this? Why? What's in it for me? How much will this cost me to defend? I'm in another state; I'll have to get outside counsel in the plaintiff's state to even answer this complaint and probably have to pay them $3,000 to $5,000 right out of the gate." Heck, you could possibly win by default if the defendant doesn't respond to the complaint. The defendant usually only has 30 days from the time of service to file an answer. Should the defendant fail to do so, the plaintiff can request a default entry.

So what can you get from this action if not money? Simply, you can get a judge to rule something that may benefit you, such as, "Neither party owes the other any money," or "This contract is null and void," or "Stop reporting this tradeline to the credit reporting agencies." This is extremely powerful. It's made even more so if a complaint can be crafted using state law claims, thus making it *nonremovable*. Personally, I like going after the furnisher with a simple contract breach or something else that's an exclusive state law claim. A contract breach may exist, since the terms of service that accompany any application or notice will likely have a provision that the creditor will report to the bureaus—assumed to be accurate information. Any action must meet jurisdiction requirements.

The use of a non-FCRA claim is unique in other ways. Even though the FCRA requires that a formal dispute must occur before civil liability exists on the part of a furnisher, other breaches of law don't necessarily share that requirement. As such, entire adverse tradelines can be removed using simple and effective causes of action—without having to contend with the bureaus. Further, many types of claims have longer statutes of limitations for legal action than within the two years post-discovery, as required by the FCRA. A breach of contract statute of limitation, for example, is often a lot longer. This varies by state, and they are listed in Appendix A. Ironically, for most entries the statute of limitation is the same as the time a creditor has to sue you for default. That's poetic.

In some states this action can be performed in municipal court (a state court), which is usually less expensive than a standard civil suit (the cost averages $130), and hearings often occur much sooner than in state circuit court (known in some states as the court of common pleas). I've been told that the wait in Ohio as of this writing is about six months in municipal court versus two years in the court of common pleas. The wait times are often a nonissue with declaratory actions, since the other party will likely settle within 30 days anyway. Yet it's a good idea to be prepared and use the most favorable court forum. It also appears that few attorneys actually know that you can use municipal court for many types of matters. (This may explain why the wait time in that court is 75 percent less.) In Ohio, cases in municipal court are for suits brought that involve $15,000 or less. In California, they used to have municipal court, but now everything falls under superior court.

> **Tip:** Remember, filing suit first will keep a lawsuit from showing up on your credit report as a public record entry. If you file first, even if the defendant files a counterclaim, by rule the suit cannot be placed on your report. If a defendant files a separate claim and not a counterclaim, then the lawsuit would end up on a credit file. (In some cases, a defendant would not have the ability to file a counterclaim to a plaintiff's action and would be forced to file a separate action.) Powerful stuff! Bear in mind that if you lose, any money judgment against you will end up on your credit report, regardless of who filed first.

Keep in mind that although a judge may issue a "summary judgment" (where he rules without a hearing) in your favor, he will require a trial if he feels that there are issues of material fact that must be litigated. This isn't something to be afraid of, just aware of. If you're dead right, can prove it, and have crafted a well-pled case, then you can go to court and stand tall. If you're *pro se*, just make sure you have the local court rules and know them well—so as not to upset the judge.

When Both Accurate and Inaccurate Data Exists

In A.D. 450, Attila the Hun sought to attack Rome yet needed a reason to rally his forces to the epic battles that would ensue. Honoria, sister of Valentinian III, the emperor of the West, had sent a letter to Attila to offer him her hand in marriage and thus a right to share in her imperial power. The Romans had discovered this, and she was imprisoned. Attila thus pretended to take up arms on her behalf, proclaiming that he was marching on Rome for his would-be betrothed. This is what's known as a pretext.

A pretext is simply an excuse. When creditors have wronged me by reporting something erroneously, then I have my reason to sue. If they are careless and callous toward me in their reporting, then I simply treat them with the same regard. I take their act and, using its own force, spin it back against them.

For example, let's say that the creditor erroneously reports, "Account Closed by Credit Grantor," and there's something else negative but also factual on the same tradeline, such as "60 Days Late." The furnisher can be sued for reporting erroneously, using a FCRA violation, contract breach, state UDAP breach, or the like. As a result, it's possible to have the whole account (tradeline) removed.

So let's look at some possible pretexts. According to the NCLC, Congress, "concerned that such reports may be read as suggesting that an account was closed because the consumer did not meet the account terms . . . required that creditors who regularly and in the ordinary course of business furnish information to the reporting agency must also notify the agency when an account has been voluntarily closed by the consumer.[40] A reporting agency which receives notice must indicate the voluntary nature of the closure in any report which includes information about the closed account."[41]

---

40. 15 U.S.C. § 1681s-2(a)(4). The notification is to be included as part of the information regularly furnished for the period in which the account was closed. Some state FCRAs also require that a furnisher indicate voluntary closure of accounts. Maine is one such state (Me. Rev. Stat. Ann. tit. 10, §§ 131 to 1329). California is another (Cal. Civ. Code § 1785.13(c),(e)(West)).

41. 15 U.S.C. § 1681c(e); NCLC *Fair Credit Reporting* § 3.8 (5th ed. 2002 and 2005 Supp.).

I've used this pretext several times in declaratory actions and always with success. At first, I believed creditors would often not even respond to such an action, since it costs them money. But with the exception of one who didn't respond, each one of them contacted me right away and agreed to remove the tradeline in exchange for my dismissal. Usually it was an in-house attorney, and I couldn't help but ask, "Why don't you guys just let this thing go and permit a default entry? There's no money involved, except perhaps court costs in some cases." They claimed that they didn't want judgments out there piling up against them as public record entries, so they opted to contact me and attempt to settle out of court before an answer was due the court.[42]

Warning: It's important to note that with banks and similar types of creditors, declaratory judgments only work when (a) you don't owe them any money, or (b) you owe them money but aren't in arrears (in which case you have leverage and can bargain the bad mark off anyway). If you owe them money and you're delinquent, then it's likely that your action will cause a set-off; they'll countersue and get a judgment against you (assuming that the matter isn't settled out of court before trial and then dismissed).[43]

This is even better than a default judgment, since (a) there's no guarantee that a judge will rule that the tradeline be removed even if a default is granted, and (b) if the judge orders it removed, then what other legal entanglement would I face if the bureau(s)/furnisher fail to comply with the court's order, and (c) the speed at which the tradeline is removed is greatly increased, since I don't have to wait on the court

---

42. They also don't want people searching court records on WestLaw and LexisNexis, discovering a bunch of default judgments that announce, "Banks don't respond, and this technique works. Sue them and get your bad credit removed."
43. Remember, for a creditor to countersue in federal court, the debt must meet the requisite amount, or $75,000, under 28 U.S.C. § 1332. Otherwise the creditor must pursue a new lawsuit in state court and perform service of process accordingly.

to rule; the furnisher will usually do it within days of the settlement agreement's being signed. An out-of-court settlement before an answer is due to the court is simply *spectacular!*

Declaratory judgments can also cause a set-off when I have a dispute with a landlord or something similar. But that doesn't mean it shouldn't be deployed in such cases. On the contrary—if I feel that I can defend myself and win, I go forward. But if the judge rules against me for the sum of even $1, that judgment just ended up on my credit report.[44] This is a very tricky business, and that's why I only use it when either (a) money isn't owed, or (b) I'm dead certain that I can withstand any counterclaim, either through a pretrial out-of-court settlement or victory in court.

Note: In every civil action I've filed, declaratory actions have always brought a good result with relative ease. Almost always, defendants (or their counsel) have contacted me right away and an out-of-court settlement has been reached. (On one occasion the defendant didn't file an answer, and I went for a default judgment and obtained it.)[45] On the other hand, every time I've gone for money I've had a big fight on my hands.

Most often, all consumers want is for bad information to come off their report. This is true even when they may have a money claim. This is what makes declaratory judgments so useful. It's the least aggressive form of legal action, and defendants get the message without feeling the need to pour money into defending it.

Always bear in mind that declaratory judgments do not involve money damages of any kind, and in some states, only court costs can

---

44. Worse, if you lose and you've filed cause of action for either (a) a contract breach that contained a provision for the loser to pay attorney's fees or (b) a FCRA violation, then you would have to pay the defendant's attorney's fees.
45. See Chapter 15; Provident Bank (Declaratory Action; FCRA).

be recovered, not attorney's fees. This may also depend on whether the fees are recoverable by contract or statute.

This issue, among others, may impact what type of cause of action to claim in a declaratory suit involving credit reporting. If there's a contract breach with the furnisher and you're looking for deletion of credit bureau entries using a declaratory judgment, then it would seem that a cause of action in state court for contract breach (if permissible in your state) would be more suitable. I'll give you three or possibly four reasons, some of which I've already explained. First, when you're not seeking money damages, then a FCRA cause of action isn't necessary. Second, a contract breach cause of action isn't removable to federal court on its face.[46] Third, a contract breach doesn't require that a dispute be filed with the bureaus, and, fourth, many states have longer statutes of limitations for contract breach than that prescribed by the FCRA. But be advised, state laws require that actual damages must have occurred in order to have a valid claim of contract breach. This would have to come in the form of a denial of credit of some kind, a higher interest rate, or denial of employment as a direct result of the erroneous reporting. If this isn't possible, then a state UDAP claim would be the next place to look as it has the same favorable characteristics. (Though some states require a demand letter to be submitted to the offender before a UDAP claim can be filed.)

There are other considerations for a plaintiff, such as the ability to amend the case and go for money damages, possibly punitive, in the event that the defendant wants to duke it out.[47] A poorly planned complaint that starts out as a simple declaratory action and lacks the ability to counterpunch in such an event can effectively hamstring a plaintiff—a person who only wanted a simple deletion.

And if a declaratory complaint is not drafted properly, a defense attorney can argue that it's a FCRA claim even if the complaint doesn't

---

46. Not an issue with declaratory actions, but any action over $75,000 is removable (28 U.S.C. § 1332).

47. Punitive damages are not only relative to the offense, but also relative to the total market value of the company being sued. In other words, a lot of money could be involved. For a FCRA claim, the violation must be willful.

specify it, and thus have it removed to federal court. However, this is unlikely, since it risks giving any plaintiff the opportunity to amend the complaint and possibly seek money damages—perhaps punitive if the action is found willful. Remember, money damages aren't even possible under the FCRA if the entry in question wasn't first disputed with the bureaus. (Many furnishers will likely know this and will have on file any disputes that were made with the bureaus.) But as explained, there may be breaches of other laws that have additional money damage remedies.

Regarding strategy and law, my theories aren't worth much, of course. Yes, a fight would seem unlikely when the suit contains no money damage claim anyway, but you never know. As stated previously, in the case of *pro se* litigants, sometimes creditors are trying to make new law, and they'll pay big money to do that—even when they know they're dead wrong.

The smart thing is to get a FCRA attorney in all cases. Though success as a *pro se* litigant has emboldened me, I'm lucky to have my hide after the mistakes I've made. Thank goodness some opposing attorneys haven't noticed some of my bonehead errors, or they could have really put the hurt on me. A crackerjack FCRA attorney pointed this out to me in one case, which enabled me to extract myself before the opposing counsel got smart. Each case that got tricky involved money damage claims, by the way, which are always troublesome— especially when creditors have more money than God. As such, never file a claim unless you are prepared for every possible eventuality.

I should also disclose that I've initiated state declaratory actions using FCRA claims and always with success. However, any future actions will have exclusive state claims whenever possible so as to preclude removal. Avoiding the formal dispute process with the bureaus is also desirable in my opinion, as multiple disputes only bring unwanted attention. As such, I prefer to keep disputes to an absolute minimum.

Incidentally, declaratory actions also work well after bankruptcy, since creditors are notorious for reporting that debts are in arrears and balances owed long after debts are discharged.[48] Remember, any false aspect of a tradeline is a pretext. Sound ruthless? I don't think so. After

---

48. See Chapter 10.

all, a declaratory action is not a money damage claim. Moreover, erroneous furnishing should be met harshly.

Searching for a Pretext

Credit reporting is so unbelievably inaccurate that it boggles the mind, especially when it comes to delinquent accounts. Even when I look at an account entry over and over and can't find something erroneous, I know it's there—somewhere. There always is.

And then sure enough, sometimes after days of letting it cool off and then going back to give it a fresh look, it's there right in front of my eyes. In fact, sometimes I can find multiple problems with an entry even after not being able to find one on the first pass.

Take this scenario, for example: A person files for Chapter 7 bankruptcy, and it's discharged three months later. One of the creditors listed in the bankruptcy petition, Discover Card, reported the account to both Experian and Trans Union (Figure 12).

Can you see the problems with this tradeline? Discover failed to do two things as required by the FCRA. First, the account shows a status of "Petition for Chapter 7 Bankruptcy." That's false, since the bankruptcy discharged this debt. In accordance with the FCRA, it should read, "Included in Bankruptcy." Second, accounts included in bankruptcy are supposed to show a zero balance, and this account shows "NA." As such, a declaratory action can be used to delete the whole tradeline, providing the action is performed within the statute of limitations for the particular action. (In this case, the Discover tradeline was deleted using a contract breach in state court.)

If you look hard enough, you'll find that most entries contain inaccuracies. Yet there are other considerations with this particular tradeline. It's "technically accurate" because it was reported on 05/02, and that was during the petition phase of the bankruptcy. Courts are split on technically accurate entries, but it's my belief—though I'm not a lawyer—that an action in this circumstance would fly in any court, since there are additional provisions within the law that require furnishers to report specific things with regard to bankruptcy entries. In other words, technical accuracy may be OK in some circumstances, but where there are additional laws that spell out the way an entry is supposed to be reported, the technical accuracy defense on the part of

DISCOVER FINANCIAL SVCS

Address:
PO BOX 15316
WILMINGTON, DE 19850
(800) 347-2683

Account Number:
601100944061....

Status: Petition for Chapter 7 Bankruptcy.

Date Opened: 05/1999	Type: Revolving	Credit Limit/Original Amount: $15,002
Reported Since: NA	Terms: NA	High Balance: $15,361
Date of Status: 05/2002	Monthly Payment: $0	Recent Balance: NA
Last Reported: NA	Responsibility: Individual	Recent Payment: NA

Your statement:
Account closed at consumer's request

Account History:
Filed Chapter 7 Bankruptcy on May 22, 2002

Figure 12.

any furnisher would not likely hold up. But then again, who knows what a judge will do?

In any event, a declaratory action in similar cases isn't likely to cause a fight; however, as I've mentioned, anyone who files suit should be prepared for any eventuality.

PUBLIC RECORD PRETEXTS AND PITFALLS

Usually the furnisher of public record information is a service bureau. It takes a little bit of work, but once you discover the identity of the service bureau, you can bring a suit against it for failing to report accurately. You must take care, however; there might indeed be an inaccurate public record document that it transposed correctly, in which case the party that actually filed the document is at fault. The best way to determine this, of course, is to check the public record entry against the information the service bureau furnishes.

If it's a courthouse or county office mistake, be careful. It's best to avoid suing local courthouses and the like, lest you raise the ire of the judges. Moreover, many attorneys don't want to take cases that involve suing people in the yard they play in. And although many state judges are often happy—even impressed—when a *pro se* plaintiff can follow the complex rules and get things done, they can also make things very difficult on someone they believe to be messing on their turf.

To find out which service bureau is furnishing the entry, you can often contact the courthouse or county office and ask what company scans its records for the bureaus. You can also simply inquire with the credit bureaus as to who furnished them with the data, since you have the right to know under the FCRA.[49] Any information gleaned from demanding disclosure of the description of procedure used to determine accuracy and completeness can be used in a civil action.

If it's the service bureau's mistake, then I believe a declaratory action can be taken against it, assuming that it is not also a credit reporting agency, as no private cause of action exists for injunctive relief against a credit bureau. But a contract breach cannot be employed, since none exists. I would first look for something outside of a FCRA violation, such as violation of a state UDAP law, intentional interference with contractual relations, or injurious falsehood, and use a FCRA violation only as a last resort.

I haven't ever filed a declaratory action against a service bureau, and I have no idea what the outcome would be. But if given the opportunity, I'd surely give it a try. They don't want to fight, of course, and if they were facing a nonmonetary action for faulty reporting, it's my belief that they would run for cover like everyone else.

---

49. 15 U.S.C. § 1681i(6)(B)(iii), a notice that, if requested by the consumer, a description of the procedure used to determine the accuracy and completeness of the information shall be provided to the consumer by the agency, including the business name and address of any furnisher of information contacted in connection with such information and the telephone number of such furnisher, if reasonably available. 15 U.S.C. § 1681i(7), description of reinvestigation procedure. A consumer reporting agency shall provide to a consumer a description referred to in paragraph (6)(B)(iii) by not later than 15 days after receiving a request from the consumer for that description.

LEGAL OPTIONS FOR DEBT COLLECTOR ABUSE

As explained in Chapter 7, the FDCPA governs certain types of collectors and certain types of debts. However, what if the debt collector doesn't fall under the FDCPA? Just because a collector doesn't fall under the FDCPA doesn't mean there aren't other legal remedies available. Further, just because a debt collector doesn't usually fall under the FDCPA, its actions may cause it to be subject to the FDCPA under certain circumstances. Here are some examples:

- *Mail fraud,* which includes false representation, fraudulent billing, or even a collector's use of deceitful statements, half-truths, and concealment of material facts.[50] "It arguably prohibits letters threatening to seize, sell, or garnish the debtor's property, when no such action has or will be taken."[51] And although a private cause of action (lawsuit by an individual) is not available for postal violations (it's reserved for the federal government), "the FDCPA makes the threat of illegal conduct actionable,[52] and some state debt collection statutes specifically incorporate prohibitions established in the federal postal laws."[53]
- *Criminal statutes for e-mail and telephone harassment.* These fall under the Communications Act of 1934, amended by the Federal Telecommunications Act of 1996 and converted to the Federal Communications Act (FCA)[54] and apply to interstate and foreign communications where the caller (1) fails to disclose his or her identity, with intent of annoy, abuse, threaten, or harass any person who receives the communications, (2)

---

50. NCLC *Fair Debt Collection* § 9.1 (5th ed. 2004 and 2005 Supp.); *Lustiger v. United States,* 386 F.2d 132 (9th Cir. 1967), cert. denied, 390 U.S. 951 (1968); *United States v. Federal Record Serv. Corp.,* 1999 U.S. Dist. LEXIS 7719 (S.D.N.Y. May 21, 1999).
51. Quoted from NCLC *Fair Debt Collection* § 9.1 (5th ed. 2004 and 2005 Supp.).
52. 15 U.S.C. §§ 1692d(1), 1692e(5).
53. Quoted from NCLC *Fair Debt Collection* § 9.1 (5th ed. 2004 and 2005 Supp.). See state debt collection laws summarized in Appendix E of same.
54. 47 U.S.C. § 223(a)(1)(C)—(E).

causes the telephone to ring repeatedly, with intent to harass any person at the number called, (3) repeatedly initiates communication with a telecommunications device in which the ensuing conversation or communication serves only to harass any person who receives the communication, or (4) knowingly permits any telecommunications facility under his or her control to be used for any of the above purposes with the intent that it be used for such activity.[55] Any of the aforementioned is a criminal activity, and anyone found guilty can be sentenced to prison for up to two years for each count.[56]

- *Truth in Lending Act (TIL) disclosures.* The Truth in Lending Act may require a debt collector to provide a debtor with a new TIL disclosure if a new debt payment schedule is worked out ("workout agreement") or if the amount financed or the finance charges are increased.[57]

- *Racketeering Influenced and Corrupt Organizations Act (RICO).* While RICO doesn't apply to unlawful debt collection, it does apply when such activity is taken to another level, where criminal acts relate to an "enterprise" in a forbidden manner.[58] RICO requires one of two types of qualifying conduct, "collection of an unlawful debt" and "racketeering activity" (extortion of money or advantage by threat or force). An unlawful debt can be two things: (1) unlawful gambling debt or (2) debt that arises from an unenforceable loan due to a breach of usury law (charging interest exceeding that allowable by law) and bears an interest rate that is twice the enforceable rate.[59] There

---

55. NCLC *Fair Debt Collection* § 9.3 (5th ed. 2004 and 2005 Supp.).

56. 47 U.S.C. § 223(a)(1) and U.S. Sentencing Guidelines, § 2A6.1 in 18 U.S.C., re: Threatening or Harassing Communications.

57. TIL disclosures must occur before consummation of a written, prelitigation "workout agreement" that allows the consumer to pay the obligation. Must be for a "creditor" and "credit transaction." Debts paid in full don't fall under this category. There are other requirements as well. See NCLC *Fair Debt Collection* § 9.4 (5th ed. 2004 and 2005 Supp.).

58. 18 U.S.C. § 1962(c).

59. 18 U.S.C. § 1961(6). See NCLC *Fair Debt Collection* § 9.5.2 (5th ed. 2004 and 2005 Supp.).

are qualifying elements to a RICO claim, including a requirement that injury must have resulted. For unlawful gambling debts, a collector only has to have performed the collection of such a debt one time. Yet for issues not surrounding the collection of an unlawful debt, a pattern of qualifying conduct (not just one violation) is required.[60]

• *The Equal Credit Opportunity Act (ECOA).* Violations under the ECOA deal with collection actions that discriminate against a debtor based on race, color, religion, national origin, sex, marital status, age, receipt of public assistance, and exercise of rights under the Consumer Credit Protection Act. Debt collectors who use tactics that are abusive based on any of the aforementioned are in violation of the ECOA, and any such violations apply to the entire credit transaction, including collections, not just application.[61]

• *The FCRA.* The Fair Credit Reporting Act may apply if the collector has erroneously reported the debt to a credit reporting agency.

• *The Servicemember's Civil Relief Act (SCRA).* The SCRA applies to active-duty military and limits collections on servicemembers, such as prohibiting default judgments (such as when a collector sues and a debtor fails to answer the complaint and a judge finds for the collector by default), reduction of obligations incurred prior to active-duty military service to 6 percent,[62] tolling of statutes of limitations, the member's right to terminate residential and vehicle leases, and the prohibition of self-help

---

60. Elements of a RICO claim are covered in NCLC *Unfair and Deceptive Acts and Practices* § 9.2 (6th ed. 2004). Also See NCLC *Fair Debt Collection* § 9.5.4 (5th ed. 2004 and 2005 Supp.).

61. The Federal Reserve Board (FRB) defines credit transaction as "every aspect of an applicant's dealing with a creditor regarding an application for credit or an existing extension of credit (including, but not limited to . . . collection procedures)." FRB Reg. B, 12 C.F.R. § 202.2(m).

62. SCRA § 207 (50 U.S.C. app. § 527). Minimum payments must also be adjusted accordingly. The 6 percent maximum rate applies to all debts incurred before active duty, even debts included in Chapter 13 bankruptcy, with the exception of student loans.

repossession and nonjudicial foreclosure. Self-help repossession is when creditors "help themselves" to property used as collateral by debtors in default; that is, seize property without the use of courts or lawyers, as long as it doesn't breach the peace. Nonjudicial foreclosure is employed by creditors that don't have to file suit to seize real property. This can be performed in states that use deeds of trust or when a "power of sale" clause exists in a mortgage clause, though the state must also permit nonjudicial foreclosure, such as California.

- *Bankruptcy Code.* When a debtor applies for bankruptcy protection, he or she is given an automatic stay. That is, collection activity must cease. Any violation of the stay constitutes a breach of bankruptcy law.[63]

- *Constitutional torts.* Where a state or local government official (including law enforcement officials) is involved in debt collection abuse, this is a constitutional tort. A tort is a wrongful act other than a breach of contract that injures another. An example of a constitutional tort would be a breach of the Fourth Amendment, which addresses unreasonable search and seizure.

- *Other torts.* Malicious or reckless behavior on the part a collector can be considered tortuous. This may include intentional or negligent infliction of emotional distress or mental anguish, invasion of privacy, intentional interference with employment relationships, defamation, malicious prosecution, and abuse of process.[64] Torts that don't involve government officials can be applied using state law.

While the aforementioned examples may confuse some, the list serves to illustrate that there are many remedies outside the FDCPA when a debt collector doesn't fall under the third-party definition. Furthermore, although some debt collectors may not fall under the

---

63. 11 U.S.C. § 362(a)(6).
64. See NCLC *Fair Debt Collection* § 10.1.1 (5th ed. 2004 and 2005 Supp.) for in-depth analysis of each type of claim.

FDCPA, civil action under the Act may still be available if debt collectors conduct themselves in a certain way.

The information I provide on debt collection is only a primer. There are legal manuals dedicated to the subject of debt collection, such as the one cited here frequently, the NCLC *Fair Debt Collection* manual. The book, like the Fair Credit Reporting manual, has more than 1,000 pages and covers a wide range of issues with specificity. Anyone serious about debt collection should obtain it through the NCLC at www.nclc.org.

SMALL-CLAIMS COURT

Small-claims court isn't the place for credit report issues. You can't get punitive damages, you can't get a declaratory judgment, and there's a money-damage cap. Plus, any creditor that is sued for money damages under the FCRA will likely have the case removed to federal court anyway, and any bureau will surely have it removed.

It's an option in some circumstances, such as disputes involving landlords and contractors but is mainly for preemptive action (to avoid a civil action showing on your credit report) or collection of a debt that you are owed.

Note: Most small-claims courts have very narrow jurisdiction guidelines, meaning that the offense has to have occurred in the state where you file, and both parties must reside in that state. (Suing a collection agency based in New Jersey when you live in Oregon, for example, isn't possible, even if the offense occurred in Oregon.) Other small-claims courts have jurisdiction simply based on where the offense occurred. Of course, for written contracts the venue will be that which the contract calls for. Check your small-claims court for its local rules.

The rules are far looser in small-claims, and you aren't frowned upon by the court for not having a lawyer. Simple, easy-to-file forms are provided, and you can take many types of civil issues before the court, as long as they meet the state's venue guidelines and fall within the money and/or property cap.

Other cases commonly heard in small-claims include disputes over billing/overbilling for services, unlawfully issued checks, traffic accidents that don't involve serious injury, and dog bites. The awards in most states consist of a monetary judgment (with a cap based on local law), and other states will permit recovery of property (with a cap). Most have monetary damage limits ranging from $3,000 to $6,000. Check with your local small-claims court to see if your case can be heard there.

SERVICE OF PROCESS

As explained in Chapter 6, after you file suit, the defendant must be served with a summons and a copy of the complaint. This is called service of process. Although Chapter 6 deals with avoiding being served, it's useful to know how to serve the other party when you're the one filing suit.

In the case of businesses, it's simply a matter of contacting the secretary of state for the state in which the defendant lives. They will have the business' "agent for process service," and most provide this information for free, yet some will charge a fee just to look it up. Most businesses list an attorney with the secretary of state as their agent for receiving court papers, but many others will list a third party company that specializes in receiving such documents on behalf of another. Once you have identified the correct party to receive a summons, you must then determine how to best serve the papers. This is done with a third party, called a process server, who must be in the same location as the party being served the papers. Sheriffs in all counties across the United States are process servers for the counties in which they operate and can perform this function for a fee. Every state has companies that specialize in process service, and a simple search of the net using the county plus "process server" will yield many results. Whether you are using the county sheriff (where the defendant resides) or a company, you simply call and ask for instructions as to how to get the party you are suing served with a summons.

Many banks and credit unions can be served in this way, by using a billing statement (or Web search) to determine where the bank is incorporated and then contacting the secretary of state to determine who the agent is. However, many large banks are national associations (NA) and won't be listed with any secretary of state.

One way to determine if a bank is a NA is to use the FDIC's search tool, found at www2.fdic.gov/structur/search/findoneinst.asp. (If this link gets broken, go to ftc.gov and search under "Is my bank insured.") This is normally used for determining whether a bank is insured by the FDIC, but it also tells you where the bank is headquartered and whether or not it's a NA. If it's not a NA, then you'll know what state it's headquartered in and can then contact the appropriate secretary of state, and so on.

If the bank is a NA, there's no need to contact the secretary of state, as it can be served at the address listed with the FDIC, and no particular person is required to be listed in the summons. For example, if you want to sue Bank of America, NA, you'll search "Bank of America," and then click "Bank of America, National Association" in the search results. The address provided is acceptable for service.

As explained, there are process service companies that operate in every state, but in my experience county sheriffs are preferable because they're easy to find and reliable. To look up the sheriff's office, simply perform a Web search for its Web site (they all have them) and then contact it using the telephone number on the contact page.[65] Once you know who is to receive the summons and complaint, contact the sheriff's office by telephone and ask (a) how much for process service, (b) what form of payment is accepted, (c) how many copies of the summons and complaint are required, and (d) anything else that's required. The sheriff's office will want a cover letter with instructions for service and an address for returning the processed papers to you.

Remember, every state has its own laws. For example, in Oregon a process server (or sheriff) must serve a summons and complaint. But

---

65. The area code utility online is useful (www.intrepidsoft.com/acjava.html). Once you have the area code, contact directory assistance (area code + 555-1212) and request the number. Of course, directory assistance (411 or 555-1212) will also provide you with the area code for any location, but then you'll be charged for two directory assistance calls.

whenever anything is filed with the court subsequent to that, copies must be provided to the other party(s) and counsel, if any. For such documents, most courts require a "certificate of service" (a signed document certifying that documents were indeed provided to the opposing party(s) to be filed along with the original papers). Some states, such as California, require that whoever signs a "certificate of service" not be a party to the action. As always, check your state's laws and/or local court rules.

Many states have their entire database of corporate filings available online, while others charge a fee of $20 or so to look up the contact information of the agent for service of process, providing the information over the telephone and charging to a credit card.

PREPARE TO WIN

In all of your dealings, be a stickler for details. Put all communication to the credit bureaus in writing. Put what you can in writing when communicating with furnishers, and take detailed notes on all telephone conversations with them. Tracking correspondence is a big part of preparing any winning case. Methodically plan what your next move will be, since your actions will cause reactions; if you've played your cards right, you'll look reasonable and the other party will look unreasonable. Even the other party's failure to respond to your query would likely be interpreted by a judge or jury as unreasonable. Always employ tactics that will get the other party to tell on himself, either through writing or by taping phone conversations (if legal and admissible in your state or federal court). What better evidence than the defendant's own words and deeds? Or should I say misdeeds?

As I explained earlier, I like going it alone, particularly on the smaller cases. After all, who knows my case and cares as much as I do? Besides, I prefer to pocket the proceeds if there are any. Of course, we're all busy with our daily lives and often just want someone else who knows what he or she is doing to handle things. But sometimes the situation just won't permit this; the dollar amount involved makes legal representation impractical. In such cases, once you've done it by yourself and had success, you'll feel empowered and will not likely allow yourself to be trampled on again.

I always make certain that a positive outcome is virtually ensured no matter where my case ends up. He said/she said isn't good enough; it's hard proof that will make or break your case. Assume early on that the case will end up in court and plan accordingly. If you do retain an attorney, you'll strengthen his or her hand with your own efforts and also increase the chances that the attorney will take your well-prepared case on a contingency-fee basis.

Find the Right Lawyer

If the creditor is reporting falsely and it's impacting you negatively, consider suing for a FCRA violation in federal court and attempting to collect all types of money damages permissible under the law. If your case is strong enough and the damage egregious enough, you may want to find a crackerjack lawyer who will take the case on a contingency basis. An FCRA attorney can tell you very quickly whether you have a strong case, and if you do, he or she is likely be interested.

For me, retaining a lawyer to deal with creditors and bureaus is a last resort. It's likely that you will know far more about credit reporting than most lawyers when you are finished reading this book. Why pay someone to negotiate when you already know how? But when the terms of written agreements aren't met, when erroneous information simply won't come off your report, and when all other avenues have failed, then you should consider retaining counsel. With regard to credit reporting and debt collection claims, you should retain a lawyer under the following circumstances:

- When you've been served with a summons to appear and can't reach a settlement before the answer is due the court
- When you have any claim against a credit bureau
- When you have a money-damage claim against a furnisher
- When you have specific questions regarding debt collections, public records, and bankruptcy that a lawyer in your state can answer

Make sure that if you hire a lawyer to take on your case, you know exactly what you want him or her to do and can explain the strengths of your case succinctly. And don't search in the Yellow Pages for one.

Perform a search of the NACA Web site.[66] NACA member lawyers must never have represented creditors and cannot do so as members; you're more likely to find someone sympathetic to your cause. And since they specialize in consumer protection, many are often experts in the arena of fair credit reporting. NACA's Web site has a search tool that enables users to search by area of specialty, such as bankruptcy and fair credit reporting, as well. I've had discussions with some of them who are very advanced, crackerjacks in my opinion. In the case of faulty reporting, they can really put the hurt on those responsible—something you or I could never do.

Take, for example, NACA attorney David Szwak of Louisiana. He was writing about identity theft back in 1993, before *criminals* even knew what it was. Having been involved in hundreds of FCRA cases against credit reporting agencies and furnishers, he has vast knowledge of legal recourse. Few opposing attorneys can contend with this.

If you can't get a NACA attorney with experience in your local area, then go with an attorney who comes highly recommended by a friend or relative. Although he or she may not know the FCRA, a good attorney who's willing to learn can be very effective. There are many resources available, as well as experts in the field who will help when called upon. Have your attorney use this book as a primer and then obtain the NCLC's *Fair Credit Reporting* manual.[67] Also have him or her contact other NACA member attorneys, since many of them routinely share information with lawyers who ask. A studious attorney can become very effective if he's smart, wreaking havoc on your bureau-furnisher oppressors.

Another option is to call your state bar association for a referral. Those on the referral list will often offer 30 to 60 minutes of consultation free of charge. In addition, the bar association will often have legal aid services available to people with meager means. The wait to get an appointment with one of these attorneys can be long in some cases, but you don't know if you don't ask. Again, most of the attorneys

---

66. National Association of Consumer Advocates (www.naca.net).
67. The *Fair Credit Reporting* manual was written by attorneys who are at the top of their game. Although expensive ($140 as of this writing), every FCRA attorney should have it.

found using this option will need some schooling, and you don't want to pay for the cost of educating them.

Often lawyers are more willing to represent you when they feel confident that the defendant they are suing will pay them. If you hand them a case that is cut and dried, they will often take it on a contingency basis. In such a case, the fee they take (when and if they win) can consist of attorney's fees that you've sued for and/or a portion of what you are awarded, usually one-third. An example would be a case against a collection agency that has called you outside allowable hours (e.g., 7 A.M.) This is a slam-dunk for an attorney; all he or she has to do is subpoena the agency's phone records to prove it.

If an attorney is not yet versed in FCRA subject matter and you cannot find one locally who is, use your stellar negotiating skills to convince him or her that you have a winner. Take a copy of the FCRA and/or FDCPA with you and highlight the relevant portions so that you can wrap it all up in the first free consultation. Be sure to explain that the FDCPA and FCRA both have provisions for the recovery of attorney's fees.

Tip: Sometimes you can get free legal assistance if you meet certain income requirements. (This is OK for small cases, but not for large money-damage claims for FCRA violations.) Check with your state bar to find out more. Also, many law schools have legal clinics where students will do work pro bono. Law students are often looking for oddball cases, too, which is a category that credit sometimes falls into. Go into these clinics with an open mind; maybe you can build a rapport with someone who will be the next great American lawyer.

If you can't get an attorney to take your FCRA or FDCPA case on a contingency-fee basis, keep trying and find one who will. And in all of your written agreements with lawyers, use the phrase, "This agreement constitutes the full work that attorney will conduct, and if there are any additional services to be performed, those services will be con-

firmed in writing and a price set separately in advance of the services."
Of course, this won't apply for a contingency-fee relationship, but just
ensure that the terms of any agreements are spelled out.

Lawyers must get paid to earn a living, but it's up to you to protect yourself from overbilling and unscrupulous practices. After all, if
you're overbilled and don't have anything in writing, what are you
going to do—get another attorney who may likewise burn you? I've
seen it a hundred times: one attorney burns someone, and then that
someone gets another attorney to make it right—only to get burned
again. Unlike the rest of us, lawyers can represent themselves and forgo
legal fees, creating an environment that's ripe for abuse. Where does
that leave you?

It's easy to go to the dark side as a lawyer. The lure of easy money
is great, while what's in the best interest of the client is often the polar
opposite of human nature; the impetus is to bill hours. It's the fault of
the legal system, in my opinion. But the laws are made by lawyers for
lawyers, and reform isn't likely to come in my lifetime. A 30-year attorney summed it up best: money buys injustice.

I've made written agreements with lawyers, only to have them go
back on the deal and bill me for more than agreed. I've also had them
agree to one thing over the phone and then send me a contract that was
very different than what we agreed upon. (And they're supposed to be
working for me?) In my opinion, lawyers generally have earned their
bad reputation. Don't take anything for granted, and be prepared to
sue your lawyer and file a complaint with the state bar and attorney
general if written agreements are broken.

Some attorneys will be more receptive than others to your plight,
and some will even try to discourage you from pursuing a legal remedy. But don't let that deter you. I once consulted with an attorney who
tried to discourage me, claiming that I didn't have a case. The next one
I spoke with saw it differently and made $4,000 in the process.
Everyone has an opinion.

In another case, I sought advice from four different attorneys, all
experts in their area of practice with more than 100 years of experience
among them. I didn't like any of the advice until I spoke with the
fourth one. He was really sharp and came up with a creative way to
solve my problem.

Remember, intelligent doesn't mean smart.

I have known a good lawyer or two. It's difficult, but if you do find a one, treat him like gold. Good ones can be friends for life.

Once, I was in the middle of a serious trademark dispute, and, at the behest of a good friend, I contacted an attorney he knew. He was so helpful in providing the documents I needed, saying, "You're a smart guy and can figure this out." Then he e-mailed me the Microsoft Word templates I needed pro bono. After modifying the templates to suit my needs, I submitted an Answer to Opposition to the U.S. Trademark office, and it worked like a charm. Incidentally, the opposition in that action was a very well-financed (and well-represented) company, yet I won a very sweet trademark. (By the way, before applying for the trademark, I had two fancy trademark attorneys tell me that the word I sought to register would never be approved. Fancy shmancy.)

15

SAMPLE *PRO SE* LAWSUITS

The details of the following lawsuits are not intended as legal advice, but rather to illustrate what's possible. Consult an attorney and check your local rules for procedures.

PROVIDENT BANK, CREDIT CARD
(DECLARATORY ACTION, FCRA)

In this case, Provident Bank issued a credit card that ultimately became delinquent and was reported as such. However, once the account was no longer in arrears, the bank erroneously reported its status as past due. Some aspects of the account were being reported correctly, yet, as explained in the previous chapter, the consumer can use a single false aspect as the basis for civil action against a creditor. This works because it's not likely to cause a set-off; the consumer doesn't owe any money for which the bank is likely to countersue.

Using this aspect of erroneous reporting as a pretext, I filed suit in Oregon State Circuit Court, and when Provident failed to respond to the summons or file an answer, I first got the court to rule that the bank was in default and then filed a Request for Judgment, Declaratory Relief. Within a few days, the judge had signed my judgment—a court order requiring Provident to stop reporting.

```
PROVIDENT BANK #46752800034
                          Balance:          $0            Pay Status:       >60 Days Past Due<
PO BOX 1844               Date Updated:     10/2001        Account Type:     Revolving Account
CINCINNATI , OH 45274-0001  High Balance:   $11,026        Responsibility:   Individual Account
(800) 335-2220           Credit Limit:      $11,000        Date Opened:      06/1999

Loan Type: Credit Card
Remark: Account closed by consumer
>Maximum delinquency of 60 days in 10/2001<
Estimated date that this item will be removed:  09/2008

Late Payments                       X   X   X   30 OK OK OK OK OK OK OK OK OK OK OK OK OK OK OK OK OK OK OK OK OK
   32 months          Last 32        sep aug jul jun may apr mar feb '01 dec nov oct sep aug jul jun may apr mar feb '00 dec nov oct
   30  60  90         Months         OK OK OK OK OK OK OK OK
  >1<  0   0                          sep aug jul jun may apr mar feb
```

Figure 13.

The judgment is a court order that requires Provident to stop reporting. At this point, I disputed the entries with both Provident and the bureaus, so that I could treat any future furnishing as erroneous reporting. National City Bank had purchased Provident Bank by the time it received my dispute demanding deletion of the tradeline. Upon receipt of my strongly worded letter and a copy of the judgment, it s in-house counsel contacted me immediately and agreed to instruct the bureaus to delete the tradeline or report it as Paid/Never Late; my choice. Of course Paid/Never Late is better, but since I had already disputed it with the bureaus, they deleted it as soon as a copy of the judgment was provided. If the credit reporting agencies did their job, the account is now flagged by the bureaus to prevent reinsertion, so even favorable reporting on the part of National City won't appear.

If the account had remained after the formal dispute with the credit bureaus and National City, I would have initiated legal action in accordance with Chapter 14. Remember, I still didn't have a FCRA claim unless I filed a formal dispute with the bureaus. However, if I didn't file a formal dispute with the bureaus and simply disputed it with National City by providing it with a copy of the judgment, then I still could have used another cause of action against National City in this case, since I had a court order demanding that it stop furnishing (which requires it to either fail to affirm as accurate or furnish "delete" to the bureaus in the event of a formal dispute). Any failure to obey the court order would have given me other remedies under the law, such as contempt of court, which is punishable by fine or imprisonment.

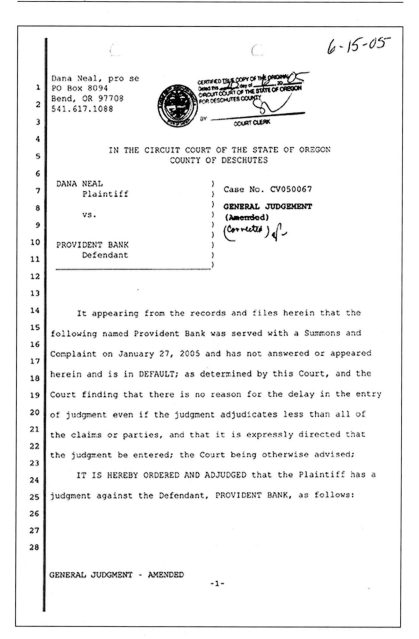

Figure 14.

DECLARATORY RELIEF

1
2   The Defendant is ordered to stop reporting the tradeline of
3 the Plaintiff, account number 4675 2800 0348 1730, to any credit
4 bureau, including TransUnion, Equifax, and Experian.
5
6 DATED this 17 day of _____ 2005.
7
8
9   Circuit Court Judge
10
11
12
13
14
15
16
17
18
19
20
21
22
23
24
25
26
27
28

GENERAL JUDGMENT - AMENDED

-2-

Figure 14a.

Notice that this judgment is corrected (Figure 14). The first one I submitted contained a mistake, wherein the declaratory relief read, "The Defendant is ordered to stop reporting the tradeline of the Defendant." I wasn't even sure what to do about this, but knowing that a new judgment was necessary and would have to be differentiated in some way, I submitted an amended judgment—which should have been a "corrected" judgment—substituting "Plaintiff" for the second "Defendant." As you can see, the judge simply inked in the correction for me and signed it. (I should have known it wasn't to be amended, since the judge wasn't ruling anything different from the original, but simply correcting a typo. But this shows that it's OK to fumble through if you're *pro se*. I've fumbled and mumbled, mumbled and fumbled.)

Judges may or may not sign *pro se* judgments as drafted, and I'll bet a dollar to a donut that this judge had never even seen a document like this. The clerk even remarked, "Interesting. I didn't know you could do that." And when I went back to get the amended . . . er . . . corrected version, there was a different clerk. She said, "Wow. You sued a bank."

In any case, as you can see, I didn't request any money—not even for reimbursement of court costs—making it a very simple request, the denial of which would have been difficult for a judge to justify. Powerful stuff!

RMA, COLLECTION AGENCY
(MONEY DAMAGES, FDCPA)

As I've already stated (and as you may have already experienced), collectors are notorious for breaking the rules. Their daily modus operandi is devoid of manners, tact, common decency, and respect for the law. Unfortunately, the law itself isn't enough of a deterrent for their hooliganism, but the legal options the FDCPA makes available to you as recourse can be useful when all other methods have failed.

I once had a bill collector from the collection agency Risk Management Alternatives (RMA) call me at 7 A.M. (Allowable hours are between 8 A.M. and 9 P.M.) He also called me three times in one day and left messages—not to mention lying. Of course, I told him I would sue if he continued to break the law, but did he believe me? Of course not—I'm a deadbeat idiot.

I sued the New Jersey-based collection agency in Oregon State Circuit Court, County of Deschutes (where I lived at the time). I could sue RMA locally, since it initiated the calls to me when I was in Oregon. Had I called RMA, I would likely have had to retain a New Jersey attorney, which might have caused me to give it up altogether. The remedies I requested were attorney fees (I didn't have an attorney but would bring one to trial if it went that far), court costs, and $20,000 in actual damages plus $1,000 in additional damages for violating 15 USC 1692k, a uniform commercial code dealing with collections. (Actual damages are subjective and relative to the amount of grief and hardship inflicted. I used $20,000, since it's best to start high.)

I picked up the book *Represent Yourself in Court—How to Prepare and Try a Winning Case* and read it cover to cover. I also picked up and studied the rules of my county's circuit court (counties' local rules often differ). Before I could file, I had to find out what type of entity I was dealing with. Was the defendant a corporation, a limited liability company (LLC), or something else? I called the New Jersey Secretary of State's office to find out, as well as to get the name and contact information for the defendant's registered agent (i.e., the attorney or third-party company required to receive a copy of the summons and complaint). This information was provided over the phone for a $20 fee, which I paid using my credit card. Now I was ready to file.

I typed up the complaint (using the techniques outlined in *Represent Yourself in Court* and copies of old cases at the courthouse) and filed it with the court at a cost of $126. (Had the damages been less than $10,000, the cost would have been $80. States differ on how much they charge, and you can call the court to find out what your state charges.) Since the defendant's registered agent had to be served (which meant typing up a summons and mailing it to the sheriff of the county in which the registered agent resided), I called the sheriff's office and asked about the procedure for service. I was told that I would need to send a check for $29 and the original plus three copies of the summons and complaint. I was also instructed to include a copy of the hearing notice, which the court provided to me (in triplicate) at the time of filing. Many state courts will perform the entire servicing process automatically if the defendant resides in your state, relieving you of the responsibility to perform service of process on your own. Check your local county's court rules or ask the clerk of courts.

Once the registered agent was served, the sheriff's office sent me "proof of service" in triplicate. I filed the original with the court, and the defendant had 30 days from the date of service in which to respond to the court.

Some crony from the defendant's legal department called me shortly thereafter and made an offer of $2,000 to settle. She also claimed that the company didn't normally operate this way and was very apologetic. After taking up her time and throwing a fit for about an hour, I told her I wasn't buying it. I felt that her company was in the business of badgering people, and now it was my turn. I told her that the price was $16,000 if she wanted to settle, explaining that her company would have to retain an Oregon attorney, and those costs alone would be from $12,000 to $15,000 if it went to trial. She told me she would think it over.

The next week I received a copy of the answer from the defendant's newly retained Oregon attorney. "Lord, these people are really stupid," I thought. "They would rather pay an attorney than pay me." (The local attorney I used for larger cases informed me that this is common; large companies are moronic when it comes to settling these matters.) The moment they lawyered up, they were in for $5,000 to $6,000 right out of the gate. *Why not just make a counteroffer of $5,000?* I wondered. *It's not a FCRA claim, there aren't any punitive damages, and I see no easily identifiable case law they might wish to write; I don't see what they can expect to gain.*

RMA's attorney did one smart thing: he made a formal "Offer of Judgment" of $2,500. This was a good tactic, since plaintiffs who decline such offers are not entitled to attorney fees, even if they win at trial, if the award is less than the Offer of Judgment. (Remember, attorney's fees are only available as a remedy if a contract or a statute calls for it. Since this case involved a violation of FDCPA § 813, 15 U.S.C. § 1692k, attorneys fees were permitted.) So, if this case had gone to trial, I had won, and the judge had awarded me $2,499 or less, then I would have had to pay my own attorney's fees, which can run somewhere in the neighborhood of $10,000 to $15,000. Of course, I could go to trial without an attorney, but that can be risky and I prefer not to.

Yet the opposing attorney was not well versed on the local court rules and made two errors. First, he submitted a "Demand for Jury Trial" (reasoning that the case would be heard by a judge by default unless a plaintiff or defendant submitted such a demand), which was not even possible because my claim didn't meet the dollar requirements in that county for a trial by jury. Second, he didn't know exactly how much time a plaintiff has to accept a formal Offer of Judgment in Oregon. In this case it was three days, and if he had done his home-work he would have known this. (In most states it's 10 days, and it must be offered within 10 days of trial. Most states also only allow the defendant to file a formal offer, while others permit either, and few per-mit only the plaintiff.)[1]

After bending his ear for about an hour and wrecking his day, I signed the Offer of Judgment, made a copy, and filed it with the court. As stated, by Oregon law I had only three days to accept the offer (which truly puts pressure on the plaintiff if the offer is good enough), and this one was good enough for me, since many such awards are, unfairly, only in the hundreds of dollars. I then created a "Stipulation of Judgment," which simply said that as soon as I received $2,500, I would dismiss the case with prejudice (meaning that the case could not be reopened in the future for any reason). Here is the exact wording I used:

> THIS MATTER coming before the Court upon the stipula-tion of the parties, by and through their respective attorney(s) of record; the Court being fully advised herein; now, therefore

> IT IS HEREBY ORDERED AND ADJUDGED that defen-dant will pay plaintiff the sum of $2,500 and plaintiff will, upon receiving the sum, request a dismissal of this case with prejudice.

---

1. American College of Trial Lawyers, Survey of State Offer of Judgment Provisions, Oct. 2004.

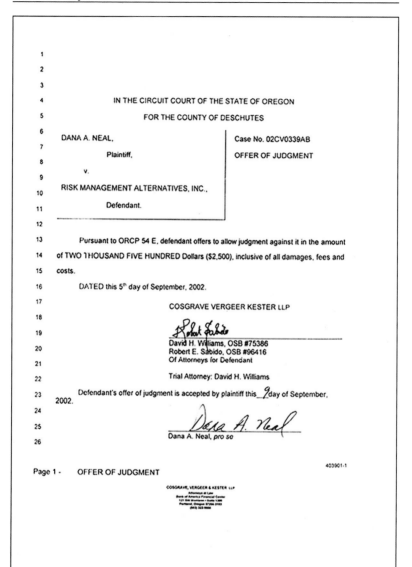

1
2
3
4
                    IN THE CIRCUIT COURT OF THE STATE OF OREGON

5
                        FOR THE COUNTY OF DESCHUTES

6
        DANA A. NEAL,   Case No. 02CV0339AB

7
                Plaintiff,   OFFER OF JUDGMENT

8
            v.

9
        RISK MANAGEMENT ALTERNATIVES, INC.,

10

11   Defendant.

12

13   Pursuant to ORCP 54 E, defendant offers to allow judgment against it in the amount

14   of TWO THOUSAND FIVE HUNDRED Dollars ($2,500), inclusive of all damages, fees and

15   costs.

16   DATED this 5th day of September, 2002.

17
                            COSGRAVE VERGEER KESTER LLP
18

19   _Robert Sabido_

20   David H. Williams, OSB #75386
                            Robert E. Sabido, OSB #96416
21   Of Attorneys for Defendant

22   Trial Attorney: David H. Williams

23   Defendant's offer of judgment is accepted by plaintiff this __9__ day of September,
        2002.
24

25   _Dana A. Neal_

26   Dana A. Neal, *pro se*

                                                                        403901-1

Page 1 -   OFFER OF JUDGMENT

                        COSGRAVE, VERGEER & KESTER LLP
                                Attorneys at Law
                        Bank of America Financial Center
                        121 SW Morrison • Suite 1300
                        Portland, Oregon 97204-3183
                                (503) 323-9000

Figure 15.

This was to be signed by the defendant's attorney and me and then filed with the court. The judge would have to sign it to make it binding. I signed it and sent it to the defendant's attorney for signature. He, in turn, sent me his own version of the Stipulation of Judgment, which read:

> Based on defendant's ORCP 54 E Offer of Judgment, which plaintiff has accepted, the parties stipulate that:
> A judgment be entered against the defendant in the amount of $2,500, inclusive of all damages, fees, and costs;
> Upon receiving proof of check from defendant in the amount of the stipulated judgment, plaintiff shall execute (a) this stipulated money judgment; and (b) a satisfaction of judgment in the form attached. Upon receiving those executed documents from plaintiff, defendant shall (a) send plaintiff the original settlement check, which plaintiff shall be authorized to negotiate; and (b) file the executed documents with the Court.

The attorney included a *copy* of the check made out to me from the defendant, along with another document, a "Satisfaction of Judgment," which I was supposed to sign and return with the stipulation.

What's wrong with this picture? Why in the heck would I sign a Satisfaction of Judgment when it wasn't really satisfied? Some people might consider signing this pile of crap and returning it to the defendant, but I am not one of them. I called the attorney and left the following message on his voice mail: "I have received your mail. These terms are unacceptable. I will dismiss the case only after I have received payment in full, and that point is nonnegotiable. Feel free to call me and let me know how you want to proceed."

If I signed the satisfaction of judgment, the case would be dismissed. What if the defendant decided not to send me the check? I didn't want to know the answer to that question. This wording only guaranteed that I would have "proof of check" in exchange for my dismissal, not actual payment. And once a suit is "dismissed with prejudice," it cannot be brought again.

What reason could the attorney have had for inserting "proof of check" instead of "payment in full?" It smelled like nothing but trouble, and I had never seen anything like this—or heard of it for that matter. Perhaps the attorney thought I was a neophyte and would bite. Perhaps I am—but this newbie surely wouldn't agree to dismiss anything without the cash in hand. Perhaps this was customary in Oregon, but I won't take the word of anyone for anything.

The attorney called me back and offered to have a local attorney (he was 150 miles away) meet with me to exchange the check/documents, which I agreed to. This satisfied both of our needs and put the whole thing back on track. He sent the new stipulation to a local attorney, and I met with that attorney, signed the documents, and was handed the check.

My resource costs totaled $175 plus time, and I received $2,500. RMA probably incurred $3,000 to $4,000 in legal fees, which put its total costs at $5,500 to $6,500. Not bad, eh? RMA got spanked for its

Figure 15a.

hooliganism, and I got a few bucks for my troubles, not to mention a good story for this book.

Of course, I had to pay income tax on the $2,500; the collection agency sent me a 1099 (a copy also goes to the IRS), but still . . . not a bad deal.

Figure 15a shows the final offer of judgment for $2,500 and the check.

SPRINT PCS, CELL PHONE COMPANY (MONEY DAMAGES, PREVENTIVE)

Ever owned a cell phone that was pure junk? I have; it was manufactured by Samsung and provided by Sprint PCS.

This particular phone had several problems, but the most aggravating was the propensity for the batteries to stop holding their charge. Every time I went to the Sprint PCS store in San Diego, I would wait in line for more than an hour, and each time an employee would inform me that the battery was defective and replace it.

After doing this three times, I decided this phone wasn't going to cut it. After all, I could not keep spending my days waiting in line at the Sprint store. Something had to give.

On the fourth visit I requested to speak with management. I informed him that the phone was defective by virtue of the batteries and that I didn't want a replacement battery, only to likely find that it too was defective. I said, "I don't want to find myself standing here again on this issue. I want a different model phone."

The manager refused to exchange my phone for a different model, to which I said, "I know you don't believe me—nobody ever does— but look into my eyes: You're going to get sued tomorrow if you don't provide me with a new model." Did he believe me? Of course not.

The next day I called Sprint PCS' 800-number customer service and requested to speak with the manager. She was nasty when I informed her of the problems I'd had with my phone, which were clearly annotated in the computer. I told her that she had one last chance to replace the phone, or I would cease doing business with Sprint and file suit that same day. She refused, and I told her to cancel service right then and there. I filed suit that day.

Meanwhile, I was sitting on a bill for service for $282.32 and didn't pay it. But by filing suit first, I made sure that any future lawsuit against me wouldn't end up on my credit report.

Not long after service of papers, someone from Sprint PCS contacted me and was very apologetic. I said to her, "Oh, now you want to be nice, eh? It's too late for that."

Anyway, she offered me $500 to go away, and I refused. In the end, Sprint PCS bought back my phone, paid my court fees, and agreed to forget about the pending bill. The company rendered me a check for $1,000 in addition to the removal of the pending bill.

SPRINT UNITED MANAGEMENT COMPANY
6580 SPRINT PARKWAY
OVERLAND PARK, KS 66251
1-888-283-4636

DANA NEAL
6172 CAMINITO DEL OESTE
SAN DIEGO, CA 92111

☐ CORRECTED (if checked)

PAYER'S name, street address, city, state, ZIP code, and telephone no. SPRINT UNITED MANAGEMENT COMPANY 6580 SPRINT PARKWAY OVERLAND PARK, KS 66251 1-888-283-4636		1 Rents 2 Royalties	OMB No. 1545-0115 **2003** Form 1099-MISC	**Miscellaneous Income**
PAYER'S Federal identification number 48-1077227	RECIPIENT'S identification number	3 Other income	4 Federal income tax withheld	**Copy B For Recipient** This is important tax information and is being furnished to the Internal Revenue Service. If you are required to file a return, a negligence penalty or other sanction may be imposed on you if this income is taxable and the IRS determines that it has not been reported.
RECIPIENT'S name, street address, city, state, and ZIP code DANA NEAL 6172 CAMINITO DEL OESTE SAN DIEGO, CA 92111		5 Fishing boat proceeds	6 Medical and health care payments	
		7 Nonemployee compensation $1,000.00	8 Substitute payments in lieu of dividends or interest	
		9 Payer made direct sales of $5,000 or more of consumer products to a buyer (recipient) for resale ☐	10 Crop insurance proceeds	
		11	12	
Account number (optional) LS346		13 Excess golden parachute payments	14 Gross proceeds paid to an attorney	
15		16 State tax withheld	17 State/Payer's state no. CA/	18 State income

Form 1099-MISC Department of the Treasury - Internal Revenue Service

Figure 16.

Margie Crawford
Senior Legal Analyst

Sprint Law Department
6450 Sprint Parkway
Overland Park, KS 66251
MailStop: KSOPHN0412-4A322
Voice 913-315-9521
Fax 913-523-0447
margie.crawford@mail.sprint.com

February 5, 2004

Mr. Dana Neal
6172 Caminito Del Oeste
San Diego, California 92111

     Re: Dana Neal v. Sprint Spectrum L.P.
             Case No. IC 820513

Dear Mr. Neal:

    Attached is the information which directs Sprint's tax department to correct the 1099 information relating to your refund. This was an oversight on my part and I apologize.

    If you require additional information, please give me a call.

                  Sincerely,

                  Margie Crawford

Attachment(s)

Figure 17.

But the story doesn't end there. Sprint PCS sent me a Form 1099 at the end of the year for the $1,000 refund! Yes, that's right. The company was trying to get a tax deduction for the amount *refunded to me*, and trying to screw me with the IRS as well (Figure 16).

I contacted the Sprint PCS agent again and informed her that I was going to file another lawsuit if she didn't withdraw the 1099 in writing. Did she believe me?

She did that time.

This whole scenario is just another example of how being proactive can be far more powerful than being a victim. If I had not filed suit, Sprint PCS would have not only wrecked my credit through collections but come after me for the unpaid bill plus a cancellation fee, since I failed to live up to the annual contract. Instead, I got all my money back and walked away unscathed. Sprint PCS, in turn, lost me as a customer—when all the agent had to do was replace the phone with something different.

AMERICAN EXPRESS, CREDIT CARD
(DECLARATORY, CONTRACT BREACH)

As mentioned earlier, American Express is notorious for listing accounts closed by consumer as "account closed by credit grantor."

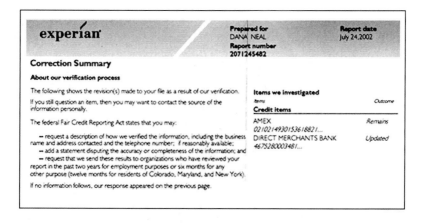

Figure 18.

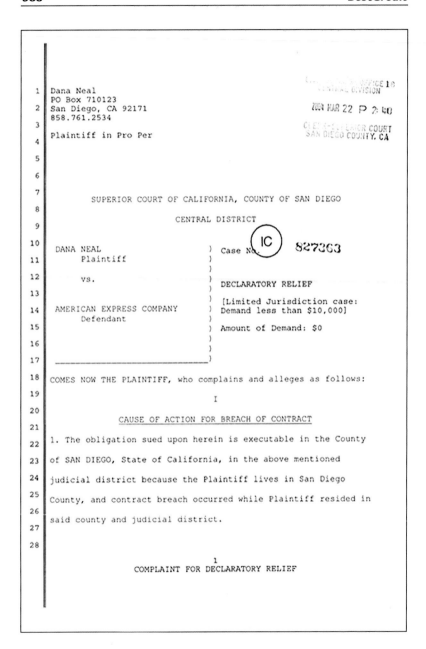

           SUPERIOR COURT OF CALIFORNIA, COUNTY OF SAN DIEGO

                              CENTRAL DISTRICT

10 DANA NEAL   )   Case No. 827363
11   Plaintiff   )
)
12   vs.   )   DECLARATORY RELIEF
13   )
)   [Limited Jurisdiction case:
14 AMERICAN EXPRESS COMPANY   )   Demand less than $10,000]
         Defendant   )
15   )   Amount of Demand: $0
)
16   )
)
17 _____)

18 COMES NOW THE PLAINTIFF, who complains and alleges as follows:

19   I

20   CAUSE OF ACTION FOR BREACH OF CONTRACT

21 1. The obligation sued upon herein is executable in the County

22 of SAN DIEGO, State of California, in the above mentioned

23 judicial district because the Plaintiff lives in San Diego

24 County, and contract breach occurred while Plaintiff resided in

25
26 said county and judicial district.

27

28
                                 1
                 COMPLAINT FOR DECLARATORY RELIEF

Figure 19.

1 2. Defendant is a corporation organized under the laws of New

2 York with offices Nationwide. Defendant's primary business is to

3 provide consumers and businesses with American Express Credit

4 Cards.

5

6 3. The Plaintiff and Defendant (hereafter referred to as

7 Parties) entered into an agreement in February of 1998, as

8 Plaintiff obtained a credit card from Defendant, Account Number

9 3723 196168 82001.

10

11 4. Plaintiff voluntarily closed said credit card by telephone on

12 July 30, 2001, speaking with Defendant's customer service

13 representative Ann Hall, operator number 54436, who is located

14 in the St Joseph, MO office of Defendant. At no time was

15 Plaintiff in arrears prior to the account being closed.

16

17 5. Defendant subsequently reported the account incorrectly to

18 the credit reporting agencies (Trans Union, Equifax, and

19 Experian, hereafter known as the "Big Three") by reporting that

20 the account was closed by Defendant; an attempt to harm

21 Plaintiff by lowering his FICO® Credit Score.

22

23 6. Plaintiff again attempted to get Defendant to remove the

24 offending data, speaking with representatives of Defendant by

25 telephone numerous times between January-March of 2002, and

26 Defendant refused. The Defendant's representative that handled

27 the matter was Angela Selma with the Credit Bureau Unit.

28

2
COMPLAINT FOR DECLARATORY RELIEF

Figure 19a.

1 7. Plaintiff disputed status with of account with the Big Three

2 from February to July of 2002. The Defendant affirmed the same

3 status with the Big Three, and the Big Three refused to update

4 the account to reflect that Plaintiff closed the account.

5

6 (Attached as Exhibit A)

7 8. Defendant is required to accurately report all account

8 information to the credit reporting agencies in accordance with

9 the Fair Credit Reporting Act. Plaintiff contends that by

10 reporting inaccurate information, Defendant first breached the

11 contract with Plaintiff.

12

13   WHEREFORE, Plaintiff prays for Declaratory Relief against

14 the Defendant, as follows:

15   1. The Defendant first breached the contract.

16   2. The Defendant be ordered to stop reporting the account

17   in its entirety to the credit reporting agencies; Trans

18   Union, Equifax, and Experian.

19

20   3. For such other relief as the court may deem just and

21   proper.

22   DATED: March 19, 2004.

23   _Dana Neal_____

24   Dana Neal

25   (Plaintiff in Pro Per)

26

27

28

                              3
              COMPLAINT FOR DECLARATORY RELIEF

Figure 19b.

This looks bad to any lender—raising the question of what happened that would cause a creditor to close an account.

This is exactly what happened to me, and when I disputed it with all three bureaus, American Express affirmed its reporting as accurate. I also contacted American Express and stated that I would sue if it didn't report the account closure correctly. Did it believe me?

Of course not.

Notice that I filed the lawsuit within two years of the erroneous reporting discovery—as required by the FCRA. I received the affirmation from Experian in July 2002 and filed the complaint in March 2004.

Within about a week of its being served, American Express had an attorney telephone me, and he was quite nasty. He claimed that I had filed suit against the wrong company, stating that American Express has a few divisions and I sued the wrong one.[2] He also said, "Your lawsuit is ridiculous. You should realize that you're going to get nowhere."

I replied, "You're free to retain a California attorney to defend it if you wish, but I'm not going to go away."

"No judge would ever grant tradeline deletion anyway," he said.

"Well, let's find out," I replied.

He softened, "Oh, hell. This isn't worth it. We'll delete the tradeline if you agree to dismiss your lawsuit immediately."

"Sounds good to me. Send me a settlement agreement, and we'll go from there."

From that point on, he was never rude or grumpy again, and we settled it.

Incidentally, my suit against Amex was my first declaratory judgment action. I've since learned a great deal about such actions and would have done a couple of things differently: (a) closing the account using the insurance method and (b) listing the proper legal reference in my complaint, as "account closed by credit grantor" is not permissible under the FCRA, 15 U.S.C. § 1681s-2(a)(4) and Cal. Civ. Code

---

2. Perhaps I did sue the wrong one, but apparently it didn't matter.

§ 1785.13(c),(e)(West). In fact, I could have brought a declaratory
action using California's state FCRA.

My complaint had other flaws, including the failure to provide a
copy of the contract with American Express, as required by law when
suing for a contract breach.[3]

---

3. "The contract must be set out verbatim in the body of the complaint or a copy
    of the written instrument must be attached and incorporated by reference."
    Otworth v. Southern Pacific Transp. Co. (1985) 166 Cal. App. 3d 452, 458-459.
    Failing to provide a copy of the contract wouldn't have stopped the case from
    moving forward, but an attorney wishing to give me a hard time could have
    slowed it by using a notice of demurrer. I would have been given time to amend
    the complaint, usually 20 to 30 days.

CONCLUSION
AND RESOURCES

It's easy to see why the quest for credit improvement can become so complicated. With the credit reporting agencies, furnishers, lenders, credit scoring nuances, collectors, state and federal laws, FTC rules, legal procedures, court rules, lawyers, and the wide spectrum of personalities and peculiarities among them all—it's easy to see why people just simply run from the problem of bad credit.

Remember, the very best results will come by dealing with the creditor. Very few ever need to resort to legal action. Readers of my first edition report an incredible success rate—over 90 percent—through negotiating, and the remaining 10 percent are situations where the creditor's expectations are reasonable but can't be met by the debtor. For example, *BestCredit* students periodically report that they're able to get seven of eight creditors to enter into a repayment plan and remove all adverse history. The single holdout refuses a repayment plan but will accept 80 percent of the debt if paid in full and remove the adverse history. This is perfectly reasonable on the part of a creditor, yet the debtor doesn't have the money to pay a lump sum. This isn't a failure of the methods, only a failure to find a meeting ground. If this happens to you, then suspend all negotiations for 60 days and go back and try again. Keep trying until you get the deal that works for you.

Creditors know that the credit reporting system favors them, which is why they're almost always willing to remove adverse history in exchange for payment. So go to them—hat in hand—and make a deal. Don't be overwhelmed or intimidated. Be steadfast and don't take no for an answer. Just apply what you've learned and create a credit profile that looks exactly the way you want. And once you get it there, always pay your bills on time!

If you think it's ludicrous the way lawmakers in this country permit banks to run all over consumers, with the use of arbitration agreements, unlimited credit card interest and late fees, and the use of risk-based pricing, you are one of millions who agree. If you think that credit reporting agencies are purveyors of identity theft, that they are absurd in the way they handle consumer disputes, you are one of millions who agree. If you think the credit reporting system unjustly puts you on par with a crackhead, by failing to have provisions for those who fall ill or have an injury and then repay their debts, you are also one of millions who agree. Contact your congressmen and tell them it's their job to look out for the people—something they've failed to do thus far. If we all contacted our congressmen, they'd be forced to take a serious look.

Finally, this book is the culmination of many years of experience and research. I've tried to address many concerns by readers of the first addition, yet it's impossible to address every scenario without turning it into a book the size of an IRS tax manual. I sincerely hope that this book has helped you, and I'm open to suggestions for ways in which the material may be improved. Your feedback is welcome and appreciated, and I'm always pleased to learn something about credit that I didn't know.

Many people desire an expert to coach them along as they implement *BestCredit* techniques. On a trial basis, I may perform some personal consulting for book readers only. If you're interested, contact me using the BestCredit web site. Good luck!

Note: While the book was at the printer, a significant development in scoring occurred that *BestCredit* readers should know about. On March 14, 2006, the Big Three announced VantageScore, a new scoring system designed jointly by the three bureaus. Designed to provide consistency in credit scores, VantageScore is a good idea, but it remains to be seen to what extent it will be adopted by the lenders. (See more at www.bestcredit.com/vantagescore/.)

BOOKS

- *Credit Scores and Credit Reports* by Evan Hendricks. Not useful for credit restoration, but Hendricks is a fine researcher and an expert on privacy.
- *Sue in California without a Lawyer* by Ron Duncan. Excellent for *pro se* litigants who reside in California. However, it doesn't deal with federal courts or Fair Credit Reporting.
- *Fair Credit Reporting* by the National Consumer Law Center. Often referred to in my book, this 1,000-plus-page book is a must have for any attorney litigating Fair Credit Reporting cases. It includes some case law with interpretations, sample interrogatories, pleadings, discoveries, and more. The cost is $140.
- *Fair Debt Collection* by the National Consumer Law Center. An excellent manual for attorneys litigating FDCPA violations.
- *The Total Money Makeover Book* by Dave Ramsey, www.daveramsey.com. This book is about becoming debt free, and it presents good (albeit unorthodox) step-by-step methods for achieving that goal.

CREDIT REPORTING

Consumer Reporting Agencies

Equifax
PO Box 740241
Atlanta, Georgia 30374-0241
www.equifax.com

Trans Union
PO Box 1000
Chester, PA 19022-2000
www.transunion.com

Experian
PO Box 2104
Allen, TX 75013-2104
www.experian.com

Business Reporting Agencies

Dun & Bradstreet
103 JFK Parkway
Short Hills, NJ 07078
www.dnb.com

Innovis
PO Box 1358
Columbus, OH 43216-1358
www.innovis.com

Checking Reporting Services

- ChexSystems: www.consumerdebit.com
- CheckRite: 800-766-2748
- TeleCheck: www.telecheck.com
- SCAN/DPPS: www.consumerdebit.com[1]
- CheckCenter/CrossCheck: www.crosscheck.com
- Certegy/Equifax: www.certegy.com
- International Check Services: 800-631-9656; acquired by TeleCheck in 2002

WEB SITES

- www.aiccca.org: The Association of Independent Consumer Credit Counseling Agencies provides information on credit counselors who are accredited.
- www.bestcredit.com: Check BestCredit for any book updates. Also search for your state's attorney general and view collection statutes by state. BestCredit also compiles information, so be sure to provide information you think should be shared with other readers.
- www.clickandbif.com: A useful reverse directory and other search utilities.

---

1. Both SCAN/DPPS and ChexSystems are owned by eFunds Corporation.

- www.daveramsey.com: Dave Ramsey is a radio talk show host and author of *The Total Money Makeover Book*. He offers some sound methods for getting out of debt and staying that way.
- www.findlaw.com: FindLaw provides lots of information about the law; fully searchable and indexed by category.
- www.ftc.gov: The Federal Trade Commission is the federal agency that oversees credit reporting, among other things. Any complaint about a furnisher or bureau should be filed with it.
- www.law.cornell.edu: Cornell University Law's site compiles many of the nation's laws (U.S. Code); a fully indexed and searchable site. Further, www.law.cornell.edu/uniform/ucc.html contains all 50 states' Uniform Commercial Codes; an invaluable resource. Cornell also has locators for the Uniform Probate Code, Uniform Code of Evidence, and uniform laws in the areas of matrimony, family and health, and business and finance.
- www.myfico.com: MyFico offers the Big Three credit reports with FICO score.
- www.naca.net: The National Association of Consumer Advocates is an invaluable resource for finding a knowledgeable consumer protection attorney in your area. For attorneys, NACA offers an array of programs, including educational seminars on the FCRA and FDCPA.
- www.nclc.org: The National Consumer Law Center has many consumer protection books for attorneys in addition to the ones mentioned above, such as ones on student loans, truth in lending, fair debt collection, and more. The 16-volume set can be purchased at a steep discount.
- www.nfcc.org: The National Foundation for Credit Counseling provides information on accredited credit counselors; yet this does not guarantee that the assistance provided by an accredited agency will be good.
- www.nolopress.com: Nolo Press offers many legal how-to books geared toward nonlawyers.
- www.privacytimes.com: *Privacy Times* is a newsletter, and its editor, Evan Hendricks, is a leading expert on privacy issues.

- www.wemed.com: Download *Punitive Damages Review* by Wilson, Elser, Moskowitz, Edelman & Dicker LLP. This 136-page guide lists the punitive damage remedies available by state and federal law.

COLLECTION STATUTE OF LIMITATIONS BY STATE

STATUTE OF LIMITATIONS[1]				
STATE	**ORAL AGREEMENTS**	**WRITTEN CONTRACTS**	**PROMISSORY NOTES**	**OPEN ACCOUNTS**
Alabama	6	6	6	3
Alaska	6	6	6	6
Arizona	3	6	5	3
Arkansas	3	5	6	3
California	2	4	4	4
Colorado	6	6	6	6
Connecticut	3	6	6	6
Delaware	3	3	6	3

(cont.)

1. Check your local statutes. Some states may also consider service complete when a debtor's residence is unknown and notice is made in a publication in the county in which the complaint is filed (e.g., Ohio Civ. R. 4.4, 4.6.—if service is refused, then regular mail is permitted; restrictions exist if the debtor is out of state, as the types of claims subject to these rule are limited).

State	Oral Agreements	Written Contracts	Promissory Notes	Open Accounts
D.C.	3	3	3	3
Florida	4	5	5	4
Georgia	4	6	6	4
Hawaii	6	6	6	6
Idaho	4	5	10	4
Illinois	5	10	6	5
Indiana	6	10	10	6
Iowa	5	10	5	5
Kansas	3	5	5	3
Kentucky	5	15	15	5
Louisiana	10	10	10	3
Maine	6	6	6	6
Maryland	3	3	6	3
Massachusetts	6	6	6	6
Michigan	6	6	6	6
Minnesota	6	6	6	6
Mississippi	3	3	3	3
Missouri	5	10	10	5
Montana	5	8	8	5
Nebraska	4	5	6	4
Nevada	4	6	3	4
New Hampshire	3	3	6	3
New Jersey	6	6	6	6
New Mexico	4	6	6	4

STATE	ORAL AGREEMENTS	WRITTEN CONTRACTS	PROMISSORY NOTES	OPEN ACCOUNTS
New York	6	6	6	6
North Carolina	3	3	5	3
North Dakota	6	6	6	6
Ohio	6	15	15	6
Oklahoma	3	5	5	3
Oregon	6	6	6	6
Pennsylvania	4	4	4	4
Rhode Island	15	15	10	10
South Carolina	10	10	3	3
South Dakota	6	6	6	6
Tennessee	6	6	6	6
Texas	4	4	4	4
Utah	4	6	6	4
Vermont	6	6	5	6
Virginia	3	5	6	3
Washington	3	6	6	3
West Virginia	5	10	6	5
Wisconsin	6	6	10	6
Wyoming	8	10	10	8

LEONARD A. BENNETT'S TESTIMONY BEFORE CONGRESS

Testimony Before Subcommittee on Financial Institutions and Consumer Credit of the Committee on Financial Services Regarding "Fair Credit Reporting Act: How it Functions for Consumers and the Economy," June 4, 2003. Submitted by Leonard A. Bennett, P.C. 12515 Warwick Boulevard Newport News, Virginia, on behalf of National Association of Consumer Advocates 1730 Rhode Island Avenue, NW, Suite 805, Washington, D.C. 20036.

Chairman Bachus, Congressman Sanders and other distinguished members of the Financial Services Committee, the National Association of Consumer Advocates (NACA) thanks you for inviting us to testify today in this early stage of considering changes to the Federal Fair Credit Reporting Act.

My name is Leonard A. Bennett. I have been asked to appear before you on behalf of NACA, its 850-plus members and the tens of thousands of consumers who we represent or on whose behalf we litigate. I am a consumer protection attorney. I have practiced law in Virginia since 1994, and in North Carolina since 1995. I obtained my undergraduate degree in Finance from George Mason University and my law degree from the George

Mason University School of Law and Economics. I have been asked to represent NACA today because of my litigation experience. More than anything else, my practice is focused on the private enforcement of the FCRA.

I have had the opportunity to review the prepared statements of the sub-committee's witnesses from your May 8th hearing. I expect that you will have heard more of the same today. The position of both the financial services industry and the credit bureaus is essentially the same—the FCRA system is perfect and you should not allow preemption to expire. The reality is far from these mis-truths. The Credit Reporting system remains seriously flawed and under present trends will only get worse. And the fear of the preemption sunset is blown out of proportion and would not jeopardize what national standards the FCRA has established.

Unlike some consumer protection statutes, the FCRA is not targeted to protect any particular group of Americans. It protects all of us. Wealthy and those of modest means alike. Husband and wife. Father and son. It protects those of us in the South as much as those of you from any other region. I practice primarily in Hampton Roads, Virginia. As a result, I have had the privilege to represent countless members of the United States Armed Forces. I represented several consumers in pending cases while they proudly served our country in Iraq. And whether an enlisted or an officer, the law protects each the same. The FCRA's protections do not know party line or ideology. It is a unique statute for a unique problem. The law must protect our privacy. It should help maintain the security of our information. It could help expand a frictionless economy. And ideally it would better guarantee that those who have earned good credit are able to keep the fruits of their efforts and responsibility.

Beyond the importance of the FCRA to consumers, you must also consider its benefits to our economy and American business. In its original adoption of the FCRA, Congress found that "the banking system is dependent upon fair and accurate credit reporting. Inaccurate credit reports directly impair the efficiency of the banking system, and unfair credit reporting methods undermine the public confidence which is essential to the continued functioning of the banking system." 15 U.S.C. Section 1681(a)(1). In considering the 1996 Amendments to the Act, Representative Kennedy explained, "[i]f these reports are not accurate, or if they are distributed without a legitimate purpose, then our whole society suffers. Consumers may be unfairly deprived of credit, employment, and their privacy. And businesses may lose out on the opportunity to gain new customers." 140 Cong. Rec. H9809, September 27, 1994. These insights are still true today. Accurate information is critical for a functioning economy. I am a believer in the free market system. The more accurate the information, the better the decisions made by our economy's actors. One of the principals [sic] I was taught in my undergraduate years studying the stock and investment markets is a concept titled "the efficient market hypothesis." The idea is that the investment markets will be fluid and frictionless only if perfect and equal information is available to all market participants. The same may be said for the consumer credit markets. Businesses need more accurate and complete information with which to make better lending decisions. Whether for the financing of an automobile, a home, or a department store purchase, sellers and lenders need access to accurate credit information so that they may transact business safely and with lower risk. These include large consumer lenders such as the credit card industry or mortgage lenders. But, it also includes more modest-sized businesses without the large margins for error available to institutional creditors. Credit file inaccuracies are damaging to businesses in both directions. Inaccurate credit reports may misstate the quality of a consumer's credit in a manner which could cause a potential seller or lender to inappropriately extend credit. The rise in consumer bankruptcies is one of the results of this false positive. On the other side of the coin, inaccurate derogatory information will keep businesses from selling and financing goods and services to consumers with otherwise excellent credit. The growing flaws in the credit system are endangering American businesses in both ways. Credit risks are inappropriately getting credit, while responsible consumers are often saddled with inaccurate derogatory histories that keep them from doing the same. The irony of the credit industry's opposition to FCRA improvement is the fact that the industry stands to gain as much as any other participant in this debate.

You have heard or will hear from countless witnesses all who express the policy view of their respective organizations or trade groups. Few if any of your witnesses will have any live experience actually using or enforcing the statute. Throughout the history of the consumer credit laws, attorneys such as myself have been titled "private attorneys general" by courts and commentators. It is our role to bring private enforcement actions to ensure compliance with laws such as the FCRA. Without these efforts, the FTC would need an army of regulators to perform the function—a possibility an advocate of limited government such as myself could not accept. You have now met one of the individuals who actually goes into federal court to implement the laws that you enact. I and other members of NACA see the flaws in the FCRA firsthand. We face the walls and obstacles placed in the way of full enforcement by the credit bureaus and their army of lawyers. We face the limitations and restrictions of the FCRA on a daily basis. I would like to take this opportunity to better inform the sub-committee on the mechanics of the FCRA system and some of the flaws within it.

Most of my litigation experience arose from claims of credit file inaccuracy. There are countless ways in which my clients' credit reports have been inaccurate. Often, my client's credit files were combined—partially or entirely—with those of another person. This may happen through the criminal acts of a third-party. I am involved in a Michigan case in which an identity thief discovered that our client, with a social security number off by one digit, had better credit. So she began to apply for credit using our client's social. Within no time, the credit files at the bureaus began to show a single identity with the thief's name as our client's alias. Despite multiple investigation demands, nothing was done about the problem or to keep it from recurring. She has been forced to sue. These cases are identity thefts and they have received the greatest notoriety. Unfortunately, they are far from the exception. The industry describes ID theft as a criminal law problem. But the only reason that identity theft is so prevalent and so easy to accomplish is because of the lack of any industry safeguards to stop it.

As common in my case portfolio are those claims we describe as "merged identity" cases. As easy as it is for an identity thief's credit files to be combined with that of an innocent consumer, it is even more likely to happen to persons of similar name and address or Social Security number. The credit reporting industry is now almost entirely automated. Its file searches do not require full identifying information—either to obtain a credit report or to furnish information to the bureau. As a result, I have been asked to help Sandra K. Brown, who had perfect credit, when Equifax could not keep the files of Sandra M. Brown from merging. And Mary E. Jones and Mary W. Jones, who because of their similar names and addresses had both of their identities combined by Trans Union. Or Teresa B. Davis, who lived on the same street as had Teresa G. Davis several years prior and had much better credit before Equifax merged the two files. These are my cases, solely out of Newport News and Hampton, Virginia. But, there is nothing about this problem which is unique to my community. It is happening everywhere throughout America. And while no one consumer is truly immune from it, the problem is much worse for consumers with common surnames, particularly those who share their name with multiple generations.

I also see a large number of pure inaccuracy cases—those in which an individual item within a credit report is inaccurate. These types of problems, though lacking the glamour and intrigue of an identity theft, are far more common and just as damaging. The Consumer Federation of America study, already made a part of the sub-committee's record by Representative Hinojosa on May 8, found that 1 in 10 credit scores were inaccurate. This is because of inaccurate information within the credit files used to calculate such scores. At the present, there are far more FCRA cases in my community than I can accept and litigate. Some examples which repeat again and again include Mr. Jeffreys, who refinanced his Bank of America mortgage in early 2002. Within his credit report the creditor and bureaus continue to report the account as a charge off and pending foreclosure with a full balance. This is despite the fact that he has mailed to all parties a copy of the original note marked paid in full by the creditor, a letter from the bank stating as much, and a letter from his real estate attorney. Or Linda Johnson, whose ex-husband filed bankruptcy on a credit card for which she was never responsible. When he filed bankruptcy, MBNA added Ms. Johnson as a cardholder and would not remove the account from her credit files until it was sued. These are only examples and they are far more typical of these problems than not.

The FCRA, as amended, includes a system of reinvestigation which Congress had hoped could provide a remedy by which consumers could obtain a correction of an inaccuracy within their credit files. Unfortunately, the system does not work. Of all of the provisions within the Act, no other is more fatally flawed than the investigation requirement. Let me first explain the real world mechanics of the system.

When a consumer discovers an inaccuracy within his or her credit report, they may initiate a dispute in one of two ways—by contacting the furnisher directly or by contacting the credit reporting agency. If the consumer contacts the furnisher directly, he does so at his own peril. Despite the 1996 amendments, the FCRA has left the furnisher largely immune from effective oversight. Without a private cause of action, the broad and admirable accuracy standards of Section 1681s-2(a) are merely aspirational. The only furnisher liability under the FCRA is under Section 1681s-2(b) and this is only triggered through a contact from the credit reporting agencies. No FCRA case has survived even the earliest stages of litigation without the consumer establishing that the dispute was initiated through the bureaus.

Approximately 80% of all consumer disputes received by the credit reporting agencies are made in writing. The remaining 20% come in by telephone. Each agency has a different process for handling these disputes, but all three use a similar system. The three bureaus collaborated through their trade organization to automate the entire reinvestigation process using an online computer program, E-Oscar. Upon receiving a written dispute, often in the form of a detailed letter with documents attached, the CRA assigns the dispute to its dispute department. The employees within the department are usually hourly employees and are minimally paid. In the case of Equifax, things are even worse. The CRA contracts out its FCRA responsibilities to a foreign company based in Jamaica which uses only foreign labor for its "investigations." The job of a CRA dispute department employee, even if titled "investigator," is solely data entry. No matter how detailed the written dispute, the CRA will merely translate it into a two digit code and, usually by automated means (ACDV), send a message to the furnisher identifying the code its employee believes best describes the dispute. The employees of all three CRAs operate under a quota system whereby each employee is expected to process all of the disputes of an individual consumer in less than four minutes. Worse still, the "codes" used by both the CRAs and their subscribers (the furnishers) are limited in number and rarely describe the actual basis for the consumer's dispute. For example, in two of my recent cases, both identical, consumers Van Evans and Ray Bailey wrote dispute letters to all three bureaus. The disputes were conveyed in great detail and explained that the consumers were not responsible for the disputed accounts and that any signatures claimed to be theirs were forgeries. Each consumer dispute letter also enclosed copies of handwriting exemplars such as signatures on driver's license, military IDs and other credit cards. Van Evans had also obtained a copy of the forged note and included it in his dispute letter. When Equifax and Trans Union received the letters, their employees simplified the disputes to a code and the description "not his/hers." This was all the furnishers received. In a deposition taken in a Pennsylvania case, Trans Union's responsible employee explained the CRA's "investigation procedure."

Q. [T]he dispute investigator looks
9 at the consumer's written dispute and then
10 reduces that to a code that gets transmitted
11 to the furnisher?
12 A. Yes.
13 Q. Does the furnisher ever see the
14 consumer's written dispute?
15 A. No.

• • •

Q. Are there any instances in which the
22 dispute investigator would call the consumer
23 to find out more about the dispute?
24 A. No.

This is consistent with CRA testimony in every other case of which I am aware. The bureaus do not convey the full dispute or forward any of the documents to the furnishers. As an expected result, nearly all consumer disputes are verified against the consumers.

However, while the CRAs are the cause of many of the FCRA problems, they are not solely responsible. Despite the 1996 Amendments, the furnishers continue to neglect or ignore their role in the credit reporting system. It is not an unfair characterization to describe the investigation process as a shell game wherein the CRAs and furnishers have worked in concert to protect one another from their already minimal liabilities under the FCRA. In nearly every case against a credit reporting agency in which I have been involved, the bureau has asserted as its defense the fact that the furnisher verified and re-reported the inaccurate information. Contrary to the plain language of the FCRA and the unanimous judgment of the federal judiciary, the CRAs do not believe they have any duty under the FCRA to independently evaluate the documents and disputes before them. Rather, they continue to assert the position that their only duty in conducting an investigation is to confirm that the furnisher wishes to maintain the disputed item. The CRAs continue to blindly mirror whatever the furnishers provide. In its deposition, Trans Union brazenly admitted this fact on the record.

21 Q. What happens when a dispute
22 investigator gets some type of documentation,
23 other than the consumer's dispute, that comes
24 from a third party, but doesn't come from the
1 furnisher?
2 A. We wouldn't be able to act on any
3 instructions or anything in there.
4 They're not the furnisher of
5 the information.

Trans Union's policy is identical to that of Equifax and Experian. The CRAs simply parrot whatever they receive from the furnisher. At the same time, the furnishers are relying heavily on the fact that there is no private cause of action under Section 1681s-2(a) and no standard for the furnisher investigation under Section

1681s-2(b). Nearly all institutional furnishers have the same procedures. On January 21, 2003, I represented a consumer in a jury trial against a furnisher in a Richmond federal court. In Johnson v. MBNA, we obtained the first plaintiff's verdict in the country under 15 U.S.C. Section 1681s-2(b). In pre-trial depositions and in evidence at trial, MBNA admitted that its sole procedure for handling consumer disputes under the FCRA was to compare the CRA data to its own summary of the account in its computer. That itself was the subject of the consumer's dispute. MBNA's 12 "investigators" were expected to perform an average of 250 investigations per eight-hour day. They were never to consult original documents and were not provided any means by which to determine if the account summary within their computer was in fact accurate. Throughout the litigation of this case and now on MBNA's appeal, the furnisher has made two arguments: 1. The furnisher duties under Section 1681s-2(a) are not enforceable by any means and are separate and apart from the duties under Section 1681s-2(b); and 2. There is no qualitative national standard for furnisher compliance under the FCRA. MBNA has opposed even the imposition of a "reasonable investigation" standard under the Act. In its Appellant's Brief, the furnisher argued,

The words "reasonable" and "procedures" are plainly absent from Section 1681s-2. Thus Congress did not intend to impose upon any furnisher the duty to defend its investigation or records qualitatively under Section 1681s-2(b). Indeed, the requirements of accuracy as they relate to mere furnishers of information are contained in Section 1681s-2(a), a section which is expressly made non-actionable by consumers like Johnson under Section 1681s-2(c)-(d). . . . If Congress had wanted to subject furnishers to a qualitative standard, it easily could have done so.

This position, taken by MBNA, the largest credit card company in America, exposes the distinction between the industry's cry for Congress to maintain preemption and the reality in which furnishers actually operate—one which still lacks any enforceable national standard.

Rather than comply with the spirit and intent of the FCRA, furnishers continue to fight its application or ignore its accuracy objectives. Nearly every major furnisher who has been deposed has confessed to a policy of automated investigations in which the consumer has almost no hope of obtaining relief. The furnishers merely proofread the form from the CRA and match it to the data within their computer's account screen. There is no other means by which to verify and correct a credit reporting dispute once the error has worked its way into the furnisher's computer account record. None of the major furnishers of which I am aware reviews original documents or paper records. In a May 21, 2003 deposition, Capital One's representative confirmed this fact for her employer.

7 Q Okay. What kinds of information do your
8 ACDV operators have available to them through the
9 interface of the Odyssey system?
10 A Name, address, ECOA, pay history, cycle
11 date, last date paid. Statements, action or activity
12 on the account, late fees, past-due fees, membership
13 fees, etc.
14 Q What about original application information?
15 A That, we cannot see in Unisys.
16 Q All right. Is there a reason why it is that
17 your ACDV operators do not have access to all of the
18 other systems that I mentioned, being Tandem, CHIA,
19 Retain One, Casper, Baltrax, Amdahl, Capstone, and
20 Rocky?
21 A Yeah, I'll give you the simplified answer
22 first. Based on what my associates do, which is to
23 verify the information, the — some of the systems
24 that you mentioned there are for in-depth research; my
25 associates do not complete in-depth research.

When questioned further as to why Capital One would never conduct "in-depth research" of FCRA disputes, the representative explained that the furnisher's procedures were developed in collaboration with the three bureaus, and that this is the policy which was developed through such involvement.

1 Q Okay, why is it that your associates do not
2 complete in-depth research?
3 A They do that because, when the — we had

4 three bureau reps actually come to Capital One in — I
5 can verify this, I want to say it was like February of
6 2000 —
7 Q When you say — let me stop you here for a
8 minute and interrupt, I'm sorry — you say three
9 bureau reps, do you mean a rep from each of the
10 different bureaus or from combinations thereof?
11 A I'm sorry, a representative from each bureau
12 came on three separate visits, so a Trans Union rep
13 came, Experian rep, and then an Equifax rep.
14 Q Okay.
15 A And they came to explain to my team how to
16 more properly and more accurately work accounts, the
17 cases. One of the questions that I had for them, as a
18 manager, was should we verify the accounts — and I
19 even explained to them what my definition of verify
20 is — which is, we pull up our system of record, in
21 this case Unisys or Beast, we look at what the bureau
22 has sent us on the ACDV. If there are any
23 discrepancies, we make sure that what the bureau has
24 mirrors exactly what we, as Capital One, have. That's
25 verifying.
1 Q That was what you described to the
2 representatives as verifying?
3 A Yes.
4 Q And what did they say in response to that?
5 A Well, I actually followed that up with, Do you want
6 us to do that, or do you want us to do things
7 such as pull statements, etc., actually do the
8 research which would involve CHIA. And in each case,
9 the bureau rep said, No, we want you to verify it. We
10 want you to make our system look like your system. So
11 that's what we've been doing.

As long as consumers remain stuck in the catch-22 of the CRA-furnisher responsibility dodge, the FCRA will continue to offer little relief for your constituents. The bureaus will continue to issue flawed and inaccurate credit reports to the many innocent users who must rely on same for their daily business decisions. Whether or not the industry lobby accepts this truth, the financial services industry has far more to gain by improving the credit reporting system than by accepting its serious flaws.

The continuing drumbeat from the other side of this issue is for extension of the FCRA's preemption of state credit reporting statutes. The argument that was made on May 8 and will be repeated today is that our economy would be badly harmed if we replaced the FCRA's "national standards" with a patchwork of state substitutes. This argument is founded upon several false assumptions. First, the argument assumes that the FCRA in its current form is working. It is not. Disputes are up, identity theft is rampant, and consumer complaints to the FTC in the FCRA and identity theft areas are overwhelming all other matters. Businesses cannot now comfortably rely upon the credit reporting industry to produce an accurate predictor of default or bankruptcy. Despite the efforts made in 1996, the FCRA still has failed to place and keep pressure upon either the credit reporting agencies or the furnishers to maintain accuracy in the information they report.

Industry's preemption argument assumes that the FCRA's "national standards" are in competition with certain, unstated state standards. They are not. At a minimum, even with the scheduled sunset, Section 1681t(a)'s preemption of "inconsistent" state laws will remain. Furthermore, the FCRA establishes for furnishers a "national standard" of completeness and accuracy. (The standard for CRAs remains "maximum possible accuracy.") I am unaware of any state laws whose standards exceed those of the FCRA. The issue is not competing state standards but more generous state remedies that protect consumers better than the FCRA does. Industry ought to be forced to identify the purported "unworkable" state standards that form the foundation of its position. If there really is a legitimate problem with competing state law standards, NACA would join with industry and this Committee in accommodating those concerns. Otherwise, the national standards established by the FCRA need simply to be followed. This objective will not be furthered by adopting industry's proposed amendment.

APPENDIX

C

SAMPLE LETTERS

It is very important that you use the letters provided here only as a guide. Never use the exact wording or structure, as doing so may tip the reader that you are using a credit restoration technique or program. Always review the appropriate section of this book before sending any letter contained herein. And be advised, any information to a credit bureau can be viewed by collectors (e.g., telephone number, address, place of employment).

Remember, bureaus are notorious for stalling and will use whatever means available to keep from having to do something. The most common delay tactic is to respond to your letter by asking you to verify that "you are who you say you are." They will ask you to resubmit your request and include a copy of a utility bill to verify your address. To preclude this delaying tactic, always include a copy of a utility bill in your first correspondence. For those wishing to be "lost," use a bill that has been sent to your PO Box, not to your home address. If you use your home address, it will end up on your credit report, and collectors will have found you.

CEASE COMMUNICATION LETTER—FOR CREDITORS

This letter is for creditors, not debt collectors. Send it when requesting that a creditor stop contacting you. Always review the appropriate section of this book before sending this or any other letter. Use your own words; these words are a guide only.

[date]

Mr. Homer Hancock
First Bank of Simpsons
555 Ruff Ruff Road
Denzel, WA 00000

RE: First Bank of Simpsons, Acct # 0000 0000 0000 0000

[Creditor]:

I request that you cease communication regarding [account #] immediately. I'm familiar with the Fair Debt Collection Practices Act, and you must comply with this request.

Sincerely,

Joe P. Snuffy

CEASE COMMUNICATION LETTER—
FOR DEBT COLLECTORS (COLLECTION AGENCIES)

This letter is for debt collectors (Chapter 7), not creditors. It is to be used when demanding that a debt collector stop contacting you and/or when you want the matter referred back to the original creditor.

[date]

Mr. Homer Hellhound
First Collection Agency of Snakes and Worms
555 Cya Later Road
Denzel, WA 00000

RE: [Original Creditor Name, Account Number]

[Debt Collector]:

I demand that you cease communication immediately and refer the matter back to [Original Creditor]. I'm familiar with the Fair Debt Collection Practices Act, and you must comply with this demand.

Sincerely,

Joe P. Snuffy

VALIDATION LETTER—
FOR DEBT COLLECTORS (COLLECTION AGENCIES)

This letter is for debt collectors (Chapter 7), not creditors. It is to be used within 30 days of receipt of a collection letter from a debt collector.

[date]

Mr. Homer Hellhound
First Collection Agency of Snakes and Worms
555 Cya Later Road
Denzel, WA 00000

RE: Validation [Original Creditor Name, Account Number]

[Debt Collector]:

I'm in receipt of your collection notice dated [date of notice] concerning [Original Creditor Name, Account Number]. I dispute this debt.

Sincerely,

Joe P. Snuffy

DEMAND FOR A CREDIT BUREAU TO REMOVE INQUIRY

This letter is for credit reporting agencies. It is to be used when demanding that they remove an inquiry from your report.

[date]

[name of bureau]
[address of bureau]
[city, state, ZIP of bureau]

RE: Remove Unauthorized Inquiries

[Bureau]:

I have recently received a copy of my credit file and noticed that there are unauthorized inquiries on it. This is illegal. I didn't authorize this, and it is a violation of the Fair Credit Reporting Act.

[If you know that the inquiry was supposed to be for a periodic review and not for extension of credit, state it here.]

This has hurt my chances of getting credit and caused me to be denied. I demand that you remove the following inquiries immediately:

[name of creditor]
[date of inquiry]
[subscriber code, if there is one]

I expect your compliance. If you do comply, I will consider the matter closed and will take no legal action against you. If you do not, I will take legal action [if that is your course].

Consider this a formal notice. I expect your compliance of my request, as well as a copy of the corrected report provided to me within 30 days.

Sincerely,

Joe P. Snuffy
[current address]
[previous address]
[date of address]
[SSN]

DEMAND FOR CREDITOR TO REMOVE INQUIRY

This letter is for creditors only. It is to be used when demanding that they remove an inquiry from your report.

[date]

[name of creditor]
[address of creditor]
[city, state, Zip of creditor]

RE: Remove Unauthorized Inquiries

[Creditor]:

I have recently received a copy of my credit file and noticed that there [is an/are some] unauthorized [inquiry/inquiries] on it. This is illegal. I didn't authorize this, and it is a violation of the Fair Credit Reporting Act.

[If you know that the inquiry was supposed to be for a periodic review and not for extension of credit, state it. Example: "I understand that you have the right for a periodic review of my credit report; however, those inquiries are supposed to be private and not for potential lenders to review, and (name of credit bureau) lists the inquiry as public."]

This has hurt my chances of getting credit and caused me to be denied. I demand that you remove the following immediately:

[date]

[name of creditor]
[date of inquiry]
[subscriber code] (if there is one)

I expect your compliance. If you do comply, I will consider the matter closed and will take no legal action against you. If you do not, I will take legal action. [If that is your course.]

Consider this is a formal notice. I expect your compliance, as well as a copy of the corrected report, provided to me within 30 days.

Sincerely,

Joe P. Snuffy

REQUEST FOR CREDIT BUREAU TO REMOVE
ACCURATE ADVERSE INFORMATION (FIRST LETTER)

This letter is for credit reporting agencies. It is to be used the first time you request that accurate adverse information be removed from your report.

[date]

[name of bureau]
[address of bureau]
[city, state, ZIP of bureau]

RE: Reporting of Creditor Information (Name of Creditor, Account Number)

[Bureau]:

I request that you remove any negative credit information regarding [creditor name, account number]. This account is not mine, and in accordance with the Fair Credit Reporting Act, you are not permitted to report false information.

By reporting this information, you've caused me to be denied credit.

This is a formal notice, and I expect your compliance of my request, as well as a copy of the corrected report provided to me within 30 days.

Sincerely,

Joe P. Snuffy [full name with suffix]
[current address]
[previous addresses last 12 months]
[date of address]
[SSN]

DEMAND FOR CREDIT BUREAU TO REMOVE
ACCURATE ADVERSE INFORMATION
(SECOND AND SUBSEQUENT LETTERS)

This letter is for credit reporting agencies. It is to be used the second and subsequent times you demand that accurate adverse information be removed from your report.

[date]

[name of bureau]
[address of bureau]
[city, state, ZIP of bureau]

RE: Reporting of Creditor Information (Name of Creditor, Account Number)

[Bureau]:

On [date], I sent you a letter requesting that you remove any negative credit information regarding [creditor name, account number]. The information you are reporting is not mine, and in accordance with the Fair Credit Reporting Act, you are not permitted to report false information.

Your continued negligence has caused me harm, since it has affected my ability to [specify the harm it has caused].

You have failed to comply with my request, and you may now consider it a demand. This is a formal notice, and I expect your compliance, as well as a copy of the corrected report provided to me, within 30 days. If you fail to do so, I will take legal action against you. [If that is your course.]

I also demand that you provide me with a description of the reinvestigation procedure you used in my first dispute within 15 days, in accordance with 15 U.S.C. §1681i(6)(B)(iii).

Sincerely,

Joe P. Snuffy [full name with suffix]
[current address]
[previous addresses last 12 months]
[date of address]
[SSN]

REQUEST FOR CREDIT BUREAU TO REMOVE
INACCURATE ADVERSE INFORMATION (FIRST LETTER)

This letter is for credit reporting agencies. It is to be used the first time you request that inaccurate adverse information be removed from your report.

[date]

[name of bureau]
[address of bureau]
[city, state, ZIP of bureau]

RE: Reporting of Creditor Information (Name, Account Number)

[Bureau]:

Attached you'll find a copy of my credit report dated [date]. I've highlighted the account that is false, and I request that you remove any negative credit information regarding [creditor name, account number]. This account is [not mine *or* is mine but never paid late], and in accordance with the Fair Credit Reporting Act, you are not permitted to report false information.

By reporting this information, you've [caused me to be denied credit, lost sleep, etc.].

This is a formal notice, and I expect your compliance of my request, as well as a copy of the corrected report provided to me, within 30 days.

Sincerely,

Joe P. Snuffy [full name with suffix]
[current address] (announces it to collectors)
[previous addresses last 24 months]
[date of birth]
[telephone number] (announces it to collectors)
[SSN]
[spouse's name if married]
[current employer—*be aware that this announces it to collectors*]

DEMAND FOR CREDIT BUREAU TO REMOVE INACCURATE ADVERSE INFORMATION (SECOND AND SUBSEQUENT LETTERS)

This letter is for credit reporting agencies. It is to be used the second and subsequent times you demand that inaccurate adverse information be removed from your report.

[date]

[name of bureau]
[address of bureau]
[city, state, zip of bureau]

RE: Reporting of Creditor Information [Name of Creditor, Acct #]

[Bureau]:

On [date], I sent you a letter requesting that you remove any negative credit information regarding [creditor name, account number]. The information you are reporting is false, and in accordance with the Fair Credit Reporting Act, you are not permitted to report false information.

Your continued negligence has caused me harm, since it has affected my ability to [specify the harm it has caused].

You have failed to comply with my request, and you may now consider it a demand. This is a formal notice, and I expect your compliance, as well as a copy of the corrected report provided to me, within 30 days. If you fail to do so, I will take legal action against you. [If that is your course.]

I also demand that you provide me with a description of the reinvestigation procedure used in my first dispute within 15 days, in accordance with 15 U.S.C. § 1681i(6)(B)(iii).

Sincerely,

Joe P. Snuffy [full name with suffix]
[current address] (announces it to collectors)
[previous addresses last 24 months]
[date of birth]
[telephone number] (announces it to collectors)
[SSN]
[spouse's name if married]
[current employer] (announces it to collectors)

DEMAND FOR CREDITOR TO REMOVE
INACCURATE ADVERSE INFORMATION

This letter is for creditors only. Send it when demanding that they stop reporting inaccurate adverse information.

[date]

Mr. Homer Hancock
First Bank of Simpsons
555 Ruff Ruff Road
Denzel, WA 00000

RE: First Bank of Simpsons, [Account Number]

[Creditor]:

Enclosed you'll find a copy of my credit report. The report contains the following false information: [state the false information]. I demand that you instruct the credit bureaus to delete this information immediately and provide me a copy of a UDF instructing deletion.

By reporting this information, you are in violation of the Fair Credit Reporting Act. This is hurting me [state how it is hurting you], and I expect your compliance within 30 days, If you do not, you will face legal action. [If that is your course.]

Sincerely,

Joe P. Snuffy

VICTIM STATEMENT LETTER

You don't have to be a victim to send this letter. It requires that a potential lender notify you when someone requests credit extended in your name. There are two downsides to this sending this letter: (1) you will not be able to get credit approval as quickly as you would otherwise, and instant credit will be impossible; and (2) you will not be able to get your online credit report. (CRAs often change their numbers and addresses to avoid filing these papers, since it costs them money. Be sure to contact the CRAs to get their current address for filing victim statements, and notify the FTC if there is any monkey business.)

[date]

[name of bureau]
[address of bureau]
[city, state, ZIP of bureau]

RE: Victim Statement Letter

To whom it may concern:

Since fraudulent applications may be submitted in my name using accurate personal information, please verify with me that applications for credit are legitimate.

    Last Name:
    First Name:
    Middle Initial:
    Social Security Number:
    Date of Birth:
    Driver's License Number:
    Street Number:
    City:
    State:
    ZIP:
    Former Address:
    Day Phone:
    Evening Phone:

I've enclosed a copy of my [insert type of document that was formerly addressed to you at the address listed above, e.g. utility bill, etc.] for verification of my identity.

Thank you for your attention in this matter.

Sincerely,

Joe P. Snuffy

APPENDIX

D

GLOSSARY

account—A relationship between a creditor and consumer; the consumer purchases a product or service in such a way that causes the transfer of money over time from the consumer to the creditor.

account reviews—Inquiries by creditors that have an ongoing relationship. (Not included in the business version of a consumer's credit report.)

acct clsd/grantors req—Account closed at grantor's request; creditor canceled charge privileges; adverse/bad credit.

adverse action—The denial of credit, insurance, or employment, taken by a creditor or other entity, affecting a consumer.

adverse entry—Derogatory information furnished to a credit reporting agency.

bank card—A credit card issued through a bank. (See credit card.)

bankruptcy—A legal proceeding to give a person or business some relief from debts. (See Chapter 7 bankruptcy, Chapter 11 bankruptcy, Chapter 12 bankruptcy, and Chapter 13 bankruptcy; adverse/bad credit.)

bk—See bankruptcy; adverse/bad credit.

bk liq reo—Account written off in bankruptcy; adverse/bad credit.

business version (of a credit report)—An abbreviated version of a consumer credit report. The business version of a credit report is what creditors see and does not contain promotional inquiries or account reviews.

Chapter 7 bankruptcy—For individuals or businesses, this chapter of the bankruptcy code provides for court-administered liquidation of the assets. Debts listed in the bankruptcy petition are dissolved; adverse/bad credit.

Chapter 11 bankruptcy—For businesses, this chapter of the bankruptcy code is usually used for the reorganization of a business in financial trouble. Used as an alternative to liquidation under Chapter 7; adverse/bad credit.

Chapter 12 bankruptcy—The chapter of the bankruptcy code adopted to address financial difficulties of the nation's farming community; adverse/bad credit.

Chapter 13 bankruptcy—The chapter of the bankruptcy code in which debtors repay debts according to a plan accepted by the debtor, the creditors, and the court; adverse/bad credit.

charge-off—Creditor has written the debt off, assuming that it is not collectible. Creditors often will sell the debt to a third party at a discount, i.e., send it to a collection agency. The creditor can get tax credit for charge-offs; adverse/bad credit.

charge card—A credit card that requires full payment of the bill each month; no interest is charged. Some versions of the American Express Card and Diners Club Card are examples.

collection account—Creditor has given up on collecting and has sold the debt to a third party (often a collection agency); adverse/bad credit.

consumer version (of a credit report)—The consumer version of a credit report lists all inquiries, including promotional and account review. Only the consumer can request this version of his or her credit report. Creditors cannot see this version; they see only the business version of credit reports.

CRA—Credit reporting agency, also known as a credit bureau.

credit—A consumer's ability to make purchases, obtain services, or borrow money based on his or her promise, ability, and demonstrated willingness to repay.

credit bureau—A company that gathers information about how consumers use credit, which the credit bureau in turn provides to potential creditors, employers, and others who have a legally recognized reason (permissible purpose) to inquire about the creditworthiness of an individual.

credit card—A charge account that allows a consumer to pay a portion or all of the outstanding balance each month (revolving account) and has a credit limit. Visa, MasterCard, and Discover are examples.

credit check—An inquiry to confirm a consumer's credit payment history.

credit fraud—A case when someone has stolen a consumer's identity by fraudulently using that consumer's SSN or other personal information to acquire credit in his or her name.

credit history—The record of a consumer's credit accounts and manner of payment (MOP). Credit history includes high credit, current balance, credit limit, and 24 months of MOP history.

credit report—Information extracted from a database that is housed by a credit bureau, which contains past payment activity for accounts and other additional facts about the consumer that will help creditors judge the consumer's creditworthiness.

credit risk—An assessment of a consumer's likelihood of fulfilling the terms of a credit agreement.

credit score—A mathematical calculation that reflects a consumer's creditworthiness. The score is an assessment of how likely a consumer is to pay his or her debts.

creditor—One who loans money; a person or business to whom a debt is owed.

creditworthiness—A description of a consumer's credit behavior and management that leads to a creditor's decision whether to make an offer of credit.

current account—All payments to date have been on time.

current was 60/90—Late both 60 and 90 days (how many times for each occurrence will also be shown on a report); adverse/bad credit.

date closed—The date a credit agreement or account was terminated.

date opened—The date a credit account was established.

debtor—One who owes money to a creditor.

default—Failure of a consumer to make loan or credit repayments as agreed in a loan or credit agreement. A loan or credit default may be identified by a high MOP rating (see manner of payment); adverse/bad credit.

defendant—The party against whom a legal action is brought.

delinquent—Past due; adverse/bad credit.

derogatory (syn. adverse)—Negative information that indicates an increased credit risk to a creditor and lowers a score.

discharged bankruptcy—A bankruptcy that has concluded legal proceedings so that the debts are resolved by the court through a payment plan (Chapter 13) or dissolved entirely (Chapter 7); adverse/bad credit.

dismissed bankruptcy—Person failed to complete the bankruptcy.

dispute—To question the accuracy of information in a credit report.

Fair and Accurate Transactions Act (FACTA)—Congressional legislation in December 2003 designed to extend provisions of the Fair Credit Reporting Act and strengthen identity theft provisions.

Fair Credit Billing Act (FCBA)—Congressional legislation intended to protect citizens by providing operational guidelines for those connected with billing of certain types of credit accounts. The law applies to "open end" credit accounts, such as credit cards, and revolving charge accounts, such as department store accounts. It does not cover installment contracts—loans or extensions of credit that the consumer repays on a fixed schedule.

Fair Credit Reporting Act (FCRA)—Congressional legislation intended to protect citizens by providing operational guidelines for those connected with the credit reporting system.

Fair Debt Collection Practices Act (FDCPA)—Congressional legislation intended to protect citizens by providing operational guidelines for those connected with the debt collection system.

fraud—Intentional twisting of truth in order to cause another to part with something of value or to surrender a legal right.

furnisher—A creditor who provides information to a credit bureau.

identity—The distinguishing character or personality of a consumer. Also includes any unique information about a consumer, such as an SSN.

identity confirmation—The successful verification of a consumer's identity.

inc in bk—Account written off in bankruptcy; adverse/bad credit.

inquiry—An examination of a consumer's credit history.

installment loan—A credit account in which the debt is divided into amounts to be paid successively at specified intervals set by the terms of the loan.

insurance method—The method all consumers must use when dealing with creditors and credit reporting agencies: all promises are set forth in writing and spelled out, and all correspondence via mail is sent to creditors using certified mail, return receipt requested.

judgment—You have a judgment against you when someone has taken you to court and won the suit. The judgment is a piece of paper that gives the plaintiff the right to collect an amount of money through legal means (see paid judgment, unpaid judgment); adverse/bad credit.

lien—An interest that a creditor has in a debtor's property that lasts until the satisfaction of some debt or duty; adverse/bad credit (e.g., a secured interest created by a mortgage, usually filed with the county in which the property is located).

line of credit—Credit limit established by a creditor.

litigate—To engage in legal proceedings.

manner of payment (MOP)—A series of codes or statements used to show the payment habits (prompt, delinquent, etc.) of a consumer.

mortgage—A document in which the owner pledges his/her/its title to real property to a creditor as security for a loan.

National Association of Consumer Advocates (NACA)—A group of consumer-friendly attorneys who only represent consumers, not creditors.

National Consumer Law Center (NCLC)—A company that specializes in the publication of consumer protection manuals for attorneys.

open account—An account that is active, still in use, or is still being paid.

paid as agreed—Consumer has made and is making payments in accordance with the terms.

paid charge-off—Charged-off account that was eventually paid; often a ploy by the creditor to get you to pay in exchange for this rating. Better than a charge-off, but still negative; adverse/bad credit.

paid collection account—Same as paid charge-off but performed by a collection agency instead of a creditor.

paid judgment—A judgment that is paid in accordance with the order; adverse/bad credit.

paid satisfactory—Loan paid in accordance with terms.

paid settlement—Debtor owed more than the account was settled for; adverse/bad credit.

paid was 60/90/120—Consumer paid off the debt, but not until it was 60, 90, or 120 days late; adverse/bad credit.

permissible purpose—The particular circumstances under which a consumer credit report may be disclosed by a credit bureau in accordance with the Fair Credit Reporting Act.

plaintiff—The one who initiates (files) a lawsuit (complaint).

pro se—Representing on one's own behalf in a lawsuit, without an attorney.

promotional inquiry—An inquiry made into a consumer's credit report for purposes of a promotional offer.

public records—Information that is available to the general public, including tax liens, court judgments, and bankruptcy.

re-aging—a furnisher's deliberate attempt to place a debt for collection outside of the seven-year statute of limitations by erroneously changing the date of last transaction.

refinanced—Additional money was borrowed from the same creditor, combining the first loan with the second.

repossession—When the creditor takes back an item used as collateral for a loan; adverse/bad credit.

retail card—A credit card issued by a retail store.

revolving charge account—Credit automatically available up to a predetermined limit as long as a consumer makes regular payments.

scnl—Subscriber cannot locate. Debtor has skipped and failed to pay; adverse/bad credit.

score—See credit score.

secured credit card—A credit card that requires a cash balance in an account. The cash balance is usually also the credit card limit.

settled—Debtor owed more than creditor settled for; adverse/bad credit.

tax lien—Usually reported for back taxes owed, associated with property; adverse/bad credit.

tradeline—Any credit account, such as a bank loan, credit card, or mortgage.

universal default—An existing creditor's use of a consumer's credit history with another creditor to determine or change interest rates and fees. (Such a change may be performed with 15 days' notice to the consumer.)

unpaid judgment—a judgment that hasn't been paid (satisfied) under the terms of the court order; adverse/bad credit.

unrated—The rating isn't negative or positive, but neutral. Usually reported as I0, R0, or UR (installment unrated, revolving unrated, or simply unrated). It can be negative if looked at by human eyes, but it doesn't affect a credit score.

written off in bk—Debt removed due to bankruptcy, requires a zero balance; adverse/bad credit.

ABOUT THE AUTHOR

In the early 1980s, Dana Neal learned all the ins and outs of the credit game while collecting debts for the Greater Lakes Higher Education Corporation. He quickly became disenchanted with the way his peers conducted themselves and with the state of credit reporting in the United States in general.

After graduating from Ohio State University in 1991 with a degree in aviation, Neal went on to active duty, piloting several types of aircraft, including the UH-60 Black Hawk helicopter and various multi-engine airplanes.

He was injured in the line of duty and medically retired from military service, and his subsequent financial hardships led him to become a consumer advocate, dedicated to championing the cause of individual consumers. His mission: to inform others of their rights and to demonstrate that they wield significant power over their credit report. In keeping with that goal, he founded BestCredit in 1999. He now spends his time teaching others what his experience as both a collector and a debtor has taught him about debt collection and credit reporting.